The Catacombs
and the Colosseum

The CATACOMBS and the COLOSSEUM

The Roman Empire as the Setting of Primitive Christianity

STEPHEN BENKO
JOHN J. O'ROURKE

Judson Press, Valley Forge

Foreword

In the spring of 1968 the Philadelphia Seminar on Christian Origins (PSCO) voted to devote the academic year of 1968/69 to the study of the imperial Roman background of primitive Christianity. Stephen Benko and John J. O'Rourke were elected cochairmen. Immediately afterward the cochairmen and the coordinator of PSCO, Robert A. Kraft, met and decided to use the time available more for research than for discussion.

It also seemed advantageous to establish certain chronological limits and to focus attention upon one definite period of imperial Roman history. These limits are the beginning of the Principate of Octavian Augustus and the death of Hadrian. Although the selection may seem arbitrary, it does in fact constitute a unit since the death of Hadrian (138) and the end of the second Jewish revolt (135/136) are very close in time, and it is obvious that these dates are a milestone in Judeo-Christian tradition.

At each of the five meetings of PSCO two papers were presented, and in essence these papers constitute the greater part of the present volume. Since the general approach to the topic was historical rather than philosophical, sociological, or religious, the editors deemed it proper to exclude from this volume papers which did not follow the strictly historical approach; on the other hand, a few articles which were not read at a meeting of the PSCO are included, in order that the reader may get as broad a view of imperial Roman civilization as is possible within the limits imposed. Each author is responsible for his own contribution. The editors take no credit or responsibility except for their own articles and the collecting, ordering, and other mechanics of editorship. They wish to thank, in addition to the authors, the members of the seminar who contributed to the development of the papers by their criticisms, and especially John T. Townsend who gave valuable help in the arrangement of the material.

Since the various chapters were contributed by different authors, there was need to create uniformity not so much in style as in format. This tedious job was done by Mrs. Eileen James, Mrs. Elizabeth Johnson, and co-workers of Judson Press, whose efforts are gratefully acknowledged.

The Introduction by Robert M. Grant outlines the value of the approach taken in this volume. The editors hope that the book will contribute to a better understanding of primitive Christianity and that it will encourage students of all kinds interested in this subject to do further research in this area.

STEPHEN BENKO
JOHN J. O'ROURKE

Contributors

EDITORS:

Stephen Benko is teaching Ancient History at Fresno State College, Fresno, California. Formerly he taught at Temple University. He is a graduate of the University of Basel, and he also did graduate studies at the University of Zurich and Yale. He is the author of several books, among others, *The Meaning of Sanctorum Communio; Protestants, Catholics, and Mary;* and *My Lord Speaks.* He has published widely in scholarly journals in America and Europe.

John J. O'Rourke is chairman of the Faculty of Theology and Professor of Sacred Scripture, Saint Charles Seminary, Overbrook, Philadelphia. He is author of "2 Corinthians" in *Jerome Biblical Commentary* and "1 Corinthians" in *A Catholic Commentary on Sacred Scripture,* 2nd ed.

CONTRIBUTORS

John G. Gager is Assistant Professor of Religion at Princeton University having taught previously at Haverford College. Educated at Yale and Harvard and several European universities, he is a Kent Fellow and a member of the Society for Religion in Higher Education. His field is Christian Origins, with special interest in Hellenistic Judaism and relations between early Christianity and Greco-Roman paganism.

Robert M. Grant is Professor of New Testament and Early Christianity at the Divinity School, University of Chicago, and author/editor of eighteen books, several published in Dutch, French, German, and Japanese translations. His latest books are: *The Formation of the New Testament* (London — New York, 1965) ; *The Early Christian Doctrine of God* (Richard Lectures, University of Virginia, Charlottesville, 1966) ; *After the New Testament* (Philadelphia, 1967) ; *Augustus to Constantine* (New York, 1970). Dr. Grant is a member of several scholarly societies and a coeditor of *Church History*.

James L. Jones is the Talbot Professor of New Testament and Greek at the Philadelphia Divinity School. After several years of military service as an infantry officer before and during World War II, he left the army as a lieutenant colonel. He entered seminary and received the B.D. degree in 1949 and the Th.D. in 1956. His course of study was interrupted by a recall to active military duty, and he served in Korea and Japan as a chaplain. Dr. Jones has studied Roman military history with special work on the subject at Oxford University and with field work in Britain and the Middle East.

Robert A. Kraft is Associate Professor of Religious Thought at the University of Pennsylvania, specializing in the areas of Christian origins and of Judaism in the Hellenistic era. Previously he taught at the University of Manchester in England. He received his Ph.D. from Harvard University. Dr. Kraft is an active member of many American and international scholarly societies and is editor of the *Journal of Biblical Literature Monograph* series. He is author of the volume on Barnabas and the Didache (1965) in the series *The Apostolic Fathers: A New Translation and Commentary,* edited by Robert M. Grant.

Gerhard Krodel is Professor of New Testament at the Lutheran Theological Seminary in Philadelphia, Pennsylvania. Prior to his present post he taught at Wartburg Theological Seminary, Dubuque, Iowa, and Capital University, Columbus, Ohio.

Clarence L. Lee is Associate Professor of Church History at the Lutheran Theological Seminary at Philadelphia, Pennsylvania. He is a graduate of Harvard Divinity School and has contributed articles to *Masterpieces of Christian Literature* (edited by Frank Magill) and numerous articles and reviews to *Lutheran Quarterly* and *Dialog.* He is the editor of the series on the early church in Facet Books by Fortress Press.

John T. Townsend majored in Classical Language at Brown University. He did postgraduate studies at Wycliffe College, University of Toronto, and Harvard Divinity School where he earned his doctor's degree. Presently he is Associate Professor in Biblical Languages and

New Testament at the Philadelphia Divinity School. His articles have appeared in the *Journal of Theological Studies, Harvard Theological Review,* and other scholarly journals.

William White, Jr., teaches History at Philadelphia College of Textiles and Science. Prior to this position he taught in Japan, Israel, Belgium, and Holland. He is the author of many scholarly articles in the field of Ancient History, Linguistics, and the History and Philosophy of Science.

Robert L. Wilken is Assistant Professor of Patristics, Fordham University, New York, New York. Formerly he taught at the Lutheran Theological Seminary, Gettysburg, Pennsylvania. Dr. Wilken received his Ph.D. from the University of Chicago, after which he studied in Germany. He is the author of *Judaism and the Early Christian Mind* and *The Myth of Christian Beginnings.*

Donald Winslow received his graduate degrees from Harvard University. He spent four years in Japan teaching in a Japanese Episcopal Theological college. Currently he is teaching Historical Theology at the Philadelphia Divinity School.

Contents

The Catacombs
and the Colosseum

Robert M. Grant

Introduction:
Christian and Roman History

Forty years ago B. H. Streeter began his lectures on *The Primitive Church* with this personal testimony.

> When I first began to read Theology more than thirty years ago, I found Church History so dull—especially after reading Greek and Roman history for "Greats"—that I dropped the subject, and offered for examination Textual Criticism instead. I discovered later what the matter was; it was not that "Church" history was dull, but that what was then presented to me as such was not really history.[1]

Today the situation is somewhat different, but the movement to make real history out of church history still has some distance to go, particularly in regard to the history of the church in its formative period as it moved out from Palestine into the rest of the Roman world, as the Spirit-guided witnesses passed from Jerusalem to all Judea and Samaria and then to "the end of the earth" (Acts 1:8). Indeed, the programmatic episode at Pentecost cannot adequately be understood unless one recognizes that the "devout Jews" who were present "from every nation under heaven" (Acts 2:5) were under heaven in the sense that they came from lands regarded as especially related to the twelve signs of the zodiac (Acts 2:9-11).[2] Franz Cumont found the list of lands in the work of Paul of Alexandria in the fourth century, but parallels show that the sources of Paul go back at least to the second century.[3]

This is not to say that the apostolic mission was planned along astrological lines, or even that the statement in Acts comes from an early Christian astrologer. For that kind of thought we have to wait for the Valentinian Gnostics to tell us that "the apostles replaced the signs of the zodiac, for as birth is governed by them, so rebirth is directed by the apostles."[4] The author of Acts simply uses geographical materials related to the signs of the zodiac. He has no more interest in their astrological significance than does Tertullian, who expands the passage in his treatise *Adversus Iudaeos.*[5] The astrology is there and deserves our attention, but it is not significantly there. Conceivably something similar underlay the fragmentary list given by Eusebius to show how the apostles divided up the world-mission: Parthia was allotted to Thomas, Scythia to Andrew, Asia to John;[6] and perhaps we should add Bartholomew's Indian expedition to the list.[7] But the list is too short for making comparisons. We note only that the basic emphasis, as in Acts, is still on the eastern half of the "inhabited world."

Not surprisingly, when we encounter a Roman Christian writer of the end of the first century, the emphasis is somewhat different. According to 1 Clement, the apostle Paul was a herald "both in the east and in the west"; he "taught the whole world righteousness and reached the limits of the west." [8] In the Psalms of Solomon (17:14) "the west" means Rome; but there we are dealing with a Palestinian viewpoint. Clement, who refers to the ocean as impassable by men, must have Spain in mind. His horizon has been expanded westward, in part just because he had read Paul's letter to the Romans with its reference to Spain.

The spread of Christianity encouraged concern for geographical information, and Justin Martyr tells how Christians have fulfilled the prophecy of Malachi 1:11: "from the rising of the sun to its setting." Christians are to be found even among such exotic barbarian tribes as the Hamaxobioi (wagon-dwellers), the Aoikoi (nomads), and the "tent-dwelling shepherds" mentioned in Genesis 4:20.[9] I suspect that Justin may have the descendants of the Old Testament Lamech in mind, but the Hamaxobioi actually lived north of the Danube,[10] the nomads in Numidia or India or Ethiopia,[11] and the tent-dwellers in Syria.[12] Among all these tribes, Justin says, "prayers and thanksgivings are offered to the Father and Maker of all through the name of the crucified Jesus." Was Christianity actually crossing the Roman frontiers? We cannot be quite sure. In relation to Justin we can only add that among the various endeavors despised by his anti-cultural pupil Tatian was the work of geographers; Tatian insisted that they had no real idea of what lay at the boundaries of their maps.[13]

For our present purposes there is no reason to describe the geographical ventures of Theophilus, Irenaeus, Tertullian, and Hippolytus.[14] It is enough to point out that as the mission advanced so did concern with the world in which it was advancing. Christians developed a genuine, if not always profound, interest in the geography of the Roman world. Apart from the mission, there was practically no interest of this kind among them, although we do not know precisely why the author of Acts represents Paul as saying, "I must also see Rome" (Acts 19:21). In a later passage the expression comes to be I "must bear witness also at Rome" (Acts 23:11; cf. Romans 1:13), and if this passage interprets the earlier one, the emphasis is still on the mission.

This concern for geography in relation to mission took place because the mission was primarily directed to the inhabitants of the Greco-Roman world and therefore cannot be understood without constant reference to that world. To this day the discoveries of Sir William Ramsay and others remain significant because the Roman world was real to them, as it becomes real to anyone who visits it or explores museums or even looks at slides. The student of early Christianity who visits Roman space does so not only because as a human being he cannot help being moved by the Roman works which still stand, though largely in ruins; he does so also because in imagination he can recapture a glimpse of the historical life the monuments attest.

This historical life, to which the Philadelphia Seminar on Christian Origins has devoted its attention in these papers, is a life in which early Christians inevitably shared. Their sharing becomes vivid, of course, in what can be discovered of the historical mission of Jesus and his disciples, which seemingly ended when he was crucified by Pontius Pilate, the Roman prefect of Judea whose true title has been discovered on an inscription from Caesarea.[15] Our understanding of early Christian experience is aided further by an inscription from Delphi that makes it possible to date, within a year, the presence of Gallio at Corinth as proconsul of Achaea.[16] And the *memoria* found underneath St. Peter's at Rome show that from about the middle of the second century the apostle's relics were probably venerated on the Vatican Hill. The art of the oldest catacombs gives some insight into Christian piety about the same time, and this art can be understood best when it is compared not only with Jewish counterparts but with Greco-Roman art as a whole.[17]

This seems clear enough, but it should be added that Christians shared a common past with others. To be sure, they enjoyed a special past based on the history of salvation in the Old Testament. But we sometimes neglect the fact that they also shared a Greco-Roman past. This participation in a wider history is one inference to be drawn from the chronology of Luke 3:1-2, with its references to Tiberius, Pilate, Herod, Philip, Lysanias, and even Annas and Caiaphas. These actors owe their position on the stage to the performance of the new drama of salvation, in which they have merely supporting parts. But without them the drama would be a mere fiction. They are persons who must be part of the common past shared by the evangelist with his readers.

Unfortunately for our attempt to find Roman history in Christian writers, our next candidate, the apologist Justin, is not very well informed. He naturally knows about Tiberius and Pontius Pilate, and about the emperors in his own day. He can date Simon Magus at Rome under Claudius and knows of the famous inscription to the god Semo Sancus, which he supposes was dedicated SIMONI DEO SANCTO.[18] He has heard of Hadrian's favorite Antoninus and of the Jewish revolt under Bar Kochba.[19] He can even say that the incarnation took place 150 years earlier, under Quirinius; but he thinks, perhaps misreading Luke 2:2, that Quirinius was the first Roman prefect or procurator in Judea.[20] He goes much farther astray when he describes "Ptolemy the king of the Egyptians" as requesting the books of the prophecies from Herod, then king of the Jews.[21] W. Schmid may have been right in deciding to delete Herod's name, but one cannot be sure.[22] Whatever the extent of Justin's knowledge, it is worth noting that once again the information is almost entirely related to the history of Judaism and Christianity. One might say that Justin is somehow creating a common past for the benefit of both his non-Christian readers and the Christians — just as in dealing with the history of philosophy, he takes over current ideas and uses them to point toward the goal of philosophy, the vision of God or, rather, the incarnation of the Logos.[23]

We need not deal with the attempts made by Christians to demonstrate the priority of Moses over all Greek literature, for in making these attempts they used models and, largely, materials provided by Hellenistic Jewish writers.[24] Instead, we should say something about the beginnings of "imperial history" among the Christian apologists.

First, of course, comes Melito, bishop of Sardis, with his claim that Christianity and the Empire grew up together and that the Empire should pay its debt to Christianity by recognizing it as the true (i.e., official) "philosophy." Only Nero and Domitian, misled by others, were persecutors. Both Hadrian and Antoninus Pius protected the church.[25] A similar sketch, with an even more drastic revision of history, is to be found in Tertullian's *Apology*,[26] and the synchronism Jesus/Augustus is discussed by Origen.[27] Some Christians took a slightly different tack: Theophilus says that God was aiding the growth of Rome from the time when the kings were replaced by magistrates, and he does not refer to the birth of Jesus under the emperor Augustus.[28] However, Theophilus was no republican; in his view the emperor, like the apostle Paul, had been entrusted with a stewardship by God.[29]

The historical approach to the Roman Empire on the part of these Christians was nothing but a variant on the theme of the greatness of Rome, expressed not only by second-century rhetoricians like Aelius Aristides[30] but also by Christian writers. We need mention only the claim of Apollinaris that Christians had made victory over the Quadi possible,[31] the praise given Empire and emperors by Athenagoras (who even compares Marcus Aurelius and Commodus with the Father and the Son),[32] and the statement by Irenaeus that the world enjoys peace because of the Romans, who make travel safe by land and by sea.[33] Here the needs of the mission (geography again!) join the work of the imperial government. To be sure, there were other views of Rome, to which Ramsay MacMullen has drawn attention; we find them in Tatian and sometimes in Tertullian.[34] Favorable or unfavorable, however, the Roman world was the one in which Christians had to take a stand, from New Testament times onward. The problem is already posed in the tradition about Jesus and the denarius with the image of Caesar on it. It is solved in one way in Romans 13 and in the book of Acts, in another way in the book of Revelation. And indeed the problem was not absolutely new when it was raised among Christians. The history of Jewish revolts against Roman power, especially as this power was expressed in taxation, provides a primary setting for the mission of Jesus himself,[35] and the early Christian solutions are paralleled in the attitudes of various groups of Jews.[36]

All this is to say little more than what the apostle Paul said in 1 Corinthians 5:9-10: "I wrote to you in my letter not to associate with immoral men; not at all meaning the immoral of this world, or the greedy and robbers, or idolaters, since then you would need to go out of the world." The Christians of the late second century prided themselves on being like everyone else in many respects, a point made clear in the *Epistle to Diognetus* and in Tertullian's *Apology*. As Paul and the others made clear, however, there was an ethical difference between Christians and non-Christians. Let the author to Diognetus express it:

> They live in their own countries but as sojourners. [Should we say "resident aliens"?] They participate fully as citizens and endure everything as foreigners; every foreign land is theirs. . . . They live on earth but are citizens of heaven; they obey the laws as laid down and in their own lives they transcend the laws. They love all and are persecuted by all.[37]

Origen has no real doubt about the gospel miracles wrought by Jesus, but in reply to Celsus' criticism of them he insists that "the whole human world has evidence of the work of Jesus since in it dwell the churches of God which consist of people converted through Jesus from countless evils." The greatest of miracles is this transformation of character.[38] Once more, however, the church cannot be completely separated from the world in which it was living. The transformation was in relation to principles known to Greek and Roman moralists, as Justin already pointed out. "What has been well spoken by all belongs to us Christians." [39] Origen refers to "the law written in their hearts" (Romans 2:15) and says that those who affirmed the righteous judgment of God could not have believed in a penalty for sins "unless in accordance with the universal idea all men had a sound conception of moral principles." [40] He is referring to the Stoic idea of "common notions," as Chadwick points out; and to understand his thought is impossible without reference to this idea.

Geography, history, life in society — all these aspects of early Christian life and thought need to be related to the life and thought of the Roman world in which Christians were living and thinking. Indeed, it seems fairly clear that Christianity is incomprehensible without its Roman setting. The point seems self-evident to me; but both Canon Streeter and I began our studies in church history on another basis, and so for the moment I shall assume that it is not self-evident and defend it by analogy. How could you possibly understand the life of the church today unless you took into account the two world wars and their consequences, the various kinds of liberation movements, the trends in the sciences and philosophy and the arts? It is almost amusing to think that not so long ago an ecumenical group had to plead for a consideration of "nontheological factors" in Christianity. Theology itself has undergone a tremendous period of testing and reformulation, and the end is not yet. At this point there are those who plead for a renewal of emphasis on the Christian tradition as such and on its theological expression in our day. This plea is misguided. The tradition, yes; the tradition in a vacuum, no; for the tradition has never been transmitted in some kind of pristine purity but always in relation to the life of the times in which it was being transmitted. To isolate it is impossible.

If we look back at the beginnings of Christian theology in the New Testament itself, we find at its base a hope and a movement. The hope is for the coming reign of God, as differentiated from Herodian and Roman rule in Palestine. The movement is that of Jesus and his disciples, calling upon Palestinian Jews to repent and prepare themselves for the coming of God's reign, i.e., for the theocracy. When we go beyond this stage to the thought of the apostle Paul, we find him using the commonplaces of Greco-Roman rhetorical theology to speak of the one God, from whom and for whom everything exists, and the one Lord Jesus Christ, through whom everything exists and through whom the Christian community came into being (1 Corinthians 8:6). A little farther on in Christian experience the implications of this kind of statement are drawn out by Ignatius of Antioch. What he says about Jesus Christ — "the eternal; the invisible, visible for us; the intangible; the impassible, passible for us; the one who endured for us in every way" — is an answer to Christian Docetists, who held that since Jesus was God he was eternal, invisible, intangible, and impassible. Their idea of God was based on Greek philosophical ideas, perhaps as mediated through Hellenistic Judaism. [41] By applying these ideas to Christ, they emptied the Incarnation, i.e., the fact of Jesus, of its historical meaning. Ignatius accepts their ideas in regard to both God and Christ. In order to save the reality of Jesus, he had to resort to paradox by saying that the invisible became visible, the impassible, passible.

Other early Christians worked out the doctrine of the Son of God in other ways, but without exception they did so in relation to the Greco-Roman philosophical milieu in which they were living and to which they addressed their writings. Again, this milieu was a general one, but it can be understood as quite specific if we recall that many of the Christian apologies were addressed to Roman emperors. Too often we see the emperors and their staffs as providing nothing but a backdrop before which the drama, the real drama, of Christian history is being played. But they were real men, and Christian history (if there is such an entity) fades into unreality when they are neglected. Remember Justin Martyr. He addressed his apology to the emperor Antoninus Pius and to his adopted sons, Marcus Aurelius and Lucius Verus. He called Marcus by the nickname "Verissimus" which Hadrian had used because of the boy's love of study; he addressed both heirs to the throne as philosophers because during the past few years Marcus had definitely and publicly turned from rhetoric to philosophy. Many years later Marcus Aurelius wrote down the things for which he owed gratitude to his family and his friends, and he gave thanks to a certain Rusticus for keeping him away from zeal for rhetoric and for teaching him to avoid rhetoric, poetry, and preciosity. Rusticus had lent him a copy of the *Discourses* of Epictetus.[42] It was before Rusticus, prefect of Rome in about 165, that Justin appeared on the charge of being a Christian; it was Rusticus who condemned him to death.

The relation between the Christian apologist and the Roman world did not consist simply of an address to a philosopher-king and a condemnation by his adviser. Justin also describes the legal procedure followed by a Christian, perhaps Gnostic-minded, youth at Alexandria who presented a *libellus* to the prefect of Egypt asking for permission to be castrated. His intention was to prove that Christians did not practice promiscuous intercourse as a sacred rite *(mysterion)*. The prefect, L. Munatius Felix, refused to endorse the petition, for it was contrary to Roman law.[43] This brief episode raises innumerable questions bearing on the setting of Christianity in the Roman world. Why did non-Christians suppose that promiscuous intercourse was a Christian rite? Why did the youth think that castration was advisable on Christian grounds, permissible in Roman procedure? Did Christianity at Alexandria have sacred rites called "mysteries"? What was a *libellus?* What was the office of the prefect of Egypt? Would a record of the youth's petition be kept, and would it prejudice the attitude of the state, at least in Egypt, toward Christians? Finally, the date of Felix as prefect is determined not from Christian writings or Roman literary sources but from papyrus documents found in Egypt. These show that another man held office on November 11, 148, while Felix himself was prefect on April 17, 150 (P. Ryl. 75) and during the sixteenth year of Antoninus Pius (152/153, P. Oxy. 800).[44] By August 29, 154 another man was prefect. To these points we can then add that in Justin's opinion the birth of Christ had occurred a hundred and fifty years before the apology was written.[45]

Another set of questions arises out of Justin's description of the martyrdom of a Christian teacher named Ptolemaeus. This is to be found at the beginning of the so-called "second apology," a booklet which Justin himself describes as a *libellus,* asking the emperor or emperors to endorse it.[46] Ptolemaeus had been the teacher of a Christian woman whose husband finally gave information against both her and the teacher. (This happened after she had given her husband a *repudium* or bill of divorcement.) The judge before whom Ptolemaeus came is especially interesting, for he was the famous Q. Lollius Urbicus, an African who was sufficiently famous before 138 to erect an inscription concerning his *cursus honorum.*[47] Urbicus had already been the legate of Hadrian during the "Jewish expedition" and legate of Germania Inferior, as well as *consul suffectus.* Under Antoninus Pius he became legate of Britain and undertook the construction of the Antonine Wall or earthworks between the Firth of Forth and the Clyde. Many inscriptions from Britain record his name and his work. Later he became *praefectus urbi,* about 150, and Apuleius mentions a case heard before him. Given this background in his career, it is hardly surprising that when Ptolemaeus came before him, he did not investigate anything but the question of his being a Christian. The background also illuminates the protest made after the sentencing by another Christian. "What is the basis on which you have sentenced this man, who acknowledged being a Christian, when he was not convicted . . . of any crime at all? Your decision is unworthy of the emperor Pius or the philosopher Caesar or the son of a philosopher." This Christian was appealing to the Roman justice which Urbicus was representing in his office as prefect. Urbicus, concerned with the maintenance of the order to which he had devoted his life, sentenced him to death also, after he had acknowledged being a Christian.[48]

The kinds of materials to which I have been pointing are not, of course, fully listed here. All I have been trying to do is to provide a few examples of the kind of work I see as relatively fruitful. R. P. C. Hanson, editing the papers presented at a conference on "Christianity in Britain, 300–700," has put a rather similar point with his customary

vigor. Speaking of "Gildas the Wise," one of the few literary sources
for the early history of Christian Britain, he says that far more research students should be urged to turn their attention to Gildas.
"Several dozen could well [dare I say it?] be profitably drafted from
pursuing fairly useless researches on the New Testament." [49] I do not
know that I should "dare say it," but I am convinced that either the
traditional methods or the much-advertised new approaches to biblical
study or, for that matter, to church history are unlikely to produce
results proportionate to the labors involved. It is time for students
of the New Testament and early Christianity to come out of the
sacred texts into the world to which and in which the Christian mission was addressed and achieved results. To put it another way, two
centuries of work with the microscope have been enough, so that
attention can now be directed to other objects in the same field. The
title of the Philadelphia Seminar, with its reference to Christian
Origins, surely implies that beginnings and sources are not the only
objects to be considered. The point of considering the origin of
something is that there was a movement and a life that somehow
grew out of the origin. In my opinion, it would be a disaster for New
Testament studies if they were to continue to be concentrated solely
upon the New Testament itself without any meaningful context.

I see several attempts as having been made in fairly recent times.
One was the theological interpretation of the Bible, undertaken
chiefly within the confines of the Christian community. It was intended to support various forms of traditional Christianity or non-
traditional Christianity. Its adherents often believed that they could
identify their own conclusions with a primitive norm from which
their opponents had departed. This approach was often accompanied
by an insistence on the subjectivism in the work of their predecessors,
a subjectivism which masqueraded as a search for objectivity. They
themselves, aware of this difficulty, could then claim to be either
objective or subjective but, in any event, right. The appeal of this
approach has tended to wane as the Christian community itself has
turned to the world outside and to recognize, once more, the importance of the secular.

A more recent approach has revived the concerns of the old "history of religions" school while claiming to represent something different. There is still a great deal to be learned from this approach, not
only in such obvious areas as Gnostic studies but also in regard to the
whole religious life of the world in which Christianity arose. Mystery
religions, fashionable half a century ago, but more recently under a
cloud, did exist and did influence Christianity, not simply as opponents. Civic cults, the worship of the emperor, the religion of the army
— all need to be considered again and more adequately.

But Christianity was not just a religion. Anyone who deals with early Christianity or Judaism or civic and national cults realizes at once that the differentiation of "religious" and "political" elements in the Greco-Roman world is virtually meaningless. Such a differentiation leads to, or results from, a kind of historical schizophrenia which makes for lopsided conclusions. For example, one cannot study even the religion of Isis without recalling the Roman official attitudes toward it and, on the other side, the Pompeian inscriptions stating that the Isiacs were in favor of Cuspius Pansa or Helvius Sabinus as *aedile*.[50] But Christianity, like Judaism, was more a political-social movement than was the religion of Isis. To understand its origins in the broadest sense means dealing not simply with theology (though theology was a part of it) or with religion (though in some aspects it was a religion) but with history in the broadest sense, with the history of the Roman world and of the barbarians who finally overcame Rome in the west. Perhaps we could put it this way. Christianity was essentially a movement, a movement of mission to the world in which it arose. It is the mission that counted. The detailed study of the books which Christians brought with them on the mission has some importance, for we certainly need to know what the missionary documents were. To spend all our time concentrating on the very beginnings, however, especially since the records were compiled only in part to provide historical information,[51] would be like studying American history with reference only to the Constitution and perhaps the Federalist Papers.

The early history of Christianity is Roman history, and I should claim that Roman history itself needs the collaboration of those who try to relate the Christian movement to the whole life of the Empire, not explaining everything Christian in Roman terms or everything Roman in Christian terms but trying to understand identities, similarities, and differences. Otherwise, Roman history fades away into the past, and Christian history remains a myth. To put it another way, what early church history needs is demythologizing.

NOTES

[1] B. H. Streeter, *The Primitive Church* (New York: The Macmillan Company, 1929), p. 7.

[2] E. Haenchen, *Die Apostelgeschichte* (Göttingen: Vandenhoeck & Ruprecht, 1959), pp. 133-134; cf. S. Weinstock in *Journal of Roman Studies* 39 (1949), 43-46.

[3] *Klio* 9 (1909), 263-273; cf. F. Boll, C. Bezold and W. Gundel, *Sternglaube und Sterndeutung* (Leipzig: Teubner, 1926), pp. 64; 157-158.

[4] Clement, *Excerpta ex Theodoto* 25. 2.

[5] *Adversus Iudaeos* 7. 4.

[6] *Historia Ecclesiastica* 3. 1. 1.

[7] *Ibid.*, 5. 10. 3.

[8] 1 Clement 5. 5-7.

[9] *Dialogue* 117. 5.

[10] Pliny, *Naturalis Historia* 4. 80.

[11] *Ibid.*, 5. 22; 6. 55; 6. 189.

[12] *Ibid.*, 5. 87.

[13] Tatian, *Oratio* 20 (cf. Plutarch, *Theseus* 1).

[14] See my note in *Vigiliae Christianae* 3 (1949), 225-229.

[15] J. Vardeman in *Journal of Biblical Literature* 81 (1962), 70-71.

[16] W. Dittenberger, *Sylloge Inscriptionum Graecarum*, 3rd ed. (Leipzig: Hirzelium, 1917), p. 801.

[17] Cf. A. Grabar, *Christian Iconography* (Princeton: Princeton University Press, 1968), pp. 7-13.

[18] *1 Apologia* 13. 3; 1. 1; 26. 2.

[19] *Ibid.*, 29. 4; 31. 6.

[20] *Ibid.*, 46. 1; 34. 2.

[21] *Ibid.*, 31. 2.

[22] W. Schmid in *Zeitschrift für die neutestamentliche Wissenschaft* 40 (1941), 121-23.

[23] Cf. R. M. Grant, *After the New Testament* (Philadelphia: Fortress Press, 1967), pp. 93-97.

[24] Josephus is followed by Tatian and Theophilus.

[25] Eusebius, *Historia Ecclesiastica* 4. 26. 7-10.

[26] *Apologeticum* 5.

[27] Origen, *Contra Celsum* 2. 31 (see the note of H. Chadwick).

[28] *Ad Autolycum* 3. 27.

[29] *Ibid.*, 1. 11; 1 Corinthians 9:17.

[30] Cf. J. H. Oliver, *The Ruling Power (Trans. Amer. Philos. Soc.* 43 [1953], 4).

[31] Eusebius, *Historia Ecclesiastica* 5. 5.

[32] *Legatio* 1 and 18.

[33] *Adversus Haereses* 4. 30. 3.

[34] Ramsey MacMullen, *Enemies of the Roman Order* (Cambridge, Mass.: Harvard University Press, 1966).

[35] S. G. F. Brandon, *Jesus and the Zealots* (New York: Charles Scribner's Sons, 1967).

[36] W. L. Knox in *Journal of Roman Studies* 39 (1949), 23-30.

[37] *Ad Diognetum* 5; *Apologeticum* 42. 1-3; on 1 Corinthians 5:10 cf. *De idololatria* 14. 5.

[38] *Contra Celsum* 1. 67 (trans. H. Chadwick); cf. 1. 43.

[39] *2 Apologia* 13. 4; cf. Seneca, *Epistula* 12. 11; 16. 7; Clement, *Stromata* 1. 37. 6.

[40] *Contra Celsum* 1. 4 (p. 8, Chadwick).

[41] R. M. Grant, *The Early Christian Doctrine of God* (Charlottesville, Va.: University of Virginia Press, 1966), pp. 14-15.

[42] M. Aurelius, *Meditationes* 1. 6; cf. 1. 17. 5.

[43] *1 Apologia* 29; cf. *Digest of Justinian* 48. 8. 4. 2; W. Bauer in *Neutestamentliche Studien G. Heinrici* (Leipzig, 1914), pp. 235-244.

[44] Cf. O. W. Reinmuth in A. F. Pauly and G. Wissowa, *Realencyclopädie der classischen Altertumswissenschaft* (Stuttgart, 1894-1960), 22. 2372; also in *Bulletin of the American Society of Papyrologists* 4 (1967), 96-97.

[45] *1 Apologia* 46. 1.

[46] *2 Apologia* 14. 1.

[47] H. Dessau, *Inscriptiones Latinae Selectae 1* (Berlin: Weidmann, 1892), 1065.

[48] 2 *Apologia* 2.

[49] R. P. C. Hanson and M. Barley, eds., *Christianity in Britain, 300-700* (New York: Humanities Press, Inc., 1968), p. 211.

[50] Dessau, *op. cit.*, 2. 6419 (f) and 6420 (b).

[51] The part was important, however; cf. A. W. Mosley, "Historical Reporting in the Ancient World," *New Testament Studies* 12 (1965), 10-26.

Stephen Benko

1

The Sources of Roman History Between 31 B.C.–A.D. 138

The student who wishes to learn about the history of the Roman Empire in this period of time is in the fortunate position of having at his disposal many works of contemporary historians. Several of these writers experienced personally the events which they described and thus we are in possession of many eyewitness accounts. The works which are pertinent to our period of time are as follows:

STRABO OF AMASIA (*ca.* 64 B.C.–A.D. 21) wrote in seventeen books a work entitled *Geographica,* in which he described the countries of the Roman world, their geographical features, histories, and the characteristics of their peoples. These books survived almost entirely intact. Strabo also wrote a great historical book from which only fragments remain.

RES GESTAE DIVI AUGUSTI is the only surviving work of Augustus and records the most important events of his life. It is also known as *Monumentum Ancyranum* because a copy of it was found inscribed on the wall of a temple in Ancyra. Fragments of it have been found elsewhere. The text is available in *Monumentum Ancyranum, The Deeds of Augustus,* edited and translated by William Fairly. *Translations and Reprints,* vol. 5, no. 1 (Philadelphia: University of Pennsylvania Press, 1898). A copy and translation is also included in the volume of the Loeb Classical Library containing the *History of Velleius Paterculus.*

VELLEIUS PATERCULUS (*ca.* 20 B.C.–A.D. 30) lived under Augustus and Tiberius and served as an officer under Tiberius. He took part in the campaigns in Germany and Pannonia. Around A.D. 30 he wrote a *Roman History* from the earliest times up to his own time. His work is especially important for the life of Tiberius, whom he presented in a very favorable light, in contrast to the later work of Tacitus.

PHILO OF ALEXANDRIA (*ca.* 20 B.C.–A.D. 45), the famous Jewish philosopher of Alexandria, wrote extensively. A number of books have survived from his extensive literary activity, but only two need to be mentioned here: *Legatio ad Gaium* and *In Flaccum (Peri Aretōn)* which describe the Alexandrian Jewish pogrom of A.D. 38 and the embassy of the Jews to Emperor Gaius, led by Philo.

FLAVIUS JOSEPHUS (A.D. 37–100?) was the renegade Jewish general who earned the gratitude of Vespasian and Titus and received Roman citizenship. His four books are as follows:

1. *History of the Jewish Wars (Peri tōn Ioudaikōn polemōn)* is the version or new edition in Greek of a book originally written in Aramaic. Divided into seven books, this work deals with the story of the Jews from 170 B.C., i.e., the capture of Jerusalem by Antiochus Epiphanes, until A.D. 70, the capture of Jerusalem by Titus, which Josephus himself witnessed. The bulk of the work is about the rebellion of A.D. 66–70. This work was composed soon after the conclusion of the war.

2. *Jewish Antiquities (Ioudaikē Archaiologiā)* is a history, in twenty books, of the Jews from the Creation until A.D. 66. In this work Josephus preserved for us (although sometimes in abbreviated form) many Roman edicts and rescripts, and he also gave valuable information which he took from reliable Roman sources concerning several Roman emperors. The work was written around A.D. 93–94.

3. *Vita,* attached as an appendix to the *Antiquities,* is an apology against the accusations of an historian, Justus of Tiberias.

4. *Contra Apionem* is a defense of Judaism and an attack upon Gentile morality and teachings.

DIO OF PRUSA in Bithynia, also called *Chrysostom (ca.* A.D. 40–115) , was in disfavor under Domitian, but highly esteemed by Nerva and Trajan. His *Discourses* on various philosophical and political questions contain some important references to the events of his times.

PLUTARCH *(ca.* A.D. 46–120) was a famous Greek philosopher. The *Parallel Lives (Bioi paralleloi)* of this man are widely known. For our period, however, they are only of limited value, since from the Roman emperors only the histories of Galba and Otho remained.

PUBLIUS CORNELIUS TACITUS *(ca.* A.D. 55–120) had a distinguished career as a public official including consulship, proconsulship, and governorship of a province. His five works listed below are major sources of the history of imperial Rome.

1. *Agricola* is an encomium on his father-in-law *(d.* A.D. 93) , who played an important role in the conquest of Britain by the Romans. Agricola was governor of Britain in A.D. 77 or 78 and led the British campaigns between 80–83. Tacitus relates these events praising Agricola's distinguished service.

2. *Germania* is a description of Germany including the geography

of the country, the political and social characteristics of its people. The book was written in A.D. 98, the same year *Agricola* was written.

3. *Historiae* is the history of the years A.D. 69–96 in five books, written between A.D. 104–109. The emperors who are discussed here are those from Galba to Domitian. The last part of Book 5 is lost and the narrative breaks off with the reign of Vespasian and the revolt of the Batavians under Civilis. The younger Pliny supplied Tacitus with material for this work and revised parts of it.

4. *Annales* is the history of the Empire under Tiberius, Gaius, Claudius, and Nero, written after the *Historiae*, probably between A.D. 115–117. The whole work is divided into sixteen books, of which large portions are unfortunately missing. Books 1–6 deal with Tiberius; parts of Book 5 are missing. The history of the years 37–46 is lost, and the story resumes with the second half of Book 11, A.D. 47, i.e., the seventh year of Claudius. Book 12 relates the history up to the accession of Nero in A.D. 54. Books 13–16 deal with the years of Nero's reign, but the events of the last two years of Nero are lost. Book 15 describes the fire of Rome and the persecution of the Christians.

5. *Dialogus de Oratoribus* is a dialogue on the art of oratory, important because of its many references to public life and morals.

GAIUS PLINIUS CAECILIUS SECUNDUS, better known as Pliny the Younger (*ca.* A.D. 61–114), was a contemporary of Tacitus. He held public offices under Trajan and acted as governor of Bithynia between A.D. 111–113. Two of his works are important for our study:

1. *Panegyricus* is an oration delivered in A.D. 100 in praise of Trajan. In this speech Pliny threw light on many abuses during the reign of Domitian and on the reforms under Trajan.

2. *Letters:* These consist of nine books which were published by him; the tenth was published posthumously. Particularly famous are 6. 16 and 20, addressed to Tacitus, describing the eruption of Vesuvius and 10, which contains his correspondence as governor of Bithynia with Trajan. 10. 96 is the well-known correspondence dealing with the Christians.

GAIUS SUETONIUS TRANQUILLUS (*ca.* A.D. 70–*ca.* 150) was a friend of the younger Pliny. His father served in the thirteenth legion which took part in the war between the forces of Otho and Vitellius. Suetonius himself served under Trajan as one of the imperial secretaries. Thus he had access to documents in the archives, and he consulted these carefully when he wrote his books. Of his many writings only one has survived, *De Vita Caesarum*, [Lives of the Caesars] which gives the biographies of the "Caesars" beginning with Julius Caesar up to Domitian. His book is rich in anecdotes and detailed descriptions of the emperors' daily life, hobbies, vices, etc.

DIO CASSIUS COCCEIANUS (*ca.* A.D. 155–230) was consul, and later governor of Africa and Dalmatia. He wrote a *Roman History* in eighty books around A.D. 200. He spent ten years collecting the material and another twelve years writing this work, using as his sources the works of earlier historians. The period which he covers is from the founding of the city to A.D. 229, but many parts of the work are lost. We have only Books 36-60 and 79 complete; the others are known through the summaries of Zonaras (twelfth century), who prepared an epitome of Books 1–21, and Xiphilinos (eleventh century), who wrote an epitome of Books 36–80.

HISTORIA AUGUSTA is the title of a collection of biographies dating from A.D. 117 to 284. It was probably written in the second half of the fourth century by six authors. For our study only the first biography, that of Hadrian, comes into question.

All the works thus far mentioned are easily accessible in the Loeb Classical Library. In addition, there are many critical editions, and the most important histories are available in various English translations. Many of them, for example, Tacitus, Suetonius, Plutarch, and Josephus, can also be had in inexpensive paperback editions. From the preceding list we omitted the name of Titus Livius (59 B.C.– A.D. 17) whose *History of Rome* in its original form covered the period from the foundation of the city up to 9 B.C.. Much of Livy's work is, however, lost; and from the history after 167 B.C. only fragments and summaries remain. There are, of course, later historians who wrote about the time of the early Roman Empire. Among these Orosius, a fifth century Christian author, is best known. At the request of his friend St. Augustine, he wrote a history of the world up to A.D. 417. But he, as did other later historians, relied upon earlier material and thus these writings can only be considered as secondary sources.

For the reconstruction of the early history of imperial Rome, historians can also rely upon the numerous inscriptions, papyri, and coins, of which many have been discovered, collected, systematically examined, and published. Much valuable information, especially for the social and economic conditions, everyday life, customs, and public morals of the people can be gathered from the works of contemporary authors, poets, and orators. Virgil, Horace, Tibullus, and Ovid reflect the era of Augustus. Martial lived between A.D. 40–104; Seneca the younger and Petronius the *elegantiae arbiter* were both victims of Nero in A.D. 65. Juvenal and Epictetus were active during Hadrian's reign. When we read their works, we are transported back into the times in which they lived. The best-known and most important such writers are the following:

PUBLIUS VIRGILIUS MARO (70–19 B.C.) wrote the famous

nationalist epic the *Aeneid* in which he extolled the virtues of the Augustan age. His ten *Eclogues* and the *Georgics* are also well known.

QUINTUS HORATIUS FLACCUS (65–8 B.C.) was author of the *Carmen Saeculare* which was written for the "secular games" of Augustus in 17 B.C. His *Satires* and *Odes* are no less important.

ALBIUS TIBULLUS (*ca.* 60–19 B.C.) was a friend of Horace. His poems were published in three books.

PUBLIUS OVIDIUS NASO (43 B.C.–A.D. 18) composed a large number of mythological and erotic poems in Rome. In A.D. 8 Augustus expelled him from Rome and banished him to Tomis on the west shore of the Black Sea. The reason for this judgment may have been his poem *Ars Amatoria* and his personal morals. He continued to write poetry until his death in Tomis. These poems appeared under the title *Tristia* and *Epistulae ex Ponto* [Laments and Letters from Pontus].

LUCIUS ANNAEUS SENECA, called "the elder," (*ca.* 55 B.C.–*ca.* A.D. 37) wrote books on rhetorical themes.

LUCIUS ANNAEUS SENECA, called "the philosopher," son of "the elder" Seneca (4 B.C.–A.D. 65), played a prominent role in the political world under Nero (see below). He was the author of many philosophical works of which the *Dialogues* are best known. His brother was M. Annaeus Novatus who later took the name Gallio from his adoptive father and became proconsul of Achaea (see Acts 18:12-17). Seneca's popularity is shown by the fact that in later Christian circles a correspondence between the apostle Paul and Seneca was invented, consisting of fourteen letters in all.

PETRONIUS ARBITER (*d.* A.D. 65) was the author of the *Satyricon* of which only portions survive. It is a biting satire of life under Nero.

GAIUS PLINIUS SECUNDUS (A.D. 23–79) "the elder" was a close associate of Emperor Vespasian. His one surviving work is the *Natural History* in thirty-seven books. He died at the eruption of Vesuvius which the younger Pliny described in a letter to Tacitus (6. 16). The younger Pliny was his nephew and adopted son.

MARCUS FABIUS QUINTILIANUS (*ca.* A.D. 30–96) was professor in Rome and taught, among others, Pliny the younger and children of the imperial family. His *Institutio Oratoria* gives valuable information about education in imperial Rome.

MARCUS VALERIUS MARTIALIS (*ca.* A.D. 40–100) published his short poems under the title *Epigrams*. These reflect a realistic knowledge of the society in which he lived. His language was often obscene.

DECIMUS JUNIUS JUVENALIS (*ca.* A.D. 60–140), a friend of Martial, is famous for his biting *Satires* on Roman life.

EPICTETUS (*ca.* A.D. 60–140) of Hierapolis in Phrygia was the outstanding stoic philosopher of the time period with which we deal. He was a slave who was once owned by the secretary of Nero. His doctrines survived in his *Diatribai* and *Enchiridion.* In *Diatribai (Dissertationes)* 4. 7. 6 he mentioned the "Galileans" who were not afraid when someone threatened them. This term probably referred to the Christians.

LUCIUS APULEIUS (*ca.* A.D. 125–171) is best known as the author of the *Metamorphoses* or *Golden Ass.* This is important because of the many references to oriental religions in it. Apuleius opposed Christianity; in *Metamorphoses* 11. 14 he may have referred to it. He was born in Madauros, North Africa, not far from Carthage where Tertullian was born *ca.* A.D. 155.

For those who are interested in a particular period in Roman history, or in a particular person or problem, a wealth of modern literature is available. The following bibliography attempts to offer some help in this respect. It is to be remembered, however, that this list of books represents only a fraction of what has been written and that new titles are constantly being published.

FOR ADVANCED READING

STANDARD REFERENCE WORKS

Bickerman, Elias J., *Chronology of the Ancient World.* Ithaca: Cornell University Press, 1968.

Coleman-Norton, Paul R., ed., *Roman State and Christian Church: A Collection of Legal Documents to A.D. 535.* 3 Vols. London: S.P.C.K., 1966.

Corpus Inscriptionum Latinarum. Berlin: Deutsche Akademic der Wissenschaften, 1863—. Thus far 16 volumes. (Parallel edition of the *Corpus Inscriptionum Graecarum* must also be consulted.)

Cook, S. A.; Adcock, F. E.; and Charlesworth, M. P., eds., *The Cambridge Ancient History.* New York: Cambridge University Press, vol. 10 (1934); vol. 11 (1936).

Daremberg, C., and Saglio, E., eds., *Dictionaire des antiquités grecques et romaines* Paris: 1877–1919.

Dessau, H., *Geschichte der römischen Kaiserzeit.* 2 vols. Berlin: 1924-30.

————, *Inscriptiones Latinae Selectae.* Berlin: Weidmann, 1892-1916.

Dittenberger, W., *Sylloge Inscriptionum Graecarum.* 3rd ed. Hildesheim: G. Olms, 1960. (Reprint of the edition of 1915).

Duff, John W., *A Literary History of Rome in the Silver Age.* New York: Barnes & Noble Inc., 1964.

Frank, T., ed., *An Economic Survey of Ancient Rome.* Baltimore: The Johns Hopkins Press, 1933-40.

Gordon, Arthur E. and Joyce S., *Album of Dated Latin Inscriptions.* Berkeley: University of California Press, 1958.

Harper's Dictionary of Classical Literature and Antiquities. Edited by Harry T. Peck. New York: Cooper Square Publishers, Inc., 1965.

Harvey, Paul, ed., *The Oxford Companion to Classical Literature.* Oxford: The

Clarendon Press, 1937.
Holmes, Thomas R. E., *The Roman Republic and the Founder of the Empire.* 3 vols. New York: Russell & Russell, 1967.
Lewis, Naphtali, and Reinhold, M., eds., *Roman Civilization.* 2 vols. New York: Columbia University Press, 1951, 1955. (Paper, 1966.)
Lexikon der Alten Welt. Stuttgart: Artemis Verlag, 1965.
Methuen's History of the Greek and Roman World. Edited by Max Cary. 6 vols. New York: Barnes & Noble, Inc., 1966.
Mommsen, Theodore, *Römische Geschichte.* 11 ed., 5 vols. Berlin: Weidmann, 1935. (English translation by W. P. Dickson, London: The Macmillan Company, 1913.)
_____, *The History of Rome.* rev. ed. by Dero A. Saunders and John H. Collins. New York: The World Publishing Company, 1958.
The New Century Classical Handbook. Edited by Catherine B. Avery. New York: Appleton-Century-Crofts, 1962.
The Oxford Classical Dictionary. Oxford: The Clarendon Press, 1966. (New edition 1970.)
Pauly, A. F.; Wissows, G.; and Kroll, W., *Realencyclopädie der Classischen Altertumswissenschaft.* Stuttgart: 1894. A 4 volume abbreviated edition *Der kleine Pauly,* ed. K. Ziegler and W. Southeimer, is now available.
Platner, Samuel B., and Ashby, Thomas, *Topographical Dictionary of Ancient Rome.* New York: Oxford University Press, 1929.
Propyläen Weltgeschichte. Eine Universalgeschichte. Herausgegeben von Golo Mann und Alfred Heusz. 4 Band. Rom. Die römische Welt. Im Propyläen Verlag. Berlin, Frankfurt, Wien, 1963.
Rostovtzeff, Mikhail I., *A History of the Ancient World.* trans. by J. D. Duff. New York: Oxford University Press, 1930
_____, *Rome.* (New ed. by Elias J. Bickerman of vol. 2 of *A History of the Ancient World.*) New York: Oxford University Press, 1960.
_____, *The Social and Economic History of the Roman Empire.* 2nd rev. ed. by P. M. Fraser. Oxford: The Clarendon Press. 1957.
Sandys, John E., *A Companion to Latin Studies.* 3rd. ed. New York: Hafner Publishing Co., Inc., 1935.
Schürer, Emil, *A History of the Jewish People in the Time of Jesus.* Edited by Nahum N. Glatzer. New York: Schocken Books, 1961.

THE HISTORY OF ROME

Africa, Thomas W., *Rome of the Caesars.* New York: John Wiley & Sons, Inc., 1965.
Altheim, F., *Römische Geschichte.* Vierte erweiterte und ergänzte Auflage. 2 vols. Frankfurt: Klostermann, 1951-53.
Aymard, A., and Auboyer, J., *Rome et son empire.* Paris: 1954.
Barrow, R. H., *The Romans.* Baltimore: Penguin Books, Inc., 1949.
Bengtson, H., *Grundriss der römischen Geschichte mit Quellenkunde.* Band I: Republik und Kaiserzeit bis 284 n.Chr. München, 1967.
Boak, A. E. R., and Sinnigen, W. G., *A History of Rome to A.D. 565.* New York: The Macmillan Company, 1965.
Burke, Richard, *The Ancient World (800 B.C.–A.D. 800).* New York: McGraw-Hill Book Company, 1967.
Cary, Max, *Geographic Background of Greek and Roman History.* New York: Oxford University Press, 1949.
_____, *A History of Rome.* New York: St. Martin's Press, Inc., 1954.

Chapot, Victor, *The Roman World*. New York: Alfred A. Knopf, Inc., 1928.

Charlesworth, Martin P., *The Roman Empire*. New York: Oxford University Press, 1967.

Frank, Tenney, *A History of Rome*. New York: Holt, Rinehart & Winston, Inc., 1923.

Gianelli, G., ed., *The World of Ancient Rome*. New York: G. P. Putnam's Sons, 1967.

Grant, M., *The World of Rome*. Cleveland: The World Publishing Company, 1960.

————, *Roman History from Coins*. New York: Cambridge University Press, 1968.

————, *The Climax of Rome: the Final Achievement of the Ancient World*. New York: Little, Brown & Co., 1968.

Hadas, M., *A History of Rome*. New York: Doubleday & Company, Inc., 1956.

Haywood, R. M., *Ancient Rome*. New York: David McKay Co., Inc., 1967.

Heichelheim, Fritz M., and Yeo, C. A., *History of the Roman People*. Englewood Cliffs, N.J.: Prentice-Hall, Inc., 1962.

Henderson, B. W., *Civil War and Rebellion in the Roman Empire A.D. 68-70*. London: The Macmillan Company, 1908.

Heuss, A., *Römische Geschichte*. Braunschweig: 1960.

Kornemann, E., *Römische Geschichte*. H. Die Kaiserzeit. Stuttgart: 1954.

Millar, Fergus, *The Roman Empire and Its Neighbors*. New York: Delacorte Press, 1968.

Moore, Frank G., *The Roman's World*. New York: Biblo & Tannen, 1936.

Nilsson, Martin P., *Imperial Rome*. Reprint. New York: Schocken Books, 1962.

Pareti, L., and Brezzi, P., *History of Mankind II: The Ancient World*. New York: Harper & Row, Publishers, 1965.

Piganiol, Andre, *Histoire de Rome*. 4th ed. Paris: 1954.

Rowell, Henry T., *Rome in the Augustan Age*. Norman, Oklahoma: University of Oklahoma Press, 1962.

Salmon, E. T., *A History of the Roman World from 30 B.C. to A.D. 138*. 6th ed. New York: Barnes & Noble, Inc., 1968.

Scullard, Howard, *From the Gracchi to Nero: A History of Rome from 133 B.C. to A.D. 68*. 2nd ed. New York: Barnes & Noble, Inc., 1964.

Showerman, G., *Rome and the Romans*. New York: The Macmillan Company, 1931.

Starr, Chester, *The Emergence of Rome as a Ruler of the Western World*. 2nd ed. Ithaca: Cornell University Press, 1953.

Stier, H. E., *Roms Aufstieg zur Weltmacht und die griechische Welt*. Köln: 1957.

Timpe, D., *Untersuchungen zur Kontinuität des frühen Prinzipats*. Wiesbaden: 1962.

THE ROMAN PROVINCES

General

Arnold, W. T., and Bouchier, E. S., *Roman Provincial Administration*. Chicago: Argonaut, Inc., Publishers, 1969.

Barloeven, von W. D., and others, *Abriss der Geschichte antiker Randkulturen*. München: 1961.

Birley, Eric, ed., *The Congress of Roman Frontier Studies*. Durham: University of Durham, 1952.

Millar, Fergus, *The Roman Empire and Its Neighbors*. New York: Delacorte Press, 1968.

Mommsen, Th., *The Provinces of the Roman Empire from Caesar to Diocletian*. 2 vols. London: 1909. A selection *(The European Provinces)* was edited with an introduction by T. R. S. Broughton in 1968.

Stevenson, George H., *Roman Provincial Administration*. New York: Oxford University Press, 1939.

Vittinghoff, F., *Römische Kolonisation und Bürgerrechtspolitik*. Mainz: 1952.

The Danube Area

Alföldi, A., *Die Vorherrschaft der Pannonier im Römerreich*. Frankfurt: 1930.

Klose, J., *Roms Klientel-Randstaaten am Rhein und an der Donau*. Breslau: 1934.

La Baume, Peter, *The Romans on the Rhine*. Chicago: Argonaut, Inc., Publishers, 1968.

Oliva, P., *Pannonia and the Onset of Crisis in the Roman Empire*. Chicago: Argonaut, Inc., Publishers, 1967.

Patsch, C., *Der Kampf um den Donauraum*. Vienna: 1937.

Wilkes, J. J., *Dalmatia*. Cambridge: Harvard University Press, 1969.

Britain

Birley, A., *Life in Roman Britain*. New York: Putnam's Sons, 1965.

Birley, Eric, *Roman Britain and the Roman Army*. Kendal: Wilson, 1953.

Burn, A. R., *Agricola and Roman Britain*. New York: The Macmillan Company, 1954.

_____, *The Romans in Britain*. rev. ed. Columbia: University of South Carolina Press, 1969.

Collingwood, Robin G., *Roman Britain and the English Settlements*. New York: Oxford University Press, 1937.

Durant, G. M., *Rome's Most Northerly Province: A History of Roman Britain, 43-450*. 1968.

Frere, Sheppard S., *Britannia: A History of Roman Britain*. Cambridge: Harvard University Press, 1967.

Liversidge, Joan, *Britain in the Roman Empire*. New York: Frederick A. Praeger, Inc., 1968.

Richmond, Ian A., *Roman Britain*. New York: Barnes & Noble, Inc., 1964.

Rivet, A. L., ed., *The Roman Villa in Britain*. New York: Frederick A. Praeger, Inc., 1969.

_____, *Town and Country in Roman Britain*. New York: Hutchinson, 1966.

Welch, George P., *Britannia: The Roman Conquest and Occupation of Britain*. Middletown, Conn.: Wesleyan University Press, 1963.

Gaul

Brogan, Oliver K., *Roman Gaul*. Cambridge: Harvard University Press, 1953.

Chilver, Guy E. F., *Cisalpine Gaul: Social and Economic History from 49 B.C. to the Death of Trajan*. New York: Oxford University Press, 1941.

Spain

Bouchier, E. S., *Spain under the Roman Empire*. New York: Oxford University Press, 1914.

Sutherland, Carol H. V., *The Romans in Spain, 217 B.C.-A.D. 117*. London: Methuen, 1939.

Wiseman, Francis J., *Roman Spain*. New York: The Macmillan Company, 1956.

Asia

Chapot, V., *La province romain proconsulaire d'Asie*. Paris: 1904.

Debevoise, Neilson C., *A Political History of Parthia*. Chicago: University of Chicago Press, 1938.

Gren, E., *Kleinasien und der Ostbalkan in der wirtschaftlichen Entwickelung der römischen Kaiserzeit*. Leipzig: 1941.

Jones, Arnold H. M., *The Cities of the Eastern Roman Provinces*. Oxford: The Clarendon Press, 1937.

Magie, D., *Roman Rule in Asia Minor to the End of the Third Century after Christ*. 2 vols. Princeton: Princeton University Press, 1950.

Ramsay, W. M., ed., *Studies in the History and Art of the Eastern Provinces of the Roman Empire*. London: Hodder & Stoughton, 1906.

Ramsay, W. M., *The Social Basis of Roman Power in Asia Minor* (Prepared for the press by J. G. C. Anderson). Amsterdam: A. M. Hakkert, 1967.

Egypt

Bell, H. I., *Egypt from Alexander the Great to the Arab Conquest*. New York: Oxford University Press, 1948.

Bell, H. I., *Jews and Christians in Egypt*. Oxford: The Clarendon Press, 1924.

Chapot, V., *L'Egypte romain*. Paris: 1933.

Johnson, Allan C., *Egypt and the Roman Empire*. Ann Arbor: University of Michigan Press, 1951.

Milne, J. G., *A History of Egypt Under Roman Rule*. 3rd ed. London: Methuen, 1924.

Reinmuth, O. W., *The Prefect of Egypt from Augustus to Diocletian*. Leipzig: 1935.

Stein, A., *Untersuchungen zur Geschichte und Verwaltung Ägyptens unter römischer Herrschaft*. Stuttgart: 1915.

_____, *Die Präfekten von Ägypten in der römischen Kaiserzeit*. 1950.

Wallace, Sherman L., *Taxation in Egypt from Augustus to Diocletian*. Princeton: Princeton University Press, 1938.

Zucker, F., *Ägypten im römischen Reich*. Berlin: 1958.

Africa

Albertini, E., *Roman Africa*. Alger: 1932.

Broughton, T. R. S., *The Romanization of Africa Proconsularis*. Baltimore: The Johns Hopkins Press, 1929. (Re-issue, New York: Greenwood Press, 1968).

Gsell, S., *Histoire ancienne de l'Afrique du Nord*. 8 vols. Paris: 1913-1928.

Romanelli, P., *Storia delle province romane dell' Africa*. Rome: 1959.

Stephen Benko

2
The History of the Early Roman Empire

AUGUSTUS 31 B.C. — A.D. *14*

Obviously we cannot speak about "early Christianity" during the reign of Augustus. Not only was there no church at all, but the public ministry of Jesus had not even begun. Nevertheless, Augustus is the natural starting point for our study, not only because during his reign was Jesus Christ born, somewhere between 7–4 B.C., but because Augustus laid the foundations of the political and economic order which became the background of early Christianity. His relation to the events in Palestine are well known. In 31 B.C. he confirmed Herod the Great in his kingdom[1] and after Herod's death in 4 B.C. confirmed his testament and divided his kingdom among his three sons (Archelaus, 4 B.C.–A.D. 6, ethnarch of Judea, Samaria, and Idumea; Philip, 4 B.C.–A.D. 34, tetrarch of Iturea and Trachonitis; Herod Antipas, 4 B.C.–A.D. 39, tetrarch of Galilee and Perea) ; and, finally, in A.D. 6 he banished Archelaus to Gaul and placed Judea, Samaria, and Idumea under Roman procurators. These matters, however, were only on the fringe of the interest of Augustus, who handled these problems in the same matter-of-fact way with which he dealt with the problems of many similar smaller dynasties and client kings such as those of Armenia, Cappadocia, Mauretania, and Thrace.

His main task, the one in which Augustus was supremely successful, was to bring stability to a world which was on the brink of anarchy as a result of continuous wars and civil strife. The battle of Actium in 31 B.C. cleared the air and demonstrated once and for all who was the ruler. But it also revealed signs of things to come because Octavian (that was still Augustus' name) unmistakably demonstrated his character in these events. When he entered Alexandria, he executed only a few political prisoners, among them the murderers of Julius Caesar, but he also ordered the death of Antony's young

The Julian-Claudian Dynasty

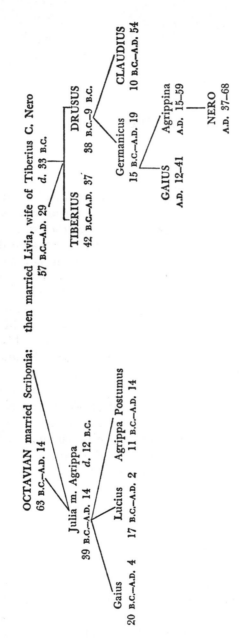

This genealogical table is highly condensed. For a more complete list see *The Cambridge Ancient History*, vol. 10; Edward T. Salmon, *A History of the Roman World*; or one of the books on Roman history listed in the Bibliography. Most contain such a table.

Compare also the table on page 50 (The Plot of Sejanus).

son, also named Antony, and the execution of Ptolemy Caesar, the son of Julius Caesar and Cleopatra. Then he coldly watched and perhaps even arranged for the suicide of Cleopatra, for there can be little doubt that Octavian did want her out of the way, preferably by her own hand; so he offered the opportunity for that.[2] He went to see the tomb of Alexander the Great but refused to visit the monuments of the Ptolemies, because, he said, he came to pay his respects to a king, not to visit corpses.[3] Historians like to exonerate him from these cruel acts by pointing out that in a cruel age Octavian actually acted magnanimously — did he not let the other children of Cleopatra live? Actually, the others constituted no immediate danger for him. Such an ethic of expediency was typical of the later Augustus, too. He was not only an arrogant and haughty man, but when it was a question of protecting his own interests and carrying out his plans, he could be as cold-blooded and ruthless as he was in Alexandria.

He was wise enough to know that the most urgent matter before him was to establish the confidence of all citizens in his government. He therefore announced that no one would be prosecuted for having supported Antony. He drastically reduced the number of his legions, and many of those remaining were assigned to public works. Since the wealth of Egypt poured into Rome, money was plentiful; soldiers were paid their wages, and all arrears in taxes were cancelled. The temple of Janus was closed in 29 B.C. when the news reached Rome that a war with Parthia had been avoided. That meant that peace had finally arrived in the *imperium* and that a new age had begun. Of course, the doors of the temple of Janus were soon reopened, and the Parthian confrontation was only delayed, not resolved. But these were only minor unpleasantnesses about which one could keep quiet in favor of a great image that was to be created. And that image was that through Octavian the long-awaited "golden age" had finally arrived. Thus when Octavian in 29 B.C. returned to Rome to celebrate a magnificent triumph, he conveniently forgot the fact that Antony had some part to play in the consolidation of the East and that all the victories were paid for with the lives of Roman citizens. Nevertheless, the reign of Augustus did have many positive achievements which cannot be minimized. His social legislation, the reorganization of the administrative machinery and the Senate, and his military reforms had a lasting effect. Eighty-two temples were restored in Rome alone during his Principate; a major road-repaving and road-building program was begun along with other public works. Law and order were restored within the boundaries of the Empire as a result of which commerce and the arts flourished.

The new governmental system established by Octavian is called the Principate. After Actium, Octavian held supreme power in Rome, but the Ides of March when Julius Caesar was assassinated probably lingered in his memory, and he was aware that an absolute monarchy would not be successful. At the same time he saw that a return to the old republican form of government was out of the question, if for no other reason, because of the vastly expanded territory of the state with its new and complex problems of diverse populations and cultures. Out of this quite realistic appraisal of the situation, Octavian, by masterful manipulations, effected a reorganization of the Roman governmental system. This system was republican in form and semblance, but imperial as far as actual executive power was concerned. The prerogatives of the Senate were restored and the old republican forms respected, but in addition to these, a new office was created, the office of the *princeps* (thus, the term Principate). The development of this system, however, was a long process, and the relationship between Senate and *princeps* is not always easy to describe. Octavian was very cautious and tried to avoid offending republican sensitivities. At the same time he was determined to strengthen his position and ruled practically as a sovereign. The official regularization of the new order took place in 27 B.C. and was subsequently revised in 23 B.C.

In January, 27 B.C., Octavian resigned his supreme power, but then at the protest of the Senate he consented to administer a certain number of provinces. The whole scene was prearranged, but it gave a semblance of legality to the arrangement. Octavian actually did not usurp any power, for the *Imperium Proconsulare* was conferred upon him by vote of the Senate. The personal inviolability of a tribune had already been granted to him for life in 36 B.C. The provinces placed under him were those with the largest contingents of the Roman army: Spain, Gaul, Syria, and Egypt; and that, of course, gave him practical control over military matters, and the person who controlled the military had the final word in other matters, too. The Senate retained control over other provinces. In the imperial provinces military government had been established, whereas the senatorial provinces were ruled by civil government. We note that in Syria and later in Judea, as imperial provinces, military government prevailed. However, this settlement remained flexible because senatorial provinces sometimes passed into imperial control, or vice versa as events necessitated. The settlement of 27 B.C. was revised in 23 B.C. after a serious illness of the emperor. At that time the *Imperium Proconsulare* of Octavian was described as *maius* (superior). It was decreed that Octavian should have this power within the city of Rome, too, and, in addition, he was granted all the ordinary, and some extraordinary, prerogatives of a tribune. He was given the power to declare war, to conclude peace, to make treaties, and to do "whatever he may deem to serve the interest of the Republic." [4] Thus his personal power was really raised above that of all others. In the meantime other honors were bestowed upon him that made his person even more unique: the title *Augustus* attached some religious significance to him; the month *Sextilis* was named Augustus; in 12 B.C. he became *pontifex maximus,* head of the state religion; and in 2 B.C. he was given the title *pater patriae.* Yet the title which he preferred was that of *princeps,* because it suggested that he was merely the first citizen of the country, first in the Senate, something like first among equals, although one is hard put to imagine who and where the equals were. He held the Senate under strict control and his personal authority clearly superseded that of the two consuls.

In this kind of setup, obviously much depended upon the personality and the character of the *princeps:* unscrupulous emperors could become tyrants, while "the good emperors," as a succession of emperors in the second century was popularly called, could do much for the benefit of the people. Augustus was not unaware of this situation, and he was earnestly trying to find a successor to himself. In this search he had to go through a series of bitter disappointments. He had only one daughter by his wife Scribonia, whom he divorced soon after her child, named Julia, was born. Julia was fourteen years old when she was married to M. Claudius Marcellus, the son of Octavia, Augustus' sister, and thus Julia's cousin. Marcellus was looked upon for a while as a likely successor; he was given important assignments after which special honors were conferred upon him by the Senate. Unfortunately Marcellus died of some disease in 23 B.C. Julia was then married to Agrippa, a longtime friend and co-worker of Augustus who, as the commander of Octavian's fleet, had had a major share in the victory at Actium. He had been married to the daughter of Octavia (Octavia was Augustus' sister), Marcella, by whom he also had children.[5] In his typical authoritarian manner, Augustus simply ordered Agrippa to divorce Marcella and marry Julia. To this marriage three sons were born: Gaius in 20 B.C., Lucius in 17 B.C., and Agrippa Postumus in 11 B.C., shortly after the death of Agrippa.

Of the three, Agrippa Postumus apparently lacked any promise of leadership, but Augustus had great hopes for Gaius and Lucius. Early in life they were given special privileges by the Senate, and Augustus did his best to raise their stature in the public eye. We read, for example, that in the absence of Augustus, Gaius took his place in the council which debated the request of the ambassadors of the Jews (in 4 B.C.), that they be freed from the Herodian dynasty and put under Roman protectorate.[6] The boys obviously developed well, but fate again intervened. Lucius died in Marseilles in A.D. 2 and Gaius in A.D. 4 of a wound received in action on the Armenian frontier. Agrippa Postumus was executed in A.D. 14 soon after the death of Augustus — some say that the order came from Augustus himself; others put the blame upon Tiberius.

No sooner did Agrippa die than Julia was married the third time (even before Agrippa Postumus was born) —to Tiberius, the stepson and later the adopted son of Augustus. The marriage was arranged with the customary ruthlessness. Tiberius was ordered to divorce his wife, Vipsania, the daughter of Agrippa, with whom he was deeply in love. To the marriage of Julia and Tiberius one child was born which died in infancy. Both parties were unhappy, and when in 6 B.C. Tiberius, temporarily and of his own will, retired from public life and left Rome to live on the island of Rhodes, Julia did not go with him. What happened was fateful for Julia. All alone in Rome she acquired a number of lovers and this fact did not remain a secret. Finally, in 2 B.C. Augustus banished her to the island of Pandateria, and we can imagine what the whole affair meant to the aging emperor. Julia died in A.D. 14 by committing suicide, after the execution of her last remaining son, Postumus.

Augustus was married again after his divorce from Scribonia. This time his choice was Livia, and the circumstances under which he took her were unpleasant. Livia was married to Tiberius Claudius Nero, who, in the meeting of the Senate held after the murder of Julius Caesar, asked that the murderers be rewarded for eliminating a tyrant. He was a praetor in 42 B.C., but, around 40 B.C., he, being a convinced republican, led an uprising of slaves which was crushed by Octavian. He was expelled from Italy, together with his wife Livia and their son Tiberius. They were permitted to return under general amnesty issued in 39 B.C., and after that Octavian fell in love with Livia. Notwithstanding the fact that she was pregnant with her second child, Octavian enforced a divorce and married her three days after her second child, Drusus, was born. The marriage took place in 38 B.C. and (let it be said to the credit of Augustus), according to all available evidence, he remained devoted to Livia to the end of his life. It is said that he died with her name on his lips.

Tiberius Claudius Nero died in 33 B.C.; his two sons, Tiberius and Drusus (later called Germanicus), were reared in Octavian's home. As stepsons of Augustus, both of them received exceptional honors and privileges from the Senate, and both of them performed outstanding services to the Republic, especially in their military campaigns in Germany. In these campaigns Drusus advanced northward as far as the Elbe River, yet without making the territory a Roman possession. For these achievements both brothers received an *ovatio* (just short of the triumph) in 11 B.C., and the title *imperator* in 9 B.C.[7] Drusus died of an accident in the same year, and Tiberius conducted the further campaigns in Germany. It was not until A.D. 4, however, when both of his grandsons were dead, that Augustus finally adopted Tiberius and designated him as his successor.

It is customary to remember the Principate of Augustus as a time of quiet, peaceful development. In Christian homilies it is a common device to refer to the birth of Jesus Christ as the time when there was no war at all in the world. Perhaps Augustus wanted to be remembered as the one who brought peace to the Empire. We know that he did accept the *Ara Pacis Augustae,* an altar dedicated to the peace which he established. The altar was built between 13 and 9 B.C. when Augustus returned to Rome after a three-year tour of Gaul and Spain, and it was meant to be a massive symbol of the *pax Romana.* But the *pax Romana* of Augustus must be qualified somewhat. It was a blessed reality within the established boundaries of the Empire itself, but a glance at the history of Augustus' reign shows that more fighting was done during this time than during the reign of any other emperor with whom we shall deal. Immediately after the conquest of Egypt there were two insurrections which had to be quelled there. Then there was a campaign against Ethiopia to create a buffer zone between Egypt and Ethiopia. This was completed by the first governor of Egypt, C. Cornelius Gallus, in 26 B.C. Augustus, in the next year, 25 B.C., ordered the invasion of Arabia, which netted him nothing but untold suffering for the invading army. While the Romans uselessly spent their energies in Arabia, the Ethiopians invaded Egypt, to which the new governor, Petronius, responded with another campaign against that southern kingdom. At the same time, during 30–29 B.C., fighting broke out on the Balkan peninsula where various barbarian tribes from the lower Danube area had infiltrated the Roman provinces. The conquest of northern Spain was completed in 25 B.C., and a rebellion in the western Alps was successfully put down. In 23 B.C. a conspiracy against the life of Augustus was discovered and the conspirators condemned. We also hear of a similar incident around the year 19. In 20 B.C. disturbances broke out in Gaul and an insurrection in Spain, while on the eastern frontier Tiberius was busy conquering Armenia and recovering the long lost Roman standards from the Parthians. (These had been lost by Crassus at the battle of Carrhae in 53 B.C. and by Mark Antony in 40 and 36 B.C.) This latter was achieved by a show of force rather than actual fighting, but it was hailed as a great victory by Augustus.

There were constant wars on the northern frontiers of the Empire. The brothers Tiberius and Drusus were especially active here. In long campaigns they added the territory up to the Danube, Noricum, to the Empire. In the same year Raetia was annexed. Hardly was this accomplished in 14 B.C. when Augustus began to plan for the *Bellum*

Pannonicum which lasted from 13–9 B.C. and brought Pannonia (i.e., the area west of the Danube) under Roman control. In the meantime Drusus went victoriously ahead in Germany, and, although he did not conquer the territory up to the Elbe, he definitely established the Rhine as the indisputable northern boundary of Rome. If this is what Augustus called "peace," one wonders what his idea was about "war." And the worst was yet to come. About this time the tribe of the Marcomanni, in what today is Bohemia, began to rise as a new power under the aggressive leadership of a certain Maroboduus, and in Transylvania the Dacians were active. The Roman army crossed the Danube and subdued the Dacians. Then an invasion of Bohemia was planned under the leadership of Tiberius and was almost completed when a serious uprising in Pannonia and Dalmatia forced a compromise settlement. All the available forces of the Romans were needed to put down the insurrection which lasted three years, during which the Romans were dangerously close to suffering serious defeat. Finally, however, the area was made secure and hostilities ceased in A.D. 9.

But disaster struck in Germany in the same year. This event was connected with the name of Quintilius Varus, who, in the latter years of Herod the Great, had been imperial legate in Syria (6–4 B.C.). He was the one who, together with Herod, sat in judgment over Herod's son Antipater and condemned him to die.[8] After the death of Herod, when the Jews revolted during Archelaus' visit to Rome to have his father's testament confirmed, it was Varus who led an expedition into Palestine and ruthlessly suppressed the revolt by burning some cities and crucifying some two thousand Jews.[9] Varus married the grandniece of Augustus and (perhaps because of this relationship) was made commander of the Roman army of the Rhine. Three legions were under his control when a German tribe under the leadership of Arminius revolted in A.D. 9. Arminius treacherously made Varus leave his summer camp, then trapped him in forest country, and totally annihilated the three Roman legions in a great massacre. Varus committed suicide, and Arminius sent his head to Maroboduus in the hope of inspiring a greater uprising against the Romans. Such an uprising did not take place, but in Rome the news of the disaster was received with great shock. It is said that the impression made upon Augustus was so deep that months later he cried out in desperation: *"Quintili Vare, legiones redde!"* ["Quintilius Varus, give me back my legions!"][10]

Worse than the military defeat were the symptoms that were laid open by it in Roman society. Augustus tried to replace the lost legions, but hardly any of the Roman youth were willing to enlist. There was prosperity in Rome; people had better things to do than

enlist in the army and spend the best part of their lives in some remote area. The former martial spirit was waning in Rome. Within
the circle of the vision of the Romans there was peace, the good life;
and the man on the street or the peasant minding his business or
his field did not understand what some war on a faraway part of the
world had to do with him. Augustus even threatened to confiscate
the goods of those of military age who refused to serve, and some may
even have been executed. But finally, he was forced to recall discharged veterans, conscript emancipated slaves, and muster as large a
force as he could from these elements to send to Tiberius in Germany.
Germanicus, the son of Drusus, had some very limited success against
the Germans, but finally the conquest of Germany was indefinitely
postponed. The weakness of the Empire was obvious, and Tiberius
saw that Rome had now absorbed just about as much territory as it
could for the time being.

By the death of Augustus the time obviously was ripe for a respite
and some consolidation. After all, the additions were considerable.
During Augustus' rule the following provinces were organized: Egypt
in 31 B.C., Illyricum in 27 B.C., Galatia in 25 B.C., Raetia and Noricum
in 15 B.C., Judea in A.D. 6, and Pannonia in A.D. 9. On August 19, A.D.
14, Augustus could close his eyes in the full knowledge that he had
created and left behind a grand Empire.

TIBERIUS 14–37

The tenure of Tiberius embraces the time during which the
events related in the Gospels took place. He is mentioned by name
only once in Scripture (Luke 3:1), but, of course, when the term
"Caesar" is used in the narratives (Mark 12:14-17; Matthew 22:17-21;
Luke 20:22-25; 23:2; John 19:12-15), Tiberius is meant.

He was born in 42 B.C. and at the time of Augustus' death he was
fifty-five years old. He did not covet the title *princeps* and we have
no reason to doubt historians' reports that he accepted the offer of
the title and office by the Senate reluctantly and only after much
protest. To understand his attitude and much of his later actions,
we must remember the many bitter disappointments he had to en-
dure in his lifetime. The opportunity came to him too late in life
to inspire him with new zeal or to give him much pleasure in his
new and exalted position. We have already discussed many events
from his early life: his parents were divorced when he was only three
years old, and a few years later his natural father died. He was never
the first choice of Augustus to be his successor although as his stepson, Tiberius was given exceptional positions. In 29 B.C. he was permitted to ride with his brother beside Octavian in the triumph, and

in 27 B.C. he accompanied Augustus in his tour of Gaul. In 23 B.C. the Senate gave him permission to become consul five years before the legal age, and he was elected *quaestor* for the year 22. In 23 he was the prosecutor in the case of the conspiracy against Augustus, and tribunician power was conferred upon him in 6 B.C.

But all these honors could hardly compensate for the many humiliations he had to suffer: by imperial command he was forced to divorce his wife in order to supply a husband for the widowed Julia and a foster-father for the grandsons of Augustus. When in 12 B.C. he successfully settled the affairs of Pannonia and the Senate voted a triumph for him and his brother, Augustus would not permit it. Only after the death of his brother, when the German and Pannonian campaigns were finished (in 7 B.C.), was Tiberius given permission for the triumph. It was becoming increasingly clear that Augustus wanted his direct descendants (i.e., the children of his daughter Julia, Gaius and Lucius) to become his heirs, and the thought that, in spite of his many services, he was being pushed aside in favor of much younger men was a severe wound to the pride of Tiberius. In 6 B.C. he refused a commission to go to Armenia and withdrew instead to the island of Rhodes where he remained until A.D. 2. Finally, at the request of Livia, Augustus permitted him to return. In the meantime, his wife was banished from Rome because of immorality, and in 1 B.C. the Senate refused to renew his tribunician powers. The town of Nemausus overturned his statues,[11] and he became an object of scorn to Gaius Caesar and his friends. The change in his fortunes came after Gaius and Lucius were dead and Augustus adopted him as his heir apparent. Even then strings were attached: he was required to adopt Germanicus, the son of his brother Drusus, and put him in his family ahead of his own son.

Immediately afterwards he went to Germany where the troops received him with great joy. The military genius of Tiberius won again, and he pushed the Germans back to the Elbe River. Then came his campaign against Maroboduus and the suppression of the Pannonian revolt. In A.D. 13 his tribunician power was renewed by the Senate for ten years, and he was given *Proconsular Imperium,* equal to that of Augustus. He therefore had equal rights with Augustus in the administration of the provinces and in the armies, which meant that he was now co-regent. In A.D. 14 he went to put the affairs of Illyricum in order, but had to hasten back at the news of Augustus' death. Historians agree that he found Augustus still alive and spent a day in private conversation with him.

After the funeral of Augustus and his own election as the new *princeps,* Tiberius turned his attention to the consolidation of the Empire. On the German frontier his recently adopted son, Germanicus, was still fighting some questionable battles with Arminius to avenge the defeat of Varus. In A.D. 16 Tiberius put an end to this campaign, recalled Germanicus, and let him celebrate a triumph in A.D. 17. From that time on there was quiet in this end of the Empire during Tiberius' reign, except for the Frisian revolt in 28. The Frisians enjoyed their freedom until 48 when they were subsequently subjugated under Claudius. By and large, however, the Rhine remained the frontier. The great Pannonian uprising did not escape the memory of Tiberius either, and he made provisions to consolidate the position of the Roman Empire in this area also. Early in his reign the legions built a series of roads in Dalmatia, and one legion was stationed in Carnuntum on the Danube, about twenty miles east of Vienna. More difficult was the situation in the East. There was internal political unrest in Armenia, Cappadocia, Commagene, and Cilicia. Parthia threatened war if Rome permitted a recently exiled ruler, Vononus, to live in Armenia. Tiberius had Vononus interned in Antioch, and, to settle the other affairs, he sent Germanicus to the East in A.D. 18. He was given proconsular authority, superseding the authority of all provincial governors. Consequently Commagene was incorporated into the province of Syria, and Cappadocia was annexed as a province. In Armenia Germanicus crowned a new king, Artaxias, with whom the Parthians were also satisfied. Toward the end of his life, the Parthians again made some trouble for Tiberius, but he resolved it with quiet but firm diplomacy. The trouble ended when the Parthian king acknowledged Roman authority in Armenia and sent his son Darius as a hostage to Rome.

In A.D. 19 however, Germanicus died suddenly in Antioch. It was rumored that the governor of Syria, Piso, poisoned him. On this and various other charges, Piso was tried before the Senate and soon afterwards committed suicide. To the matter of the eastern provinces belongs also the fact that in A.D. 34 Philip the tetrarch died, and his territory, Gaulanitis, Trachonitis, and Batanaea, was incorporated into the province of Syria, with the proviso that the revenues from it should be handled in a separate account. In Africa there were disturbances in A.D. 20 and Tiberius had to send a legion there to restore order.

The internal affairs of Tiberius were less peaceful. In the first part of his Principate he was careful to cooperate with the Senate and consult it in any major decision in the typical Augustan tradition. In the year 26, however, he left Rome and took up residence on the island of Capri and never again attended a meeting of the Senate in person. From then on he communicated with that body through letters which he sent regularly and which more and more appeared to be the orders, not the propositions or recommendations, of someone who was supposed to be first among equals. The degeneration of the Roman Senate is revealed in that its members not only submitted to such autocratic treatment but also that their response was to give more honors to Tiberius.

Why Tiberius withdrew to Capri is an open question. Once before he went into self-imposed exile to Rhodes, and it appears that by nature he was melancholic. He disliked theater and imposed restrictions on gladiatorial games. In A.D. 23 actors were expelled from Italy, much to the regret of the population. In 19 the Jews were expelled from Italy because of a simple incident: a Roman noblewoman was cheated out of a large sum of money by some Jews who pretended that the money was for the temple but made off with it instead. Suetonius, however, says that the expulsion took place because of the sharp numerical increase of the Jews in Rome who converted many native Romans to their religion.[12] The incident was reported to Tiberius who not only expelled the Jews, but also sent four thousand Jewish men as conscripts to Sardinia. (In 49 Claudius renewed the edict.) When Germanicus died and the land was in mourning, Tiberius did not attend the funeral; he displayed similar tactlessness when Augustus' widow, Livia, died at the age of eighty-six in the year A.D. 29. By such actions he offended the feelings of many people, perhaps without really wanting to do so or even noticing it. Perhaps the fatal blow was struck to the emotionally disturbed, heavily tried Tiberius, when his own son Drusus (born to him and to his first and beloved wife, Vipsania) died in A.D. 23. After the death of Germanicus, Drusus was the logical heir apparent, and Tiberius was especially pleased when the wife of Drusus, Livilla, gave birth to twin sons, Gemellus and Germanicus, in A.D. 19. He was prepared to train Drusus to be his successor when Drusus suddenly passed away. Later Tiberius found out that Drusus had been murdered; Livilla, his wife, and Lucius Aelius Sejanus, the Prefect of the Praetorian Guards, had committed adultery and together had Drusus killed.

This Sejanus appears to have had an evil influence upon Tiberius. Tiberius had trusted him completely and Sejanus in turn was loyal to Tiberius, even once saving Tiberius' life at the risk of his own. Sejanus was strongly anti-Semitic, and up to the time of his fall his anti-Semitic influence was clearly perceivable in the matters in which the procurators of Judea handled the affairs of their provinces. Tiberius permitted Sejanus to appoint procurators who were, therefore, obedient in carrying out his policies.[13] Sejanus was also responsible for a stricter application of the law of treason (maiestas). This law was revised under Augustus to include insults to the majesty of the emperor, but because the law contained no specifications of what constituted *maiestas,* some emperors used the law indiscriminately. Tiberius probably did not (in spite of what Tacitus says), but Sejanus found in it a convenient means of putting many persons out of his way. He may have had some scheme of his own by which he could become guardian of the sole surviving grandson of Tiberius, Gemellus, whose twin brother Germanicus had died in 23. He began to sow dissension among the members of the imperial family and induced Tiberius to take action against several of them. Those who were in the line of succession, apart from Gemellus, were the children of Germanicus (d. 19) and Agrippina, Nero, Drusus, and Gaius. Agrippina and Nero were banished in 29, and Nero committed suicide in 30. Drusus was arrested but later, when the plot of Sejanus was discovered, he was accused of having helped Sejanus against his own brother. Tiberius became aware of Sejanus' conspiracy and organized a counter-conspiracy from Capri, as a result of which Sejanus was arrested and summarily executed. Drusus was starved to death for his alleged part in Nero's banishment, and Livilla committed suicide. All this happened in 31, and two years later Agrippina died. (Pilate fell from favor in 36 because now he was no longer protected by Sejanus.) Now only two persons remained whom Tiberius could regard as heirs: Gemellus and Gaius. In 35 he wrote a will in which he made both of them heirs. In 37 he died, and when the news reached Rome, the crowds broke out in uncontrollable joy.

An interesting sidelight in the history of Tiberius that we should mention briefly was his association with Agrippa, grandson of Herod the Great through Aristobolus and Berenice. This Agrippa was sent to Rome when he was about five years old and was reared with Drusus, the son of Tiberius. When Drusus died, Tiberius could not bear to look at anyone who reminded him of his son, so Agrippa was sent away. By that time Agrippa had squandered his fortune, and he lived on borrowed funds when he could find someone willing to lend him money. For a while he lived in the East, but he returned to Capri in 36 and was cordially received by Tiberius and soon appointed tutor to Gemellus. Some instinct, however, told him that the future lay with Gaius, and he made every effort to establish friendship with him. This came to pass, but Agrippa made a mistake: one day on a chariot ride he told Gaius that he wished Tiberius were dead so that Gaius might become emperor. The conversation was overheard by the coachman, Eutyches, who reported it to Tiberius, and Agrippa was put in prison until Gaius freed him after the death of Tiberius.

Tiberius was a conscientious and good ruler. Although the Senate wanted to give him many honors, he constantly refused. In matters of judicial cases he was moderate, although his attitude had markedly hardened as in his solitude melancholy more and more overcame

PERSONS INVOLVED IN THE PLOT OF SEJANUS (DIED 31)

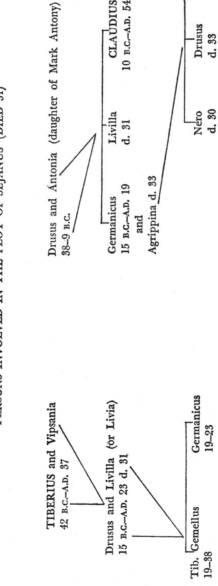

Drusus and Antonia (daughter of Mark Antony)
38–9 B.C.

Livilla
d. 31

CLAUDIUS
10 B.C.–A.D. 54

Germanicus
15 B.C.–A.D. 19
and
Agrippina d. 33

Nero
d. 30

Drusus
d. 33

GAIUS
37–41

TIBERIUS and Vipsania
42 B.C.–A.D. 37

Drusus and Livilla (or Livia)
15 B.C.–A.D. 23 d. 31

Germanicus
19–23

Tib. Gemellus
19–38

him. Some historians accuse him of sexual aberrations and other scandals in his later years, which may or may not be true. But the interests of the Empire were uppermost with him. He wanted good governors in the provinces and acted wisely to keep the government and economy in good condition. When he died, he left 2,700,000,000 sesterces in the reserves, and some sources even put that figure as high as 3,300,000,000.

GAIUS 37–41

The Senate met after the death of Tiberius and invalidated his will (in which he had named Gemellus and Gaius coheirs) on the ground that he was insane. Gaius was made *princeps,* and he promptly announced a return to the Augustan principles of government. Exiles were permitted to return, as were actors. The gloomy days of Tiberius were over. The Senate had regained its self-respect. There were no more written orders because the new *princeps* was punctual in attendance at the meetings and showed great respect to the senators. Unfortunately this ideal situation did not last. Gemellus was executed within a year and more evil was to come.

Gaius is also known under the name of *Caligula,* a nickname meaning "little boot," which was given him by the soldiers on the German frontier where his father Germanicus was active. Gaius was born in A.D. 12 and was brought up in military camps where he wore military outfits as a little boy, including little military boots, *caligae.* Later he resented the name Caligula, preferring to be called Gaius. Again, as in the case of Tiberius, a brief review of his life may give us a clue toward understanding his later actions. After a boyhood in military camps, he went back to Rome with his father and soon after that accompanied his father on his mission to the eastern provinces. In 19 his father died, and of course he must have heard the rumors of murder. He lived ten years with his widowed mother, Agrippina, under the growing shadow of Sejanus' power. When his mother and his brother were banished in A.D. 29, Gaius must have sensed that his turn might come, too. He had lost one brother by suicide and the other by police action. It was with this background that Gaius came to power.

During his short reign he attempted some innovations which were not without consequences for the future. In 39 he went to the German frontier and was somewhat successful against certain German tribes, after which he began preparations for an invasion of Britain. In this effort his political acumen is to be acknowledged because he realized that the northern frontier had to undergo a drastic reorganization. The campaign against Britain was, however, abruptly cancelled in 40 for reasons unknown. Perhaps the British had made some conciliatory gestures. For whatever reason, Gaius returned to Rome, celebrated a huge triumph, and turned his attention to the East where he made blunder after blunder and completely upset the balance created by Tiberius. The mistakes he made here had long-lasting effects. He began by sending the king of Armenia into exile, then left the throne unoccupied. This action was virtually an invitation to the Parthians to take over, and they seem to have done precisely that. Then he started to re-create client-kingdoms, which had been successfully eliminated and incorporated into the Roman provinces by his predecessor. He created a series of these client-kingdoms which by no means served to strengthen the eastern frontier; but one was used to reward his friend Agrippa I. No sooner was Tiberius dead than Gaius ordered Agrippa's release from prison and in 37 gave him the former territory of Philip the tetrarch and of Lysanias. In addition, Gaius conferred upon him the title of king. This was the immediate reason for the downfall of Herod Antipas: his wife, Herodias, could not bear the thought that Agrippa was suddenly king while her husband was a tetrarch. Finally, Antipas gave in to his wife's nagging and they went to see Gaius. But Agrippa was wise. He sent a letter to Gaius accusing Antipas of involvement with Sejanus and of maintaining in his armory equipment for seventy thousand men. While the former charge could not be proved, the latter could not be denied, and immediately Antipas was deposed as tetrarch and banished to Lugdunum Convenarum, near the Spanish frontier. His tetrarchy was added to Agrippa's kingdom.

Agrippa's return to take possession of his new kingdom was the immediate cause of the well-known anti-Jewish uprising in Alexandria. In A.D. 38 he stopped in Alexandria where he had many creditors. The Jews received him with great pomp, to which the other Alexandrians responded by parading a weak-minded person in royal robes through the streets, putting up statues of Gaius in the synagogues, burning and pillaging Jewish houses, and killing many Jews. Agrippa intervened on behalf of the Jews and the prefect of the city, Flaccus, was arrested and later executed. But an embassy of the Jews under the leadership of Philo was given an unfriendly reception by the emperor who, in spite of his friendship with Agrippa, was a great admirer of Hellenistic culture.[14] In the Jewish-Gentile *Kulturkampf*, which now grew to considerable proportions, the heart of Gaius was clearly not with the Jews.

In the meantime, the mental state of Gaius began to deteriorate noticeably. He lost all sense of reality and responsibility. The financial surplus left by Tiberius was spent foolishly on games and was given as gifts to friends. To raise new money, he imposed all kinds of taxes and resorted to extortion and confiscations. His relations with the Senate changed, too. More and more he acted as a monarch who rules by divine right. The final stage came when he became convinced of his divinity and demanded *proskynesis* [obeisance]. The Easterners and even the Romans meekly submitted, but when an altar to Gaius was erected in Jamnia in A.D. 40, the Jews tore it down. Gaius' response was the command to put up a huge statue of himself in Jerusalem. Petronius, the legate of Syria, saw that this might lead to a revolt in Judea and delayed matters as long as he could, and, in the meantime, Agrippa also interceded. Gaius rescinded his order, but a few months later renewed it and ordered Petronius to commit suicide. The ship bearing his letter was delayed by a storm, and Petronius received it only after the news reached him that Gaius had been assassinated on January 24, A.D. 41.

While this incident did contribute indirectly to the events that happened twenty-five to thirty years later in Palestine, for Christian beginnings the relationship of Gaius and Agrippa is of no real significance. It did not really matter who represented Roman rule in the Jordanian area. Two things, however, did have a lasting effect for our own concern. First, there was the transformation of the Principate into a tyrannical monarchy, and second, the deification of the emperor, which neither Augustus nor Tiberius took very seriously, became an imminent and real danger for those who would not submit to it; and when the primitive church began to spread out, this was the historical situation it had to face.

CLAUDIUS 41–54

The assassination of Gaius was followed by great confusion. Some senators had had enough of the Principate system; others wanted only to get rid of the Julian-Claudian dynasty. Claudius, the uncle of Gaius, went into hiding but some of the Praetorian guards found him and took him to their camp.[15] Negotiations were started between the Senate and the Praetorian guards, and the messenger for the two bodies was none other than Agrippa I, a longtime friend of Claudius. Soon an agreement was reached, and Claudius became *princeps* with full tribunician power and all the titles that went with his office. We notice here the first instance in which the military played a role in the selection of the emperor, a fateful precedent.

Claudius was fifty years old when he became emperor, and from the work he did, it appears that he took his office most seriously. His best-known achievement in foreign relations was the addition of Britain to the Roman Empire, a maneuver in which he himself took part and for which he celebrated a great triumph in 44. But in other parts of the Empire, too, his reign left behind many positive marks: cities were founded, highways were built, communication systems were improved, and thus the border regions were made safer and more defensible. Only in the East was his rule somewhat negative: the reinstituted client-kingdoms, which he inherited from Gaius, he left untouched. Agrippa I was rewarded for his services and was given practically the entire territory once ruled by his grandfather, Herod the Great. But the union was short lived because Agrippa I died in 44, and Claudius did not make his son his successor. The territory of Agrippa I was made into a province, and in A.D. 50 Agrippa II was made king of Chalcis, to which was added later (A.D. 53) Batanaea, Trachonitis, and Abilene. There was turbulence in Armenia and Parthia, and Armenia was lost for the rest of Claudius' reign.

It is reasonable to assume that the Jews resented the loss of their kingdom and that this action of Claudius intensified Jewish hatred against the Gentiles. This, in turn, played into the hands of Jewish extremists, and thus the establishment of the second province of Judea (the first was after the banishment of Archelaus in A.D. 6) was the prelude to the war less than twenty years later.

There were serious clashes between Jews and Greeks in Antioch and in Alexandria. The privileges of the Jews in Alexandria were confirmed by Claudius, but he also sent a stern letter to the city warning the citizens to live in peace with each other or face the wrath of an angry emperor. He warned the Jews to be content with what they had and not to try to bring more Jews into the city from Syria or Egypt. Suetonius, *Claudius* 25.4 contains the well-known passage: "Since the Jews constantly made disturbances at the instigation of Chrestus, he expelled them from Rome." This happened in 49, and Aquila and Prisca of Acts 18:2 were probably victims of this edict, in which some historians therefore see the earliest reference to the presence of Christians in the capital of the Empire. Christianity as something distinct from Judaism was hardly known under Claudius, however, and the interpretation of the Suetonius passage is not certain.

Claudius took his responsibilities toward the internal condition of the Empire with equal seriousness. He tried to undo, as much as he was able, the many evils unleashed by Gaius, including restitutions for his robberies. He was also resolved to return to the original idea of the Principate in which the Senate and the *princeps* acted in collaboration with each other. This was not an easy task because a certain degeneration of the Senate (and the senators) into a mere figurehead assembly had been in progress for a long time. Claudius did away with many time-consuming formalities of the Senate and urged the senators to get down to discussing business. He also made at-

tendance at the meetings an obligation of the senators, and absence
had to be excused. Unworthy members were dropped and new members appointed, even from the provinces, because Claudius (himself
a scholar of considerable standing and author of many respected
books) believed that the senators should be people who had the
intelligence to deal with the problems of the Empire regardless of
their place of birth.

For the same reason he was also eager to grant citizenship to many
able and worthy men who were residents of the provinces. He realized
that if the Empire were to survive as a solid unity, persons of high
training and abilities could not be treated as second-class citizens,
Citizenship under Claudius became a highly prized possession, yet
within reach of those who proved worthy of it. When the Senate
was incapable, or slow to act in certain matters, Claudius did not
hesitate to do what needed to be done, and thus, perhaps unwillingly,
he often encroached upon the authority of the Senate. This was the
case, for example, in Italy, which was definitely under the jurisdiction
of the Senate, and yet Claudius took charge of many projects (en-
larging the harbor of Ostia, building aqueducts, roads, etc.) on his
own authority. That in so doing he contributed to the elevation in
importance of the emperor at the expense of the Senate was un-
avoidable.

Probably for the same reasons, we observe during Claudius' reign
the gradual development and establishment of an imperial administration in a form not unlike our own civil service system. He organized
a department of finance and reorganized the central treasury called
Fiscus. The *Fiscus,* as the imperial treasury, was independent from the
state treasury which was called *aerarium* and was already established
by Augustus. An office dealt with petitions that came to the emperor;
another handled papers relating to judicial matters. Most important,
however, was the office which received, sorted, and forwarded all correspondence to the proper department. The heads of these offices and
departments had great responsibilities assigned to them, responsibilities which also conferred authority upon the office holders. They
soon became respected and often feared high officials, among whom
especially two names stand out: Pallas, the Secretary of the Treasury,
and Narcissus, the Secretary in charge of the central office where all
correspondence was received. Both of these were freedmen who had
achieved some notoriety because of their involvement in politics
and the daily intrigues of the court. The infamous Felix, for example,
who was procurator of Palestine, was a brother of Pallas, and we can
imagine that Felix could do many things and go unpunished, because
he had a powerful advocate where it counted. Narcissus and Pallas
also engaged in a rivalry which in some measure contributed to the

downfall of Claudius. They were reckless and greedy persons, too, and historians recorded many judicial injustices and murders which they committed against rich persons whose wealth they coveted, or whose influence they feared. These crimes naturally mar the image of Claudius' reign.

Claudius was married four times. His wives were Plantia Urgulanilla, Aelia Paetina, Valeria Messallina, and Agrippina, the sister of Gaius (Caligula), who was his own niece and the mother of Nero. When Claudius became emperor, Messallina was his wife, by whom he had a daughter, Octavia, and a son, Britannicus. Messallina is depicted by historians as an extremely ruthless person and is blamed for many of the crimes committed during this time against many people on the basis of alleged plots against the emperor, but in reality because of Messallina's greediness. She was also an immoral person who entertained many lovers. Finally, when she was caught in the act of adultery with a Roman nobleman named Silius, Narcissus denounced her to Claudius and both Messallina and her lover were executed. With the consent of the Senate, Claudius now married Agrippina, who immediately began to plot to have the rightful heir, Britannicus, replaced by her own son Nero. In character she was no less ruthless than Messallina, and she found a faithful ally in the person of Pallas. Narcissus was on the side of Britannicus. At last, however, Agrippina talked Claudius into adopting Nero and at the same time appointing him as the guardian of Britannicus. Nero was given *Proconsular Imperium* and in 53 he married Octavia, the daughter of Claudius. Narcissus attempted to make Claudius designate Britannicus as his heir, but before Claudius could make the decisive step Agrippina struck: she poisoned Claudius by putting a fatal drug into mushrooms, a dish of which he was especially fond and which were served him for dinner. He died the next morning after excruciating pain, but the news of his death was suppressed until Agrippina and her allies prepared everything for the safe succession of Nero.

NERO 54–68

The Praetorian Guards accepted Nero as emperor and thus the Senate could do little else than confirm him as *princeps*. As always, the new reign began with great promise: Nero, too, declared that he would return to Augustan policies, that toleration would be the watchword, and that inhuman practices such as the judicial murders during Claudius' reign would be abolished. In the beginning he also showed that he truly wanted to rule in harmony with the Senate, and he showed great restraint in accepting honors which a servile Senate immediately attempted to bestow upon him. Unfortunately the new atmosphere did not last long, and very soon events occurred which cast a long shadow of things to come. In the years following Nero's accession, Britannicus, son of Claudius and Messallina and the only possible threat to Nero's position, died, seemingly of an attack of epilepsy, but, in fact, he was poisoned. For this and many unpleasant things that followed, it would be easy to put the blame on Nero himself. It appears, however, that at least during this time he was completely under the influence of his mother, Agrippina, and his two advisers, Seneca (the younger Seneca, born in 4 B.C., whose brother was the proconsul Gallio mentioned in Acts 18:12) and the prefect of the Praetorian Guards, Burrus. Nero was only seventeen years old when he began his Principate, and his main concern was not politics, but having fun. A group of friends gathered around him and in their company he went on nightly trips through Rome causing mischief and disorder. Beautiful girls were not missing from the company, and among them the name of a freedwoman, Acte, is especially mentioned.

Real power lay in the hands of Agrippina, but Seneca and Burrus soon decided to undermine her influence. First, in 55 her greatest supporter, Pallas, was removed from office (Narcissus completely disappeared after Claudius' death); then she was ousted from the palace and sent to live in other quarters. In this action Nero probably had a significant part because Agrippina became increasingly critical of her son's easy life, and Nero wanted her out of the way. From that time on, Seneca and Burrus directed the policy of the Empire, until 62 when Burrus died, probably of cancer, and was replaced by a dubious character, Tigellinus. Seneca disapproved of this appointment and soon retired from public life. Now many unworthy courtiers surrounded Nero, who was easily influenced by their flattery and unprofessional advice with fateful results.

In defending the boundaries of the Empire, Nero's reign showed some significant achievements, some bad blunders, and some farsighted, long-range planning. Because of heavy taxation and generally bad policies toward the provincial population, there was an uprising in Britain which was immediately crushed. The case of Armenia, which was so badly neglected by Claudius, was opened up at the very beginning of Nero's reign. Preparations for war to regain Armenia were ordered, and one of the greatest military brains at the time, Corbulo, was put in charge of the operations. In 55 Corbulo went to the East and put the undisciplined and neglected legions in order. After initial negotiations failed, he began his campaign which resulted in the capture of the Armenian capital, Artaxata, in 58. For this victory Nero (who never went near Armenia) received triumphal celebrations and honors in Rome. An oversize statue of him was erected in Rome and thus the emperor cult was introduced into the city itself.[16] But then things began to go awry. It was decided in Rome to curb Corbulo's popularity by assigning him to Syria and withdrawing his army from Armenia. Armenia was given a client king, Tigranes V (a nephew of Tigranes IV, the great-grandson of Herod the Great), who promptly invaded Parthian territory, which immediately resulted in Parthian counteraction. Tigranes fled and the Parthians proposed lasting peace, but by this time Nero used his own judgment, instead of depending on his advisers, and decided to annex Armenia. A man named Paetus was put in charge of this project, but he was badly beaten and humiliated by the Parthians. The defeat was so thorough that for a while the province of Syria was menaced by a direct Parthian invasion. How all this may have fanned the already supercharged and unrealistic Jewish extremist emotions we can only imagine. Finally, the case was settled by the following formula of compromise: the Romans were to accept the Parthian choice, Tiridates, as king of Armenia, but Tiridates was to come to Rome and receive the crown from Nero's hands. This event took place with unprecedented splendor in Rome in A.D. 66. Tiridates knelt before Nero, called him a god, and offered him divine worship. Thus peace was established on the eastern frontier for a long time.[17]

Toward the end of his life Nero had to face a new danger that threatened the Empire. That was the Sarmatians, who previously had made occasional raids into Roman territory in the lower Danube area. Nero planned an extensive campaign against them for which he made appropriate preparations around 66, but the campaign had to be abandoned because of the outbreak of a Jewish revolt. For the same reason a planned invasion of Ethiopia was also abandoned.

The internal situation of the Empire went from bad to worse as Nero grew older. He fell in love with Poppaea, whom Josephus calls *theosebes* (God worshiper),[18] and who, therefore, may have been sympathetic to the Jewish religion. This, however, did not hinder her from realizing that she was only number three so long as Nero's mother, Agrippina, and his legal wife, Octavia, were alive. Agrippina was killed in cold blood after a prearranged accident failed to take her life in 59, and Octavia was murdered soon after Nero divorced her in 62. In both cases public opinion was on the side of the victims, but the servile attitude of the Senate helped him to stay on top of the situation.

Nero had already alienated the Roman population by sincere but excessive devotion to Greek ideas and ways of life. He organized a group of young Romans called *Augustiani,* who were a kind of artistic and sport association which presented exhibition games. He himself participated in all competitive and artistic events. In 66–67 he made an extended tour of Greece and took part in every possible game, where he naturally won the first prize and collected a total of 1808 first prizes. (In the meantime, we recall, things were really seething in Palestine.) But though his love for Greece was repulsive to the Romans, his unpopularity was greatly increased by the fire of Rome. This broke out in 64 and destroyed all but four of the fourteen districts of Rome. Countless ancient monuments and works of art perished, and many people were left homeless. In spite of the fact that Nero did everything in his power to relieve the suffering of the population (all public buildings were opened to the homeless) and to secure an adequate food supply for all, he was accused of having set the city on fire.[19] To divert attention from himself, Nero charged that the Christians were responsible for the fire and thus the well-known persecution got under way. Although there are some doubts about the basis on which Christians were put to death (arson; treason, *maiestas;* or *orium humani generis*), one significant fact clearly emerges: the *Christians* specifically were persecuted. It is therefore beyond doubt that, even before the Jewish revolt, Christianity was no longer viewed as a Jewish sect but as a religion distinct from others. There is a strong tradition, but not yet proved, that Peter and Paul fell victims of the same persecution, which, incidentally, was in all probability limited to Rome and lasted for only a brief period.

Nero displayed toward other people the same sadistic tendencies with which he persecuted the Christians. Poppaea is supposed to have died as a result of a kick inflicted by Nero in a moment of anger. Historians record many unbelievable acts of his total depravity, and it seems that he became increasingly hated by the population. A conspiracy against him was beginning to take shape in 62, but was discovered in 65, after which many, including Seneca, were either executed, driven to suicide, or exiled. From then on terror reigned, and no one was sure when the order to commit suicide would come. Another conspiracy aborted in 66, and Corbulo was one of those involved who fell victim to this attempt. In 68 Vindex, the governor of Gaul revolted, but the revolt was put down by the general of the German armies, Verginius Rufus. At the same time Galba in Spain revolted in concert with Vindex, who actually proposed Galba as the successor of Nero. Vindex, at his defeat, committed suicide; and the army of Verginius Rufus offered to make him *princeps.* Rufus declined, but in the meantime the Praetorian Guards were in rebellion and Nero fled from Rome. As soon as this news spread, the Senate declared him a public enemy and sent horsemen to pursue and arrest him. When he heard that, Nero committed suicide. The year was 68 and Rome broke out in rejoicing. But Nero's fame died slowly. Dio Chrysostom says that as late as the reign of Trajan many believed that Nero was alive and would return to reign. The *Sibylline Oracles* reflect the same view and some exegetes find a reference to this fact in Revelation 13:3, 12. (The beast whose "mortal wound was healed.") [20] Nero was only thirty years old when he died, and he left the state in a condition that the Empire had not seen for the past hundred years: in virtual civil war, in addition to a great rebellion in Judea.

From the Civil War of 68-69 to the Death of Hadrian

GALBA 68-69

In June, 68, Galba was named emperor by the Senate, and in January, 69, he was assassinated. During the seven months of his reign, he displayed no statesmanlike characteristics. Instead of rewarding those who stood by him, he neglected and insulted them, and even treated the Praetorian Guards, who were largely responsible for his election, very curtly. Galba also sent several persons to their death, but he finally sealed his own fate when choosing his successor (he was already seventy-three years old). He bypassed his long-time friend Otho and appointed a man named Piso Licinianus. Otho, who as governor of Lusitania, supported Galba when this support was badly needed, was gravely offended and won the Praetorians to his side. When the time came for action, no one protected Galba and he was slain on the Forum

> and was left lying just as he was, until a common soldier, returning from a distribution of grain, threw down his load and cut off the head. Then, since there was no hair by which to grasp it, he put it under his robe, but later thrust his thumb into the mouth and so carried it to Otho. [21]

OTHO 69

Otho was given the tribunicial authority by the Senate together with the usual powers of the *princeps*. He was well received by all, Senate and people alike, who remembered that he was the former husband of Poppaea, whom he was forced to divorce so that Nero could marry her. Even after such treatment he served his country with distinction as governor of Lusitania for ten years. He was only thirty-eight years old, and his Principate lasted only three months. The armies of the German provinces refused to acknowledge Galba and acclaimed Vitellius as emperor instead, even before Otho was elected. Vitellius immediately began his march to Italy, and during that time news of Galba's death and Otho's election reached him. To make things even worse, the Eastern provinces declared themselves for Otho, and thus, roughly speaking, the imperium was divided into two parts, ready for a civil war between East and West, not unlike the situation a hundred or so years earlier under Antony and Octavian. Otho tried to avoid war, but a compromise could not be reached. The brief war was fought in northern Italy where neither side won a decisive victory, and after losing a major battle, Otho became depressed and committed suicide. Suetonius, who says that his father took part in this war on Otho's side, describes Otho's final hours in touching detail.

VITELLIUS 69

As far as his armies were concerned, Vitellius was already the emperor, and he began to take possession of his realm. He was still in Gaul when Otho died, and from there he went to Rome with a large army, but he went as a conqueror. During the brief war with Otho his soldiers distinguished themselves by their licentious behavior and ruthless treatment of even the friendly populace. The same conduct was exhibited on their way to and in Rome. The effect of this behavior was to alienate many citizens from Vitellius. In addition to this, the new *princeps* treated some of the soldiers who had fought for Otho in a humiliating way, so that discontent was brewing among several army units as well. Vitellius and his soldiers enjoyed themselves in Rome, but in the meantime the governors and legions began to look for a new and worthier leader. Their first choice was C. Licinius Mucianus, governor of Syria, but he was not interested, and he suggested the name of Vespasian, former governor of the province of Africa, and since 67 (appointed by Nero) governor of Judea. During the summer of 69 the legions of Alexandria and Syria acclaimed him, and soon all the eastern provinces followed suit. The conduct of the war against the Jews was entrusted to Titus, the son of Vespasian (his other son Domitian was in Rome). Vespasian and Mucianus devoted themselves to the task of overthrowing Vitellius. The civil war was again in full swing.

Vitellius still had some support in Italy and good soldiers to fight for him, but a sense of defeat was in the air. One of his most trusted generals, Caecinus, made common cause with Vespasian and began to work secretly for him. The navy went over to Vespasian's side, and the Flavian armies came to the Po Valley in northern Italy. There was a night long battle by moonlight in which Vitellius' army was defeated, and the victorious army began its march toward Rome. Everything began to crumble, and finally, on a December day, Vitellius came from his palace in mourning clothes to lay down the insignia of his Principate. The populace, however, took pity on him and he had to return to the palace. The ardent adherents of Vitellius attacked those who gave up hope, among them Domitian, who escaped only with difficulty. In the meantime the Flavian army had already entered the city. There was street fighting during which Vitellius hid himself, but he was discovered and executed in December, 69. The Flavian army plundered and raped Rome until January, 70, when Mucianus arrived and restored order. Vespasian himself did not come until the late summer of 70 (perhaps even October) when things had returned to normal.

The war between the Flavians and Vitellians was not the only danger the Empire had to encounter during this time. The Jewish rebellion was at its peak; the Dacians invaded Moesia and had to be repelled, but much more serious was an uprising in the Rhine delta area led by a man called Julius Civilis. Under the pretense of supporting Vespasian, Civilis gathered a large army and used it against the Romans. The rebellion spread into Gaul where the establishment of an independent *Imperium Galliarum* was proclaimed. These movements had some initial success, but when the new government in Rome with Mucianus representing Vespasian made an organized effort, the rebellion was soon crushed. In the East, Jerusalem was captured in the same year (70), although the last seat of resistance, Masada, was occupied only in 73.

VESPASIAN 69–79

Vespasian was sixty years old when the Senate, in December, 69, conferred the Principate upon him. He had two sons, thirty-year-old Titus, just then besieging Jerusalem, and eighteen-year-old Domitian, who enjoyed himself in Rome. Vespasian found a very difficult situation in the Empire. The civil war naturally left deep scars upon the population, and his first task was to restore the confidence of the people in his government and in his own goodwill. Then, the reckless conscriptions of the latest emperors of the Julian-Claudian dynasty reduced the number of patrician families, brought the treasury to near bankruptcy, and transformed the Principate into a tyrannical, totalitarian type monarchy. Within ten years Vespasian succeeded in restoring peace, order, and prosperity. As a beginning he annulled all convictions for treason (*maiestas*) which had been passed since Nero, appointed a commission to compensate people for damages suffered during the war, and immediately began the rebuilding of Rome. The Jewish rebellion was quickly put down. In 71 a magnificent triumph was celebrated by the three Flavians (Vespasian, Titus,

Domitian) in which, along with the other booty, the seven-branched candlestick from the temple was displayed. We cannot deal here with the financial policies of Vespasian; we can only mention that strict, but just, measures were put into effect to fill the depleted treasury.

In order to insure orderly transmission of power to his heir, Titus was given *Proconsular Imperium* in 71 and shared the tribunicial power with his father. Domitian was given consulship six times and his relationship to father and brother was sufficient guarantee that, in case of an emergency, he would be the lawful successor. So far as the Senate was concerned, Vespasian added new members, some even from the provinces. In his relation with the senators he restored the principle of "first among equals." Flatterers were repulsive to him, and he maintained an "open door" policy, making himself available to all who wanted to see him without courtly formalities. We possess no reports of any judicial atrocities from his time. As a matter of fact, Vespasian tolerated free speech and criticism to a degree that is almost unbelievable.[22] We hear of a staunch republican, Helvidius Priscus by name, who did everything to make life difficult for Vespasian in the Senate and who often deliberately insulted him. Vespasian asked him only to abstain from coming to the Senate, but when Helvidius came despite this request, Vespasian tolerated his antics for many years. Finally, and very reluctantly, he had to have Helvidius banished, after which the man was executed.[23]

Similar difficulties were caused by the "Cynic" philosophers. These wandering and ascetic moralists criticized traditional mythology in favor of morality and religion, which in itself was no more than what other philosophical sects did to promote their own theses. But when the Cynics added anarchy and opposition to all government to their teaching, they went against the interests of an orderly government. Many of these Cynics also adopted an arrogant tone, mocking all authority and the entire established structure of society. Finally, Vespasian was forced to banish them, together with astrologers and philosophers, from Rome. It is possible that the Cynics had something to do with the development of later Christian monasticism and were later absorbed by that movement. There was one serious, organized plot to assassinate Vespasian; for what reason we do not know, but at any rate, Titus discovered the plot and the conspirators were summarily executed.

Suetonius characterizes Vespasian as a hardworking man who expected the same diligence from his associates. He also had a sense of humor and was often heard joking with others. Even when his health failed, he carried on his work, and when he felt death coming, remarked jokingly: "Woe is me. I think I am turning into a god."

He asked those around him to help him get on his feet, because, he said, "An emperor ought to die standing." Then he collapsed and died, at the age of sixty-nine.[24]

TITUS 79–81

Titus was eminently qualified to become emperor, for not only was he a good soldier who, before taking command against the Jewish uprising, had already seen miltary service in Germany and Britain, but he was also fluent in Latin and Greek. He had a noble face, although in stature he was somewhat short. His conduct of the war in Palestine made many Romans shudder at the thought of what would happen if he employed similar methods as emperor. We know that during the siege of Jerusalem, in full sight of the city's defenders, he crucified Jews who tried to flee the city (about five hundred a day). Later he ordered the hands of captured Jews cut off and then sent them back to Jerusalem to intimidate those who continued to resist. As emperor he did nothing like that. He retained his father's attitude toward the Senate and continued his father's policy of decency and toleration.[25] During his reign the Colosseum (begun by his father and finished by his brother) was opened, and on this occasion he sponsored games lasting for a hundred days. As a memorable event during his short reign, we must also mention the eruption of Vesuvius in August, 79, in which Pompeii and Herculaneum were buried and in which a friend of Titus, Pliny the Elder, also died. In connection with this catastrophe Titus acted with statesmanlike care for the welfare of those who survived the eruption.

One event in his life which may be of some interest to us was his relationship with Berenice, daughter of Agrippa I. This woman, great-granddaughter of Herod the Great, was married three times. She is said to have had relations with her own brother, Agrippa II, and she became the mistress of Vespasian when he was in Palestine. It is said that in addition to being very rich, she was also beautiful, and Titus fell in love with her. She lived with him in the Roman camp during the rest of the Judean campaign, and afterward she went with him to Rome. Whether Titus really promised to marry her, we do not know; she was ten years older than he. Be that as it may, Berenice made herself hated by the Romans. She was ostentatious,[26] wore huge diamonds, and behaved in an arrogant fashion, claiming privileges which did not belong to her. Perhaps Roman society also knew about her immoral life and remembered that once before an oriental princess, Cleopatra, became the cause of much distress to the Empire. Public opinion was strongly against Berenice and finally Titus, although reluctantly, sent her away from Rome.

When Vespasian died and Titus became emperor, she returned to Rome but was sent away again.[27]

Titus himself died in September, 81, after an outbreak of fever. It was rumored that his brother Domitian had something to do with his death, but all we know is that the two brothers were never close to each other, and during their lifetime there was much ill feeling between them. The death of Titus was received with genuine sorrow by the Roman people, for he was, without doubt, one of their best emperors.[28]

DOMITIAN 81–96

Domitian could hardly wait for Titus to die. On the very day his brother died, he made the Senate bestow on him the imperial powers. He could not prevent the deification of Titus by the Senate, but afterwards he made no attempt to honor his memory. Domitian was convinced that Titus had somehow tampered with the will of Vespasian, and for that reason he was eager to begin his reign and to make up for what he was supposedly deprived of previously.

Later historians, not without justification, painted such a dark image of the terror-filled Principate of Domitian that it may be advantageous to begin this account with his many positive achievements. He fought the wars of the Empire with vigor, and he did not hesitate to make far-reaching decisions when the interest of the Empire so required. As early as A.D. 83 he went to Germany and decisively defeated the tribe of the Chatti, a well-armed and disciplined German army which could have become a much greater menace had not Domitian forestalled it. Because the Romans already hated him, they treated the victory and the following triumph as a farce; yet the fact of history remains that Domitian pushed the frontier of the Empire in Germany northward to about fifty miles beyond the previously established line. Thus Rome not only acquired fertile territory that could prove helpful in case anything happened to the North-African food basket, but the defense of the frontier was also strengthened. Domitian established watchtowers, forts, and military roads, all of which made an attack from the North much easier to repel than it had been previously.

Hardly was this task finished when another had to be met in Dacia. The Dacians, under the leadership of Decebalus, became a kingdom, and during A.D. 85 broke into the province of Moesia. The governor was killed, several forts taken, and Domitian went with Cornelius Fuscus to meet the threat head-on. The situation was made graver by the fact that the Sarmatians exploited the situation by entering Roman territory and plundering. The arrival of Domitian and Fuscus restored order in the province in a short time, but then disaster came. Domitian decided to punish the Dacians for their incursion into a Roman territory. He sent Fuscus into Dacia where the Roman army suffered a crushing defeat. Fuscus died and the number of Roman casualities was great. It was a shameful retreat (Domitian watched the tragedy from Moesia), but it did not take long for Domitian to make up his mind concerning future action. Within a year he organized a well-planned attack upon Dacia which was executed in A.D. 88. He invaded Dacia through the Iron Gate Pass, where the Danube crosses the Carpathian Mountains, and reached the city of Tapae at the Bisztra River. Here, in a fierce battle, Decebalus was decisively beaten. Domitian could have exploited his victory fully by occupying Dacia, but two events interfered. One was the insurrection of the governor of Upper Germany, Antonius Saturninus, in A.D. 89. The second happened later in the same year when a punitive expedition set out against the Marcomanni (in the area which is occupied by the Czechs today) and the Quadi (in what is now Moravia) who were then joined by the Iazyges, who lived on the plain between Danube and Theiss. Thus the Dacian war was concluded with a diplomatic compromise: Decebalus paid homage to Rome and in return received recognition and yearly financial assistance from Rome.

The insurrection of Saturninus collapsed almost before it started because the governor of Lower Germany, Maximus, defeated Saturninus. The Marcomanni and Quadi quickly fell into line again. The Iazyges kept causing trouble and even invaded Pannonia in A.D. 92, but they were finally put down. Thus the achievements of Domitian in protecting the internal security of the Empire were important. In particular, it must be remembered that the idea of the *limes* (i.e., a series of watchtowers and forts), although not originating with him, was employed by him as a means of demarcating and defending the boundaries of the Empire, and after him it spread to other parts of the Empire as well.

In his domestic policies Domitian showed greatness also. His building program in Rome was considerable, and even Suetonius, who otherwise had a low opinion of him, admitted that "he administered justice scrupulously and conscientiously," [29] at least in the beginning of his rule. City officials and governors were never more honest than during his reign, and he made a laudable effort to correct, in some degree, public morals in Rome. Prostitutes were placed under various restrictions and when Vestal Virgins were found in immorality, Domitian punished them by death. The food supply in Rome was plentiful, his games were famous, and economic conditions were generally good.

This positive side of Domitian's rule is greatly overshadowed by the negative elements. Historians have put him in the class of Gaius and Nero, and because of his grim and ironic nature, they often compare him with Tiberius. He did not hesitate to impose the death penalty and often scorned his victims by letting them choose the manner of their execution, which he granted as an act of clemency. He put to death T. Flavius Sabinus, who was consul with him in 82, then married his widow, Julia, after divorcing his own wife, Domitia, whom he accused of adultery. Domitian killed the supposed lover, but a year later called back Domitia, and then lived with both women. After the defeat of Saturninus, instead of being satisfied that the insurrection was over, he went in person to Germany and conducted an investigation which claimed many victims. This event also made him more suspicious of everybody, and his cruelty reached abnormal heights. He condemned people on the testimony of informers (delatores), and the slightest offense drew heavy penalties, banishment, confiscation of property, and death. In 89 he banished philosophers and astrologers from Rome and in 95 from all Italy. His victims were mainly from the upper class, and not even his own family escaped their ranks. In 95 Flavius Clemens and his wife Domitilla, the emperor's own niece, were accused of "atheism, for which offense a number of others also, who had been carried away into Jewish customs, were condemned — some to death, others to confiscation of property." [30] Clemens was executed, and Domitilla was exiled. This incident holds particular interest for us since Judaism was a recognized religion and embracing "Jewish customs" would not be subject to the death penalty. It is possible that the term "Jewish customs" referred not to Judaism but to Christianity.[31]

That Christians may have been a special object of Domitian's persecution is also attested by Tertullian: "Domitian, too, a man Nero's type in cruelty, tried his hand at persecution; but as he had something human in him, he soon put an end to what he had begun, even restoring again those whom he had banished." [32] Eusebius, in his *Church History* states that Domitilla was exiled because of her Christian faith, and he mentions that Domitian ordered the descendents of David (i.e., the relatives of Jesus Christ) to be slain. Eusebius also gives a long quotation from Hegesippus, which tells how some relatives of Jesus were arrested and brought before Domitian who, however, dismissed them without penalty and put an end to the persecution.[33]

"Atheism" (atheotes) means nothing other than neglect of the state religion, and Christians could very well be accused of that. But others were also subject to this charge, which, in the later years of Domitian became equivalent to treason (maiestas), the most widely abused charge. Domitian had become fond of the titles *dominus et deus*,[34] and if anyone refused to offer a sacrifice before his images (with which the temples were filled), he became subject to this charge. The last years of Domitian were years of terror: no one knew when and with what crime he would be charged; secret informers were everywhere, and no one was sure whether the other person was a spy. Domitian collected incriminating evidence, and as was later discovered, he even had a secret file on his successor, Nerva, and Pliny the Younger (*ca.* 61–*ca.* 114). Finally a plot was organized in which his own wife Domitia was also involved.[35] The plotters first agreed on the successor of Domitian, and their choice fell on Nerva. Then the assassination was carried out by a freedman named Stephanus. At the news of Domitian's death the senators were so overjoyed that they held a meeting immediately, condemned the memory of Domitian, and confirmed Nerva as *princeps*. The body of Domitian was cremated by his nurse who secretly carried the ashes to the temple of the Flavian family and mingled them with the ashes of Julia, daughter of Titus, so that they would rest undisturbed.

NERVA 96–98

Nerva was sixty-six years old when he became emperor. He was distantly related to the Julian-Claudian dynasty and his previous senatorial career was impeccable, which made him more than sufficiently eligible for this highest office. There was only one thing against him: the opposition of the army. The Flavians were popular with the soldiers who resented the murder of Domitian. Nerva, however, was clearly the choice of the senators, but unfamiliar to the troops. They finally accepted him, but grudgingly, and the threat of civil war hung in the air during much of Nerva's reign. Plots were organized against him, and in 97 the Praetorians openly showed their discontent by demanding that the murderers of Domitian be executed. Nerva had no choice but to agree to the execution of those who actually elevated him to the Principate.

In foreign affairs Nerva's rule was uneventful, but in domestic policies he instituted significant and far-reaching legislation. Nerva was the first emperor who systematically attacked the problem of poverty. Two outstanding measures deserve to be mentioned. One was the agrarian reform in which the state distributed land to the needy. This measure cost approximately sixty million sesterces, and it is said that Nerva sold his own property and jewelry to help raise the money. The second was the institution of a statewide public assistance system in Italy. This provided that poor parents should receive cash grants from the municipality until their children reached the age of puberty. The money was raised by allowing farmers to borrow money from the state treasury up to one twelfth of the value of their land. On this they paid a low rate of interest, probably 5 percent, which went to the municipality.

Various other smaller measures were inaugurated to insure Nerva's popularity, but without success. In A.D. 97 he thought of abdication, but finally he was convinced to take another way out, i.e., to adopt an heir who would be fully acceptable to the military and who would be in a position to give strong leadership to the Empire. The choice fell upon the commander of the army of Upper Germany, M. Ulpius Trajanus, of Spanish descent and not related to Nerva. Trajanus was respected by the armies from one end of the Empire to the other and was also acceptable to the senators. When Nerva adopted him, the Senate gave Trajan the title of Caesar and made him co-emperor with Nerva (consors imperii). Three months later, in January, 98, Nerva died.

TRAJAN 98–117

The news of his adoption reached Trajan in Germany, and he remained there even after Nerva's death. Instead of returning to Rome, he sent letters to the Senate promising to abstain from tyranny and conveying his goodwill. He spent the winter reviewing the Danube frontier, including the lower Danube area where he ordered the construction of some new roads, obviously in preparation for a campaign against Dacia, which must have been already in his mind. Not until the spring of 99 did he finally reach Rome. He entered the city on foot, a demonstration of unostentatiousness which he and his family observed to the end.

Since Trajan is best remembered for his foreign policy, we begin with a brief review of it. Three events are of great importance in this connection: first, the Dacian wars; second, the annexation of Arabia; third, the Parthian campaigns.

The Dacian wars were fought in two stages. The first was started in 101. What reasons Trajan had to declare war we do not know, but it is certain that even Nerva was having difficulty paying the yearly subsidies to Decebalus. This foreign-aid program, which was costing the Roman taxpayers a great deal of money, failed to make Decebalus a friend of Rome. More than ever the Dacians remained a united nation and potentially dangerous enemies of Rome. Transylvania abounded (as it still does) in gold, silver, and salt mines, and that alone made the Dacian conquest a worthwhile project. He marched into Transylvania through the Iron Gate Pass, and perhaps also in a second column through the Red Tower Pass. By crossing

TRANSYLVANIA

As is obvious from this map, the natural boundaries of Transylvania are the Carpathian Mountains. Trajan's boundary on the north (broken line) was unnatural, and Aurelian (270-275) evacuated the province, establishing the Danube as the northern frontier of the Empire.

Iron Gate is the name of the narrows where the Danube River breaks through the Carpathian Mountains. **Red Tower Pass** is where the Olt River leaves Transylvania and flows into Rumania.

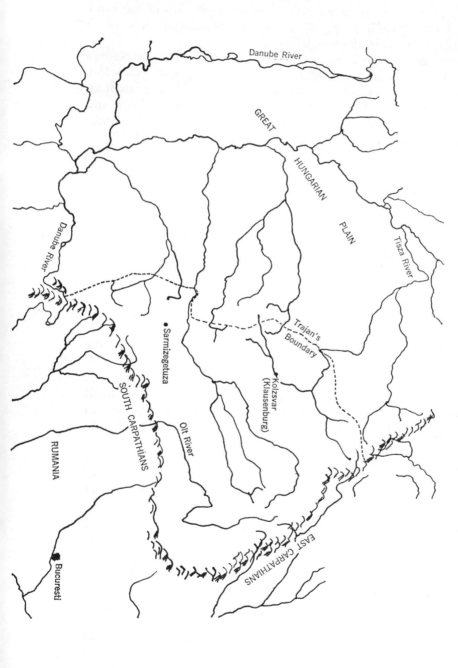

Danube River

GREAT

HUNGARIAN

PLAIN

Tisza River

Danube River

Trajan's Boundary

• Sarmizegetuza

Kolzsvar (Klausenburg)

SOUTH CARPATHIANS

Olt River

RUMANIA

EAST CARPATHIANS

• Bucuresti

the Carpathians, he was inside Transylvania, but the first encounters with Decebalus were inconclusive, and during the following winter Decebalus even counterattacked. The next year, A.D. 102, however, the capital of Dacia, Sarmizegetusa, fell; and Trajan dictated surprisingly mild terms of peace: the western part of Dacia (known as the Banat) was incorporated into the province of Moesia; Roman garrisons were left in various parts of Dacia, but Decebalus remained as a vassal king.

The peace lasted just three years. Little by little Decebalus broke his commitments and finally even attacked the Iazyges, who were allies of Rome. Trajan declared war in 105 and marched into Transylvania much as before. Only this time he was not satisfied with the capture of Sarmizegetusa, but pursued Decebalus farther north until the hard-pressed king committed suicide.

Trajan was bent on a final solution of the Dacian question. In addition to the thousands who were slaughtered, a large number of the people were exiled and forced to flee toward the north and settle in the area which is now known as the Great Hungarian Plains. Fifty thousand prisoners of war were taken to Rome to grace Trajan's triumph and later to die in the gladiatorial games. The area between the lower Danube and the Southern Carpathians was quickly repopulated by new settlers who were brought from every part of the Empire and who spoke a wide variety of languages, mostly Oriental, but also some from the West. This polyglot population under Roman rule developed into what is today Rumania, a nation which speaks a language that shows characteristics of old Latin. Dacia was secure until the Romans abandoned it during Aurelian's reign.

The annexation of Arabia went without difficulty and was accomplished in 105 by the governor of Syria, A. Cornelius Palma. Also, the client-kingdom of the Nabateans was removed, and the area was organized into a separate province with Bostra as its capital.

Trajan's third and last major war caused him considerably more problems. The immediate cause of this was Parthian infringement upon Roman prerogatives in Armenia. Here the Neronian settlement was still in force, according to which the king of Armenia would receive his crown from the Roman emperor. In breach of this agreement the king of Parthia, Chosroes, removed the king of Armenia, Exedares, and appointed his nephew Parthamasiris as king. This was a sufficient reason for war, and Trajan declared it in 113. He made the necessary preparations and left for Antioch, firmly resolved to annex Armenia. Chosroes tried to avoid the conflict and sent envoys to him. Trajan met them in Athens, but continued on his way without committing himself. In 114 he moved into Armenia where Parthamasiris met him and reminded him that, according to the

Neronic agreement, all that was needed was his investiture by Trajan. He laid his diadem before Trajan, but instead of giving it back to him, Trajan declared that Armenia was to become a Roman province. With that, Parthamasiris was dismissed, and on his way out of the country he was assassinated, whether by Trajan's order no one knows. Armenia was thus annexed, and Trajan returned to Antioch through Mesopotamia, which also fell into his hands, practically without any battle at all.

In the winter of 115, a terrible earthquake hit Syria. It destroyed a third of the city of Antioch, left many dead, and almost killed Trajan himself. From this city Trajan set out in 116 on a new campaign against Parthia. He conquered Media Adiabene easily and annexed it as the province of Assyria, then turned toward the capital of Parthia, Ctesiphon, which he took in short order. The Parthian king, Chosroes, escaped, but his treasure fell into Trajan's hands, who then declared that the new province, Parthia, was added to the Empire. The Persian Gulf, and thus the gateway to the far eastern trade, was now under Roman control, and the war seemed to be over. Trajan began to move back to Syria, leaving his garrisons behind, when suddenly news was brought to him that the Parthian army was attacking south of Armenia. Chosroes played the same trick on Trajan as the Russians did on Napoleon: while the Roman army overextended itself by occupying vast territories, Chosroes organized, and at an opportune time attacked a weakened Roman army. The Parthian resurgence quickly raised the hopes of other conquered peoples, and insurrections flared up in many places. Parthia was lost, so was Assyria, and in 117 Trajan withdrew his army to Antioch. Much of his conquest was still preserved, but he did not live to carry out his new plans for another round in Parthia.

This setback of the Romans in the East may have been the element which raised the hopes of the Jews that their time had come to take revenge on the Gentiles. At least this much is certain — around this time the Jews of the eastern Mediterranean began a revolt. It started in 115 in Cyrene where the Jews took control, slaughtered the Gentiles, burned buildings, and destroyed public property. The rebellion spread to Egypt, to Cyprus, where a terrible massacre of the Greeks took place, and in 116 the numerous Jews living in Mesopotamia joined in. Curiously enough, the Jews of Palestine were quiet. Perhaps the memory of A.D. 70 was still fresh in their minds. But those in the dispersion committed senseless barbarities and, all in all, about a million persons were killed before order was restored. Alexandria was badly damaged; Salamis, the capital of Cyprus, was practically destroyed. Trajan took stern measures, but order was ruthlessly restored later by Hadrian. So far as Cyprus was concerned, the Jews were banished and forbidden, on pain of death, ever to go there again.[36]

In his domestic policies Trajan succeeded in establishing the atmosphere of relaxed and confident security that the peoples of the Empire had long needed. Trials for treason *(maiestas)* were virtually abolished; his contact with people, particularly with senators and the soldiers, was most natural and democratic. He claimed no honors worldly or divine, and the royal ceremonies of the palace were completely done away with. His building program in Rome was considerable, and the Forum Traiani was admired by several generations. He built libraries and public baths, repaved the highways, enlarged the harbor of Ostia, and undertook many other similar projects that cannot be named within the scope of our study. He continued Nerva's public assistance program for children *(alimenta)*, and when in 99 a serious famine hit Egypt, he did not hesitate to give help from the reserves of Rome. The citizens of Rome, among whom poverty was most widespread, received on several occasions cash donations *(congiaria)* which after the Dacian victory, may have reached the sum of five hundred denaria per person, enough to help a responsible person to start something constructive. Public entertainment, especially after Dacia, was more lavish than ever. The number of gladiators and animals who fought and were killed ran into the thousands. Indeed, he brought home from Dacia about 2700 million sesterces worth of gold and silver, and the rich mines of Transylvania kept producing the precious metal for the benefit of the treasury.

Trajan was a hard-working man and required hard work of his associates. The imperial administrators were chosen from competent men regardless of their origin. His correspondence with Pliny the Younger, governor of Bithynia, survived, and it shows Trajan as a conscientious man, a humanitarian, and one who gave attention and careful consideration to small details of the provinces, too. Here we remember the well-known letter of Pliny concerning his investigation of the Christians *(ca.* 112) and Trajan's reply, which sought to combine toleration with discipline.[37] This correspondence shows that both Pliny and Trajan considered Christianity as a movement which in itself may have been harmless fanaticism, yet the *profession* of it and the refusal to recant was punishable. Actual persecutions, such as the execution of Ignatius, bishop of Antioch, which took place some time after 110, were probably isolated instances, but they did occur.

Trajan was paralyzed by a stroke in 117 in Antioch while preparing a new campaign against Parthia. He reluctantly gave up these plans and started to go back to Italy, but died on the way. The Romans long remembered him as one during whose reign the Empire reached its highest point, and indeed, the Senate in 114 had conferred upon him the title *Optimus Princeps.*

HADRIAN 117–138

Trajan had no children, and during his lifetime he did not name an heir and successor. However, when he died at Selinus in Cilicia on August 8, 117, those who were with him at the time — his wife Plotina, Hadrian's mother-in-law, Matidia, and the prefect of the Praetorian Guards, Acilius Attianus, proclaimed that on his deathbed Trajan adopted the forty-one-year-old Hadrian, his nephew and newly appointed governor of Syria, as his heir. Whether this was really true we shall never know, because in addition to these three persons who obviously would not say anything else, there was only one other person near Trajan at his death, his personal servant who died suddenly two days later, allegedly a suicide. This mystery has never been solved, but the fact remains that as soon as the news of the "adoption" of Hadrian came out, the army of Syria proclaimed him emperor. This news finally reached Rome, and in face of this the Senate had no choice but to ratify Hadrian's succession or face civil war. The senators wisely chose the first alternative, and Hadrian did his best to gain the sympathy of the Senate and the people. He apologized to the Senate for the hasty action of the army; he promised that he would never put a senator to death; and he asked that Trajan be deified. The troops received a double donative, and Hadrian showed a firm hand in restoring order in every part of the Empire. The Jewish uprisings in the eastern Mediterranean were quickly, and without much ceremony, put down, and so were the disturbances in Mauretania and Britain.

Everyone expected Hadrian to continue Trajan's policy in the East and to carry on the war against the Parthians. Instead of this, the first thing he did, when he was firmly established in the Principate, was to give up the territories which Trajan had won with such great difficulty. Armenia reverted from a Roman province into a kingdom; Parthia, as a client-kingdom, received new territories. He even considered giving up Dacia, but his friends finally dissuaded him from this plan and warned him that public opinion, already irritated at his withdrawals in the East, would tolerate no such further action. Hadrian also retained the province of Arabia Petraea. The giving up of these provinces was naturally a sacrifice, and Hadrian, who was no novice in military matters, knew this as well as his critics. Nevertheless, he made this sacrifice for a much greater end — the inner consolidation and strengthening of the territories that were firmly Roman. He realized that everything was not ideal within the Empire, and the various uprisings he had to deal with at the very beginning of his reign convinced him that further territorial addition was not the most important thing at the time. Throughout his Principate he made every effort to avoid war, up to the point where, in 118, he conducted negotiations with the Roxolani on the Lower Danube and in 123, by the same means, persuaded the Parthians to keep the peace.

His policy, therefore, was that the Empire should not undertake any further expansion; that the boundaries should be consolidated where they were; and that within these boundaries, in every part of the Empire, prosperity and peace should prevail. For this purpose he strengthened the *limites* and kept the army in perfect shape, but the role of the *limites* and of the army was now defensive and not aggressive. The best example of this policy is Hadrian's Wall in Britain, built between 122 and 128. It is about seventy-three miles long and fifteen feet high with fortlets built into it at every mile. In front of the wall was a V-shaped ditch about twenty-seven feet wide and ten feet deep. In other parts of the Empire, particularly in Germany, he also built fortifications.

His domestic policies reflect the same concern. He respected the Senate and its prerogatives and reorganized the crown council, *consilium principis,* whose duty it was to advise the emperor in administrative matters, to include not only senators but also members of the equestrian order. The codification of Roman law took place at his order, and this code, which was published in 129, had great influence upon the administration of justice and the further development of the Roman law. He enriched Italy with many new buildings; Ostia was practically rebuilt; but more than other emperors, he looked after the interests of the provinces so that they might get their proper share of the general prosperity. Aqueducts were built in Athens and Corinth, a new harbor in Ephesus; bridges and highways were constructed everywhere. New cities were founded throughout the Empire, many of which were named for him.

This interest in the provinces led Hadrian to make many journeys through the Empire. He traveled more and consequently knew more about the peoples and the places together with their problems than any other emperor. More than half of the total years of his rule he spent in visiting the provinces, and from Britain to Pannonia, from Morocco to the Euphrates, or the upper Nile valley, he visited every corner of the realm. At one time he was away from Rome for as long as five years continuously. He especially liked Greece and visited Athens three times. Here he assumed the title *Panhellenios* and *Zeus Olympios.* He was initiated into the Eleusian and Dionysiac mysteries, among others, and was also exposed to Christianity. Quadratus probably handed to him a defense of the Christian faith in the years 123,

124, or 129 when Hadrian was in Asia Minor. The Athenian philosopher Aristides may have presented him with his Apology during one of Hadrian's visits to Athens.[38]

Whether these apologies made any impression on Hadrian is doubtful. All we know is that under his reign Christians enjoyed relative peace. A letter of Hadrian, written in 125 to Minucius Fundanus, proconsul of Asia, concerning the Christians has been completely preserved in Justin Martyr's *First Apology* (68) and Eusebius' *Church History*.[39] In this rescript Hadrian ordered that Christians could be sentenced only through regular court procedures and only if the accuser could prove that the Christians had done something contrary to the laws. Penalties were to be in accordance with the character of the offenses, and false accusers must be severely punished. This ordinance is about as generous as Trajan's order to Pliny, but its weakness is the same, too, for Christians could always be accused of disloyalty to the state if they were called upon to perform those religious practices and sacrifices which they considered idolatrous.

The Jews fared far worse under Hadrian. When the emperor visited Judea in 130, he noticed that Jerusalem was still in ruins, as it was left by Titus sixty years before. He therefore decided to rebuild the city as a Roman colony called Aelia Capitolina. On the site of the temple of the Jews, a new temple dedicated to Jupiter Capitolinus was to be erected in which he himself was to be honored. The population was to be composed of Greeks and Hellenized people, and Jews were forbidden to enter it except one day in the year. As soon as Hadrian had left the East, the Jews rose in 132 in the great rebellion under Bar Kochba. The situation was so serious that in 134 Hadrian himself returned to the East. The rebellion was finally stamped out in 135. Many Jews were sold into slavery; more than half a million persons were killed; hundreds of villages were destroyed; Judea was abolished, and in its place a new province, Syria Palaestina, with two legions, was established. As a result of the dispersion of the nation the Jewish population in other provinces grew considerably, and the antipathy between Christians and Jews as well as other inhabitants of the Empire and the Jews grew considerably.

In spite of all his achievements, Hadrian was not a popular ruler. People attributed many dark motives to him, and he had a reputation of being a cruel man, a reputation for which he supplied more than sufficient material. To mention only one example, in 136 he executed his only male blood relative, an eighteen-year-old great-nephew, Fuscus, and his ninety-year-old brother-in-law, Servianus, on suspicion of plotting against him. But as he grew older, his mind darkened and physical illness attacked him also. To secure orderly succession to the Principate, he first adopted Aelius Verus, who, however, died early in 138.

Soon after that Hadrian adopted Antoninus and invested him with all the powers *(imperium proconsulare,* tribunician power) necessary to make Antoninus his heir. He died a few months later, and the ill feelings of the Senate were so strong against him that at first they refused to deify him. Finally the senators gave in at the urging of Antoninus, who then succeeded Hadrian and ruled under the name of Antoninus Pius.

NOTES

[1] Josephus, *Antiquities* 15. 194f.

[2] *Cambridge Ancient History* (New York: Cambridge University Press), 10. p. 110; Syme, *The Roman Revolution* (New York: Oxford University Press, 1960), pp. 298-299.

[3] Suetonius, *Augustus* 18.

[4] This we infer from the *Lex de Imperio Vespasiani, A.D. 69* (the law which conferred the imperial powers upon Vespasian). This decree explicitly says that Augustus also held this power as a part of his imperium. Text in N. Lewis and M. Reinhold, eds., *Roman Civilization* (New York: Columbia University Press, 1955), vol. 2, pp. 89ff.

[5] Suetonius, *Augustus* 63.

[6] Josephus, *Antiquities* 17. 229.

[7] Suetonius, *Tiberius* 9; *Claudius* 1.

[8] Josephus, *Antiquities* 17. 93ff.

[9] *Ibid.,* 17. 250f.; 286ff.; see also 17. 299 and *Jewish Wars* 1. 620; 2. 45; 2. 66ff.

[10] Suetonius, *Augustus* 23.

[11] Suetonius, *Tiberius* 13.

[12] *Ibid.,* 36; Josephus, *Antiquities* 18. 81; Dio, 57. 18. 5.

[13] Josephus, *Jewish Wars* 2. 169ff.; *Antiquities* 18. 55ff.; 168ff. See also Paul L. Maier, "Sejanus, Pilate and the Date of the Crucifixion," *Church History* 37 (1968), 3-13.

[14] Philo, *Legatio ad Gaium* and *In Flaccum* deal with these important matters.

[15] Suetonius, *Claudius* 10. 1f.

[16] Tacitus, *Annals* 13. 8. 1.

[17] Dio, *History* 63. 1. 2–63. 5. 4.

[18] Josephus, *Antiquities* 20. 195.

[19] Tacitus, *Annals* 15. 38. 1–15. 44. 1.

[20] Dio Chrysostom, *Orations* 21. 10; the *Sibylline Oracles* 4. 119; 5. 363; 8. 70. See also Tacitus, *History* 2. 8; Seutonius, *Nero* 57. 2.

[21] Suetonius, *Galba* 20. 2, from Suetonius, *The Lives of the Twelve Caesars,* ed. Joseph Gavorse (New York: Modern Library, 1959), p. 295.

[22] Suetonius, *Vespasianus* 13; 19. 2; Dio, *History* 66. 8. 2–66. 9. 1; 66. 15. 5.

[23] Suetonius, *Vespasianus* 15; Dio, *History* 66. 12. 1–66. 13. 3.

[24] Suetonius, *Vespasianus* 23; 24.

[25] Suetonius, *Titus* 7. 2; 8. 5–9. 2.

[26] Juvenal, *Satire* 6. 156.

[27] Dio, *History* 66. 15. 3-5; 66. 18. 1; Suetonius, *Titus* 7. 1-2. See also chapter 3 in this book, footnote 56.

[28] Suetonius, *Titus* 1. 1; 11. 2.

[29] Suetonius, *Domitianus* 8. 1.

[30] Dio, *History* 67. 14. 2; (the words are from Dio's epitomator Xiphilinus) .

[31] See Bo Reicke, *Neutestamentliche Zeitgeschichte*, pp. 217-225, and chapter 3 in this book, footnotes 58, 59, also chapter 4, footnote 72.

[32] *Apologia* 5; *The Ante-Nicene Fathers* (Grand Rapids: Wm. B. Eerdmans Publishing Co., 1953) , 3. 22.

[33] Eusebius, *Church History* 3. 18. 5; 19; 20; *The Nicene and Post Nicene Fathers* (Grand Rapids: Wm. B. Eerdmans Publishing Co., 1952) , Series 2. vol. 1, 148f; Hennecke-Schneemelcher 1. 423.

[34] Suetonius, *Domitianus* 13. 1-2

[35] Dio, *History* 67. 14. 5–67. 18. 2; Suetonius, *Domitianus* 17. 3.

[36] Dio, *History* 68. 32. 1-3; Eusebius, *Hist. Eccl.* 4. 2. 1-5.

[37] Pliny, *Ep.* 10. 97. 2: *"conquirendi non sunt."*

[38] Cf. Eusebius, *Church History* 4. 3. 1-3.

[39] *Ibid.*, 4. 9. 1-3. For English translation, see *Library of Christian Classics* (Philadelphia: The Westminster Press, 1960), 1. 288; *Nicene and Post Nicene Fathers*, Series 2, vol. 1, 182.

FOR ADVANCED READING

SPECIAL STUDIES ON THE EMPERORS

Augustus

Brunt, Peter A., and Moore, J., *Res Gestae Divi Augusti*. London: Oxford University Press, 1967.

Buchan, John, *Augustus*. New York: Houghton Mifflin Company, 1937.

Earle, Donald, *The Age of Augustus*. New York: Crown Publishers, Inc., 1969.

Ehrenberg, Victor, and Jones, Arnold H., *Documents Illustrating the Reigns of Augustus and Tiberius*. London: Oxford University Press, 1955.

Gagé, J., *Res Gestae Divi Augusti*. Paris, 1950.

Grenade, A., *Essai sur les origines du principat*. Paris, 1950.

Hammond, Mason, *The Augustan Principate in Theory and Practice*. Cambridge, Mass.: Harvard University Press, 1933. (re-issue New York: Russell & Russell, Publishers, 1968.)

Holmes, Thomas R., *The Architect of the Roman Empire*. 2 vols. New York: Oxford University Press, 1928-1931.

Levi, Mario A., *Il Tempo di Augusto*. Florence, 1950.

Sattler, P., *Augustus und der Senat. Untersuchungen zur römischen Innenpolitik zwischen 30 und 17 v. Christus*. Göttingen, 1960.

Schmitthenner, W., *Oktavian und das Testament Caesars*. München, 1953. (See also Charles-Picard, under *Nero*.)

Tiberius

Baker, George P., *Tiberius Caesar*. New York: Barnes & Noble, Inc., 1967.

Ciaceri, E., *Tiberio*. Rome, 1944.

Gollub, W., *Tiberius*. München, 1959.

Grant, Michael, *Aspects of the Principate of Tiberius*. New York: American Numismatic Society, 1950.

Kornemann, E., *Tiberius*. Stuttgart, 1960.

Marañon, Gregoria, *Tiberius: A Study in Resentment*. Translated by Warre B. Wells. London: Hollis and Carter, 1956.

Marsh, Frank B., *The Reign of Tiberius*. New York: Barnes & Noble, Inc., 1931.

Pippidi, D. M., *Autour de Tibere*. Bucharest, 1944.

Rogers, Robert S., *Criminal Trials and Criminal Legislation under Tiberius*. New York: American Philological Association, 1935.
————, *Studies in the Reign of Tiberius*. Baltimore: The Johns Hopkins Press, 1943.
Smith, C. E., *Tiberius and the Roman Empire*. Baton Rouge: Louisiana State University Press, 1942.
(See also V. Ehrenberg, under *Augustus*.)

Gaius

Balsdon, John P., *The Emperor Gaius–Caligula*. New York: Oxford University Press, 1934.
Smallwood, Edith M., ed., *Documents Illustrating the Principates of Gaius, Claudius and Nero*. London: Cambridge University Press, 1967.

Claudius

Charlesworth, Martin P., *Documents Illustrating the Reigns of Claudius and Nero*. New York: Cambridge University Press, 1951.
Momigliano, Arnaldo, *Claudius the Emperor and His Achievements*. New York: Barnes & Noble, Inc., 1961.
Scramuzza, Vincent M., *The Emperor Claudius*. Cambridge, Mass.: Harvard University Press, 1940.
Stähelin, F., *Kaiser Claudius*. Basel, 1933.
(See also Smallwood, under *Gaius*.)

Nero

See Charlesworth under Claudius.
Charles-Picard, Gilbert, *Auguste et Neron. Le secret de l'empire*. Paris, 1962.
————, *ET: Augustus and Nero*. Translated by Ortzen Len. New York: Apollo Editions, Inc., 1966.
Henderson, B. W., *Life and Principate of the Emperor Nero*. London: Methuen, 1903.
Levi, Mario A., *Nerone e i Suoi Tempi*. Milan, 1949.
Schiller, H., *Geschichte des römischen Kaiserreichs unter der Regierung des Nero*. Gotha, 1872.
(See also Smallwood, under *Gaius*.)

Otho

Klinger, F., *Die Geschichte Kaiser Othos bei Tacitus*. Leipzig, 1940.

The Flavians

Henderson, Bernard W., *Five Roman Emperors: Vespasian, Titus, Domitian, Nerva, Trajan, A.D. 69–117*. New York: Barnes & Noble, Inc., 1969.
McCrum, Michael, and Woodhead, A. G., *Select Documents of the Principates of the Flavian Emperors, A.D. 68–96*. London: Cambridge University Press, 1961.

Vespasian

Bersanetti, G., *Vespasiano*. Rome, 1941.
Graf, H. R., *Kaiser Vespasianus*. Stuttgart, 1937.
Homo, Leon, *Vespasien, l'empereur du bon sens*. Paris, 1949.

Titus

Fortina, M., *L'Imperatore Tito*. Turin, 1955.

Domitian

Arias, P. E., *Domitiano*. 1945.
Gsell, S., *Essai sur la règne de l'empereur Domitien*. 1894.
Pichlmayr, F., *T. Flavius Domitianus. Ein Beitrag zur römischen Kaisergeschichte*. Amberg, 1889.

Nerva

Garzetti, A., *Nerva*. Rome, 1950.
Smallwood, Edith M., ed., *Documents Illustrating the Principates of Nerva, Trajan and Hadrian*. New York: Cambridge University Press, 1966.

Trajan

Lepper, F. A., *Trajan's Parthian War*. New York: Oxford University Press, 1948.
Paribeni, R., *Optimus Princeps*. Messina, 1927.
(See also Smallwood, under *Nerva*.)

Hadrian

Birley, Anthony R., *Hadrian's Wall*. London: Ministry of Public Building and Works, 1963.
Birley, Eric, *Research on Hadrian's Wall*. Kendall, England: Titus Wilson & Son, Ltd., 1961.
Divine, A. D., *Hadrian's Wall*. Boston: Gambit, 1969.
Henderson, Bernard W., *Life and Principate of the Emperor Hadrian*. London: Methuen, 1923.
Jones, D. F., *Hadrian's Wall*. London: Cape, 1968.
d'Orgeval, B., *L'Empereur Hadrien*. Paris, 1950.
Perowne, Stewart, *Hadrian*. New York: W. W. Norton & Company, Inc., 1961.
Toynbee, Jocelyn M. C., *The Hadrianic School*. Toronto: Cambridge University Press, 1934.
(See also Smallwood, under *Nerva*.)

Robert A. Kraft

3
Judaism on the World Scene

It would be sheer folly to attempt a comprehensive and definitive overview of even the political aspects of Judaism in the early Roman period within the limited space available. The work of Josephus alone covers almost seven hundred pages in the Loeb Greek edition of the *Antiquities* (books 14-20) on the period from Pompey's intervention in 63 B.C. to the outbreak of revolt in A.D. 66, and an almost equal number of pages is used elsewhere to tell the story of the "Jewish War" in A.D. 66–73, including background information from the Maccabean revolt onward. To this extensive source material, which devotes much space to the political intrigues of the house of Herod and the general political situation in the Roman Empire, as well as to the revolt, a variety of other bits of information about Jews and Judaism can be added, such as excerpts from Greek and Latin authors, collected by T. Reinach; inscriptional evidence gathered by J. B. Frey; non-literary evidence from the Egyptian papyri and ostraca, edited by V. Tcherikover and A. Fuks; and various "symbols" used by Jews in this period, amassed by E. R. Goodenough.[1] Numerous analyses and syntheses of the available materials have appeared over the years. To mention only the most obvious general works dealing with Judaism in this period, we have the older, so to speak "classical," multi-volumed presentations by H. Grätz or E. Schürer, as well as more recent synthetic attempts by such scholars as Salo Baron or V. Tcherikover, and others.[2]

Most students of early Christianity are more or less familiar with the general chronological sequence of events in Palestine during the period:

1. The gradual disintegration of the Hasmonean High Priestly Kingdom, leading to the requested intervention of the Roman general Pompey in 63 B.C.

2. The gradual disappearance of Hasmonean Priestly Rulers and

the rise of the house of Antipater-Herod, with the latter established as "king" somewhere around the year 40 B.C.

3. The partitioning of Herod's kingdom after his death in 4 B.C., which led to placing Judea under direct Roman rule in A.D. 6.

4. The seething dissatisfaction under the Roman prefects, which was first manifest in the near revolt at the time of Gaius Caligula (A.D. 37–41) and which resulted in the "first revolt" of A.D. 66–73.

5. Finally, the less fully documented "second revolt" under Bar Kochba from A.D. 132–135, which added further encouragement for emerging Rabbinic Judaism to retreat from the world scene by building its hedges higher.

These events are all part of *Palestinian* Jewish history, but "Judaism" clearly was part of the *world* scene as well! Our traditional preoccupation with the events in Palestine should not blind us to the emphatic reality of that statement. Nor should our tendency to see Judaism from the perspective of that Pharisaic-Rabbinic Orthodoxy which flowered into Talmud and Midrash blind us to the potential variety of outlooks that can be covered in our period by the term "Judaism" when examined from a rigorously historical point of view.[3] What was "Judaism" in the eyes of Greco-Roman rulers and subjects? Who was a "Jew"? Where were "Jews" encountered, and what were they doing or thinking? How were they being treated? This chapter will deal with some of these more general questions; some of the other essays will necessarily deal in greater detail with certain specific problems outlined here.[4]

Answers are not easily found. Unless we wish to operate arbitrarily in one way or another, we must allow a man to answer for himself whether, and in what sense, he chooses to identify himself as a "Jew" or an adherent of "Judaism." Although such an approach is ideal, our available sources seldom provide the kind of information necessary to operate in that manner. Thus we are usually reduced to discussing those who are called "Jews" by a Josephus or a Suetonius or an unknown contributor to the papyri, or those whose conduct or ideas seem "Jewish" for one reason or another. Granting these difficulties, what pictures emerge when the sources are sifted?

GENERAL CHARACTERISTICS

Distribution

In the roughly two hundred years of concern to us, "Jews" are said to abound virtually everywhere in the inhabited world. There are numerous general statements to that effect from a variety of sources (mostly Jewish, admittedly!), e.g.:

Sibylline Oracle — "Every land and sea shall be full of [Jews]";[5]

Strabo, the Hellenistic geographer, as quoted by Josephus — "It is not easy to find a place in the inhabited world which this tribe has not penetrated and which has not been occupied by it";[6]

The appeal of Agrippa I to Gaius in A.D. 39 or 40, according to Philo, gives a detailed list of places where Jewish "colonies" have been established "in every region of the inhabited world — in Europe, Asia, Libya, on mainlands, on islands, both on the coast and inland";[7]

The speech of Agrippa II to dissuade Jews from revolting in A.D. 66, as reported by Josephus — "There is no people in the inhabited world which does not hold our fate in its hands";[8]

Philo — "one single country cannot support the Jews because they are so numerous";[9]

Josephus — "the Jewish race is scattered widely over the entire inhabited world among the local inhabitants, especially in Syria."[10]

Elsewhere, Josephus speaks of "not a few myriads" of Jews in the Babylonian area under Parthian rule[11] and tells not only of individuals and of particular communities there, but narrates a relatively long story of temporary but large-scale military and political success by some Jews in those eastern areas from about A.D. 20—35, as well as the better-known tale of Izates, the proselyte Jewish king of Adiabene, and his mother, Helena, at about the same time.[12] Furthermore, Josephus transcribes edict after edict dealing with Jews in various places throughout the Roman world — Sidon and Phoenicia, Asia Minor (Parium, Ephesus, Delos, Cos, Sardis, Melitus, Pergamum, Halicarnassos, and Ionia), Alexandria and Egypt, Cyrene, Rome.[13] Numerous papyri from Egypt attest the extent of Jewish occupation and/or influence there.[14]

In our statistically conditioned society, we would very much like to know how many Jews lived where! But the sources contain very few figures that would be helpful in such a game, and even these are probably unreliable, for the most part. Indeed, perhaps the first official census capable of answering that question on a large scale would be from the time of Vespasian when the special Jewish tax was imposed throughout the Empire after the first revolt (see p. 90). But to my knowledge, these figures are unavailable. Various estimates of Jewish population and distribution have been attempted and vary from a minimum of three to four million to a maximum of eight million total around the time of Jesus, with anywhere from 30 percent to 70 percent estimated as living in Palestine itself. The consensus seems to be that about two thirds of the Jews lived outside of Palestine, especially in the adjacent areas in the eastern Mediterranean.[15] Nor should we forget that the Jewish "Diaspora" includes Parthian East as well as Roman West. And Parthia had her Hellenistic cities, inherited from Alexander and the Seleucids, as well as her less Hellenized areas. Josephus mentions one episode relating to Jews in Greek cities in Parthia,[16] and speaks of numerous other Jewish settlements in the Parthian part of the Diaspora, but on the whole our information is slight. Jacob Neusner conjectures that in our period "the Jews must have formed minority communities in almost every city of the Euphrates valley and throughout the western satrapies of Parthia (some were in the east as well, in Afghanistan, and in India, but we do not know when they reached there)." [17]

Image, Definition

When we search the sources to determine how a "Jew" appeared to his contemporaries and who was considered to be a "Jew" in our designated period, the answer is not always as clear as we might like. The popular press in the Hellenistic-Roman world tended to picture the Jews as an uncultured and uncivil lot who scorned the gods of the cultured world and followed a "barbaric superstition" — haters of mankind, with odd customs and practices; they were to be shunned as foreigners by Hellenistic purists.[18] On the other hand, Jewish apologists like Philo and Josephus claim that much of the world responded in a positive way to Judaism.[19] Unfortunately, we know very little in detail about the Jewish "common man" on whose shoulders such calumnies regularly must have fallen. Nor do we know to what extent the same sorts of attitudes toward Jews were prevalent among other non-Hellenistic groups like the native Egyptians or Syrians, who were themselves looked down upon by the more cultured "Greeks" of the eastern Mediterranean.[20] Indeed, "Jews" are sometimes lumped together with "Syrians" in the sources from this period.[21] But we can safely assume that there was a deeply rooted and widely known general grass-roots polemic against "Judaism" (as against analogous groups in the ancient world), which would hardly be sufficiently offset by the presence and activity of cultured, often Hellenized, Jews like the Herods or Philo or Josephus.[22]

When we turn to Josephus, our most instructive contemporary Jewish source on this matter of Jewish identity, we find that for the most part, a Jew appears to be one who lives by the "ancestral customs" and "sacred rites" as they are sometimes enumerated in the decrees which Josephus cites — e.g., sabbath observance, food laws, temple support and sacrifices, and "common meals," to which list we also should add circumcision, although it is not mentioned as such in the decrees or emphasized by Josephus.[23] Nevertheless, there are some passages in Josephus which complicate the issue: e.g., his references to Samaritan-Jewish relationships, when he claims that Samaria-Shechem was inhabited by "apostates" from Judaism who were expelled for breaking food or sabbath or some other law,[24] and that when it seemed to their advantage, the Samaritans would identify themselves with the "Jews." [25] The relationship between apologetic and reality in such passages is not always clear. Again, Josephus vacillates on what to call Herod and his ancestors although he cites the data from Herod's close associate, Nicolas of Damascus, that Herod's immediate ancestors were prominent Jews from Babylon,[26] he seems to prefer labeling Herod as "half-Jewish," at best,[27] and an "Idumean" commoner.[28] Another problem arises with the figure of Tiberius Julius Alexander, son of Philo's brother, the wealthy Alexander, "the alabarch" of Alexandria; Tiberius is contrasted with his father and accused of "not abiding by the ancestral customs." [29] But does this mean that Josephus would exclude Tiberius from the category of "Jew"? And would Tiberius exclude himself? Elsewhere we learn of "Jews" who for various reasons adopted a less than strict attitude toward literal observance of the law, in part or in whole: e.g.:

> Sabbath is broken for the sake of self-defense.[30]
>
> Izates is advised by a leading Jew to become Jewish *without* being circumcized.[31]
>
> There is a certain ambiguity in the grammatical structure of some decrees cited by Josephus exempting from military service certain "Jews of Roman citizenship (who are) accustomed to practice Jewish rites" [32] — are the phrases in apposition, or were there also Jews of Roman citizenship who were *not* accustomed to observe the rites?

We have clear evidence from Philo that there were some "Jews" for whom an understanding of the symbolic meaning of the laws sufficed, and, thus, for whom literal obedience was not considered necessary.[33] Such issues as these, plus passing references to Jewish magicians and the like,[34] make it difficult to reconstruct with accuracy the many faces of "Judaism" in the early Roman period. The clues are preserved; what we do with them depends on our larger perspective and our inclinations!

Activities and Occupations in General

Our specific information about Jewish life in the various areas of the Hellenistic-Roman world during the early Roman period is limited. Apart from Palestine (and especially Jerusalem), we probably know most about Alexandria, where Philo refers to the presence of numerous Jews who were deprived of their houses, shops, and other property during the disturbances in the reign of Gaius Caligula (A.D. 37–41). These people were Jewish suppliers (or investors?), farmers, ship-merchants, merchants in general, and craftsmen.[35] We also hear about the wealthy Alexandrian Jewish "alabarch" Alexander (see also above), who was in a position to lend large sums of money and perhaps was an outstanding representative of Hellenistic Jewish "bankers." [36] That there were also numerous Jews who were poor and in debt is well attested by the Egyptian papyri.[37] On the whole, the evidence from Egypt and Asia Minor points to farming as perhaps the single most important Jewish occupation among the masses, with weaving and dyeing also mentioned frequently among the trades.[38]

THE RELATIONSHIP OF JEWS TO THE EMPIRE

Involvement in Roman Governmental Posts

We know far too little about the role of Jews in official government posts in the early Roman Empire, and virtually nothing of the parallel situation in Parthia.[39] Tcherikover would have us believe that, at least for Egypt, "there is very little evidence of Jewish officials in the early Roman period. It would appear that some financial and police offices were entrusted to Jews. . . . Some tax-collectors in Edfu, especially those collecting the 'Jewish tax' (after A.D. 70), might have been Jews, but we have only one definite instance." [40] Six Jewish *sitologoi* (wheat accountants?) are mentioned in a document from A.D. 101/102.

> As for posts in the Roman administration in the proper sense, there was, in theory, no obstacle to a Jew entering upon the career of a Roman official and reaching even the highest ranks. Yet in practice this was open only to those who were ready to renounce the Jewish faith [sic] and to sever any links with the Jewish community [sic]. Such a break with Jewish tradition was not easy and the number of Jewish renegades appears to have been very small.

Only Tiberius Alexander, who became procurator of Judea, staff general under Titus, and ultimately governor of Alexandria and Egypt, is well known and "his career was in every sense extraordinary." [41]

Further, Tcherikover concludes that at least in Egypt, where Rome abolished the Ptolemaic army, "Rome was not interested in engaging Jews for military service," [42] despite the importance of Jewish soldiers and military settlers in early times. It is debatable whether this policy was general throughout the Roman Empire, although the evidence is scanty. Josephus tells of the drafting of four thousand Jews (probably exaggerated) in Rome by Tiberius, in connection with his expulsion of Jews from the city;[43] earlier, Herod is said to have sent a force of five hundred men from his own bodyguard to fight under a Roman general.[44] There is mention of a Jewish centurion in an Egyptian ostracon from A.D. 116,[45] in addition to our knowledge of the military career of Tiberius Alexander. As we have already noted (see also below), there is evidence that Rome sometimes exempted at least certain Jews from military service, which may suggest that others were *not* exempted! The existence of Jewish soldiers in Parthia has already been mentioned, but they seem to be presented as a special case.[46]

Involvement in International Politics in General

That the Hasmoneans left a tradition of active participation in international politics is abundantly clear from the frequent references in Josephus to envoys sent to Rome, Parthia, and other nearby kingdoms.[47] The history of the Herods is best understood against this background, for Herod's father, Antipater, served as a special ambassador of the Hasmoneans to both East and West.[48] The Herods and other Jewish leaders seem to have moved relatively freely in and out of Rome. Indeed, if Josephus is to be trusted in this matter, Julius Caesar honored Herod's father, Antipater, by awarding him Roman citizenship and tax-free status, as well as appointing him "procurator" (epitropon) of Judea;[49] Caesar also is said to have granted the right to one of the last Hasmoneans, Hyrcanus II, his children, and his envoys (presbeutai) "to sit with members of the senatorial order as spectators of the contests of gladiators and wild beasts" [50] and to be admitted to the Senate chamber at his request for the purpose of making petition.[51] Whether such privileges were unusual or not need not detain us here; what is clear is that at least some of the leaders of the Jews clearly were "on the world scene" in a political sense and must have had some sort of established embassies in cities such as Rome. And there is no reason to suppose that the number of Jews capable of serving as ambassadors, envoys, and advocates in such a setting was small. We hear of Jewish envoys from the Diaspora[52] as well as from Palestine; and after the death of Herod the Great, as many as fifty Jewish envoys are mentioned as sent from Jerusalem to Rome to protest the continuation of Herodian rule under Archelaus.[53] To what extent there was an active training program for such persons is not clear, but a few tantalizing hints survive — e.g., reference to extensive Greek studies under the Pharisaic teacher Gamaliel II.[54] Occasionally we even catch a glimpse of an identifiable "Jewish" personality in addition to the Herods at work in these diplomatic spheres, such as Nicolas of Damascus or Philo or Tiberius Alexander

— perhaps we can include also Josephus, and possibly even Paul? That their "Jewishness" was not always consistent with later Rabbinic-"orthodox" perspectives ought not concern us here!

Some Jews who may have had some influence on the international political scene, but in a less official way, would have been such individuals as the somewhat obscure Poppaea who was first the wife of Otho and then of Nero, and whom Josephus describes as a "pious woman *(theosebes)* who pleaded [with Nero] on behalf of the Jews";[55] or Berenice, the daughter of Agrippa I, who is said to have been a mistress to Titus in Rome, if not already earlier in Palestine.[56] Drusilla, the sister of Berenice, married a Roman governor of Judea, Felix.[57] Possibly Flavius Clemens, a Roman consul, and his wife Domitilla[58] also deserve mention because he was executed and his wife exiled by their cousin Domitian *(ca.* A.D. 95) on the charge of "atheism," a charge often used against those who followed "Jewish customs." [59]

Jewish Citizenship and "Rights"

When we approach the problem of the legal and civil status of Jews in the eyes of the Roman officials in general, we are faced with several problems of interpreting the sources. What was involved in the word "citizen" *(polites)*? In what sense were Jews "citizens" of Alexandria, for example, and what did it mean to be a "Roman citizen"? In many places, Josephus seems to display a studied vagueness in his use of the term "citizen," e.g., he argues against Apion that there is a type of citizenship *(tropon tes politeias)* that consists of bearing the name of the area (or government) in which one resides — e.g., Antiochenes, Ephesians, Romans, Alexandrians.[60] This seems to be equated with "honorary citizenship" *(tes kata dosin politeias)* which Apion also enjoyed. But was it in any way "legal" citizenship? The edict of Claudius in A.D. 41 raises strong doubts in that it seems to discourage the hope that some significant segments of the Alexandrian Jewish inhabitants addressed by it were legally entitled to the designation "citizen of Alexandria," which seems to have been a prerequisite for being a Roman citizen,[61] and which depended on successful participation in the Greek gymnastic education.[62] Doubtless Tiberius Julius Alexander qualified; it would be interesting to know the background and status of Philo and his brother Alexander in this connection. Other references to specific Jews holding Roman citizenship include Antipater (thus also many of the Herods?),[63] Paul,[64] and Josephus.[65]

Josephus also refers to an incident in Caesarea at the start of the first revolt in which the right of "equal citizenship" *(isopoliteian)* was taken away from the Jews by Nero at the instigation of the Syrian populace.[66] Elsewhere, he cites several Roman edicts concerning especially Asia Minor in which "Jewish Roman citizens" are granted special rights — specifically exemption from military service[67] and the right of self-determination in general.[68] It is also claimed that the Jews of Asia and Cyrenean Libya had been granted "legal equality" (isonomia) by former kings, although there is no reference to Roman citizenship in the decree of Augustus that follows.[69] With respect to the edicts concerning military service, we may ask whether the exemption of "Jews who are Roman citizens" (in Ephesus and Delos, see n. 67) held true in general also for non-enfranchised Jews throughout the Empire,[70] or even in western Asia Minor? In any event, these edicts suggest that there was a sizable group of Jews in western Asia Minor who enjoyed Roman citizenship and who also observed the ancestral customs. Philo adds an allusion to emancipated Jewish captives who enjoyed Roman citizenship in the city of Rome at the time of Augustus.[71] Little else can be said with certainty.

In Egypt, at least, the problem of citizenship and civil status also had definite financial overtones. Near the beginning of Roman rule in Egypt (ca. 24/23 B.C.), a special tax seems to have been established for all "non-Greek" inhabitants — the laographia of sixteen drachmae annually.[72] Those Jews unable to support convincingly their claim to legal citizenship in the Hellenistic city of Alexandria probably were legally lumped together with other non-Greek inhabitants (especially the native "Egyptians") and subjected to the tax. Although in the fragmentary account of a dispute between King Agrippa I and Isodorus, Agrippa claimed that the Jews did not pay the tax, Tcherikover is convinced from the other evidence that, in general, the Jews did pay it.[73] This distinction was one way for the Greek Alexandrians to maintain a relatively pure pattern of culture and citizenship. Whether similar measures were taken elsewhere in the Roman world, not to mention the Parthian world, is not clear.

Some of the specific rights supposedly granted to Jews in the early Roman Empire — or at least to some Jews in some places and times in the period under consideration — are of special interest in relation to the general structure of usual Roman policy. There is, for example, the claim that despite a general prohibition of "religious societies" by Julius Caesar, the Jews alone were permitted their thiasoi.[74] Special financial considerations also are claimed such as exemption from certain "civic" expenses contrary to Jewish ideas[75] and permission to support financially the Jerusalem cult,[76] as well as local Jewish "communal" activities.[77] As we have seen (n. 70), there seem to have been circumstances in which exemption from military service was provided at least to some Jewish Roman citizens at one point, and normal court and related legal procedures were suspended with reference to Jews on the sabbath.[78] With respect to the Roman Emperor cult, the sources suggest that Jews were allowed some sort of compromise solution in view of their monotheistic orientation.[79]

One aspect of the supposed privileged status of Jewry under Rome changed radically after the first revolt in A.D. 70, when instead of permitting contributions to continue to flow into the now destroyed city of Jerusalem, Vespasian instituted a special tax on Jews, as a sort of reparation for the war, and financed the rebuilding of the Temple of Jupiter of Rome with this money — the "Jewish tax" (Ioudaikon telesma) or fiscus Iudaicus, also known as the denarii duo Judaeorum and the didrachmon or half-shekel tax.[80] This tax was levied on every Jew from the ages of three to sixty/sixty-two throughout the Roman world, male and female, slave and free.[81] Thus for large families, the tax may have created considerable economic hardships. Our main detailed knowledge of the tax comes from Egypt, where it was collected at least to the middle of the second century.[82] In connection with this tax, a separate census of Jews would have been necessary. Whether the tax was a significant factor in influencing any individuals or groups to separate from Judaism (e.g., "Jewish Christians") is a question worth pursuing elsewhere. The Jewish tax was in addition to the other regular taxes, such as the laographia, guard-tax, bath-tax, and others.

After the First Revolt

In closing, a word is in order about the history of Judaism subsequent to the events of 66–73, for which we have no Josephus to guide us. From Egypt, we get little information except what relates to the revolt in the last days of Trajan, 115–117. "The political history of the Egyptian Jews from A.D. 70 till A.D. 115 is almost a blank," writes Tcherikover, and the "almost total annihilation of Egyptian Jewry" after the revolt is indicated; Egyptian Judaism does not re-emerge in force until the fourth century, in a relatively conservative form compared with the period of Philo![83]

Apart from Egypt, we have some awareness of the general events in Palestine, and a few references to Jews elsewhere — such as Justin's courteous opponent Trypho, with his disciples.[84] The Palestinian Hillelite Pharisees seem to have been solidifying their hold on the religious life and traditions of Judaism through their deliberations and decisions in the Academies of Jamnia, Joppa, Lydda, and others, which were established on the basis of a policy of peaceful coexistence and cooperation with Roman rule.[85] The revolt under Trajan extended from Cyrene to Cyprus, and even on into Mesopotamia; but there is little evidence that Palestine provided any large-scale support. That some of the rabbinic leaders, including the famous teacher Aqiba himself, should take up the messianic cause of Bar Kochba against Rome some fifteen years later would seem to be a tribute to the image projected by that "Son of the Star," as well as an extreme display of dissatisfaction with the new conditions instituted by Hadrian after the Trajan revolt. But the results were disastrous — Jews were expelled from the city area; cultic practices were forbidden as well as Rabbinic ordination; and at last Jerusalem was transformed into a Hellenistic-Roman city, Aelia Capitolina. Henceforth, many survivors in Palestinian Rabbinic Jewry began to look toward Parthian Babylon for solace and the hope of a brighter future. It is striking that there is virtually no evidence for Babylonian support of either of the two major Palestinian revolts against Rome in 66 and 132, although Babylonian Jews did oppose Trajan's armies in the revolt of 115. The reasons for such seeming inconsistencies are not apparent,[86] especially since there is evidence that Parthian interests, as well as the interests of Babylonia Jewry would have been well served by a defeat of the Roman legions in Judea.

On this paradoxical note, and with Judaism entering what proved to be a new era, perhaps it is fitting to end our all too brief overview of a frequently paradoxical period of Jewish history.

NOTES

[1] Theodore Reinach, *Textes d'auteurs grecs et romains rélatifs au Judaïsme* (1895; reprint 1963 by Georg Olms). See also the corrections and suggestions contained in the review of Reinach's work by H. Willrich in *Berliner philologische Wochenschrift* of 1895; *Corpus Inscriptionum Judaicarum*, ed. J. B. Frey in 2 vols., 1936, 1952. See also J. Gray, "The Jewish Inscriptions in Greek and Hebrew at Torca, Cyrene and Barce," in A. Rowe, *Cyrenaican Expedition of the University of Manchester, 1952* (Manchester: University Press, 1956), pp. 43-59; *Corpus Papyrorum Judaicarum* [henceforth *C.P.J.*] ed. V. Tcherikover and A. Fuks, 3 vols. (Cambridge: Harvard University Press, 1957-1964); E. R. Goodenough, *Jewish Symbols in the Greco-Roman Period*, 12 vols., (New York: Pantheon Books, Inc., 1953-1966).

[2] See the bibliography appended to this chapter for fuller information and further suggested reading. At an introductory level, the treatment by Hans Lietzmann in chapters 1-2, and especially in chapter 6 of the first volume of his *History of the Early Church* (New York: The World Publishing Company, 1937, 1949), is highly recommended as a convenient and readable capsule presentation.

[3] See, e.g., M. Simon, *Jewish Sects at the Time of Jesus* (Philadelphia: Fortress Press, 1967) (French, 1960).

[4] E.g., Jews as a Social Class (chap. 4 of this book); Jews and Education (chap. 6 of this book).

[5] *Sibylline Oracle* 3. 271f. This passage contrasts the omnipresence (and offensiveness) of the Jewish people in exile with the emptiness of the Holy Land because

of their failure to fear God (3. 265ff.) . Lanchester (in Charles, *Pseudepigrapha* 372) dates the passage to about 140 B.C. (See bibliography.)

[6] Josephus, *Antiquities* 14. 115. Strabo died around 21 B.C., and in this quotation is referring to events that took place around 86 B.C.

[7] Philo, *Embassy to Gaius* 281-283: Egypt, Phoenicia, Syria, Pamphylia, Cilicia, Asia Minor (to Bithynia and Pontus) , Europe, Thessaly, Boeotia, Macedonia, Aetolia, Attica, Argos, Corinth, much of the Peloponnese, Euboea, Cyprus, Crete, Babylonia, and the other satrapies beyond the Euphrates are explicitly mentioned.

[8] That is, worldwide slaughter of Jews could occur if the nations are roused against them; Josephus, *Jewish War* 2. 398.

[9] Philo, *Flaccus* 45.

[10] Josephus, *Jewish War* 7. 43.

[11] Josephus, *Antiquities* 15. 39; see also 15. 14; 18. 313 and 339.

[12] *Ibid.*, 18. 310ff.; 20. 17ff.

[13] *Ibid.*, 14. 190-264; 16. 27ff. and 16ff.

[14] See the material in *C.P.J.*, and in Tcherikover, *Hellenistic Civilization and the Jews* (Philadelphia: Jewish Publication Society, 1959) , pp. 284ff.

[15] Tcherikover, *Hellenistic Civilization*, pp. 284-295, discusses the problem in some detail, and in n. 86 (p. 504) refers to particular estimates made by various scholars. See also Lietzmann, *History* I, p. 76, and the very valuable older discussion by A. Harnack, *The Mission and Expansion of Christianity in the First Three Centuries.* I (London: Williams and Nargate, 1908 [reprinted as Harper Torchbook, 1962]) , pp. 1-9.

[16] *Antiquities* 18. 373-379. More than 50,000 Jews are said to have lived in the Greek-Syrian city of Seleucia for five years (*ca.* A.D. 35–40?) , and some of them later fled to the nearby Greek city of Ctesiphon.

[17] J. Neusner, *A History of the Jews in Babylonia: I The Parthian Period.* (Leiden: E. J. Brill, 1965) , p. 15.

[18] Relevant materials may be found in Reinach's collection of texts: e.g., the fragment from Hecateus of Abdera (early third century B.C., pp. 14ff.) ; the fragment from Posidonius (early first century B.C., pp. 56ff.) ; Cicero, *Pro Flacco* 28. 66-69 (first century B.C., pp. 237ff.) ; the fragment from Damocritus (date uncertain, p. 121) ; Juvenal, *Satire* 14. 96-106 (second century A.D., pp. 292ff.) . See also the apologetic offered by Josephus, *Against Apion* (especially in book 2, sections 80ff., 121ff., 137ff.) .

[19] Josephus, *Against Apion* 2. 280ff.; Philo, *Life of Moses* 2. 19f.; see also Seneca, quoted in Augustine, *City of God* 6. 11. For other reactions to Jewish propaganda and the activity of some Jews to make converts ("proselytize"), see Horace, 1 *Satire* 2. 142; Josephus, *Antiquities* 18. 81-84; Matthew 23:15; Juvenal, *Satire* 6. 542f., and 14. 96ff. For an overview of Jewish propaganda and missionary activity in general, see Lietzmann, *History* I, pp. 80ff.

[20] Strained relationships between Jews and Egyptians or Jews and Syrians are hinted at in such passages as *Antiquities* 18. 373f. and 20. 184, but few details are available.

[21] "Syrian" often includes "Palestinian"; see the evidence listed in *C.P.J.* I, 4f. and n. 13, such as the Edict of Claudius in A.D. 41, or the reference to Agrippa I as a "Syrian" in Philo, *Flaccus* 39.

[22] Josephus' work *Against Apion* stands as an excellent example of Jewish attempts to deal with the problem (e.g., 2. 190ff.) . Much of Philo's literary activity also may have had such a purpose in view.

[23] A rather "liberal" attitude to circumcision by Josephus may be hinted at in *Life* 113 (compare *Antiquities* 20. 41; n. 30 below). In *Antiq.* 1. 192 and 214, Joseph-

us promises to expound on the rite elsewhere (probably in his proposed treatise on "Customs and Causes"—see *Antiquities* 4. 198), but this material is not extant. (The only reference to circumcision or uncircumcision in the papyri collected in *C.P.J.* is in #4.) Josephus also mentions that it is "Hebrew custom" *not* to marry a Gentile wife *(Antiquities* 18. 345); on Hebrew women marrying non-Hebrew men, see *Antiq.*, 20. 139-146 (especially 143).

²⁴ *Antiquities* 11. 340, 346; see also the story about Samaritan origins presented in the *"Paralipomena Jeremiou"* (or "4th Baruch") 8, where those Jews returning from exile who refused to separate from their Babylonian spouses were excluded from reentering Jerusalem and thus found Samaria.

²⁵ *Antiquities* 11. 340ff.; on Samaritans in Egypt, see *C.P.J.* III, #'s 513-514, and especially p. 103.

²⁶ *Antiquities* 14. 9; cf. 14. 283 and 20. 173.

²⁷ *Ibid.*, 14. 403.

²⁸ *Ibid.*, 14. 403, 489, 491; 15.2, 17, 81, 220, 374; 17. 192. What may have originated as an ancient, inner Jewish polemic, has had a far-reaching influence on modern descriptions of Herod; see, e.g., Lietzmann, *History* I, pp. 19-20 ("Idumean," "not native born," etc.). Interestingly, "Slavonic Josephus" calls Herod an uncircumcised Arabian (Loeb, vol. 3, p. 636 to *War* 1. 364ff.) while some Christian commentators apparently dubbed him a Philistine (see Thackeray's note *ad loc.*)

²⁹ *Antiquities* 20. 100. For a good digest of information on Tiberius Alexander, see *C.P.J.* II, 188-190 (on #418).

³⁰ *Antiquities* 12. 276 (the Maccabean revolt), in agreement with 1 Maccabees 2:41 and 9:43—see also *Antiquities* 14. 63f. Indeed, in *Jewish War* 2. 517ff., offensive warfare on sabbath is mentioned. But in *Antiquities* 18. 319ff., Josephus is critical of even self-defense on the sabbath, which may accord with such general prohibitions as those found in Jubilees 50.12 (compare 1 Maccabees 2:38, 2 Maccabees 6:11). See also 2 Maccabees 8:26ff., where offensive warfare is suspended on the sabbath.

³¹ *Antiquities* 20. 41 (See also n. 23 above). But later in 20. 46 he decides to become circumcised.

³² *Ibid.*, 14. 237, 240.

³³ Philo., *Migration of Abraham*, 89ff.

³⁴ E.g., *Antiquities* 20. 142 (see Feldman's Loeb note). On Jewish phraseology in the magical papyri, see the collection of *Papyri Graecae Magicae* by K. Preisendanz (only 2 of the 3 volumes were published; Leipzig: Teubner, 1928, 1931); W. L. Knox, "Jewish Liturgical Exorcism" in *Harvard Theological Review* 31 (1938), 192ff.; W. L. Knox, "Jewish Influence on Magical Literature" in *St. Paul and the Church of the Gentiles* (New York: The Macmillan Company, 1939), pp. 208-211; *C.P.J.* I, 110f., and 3, section 15. Recently M. Margaliouth of Jewish Theological Seminary in New York has recovered an extensive Hebrew work of "magical" orientation from the remains of the Cairo Geniza (see *New York Times*, Dec. 29, 1964); his edition of the materials is forthcoming.

³⁵ *Flaccus* 56-57. See also 3 Maccabees 3:10 (Jews in business) and the general treatment by Tcherikover, *Hellenistic Civilization*, pp. 337-339. At one point, Josephus mentions an actor of Jewish descent in Rome *(Life* 16).

³⁶ Josephus, *Antiquities* 18. 159f.; see also *ibid.*, 20. 100 and *Jewish War* 5. 205. There also seems to be a warning against taking a loan from "the Jews" in a papyrus letter sent to an Alexandrian businessman in A.D. 41 *(C.P.J.* II, #152). On the probable connection of the position of "alabarch" (or "arabarch") with fiscal matters, see Tcherikover, *Hellenistic Civilization*, pp. 339f. (520, n. 26); Josephus refers to another Alexandrian "alabarch," Demetrius, as also being wealthy and

prestigious (*Antiquities* 20. 147). There is evidence that Alexander's son Marcus Julius Alexander also was an "international" businessman of sorts; see L. Feldman's note to *ibid.*, 19. 276f. (Loeb), and *C.P.J.* II, 197f. (introduction to #419).

[37] *C.P.J.* I, 48ff. and section 7 (also Tcherikover, *Hellenistic Civilization*, p. 340 and pp. 520f. notes 30-31). See also Juvenal, *Satire* 3. 14-16 on Jewish beggars in Rome. On the infrequent references to Jewish slaves in our period, see Tcherikover, *Hellenistic Civilization*, p. 342.

[38] See Lietzmann, *History* I, pp. 79f. for a summary of the older evidence, and Tcherikover in *C.P.J.* I, 48f. and *Hellenistic Civilization*, pp. 333-343, especially for the Egyptian evidence.

[39] Neusner conjectures that Zamaris of Babylonia may have served Parthia officially (*Jews in Babylonia* I, pp. 38f.)—see *Antiquities* 17. 23ff. Parthian involvement in Jewish-Palestinian affairs also is mentioned, e.g., in *ibid.*, 14. 340ff. and 384 (see also n. 46 below).

[40] *C.P.J.* I, 53; see *C.P.J.* II, 240.

[41] *C.P.J.* I, 53; see also II, 188ff. (above, n. 29), on Tiberius Alexander.

[42] *Ibid.*, I, 52.

[43] *Antiquities* 18. 84 (the draftees were assigned to Sardinia); notice that some of the Jewish draftees refused to serve. Tacitus, *Annals* 2. 85, claims that Egyptian religionists also were banished at that time under the same conditions.

[44] *Antiquities* 15. 317.

[45] *C.P.J.* II, #229.

[46] The military rule by the Jewish brothers in *Antiquities* 18. 310ff. (above, n. 30). See also the story of the Jewish troop from Babylonia hired by Herod the Great to settle in Batanaea as a buffer-zone (*Ibid.*, 17. 23ff.).

[47] E.g., *ibid.*, 14. 29f., 34, 37, 146 (see 1 Maccabees 14:24), 222, 223-226, 233, 243, 247, 302, 304, 307, 314; 16. 160f, 299; 17. 219ff., 299f., 328, 343; 18. 109f., 143.

[48] To Aretas of Syria (*Antiquities* 14. 15, 81, 122); to the Roman leaders Pompey (14. 37) and Julius Caesar (14. 137-16. 53).

[49] *Antiquities* 14. 137; 14. 143.

[50] Herod the Great later established similar contests in Jerusalem every four years; see *ibid.*, 15. 267-276.

[51] *Ibid.*, 14. 210.

[52] E.g., *ibid.*, 16. 160, from Asia and Libya; 18. 257ff., from Alexandria.

[53] *Ibid.*, 17. 299f. Later, after a decade of rule by Archelaus, a delegation of "Jews and Samaritans" successfully petitioned Caesar to remove Archelaus.

[54] See *Sota* 49b concerning the 500 pupils studying "Greek wisdom" under Gamaliel II (*ca.* A.D. 90). See also S. Lieberman, *Greek in Jewish Palestine* (New York: Jewish Theological Seminary, 1942), 1f. and 20, and *Hellenism in Jewish Palestine*, 1950, and more recently, "How much Greek in Jewish Palestine?" in *Biblical and Other Studies*, ed. A. Altmann, Brandeis University Studies and Texts I (Cambridge, Mass.: Harvard University Press, 1963), pp. 123-141; on the sending out of "apostles" from Palestinian Judaism to the Diaspora in the latter part of our period, see Neusner, *op. cit.*, I, p. 43 (and n. 1).

[55] *Antiquities* 20. 195; see also *Life* 16.

[56] Tacitus, *History* 2. 2; Suetonius, *Titus* 7; Dio Cassius 66. 15 and 18; A. J. Cook, "Titus and Berenice," *American Journal of Philology* 72 (1951), 162-175. Josephus is silent about this aspect of Berenice's involved life. See *Antiquities* 20. 145ff.

[57] *Antiquities* 20. 142-144.

[58] A virgin "niece" of Clemens, named Domitilla, was later named as a Christian by Eusebius. Eusebius, *Ecclesiastical History* 3. 18, 4-5. See also in this book Chapter 2, page 67 and Chapter 4, page 119.

[59] Dio Cassius 67. 14; see also Suetonius, *Domitian* 15.

[60] *Against Apion* 2. 41.

[61] See Pliny the Younger, *Epistle* 6 to Trajan (and Trajan's reply, *Ep.* 7), which admittedly dates from several decades later. This particular problem (see p. 514 n. 84) and the problem of Jewish "civic rights" in general are discussed at length in Tcherikover, *Hellenistic Civilization,* pp. 309-332, with the conclusion that in the early Roman period, the Alexandrian Jews fought for their civic rights and lost, Josephus' apologetic claims notwithstanding (pp. 325f.), while elsewhere in the Diaspora "the organized Jewish community as a whole stood juridically outside the Greek city," although throughout the Greco-Roman world "isolated Jews could acquire civic rights individually" (p. 331).

[62] See *C.P.J.* II, 46ff. (#153. 52ff.).

[63] Josephus, *Jewish War* 1. 194 (*Antiquities* 14. 137).

[64] Acts 22:25-29; 23:27 (see also 21:39); but Paul never claims this for himself in his preserved writings, and this may give cause for serious doubt.

[65] See *Life* 423.

[66] *Antiquities* 20. 184.

[67] *Ibid.,* 14. 228-234, 232, 237, 240; at Ephesus and Delos.

[68] *Ibid.,* 14. 235, at Sardis; but 14. 259 casts some doubt on the civil status of these Jews of Sardis.

[69] *Ibid.,* 16. 160.

[70] So it is usually claimed, at least for *Palestinian* Judaism; see, e.g., Lietzmann, *History* I, 23 (based on Schürer I, 458) —but on p. 79, Lietzmann is much more cautious about the subject with respect to the *Diaspora* Jews.

[71] Philo, *Embassy to Gaius* 155, 157.

[72] See *C.P.J.* I, 61ff. and 81; Tcherikover, *Hellenistic Civilization,* p. 311ff.; S. L. Wallace, *Taxation in Egypt from Augustus to Diocletian* (Princeton: Princeton University Press, 1938), p. 116.

[73] *C.P.J.* II, #156c.

[74] *Antiquities* 14. 215.

[75] *Ibid.,* 16. 28; 16. 45.

[76] *Ibid.,* 16. 27. 163. For evidence of the temple tax being collected in Parthia, see *Antiquities* 18. 312. Philo refers to these "first fruits" or "ransom" contributions, e.g., in *Special Laws* 1. 78 and *Embassy to Gaius* 156. 316. The religious situation in Jerusalem at this time is not always easy to assess because of Josephus' preoccupa-tion with the more political (and entertaining?) aspects. However, numerous Jews throughout the Roman and Parthian worlds sacrificially sent their annual contribu-tions to Jerusalem until the very end.

[77] *Antiquities* 14. 214f; 14. 260.

[78] *Ibid.,* 14. 264; 16. 27, 45, 60 (?), 163, 168 (?).

[79] See Josephus, *Against Apion* 2. 77; *Jewish War* 2. 197, 409; Philo, *Embassy to Gaius* 152-158, 317.

[80] See *C.P.J.* I, 81; Josephus, *Jewish War* 7. 218; Dio Cassius 66. 7. 2.

[81] See *C.P.J.* I, 80ff. (including Jewish Roman citizens; see 82 and n. 66). On the rather strict methods of determining whether an individual was liable to the tax or not, see Suetonius, *Domitian* 12.

[82] *C.P.J.* II, introduction to section 9.

[83] See *C.P.J.* I, 85-93, for a listing of primary and secondary sources dealing with this period; also Neusner, *op. cit.,* I, 70ff. (especially the notes).

[84] Whether Justin's Trypho is to be identified with Rabbi Taraphon (see, e.g., J. Quasten, *Patrology* I, Glen Rock, N. J.: Newman Press, 1951, p. 202) is problem-atic; Eusebius calls Trypho "the most distinguished Hebrew of that time" (*Eccl. Hist.* 4. 18. 6).

[85] It is unfortunate that in Christian circles, the word "council" (e.g., "Council of Jamnia") has come to be associated with these Pharisaic Jewish communities and their discussions. These were *not* "Councils" in the later Christian sense (e.g., "Council of Nicaea").

[86] Neusner, *op. cit.*, 1, pp. 66 and 73, attempts to suggest possible explanations.

FOR ADVANCED READING

For further bibliography, see R. Marcus, "Selected Bibliography (1920-1945) of the Jews in the Hellenistic-Roman Period," *Proceedings of the American Academy for Jewish Research* 16 [1946/47], 97-181; also the appended notes in Loeb, Josephus volumes; and G. Delling, *Bibliographie zur jüdisch-hellenistischen und intertestamentarischen Literatur 1900-1965* (Texte und Untersuchungen 106; Berlin, Akademie-Verlag, 1969).

Primary Source Collections

Altjüdisches Schrifttum ausserhalb der Bibel. Edited by P. Riessler. Augsburg: Filser, 1928. Reprinted Darmstadt, 1966.
Apocrypha and Pseudpigrapha of the Old Testament. Edited by R. H. Charles. 2 vols. New York: Oxford University Press, 1913.
Corpus Inscriptionum Judaicarum. Edited by J. B. Frey. 2 vols. Rome: Pontificio instituto di archeologia cristiana, 1936, 1952.
Corpus Papyrorum Judaicarum (C.P.J.). Edited by Victor Tcherikover and A. Fuks. 3 vols. Cambridge, Mass.: Harvard University Press, 1957-1964.
Jewish Symbols in the Greco-Roman Period. Edited by E. R. Goodenough, 12 vols. New York: Pantheon Books, 1953-1969.
Textes d'auteurs grecs et romains rélatifs au Judaisme. Edited by Theodore Reinach. Paris: Leroux, 1895; reprint Hildesheim: Georg Olms, 1963.
The "Dead Sea Scrolls." Translated by Millar Burrows in *The Dead Sea Scrolls* and *More Light on the Dead Sea Scrolls: New Scrolls and New Interpretations.* New York: The Viking Press, 1955 and 1958.
The Works of Josephus. Edited by H. St. J. Thackeray, R. Marcus, A. Wikgren, and L. Feldman in the Loeb edition, 9 vols. Cambridge, Mass.: Harvard University Press, 1926-1965.
The Works of Philo. Edited by F. H. Colson, G. H. Whittaker, and R. Marcus in the Loeb edition, 12 vols. Cambridge, Mass.: Harvard University Press, 1929-1962.

Selected General Treatments

Baron, Salo W., *A Social and Religious History of the Jews.* 14 vols. thus far. New York: Columbia University Press, 1952.
Bickerman, Elias J., "The Historical Foundations of Postbiblical Judaism," in *The Jews: Their History, Culture and Religion.* Edited by L. Finkelstein, vol. I. New York: Harper & Row, Publishers, 1960; pp. 70-114.
Bonsirven, Joseph S., *Palestinian Judaism in the Time of Jesus Christ.* Translated by Wm. Wolf. New York: Holt, Rinehart & Winston, Inc., 1964.
Bousset, W., and Gressmann, H., *Die Religion des Judentums in späthellenistischen Zeitalter,* Tübingen: Mohr, 1926.
Foerster, Werner, *Palestinian Judaism in New Testament Times.* Translated by Gordon E. Harris. Philadelphia: Fortress Press, 1964.

Grätz, H., *History of the Jews.* 11 vols. Philadelphia: Jewish Publication Society of America, 1891, ET in 6 vols.

Juster, Jean, *Les Juifs dans l'Empire romain—Leur condition juridique—économique et social.* 2 vols. Paris: Geuthner, and New York: Burt Franklin, 1914.

Leon, Harry J., *The Jews of Ancient Rome.* Philadelphia: Jewish Publication Society, 1961.

Moore, George F., *Judaism in the First Centuries of the Christian Era, the Age of the Tannaim.* 3 vols. Cambridge, Mass.: Harvard University Press, 1927-1930.

Pfeiffer, Robert H., *History of New Testament Times, with an Introduction to the Apocrypha.* New York: Harper & Row, Publishers, 1949.

Reicke, B., *The New Testament Era: The World of the Bible from 500 B.C. to 100 A.D.* Translated by David Green. Philadelphia: Fortress Press, 1968.

Schürer, Emil, *Geschichte des jüdischen Volkes im Zeitalter Jesu Christi.* 4 vols. Leipzig: Hinrichs, 1901-1911; ET, *A History of the Jewish People in the Time of Jesus.* New York: Schocken Books, Inc., 1961.

Simon, Marcel, and Benoit, A., *Le Judaisme et le Christianisme Antique.* Nouvelle Clio 10. Paris: Presses Universitaires de France, 1968.

Tcherikover, Victor A., *Hellenistic Civilization and the Jews.* Philadelphia: Jewish Publication Society of America, 1959.

Zeitlin, Solomon, *The Rise and Fall of the Judean State: A Political, Social, and Religious History of the Second Commonwealth. 332. 37 B.C.E.* 2 vols. Philadelphia: Jewish Publication Society of America, 1962.

Some Specific Aspects (see also the bibliographies appended to Loeb, volumes 6-9 of Josephus, by R. Marcus, A. Wikgren, and L. Feldman)

Askowith, D., *The Toleration and Persecution of the Jews in the Roman Empire . . . Under Julius Caesar and Augustus.* New York: Columbia University Press, 1915.

Bell, H. I., *Jews and Christians in Egypt.* London: Oxford University Press, 1924.

Clark, K. W., "Worship in the Jerusalem Temple after A.D. 70," *New Testament Studies* 6 (1960), 269-280.

Farmer, W. R., *Maccabees, Zealots, and Josephus: An Inquiry into Jewish Nationalism in the Greco-Roman Period.* New York: Columbia University Press, 1956.

Finkelstein, Louis, *The Pharisees.* 2 vols. Philadelphia: Jewish Publication Society of America, 1962.

Harnack, Adolf, "Judaism, its Diffusion and Limits." Book 1, chapter 1 in *The Mission and Expansion of Christianity in the First Three Centuries.* ET by J. Moffatt. London: Willams and Norgate, 1908; reprint Harper Torchbooks; revised and expanded in the 1924 German edition.

Hengel, M., *Die Zealoten.* Leiden: E. J. Brill, 1961.

Lieberman, Saul, *Hellenism in Jewish Palestine: Studies in the Literary Transmission, Beliefs and Manners of Palestine in the 1st century B.C.E.–4th century C.E.* New York: Jewish Theological Seminary, 1950.

MacDonald, John, *The Theology of the Samaritans.* Philadelphia: The Westminster Press, 1965.

Montgomery, James A., *The Samaritans.* New York: Ktav Publishing House, Inc., 1968 (Reprint of 1907 original).

Neusner, Jacob, *A History of the Jews in Babylonia,* vol. 1: *The Parthian Period.* Leiden: E. J. Brill, 1965.

Perowne, Stuart H., *The Life and Times of Herod the Great.* Nashville, Tenn.: Abingdon Press, 1959.

Russell, David S., *The Jews from Alexander to Herod.* London: Oxford University Press, 1967.

Simon, Marcel, *Jewish Sects at the Time of Jesus.* Translated by D. Farley. Philadelphia: Fortress Press, 1967.

Thomas, J., *Le mouvement baptiste en Palestine et Syrie 150 av. J.-C.–300 apr. J.-C.* Gembloux: Duculot, 1935.

John G. Gager

4
Religion and Social Class in the Early Roman Empire

Sometime in the fifties of the first century A.D., Paul wrote a letter to the Christian community in Corinth which inadvertently provides a glimpse at the social constituency of earliest Christianity: "Not many of you were wise according to worldly standards," he says, "not many were powerful, not many were of noble birth; but God chose what is foolish in the world . . . what is weak in the world . . . what is low and despised in the world . . ." (1 Corinthians 1:26-28). More than a century later the Christian apologist Minucius Felix replied to his pagan interlocutor: "That many of us are called poor is not our disgrace, but our glory." [1] Roughly contemporary with Minucius was the pagan polemicist Celsus who characterized Christians as follows:

> Their injunctions are like this. "Let no one educated, no one wise, no one sensible draw near. For these abilities are thought by us to be evils." By the fact that they themselves admit that these people are worthy of their God, they show that they want and are able to convince only the foolish, dishonorable, and stupid, and only slaves, women and little children.[2]

Even granting the exaggerated tone of Celsus' remarks and recognizing that Paul's statement implies that there were at least some Christians of wisdom, power, and noble birth, these comments point to a general conclusion concerning the social makeup of early Christianity: Christian communities of the first two centuries derived their adherents from the lower classes of the Roman Empire — slaves, freedmen, freeborn Roman citizens of low rank, and non-Romans (*peregrini*) of various nationalities.[3] If true, this conclusion raises certain interesting questions. Was Roman society in the early Empire structured along readily identifiable class lines?[4] Was class status or affiliation a decisive factor in determining one's religious beliefs, activities, and associations? Was there any correlation between the religious character of early Christianity, its social constituency, and the attitude of "proper" Romans to it? And finally, what changes took place either in the character of the Christian religion, and/or in its social constituency, and/or in the social structure of the Empire itself such that the Roman middle and upper classes eventually abandoned their resistance and embraced Christianity?

Unlike contemporary American society where sociologists often disagree as to whether clearly defined social classes exist at all, Roman society of the early Empire presents a different picture.[5] In the period under discussion, from the last decades of the Republic through the end of the second century of the Christian era, Roman society was characterized by readily distinguishable social classes (ordines). Contrary to what one might expect, the basic criteria for determining social class were birth and legal status, rather than wealth, education, or ethnic origin.[6] Freedmen were sometimes wealthier than either equestrians or senators, but by law they could not become senators; conversely, equestrians and senators were required to show fixed levels of capital in order to qualify for their respective classes. As for the non-correlation of social class with either education or literary achievement, one need only mention Phaedrus, Livy, Terence, and Epictetus, all of whom were freedmen. Basically this system remained constant from republican to imperial times. Although the internal composition of classes varied in accordance with population shifts and economic trends, the classes themselves, as legally defined entities, did not change.

The one truly novel element in the class structure of the Empire was the immense social power of the emperor.[7] The emperor used his authority to regulate the financial requirements for senators and equestrians, to adjust the total number of senators, to delegate citizenship in his capacity as sole censor, to specify conditions under which an individual might pass from one class to another, and to introduce specific individuals into a higher class by nomination (adlectio). The resultant network of clients whose social status depended entirely on the favor of the emperor (e.g., Herod and the Herodian dynasty in Judea) and whose allegiance regularly took the form of an oath of loyalty to him became the indispensable social basis without which no emperor could hope to rule.[8]

THE SENATORIAL ARISTOCRACY

The social history of the Senate in the first two centuries of the Empire is closely tied to the gradual demise of the old Roman aristocracy. Nonetheless, the class as a whole continued to exercise considerable political and social power. Although senators represented a tiny fraction of the total population (Augustus fixed the total number of senators at six hundred), their effective power far exceeded their numbers. Readily recognizable by virtue of the broad purple stripes on their togas and by their prominent seats at all religious and civil ceremonies, they were regarded by most as the natural bearers of the ancient *disciplina Romana*. In addition, they governed most of the important provinces, occupied the chief civil magistracies (roads, treasuries, judiciary), and served as the top officers in the Roman legions. This series of responsible offices *(cursus honorum)*, with their concomitant expenses, explains Augustus' requirement that each candidate show a minimum capital worth of 1,000,000 sesterces (approximately $50,000), some of which had to be located in Rome itself. As in the republic, the main source of income among senators was agriculture. Commerce, industry, and the liberal professions (except law) were generally regarded as beneath their dignity.

Beneath this successful veneer, however, the Senate was a beleaguered body. Despite Augustus' efforts to avoid the outward signs of a tyrant, the establishment of the Principate, with enormous power vested actually, if not legally, in one man, led inevitably to bitter conflict between the emperor and the Senate. The factors involved were many: traditional aristocratic opposition to tyranny, fostered in part by the influence of Stoicism and Cynicism; close family ties with the opponents of tyranny in the last decades of the republic; reluctance to share in the imperial cult; and loss of control over the army.[9] Still another factor was the general lack of administrative skills among senators, which meant that they often served merely as titular heads of their bureaus, leaving the administrative work to socially inferior but skilled freedmen and slaves. Ironically this lack of administrative talent contributed eventually to the decline of the old aristocracy as the emperors were forced to promote men of skill to fill positions which required equestrian or senatorial status.

The result of this process was the eventual disappearance of the old Roman aristocratic families, largely as the result of purges under the Julio-Claudians (Tiberius, Caligula, Claudius, and Nero). In the thirty years between Nero and Nerva, the number of Roman senatorial families declined by one half and by A.D. 130 only one family remained.[10] The vacuum created by these bloody conflicts was filled by senators of non-Roman and ultimately of non-Italian origin. Tacitus writes:

after the merciless executions, when greatness of fame meant death, the survivors turned to wiser paths. At the same time, the self-made men *(novi homines)* repeatedly drafted into the senate from the municipalities and colonies, and even from the provinces, introduced the plain living habits of their own hearths; although by good fortune or industry many arrived at an old age of affluence, their previous prepossessions persisted. . . . Or should we say that there is a kind of cycle in all things—moral as well as seasonal revolutions?[11]

Thus the emergence of the *homo novus* and the progressive provincial-ization and de-Romanization of the Senate meant not simply new names and faces but new attitudes as well.[12] This emergent aristocracy of service, as M. Rostovtzeff calls it,[13] did not eschew entirely the old Roman virtues of liberality, equestrian skills, and reverence for the Roman deities, but their loyalties were often divided between Rome and their native lands. Apart from the simplicity in their life style noted by Tacitus, on simple matters such as place of domicile, financial contributions to civic functions, and support of religious activities, their devotion to Rome must have seemed deficient in the eyes of the old aristocrats.

In the religious affairs of the Empire, it is difficult to specify a dis-tinctively senatorial religion.[14] Naturally their basic instincts were conservative. They looked to the ancient gods who had established and continued to support their privileged position in the social hier-archy. As part of his plan to restore the old order, Augustus had installed senators in the major priestly posts *(augures, pontifices, quindecimviri,* etc.) with himself as *pontifex maximus.* But these ancient cults, like the more recent imperial cult, were primarily socio-political in character, with little evidence that their adherents re-garded them as anything but routine civic institutions. For the most part, the priestly positions demanded no training or qualification beyond senatorial status, and in all respects senator-priests continued to lead a normal civil life. According to J. Beaujeu's study of sena-torial religion, the literary and epigraphic evidence suggests that senatorial piety ranged from individual acts of deference (Pliny the Younger erected temples and statues to the gods) to reserve or even agnosticism (the same Pliny berated his uncle, Pliny the Elder, for his lack of religion) but rarely included strong religious sentiment.[15]

The case of the second century rhetor Aelius Aristides, whose pas-sionate devotion to the healing god Asclepius is chronicled in his *Sacred Teachings* or *Discourses,* is at once atypical of aristocratic re-ligiosity and indicative of new currents in his day.[16] For it was in the second century that the emperors Hadrian and Marcus Aurelius became initiates of the Eleusinian mysteries, that Antoninus Pius legalized the enthusiastic Phrygian cult of Cybele and that senatorial participation in non-Roman (Mithras, Dionysus) or Greco-Roman (Isis-Diana, Serapis-Jupiter) cults increased markedly.[17] A particularly interesting case is the Dionysiac congregation *(thiasos)* at Tusculum which numbered about four hundred members. From a social point of view the congregation is of exceptional interest because it shows the active participation in one cult of senators along with their clients, freedmen, and slaves.[18] Such cultic associations, especially those of eastern origin, seem to have been the only areas where social rank gave way to fellowship among different social groups. Even here, however, membership in the congregation included only the senators' immediate clients.

The conclusion to be drawn from the above considerations is that the new religious atmosphere of the second century, signaled by openness to non-Roman gods on the part of emperors and senators, resulted in large part from the provincialization of the Senate itself.[19] Not only did the newly designated senators of Greek blood bring their native deities to Rome, but once there they exerted considerable influence on the Italian aristocracy. Traditional Roman conservatism continued to express its scorn for many Eastern *superstitiones,* especially those of recent origin, e.g., Christianity, but internal social changes gave a new face to the religion of the aristocracy.

THE EQUESTRIAN ORDER

Just below the Senate in social dignity and legal status came the order of equestrians or knights *(ordo equester),* although in terms of wealth and education the two orders were often indistinguishable.[20] Unlike senators, their number was not limited, their title was not restricted by heredity, and the emperor could designate as equestrian any citizen of free birth provided only that the census showed 400,000 sesterces (approximately $20,000). Equestrians were the capitalists in business, commerce, and industry, with regular responsibility for overseeing the financial management of the substantial imperial farms. In such capacities they acquired considerable wealth and administrative skills, both of which made them valuable assets in administering the Empire.

The career of the equestrian, his *cursus honorum,* normally followed a fixed pattern of salaried positions: first, a series of modest commands *(praefecti)* in the army; second, procuratorial appointments involving financial administration; third, positions including responsibility for food distribution *(annona)* in Rome and for the imperial fleets; and finally, the highest posts open to equestrians, the prefectures of Egypt and of the Praetorian Guard.[21] In addition, the administration of small provinces which did not require substantial troops was normally in the hands of equestrian procurators. Thus the province of Judea was governed by equestrians from A.D.. 6–41 and again from A.D. 44–66. In time, this second aristocracy of service became an indispensable factor in the imperial bureaucracy, and the emperors regularly chose new senators from eminent knights. But the solution of the administrative problem created a new social problem. However much these newcomers *(novi homines),* most of whom were from the provinces, might seek to emulate the manners of the old aristocrats, their presence in positions of high responsibility was bitterly resented. The resultant tension was but one more element in the delicate social fabric which the emperors sought, ultimately in vain, to hold together.

On the matter of equestrian religion there is scanty information, and the subject might well warrant a separate study. In general, one would expect little difference from senatorial religion, with the obvious exception that knights could not hold the highest priestly spots in the public cults. Among those who aspired to the highest prefectures and eventually to senatorial status, there was undoubtedly dutiful adherence to the ancient gods, to the imperial cult, and to the more respectable oriental cults. To the degree that senators of provincial origin did not abandon their native gods, provincial knights probably followed the same pattern. Senators, equestrians, and the municipial aristocrats represented the established power in the Roman social order, and as such they showed little interest in religions which stood outside that order.

THE MUNICIPAL BUREAUCRACIES

We must speak a brief a word about this important group which, though not an official part of the Roman class structure, was nonetheless a crucial element in the unofficial aristocracy. From the time of the Republic, Rome had faced the problem of assuring good relations with its conquered peoples. Their efforts generally took two directions: first, the enlistment of local politicians, rhetors, and philosophers as official advisors and emissaries, and second, strong support for local aristocracies.[22] With respect to the cities, the normal procedure was for the Senate to approve municipal charters, taking account of local law and custom, and to allow the local citizens to elect municipal magistrates pretty much as they had in the past. This general Roman practice, which dated back to the time of the Republic, explains why Jewish residents in cities of the Empire and in Jerusalem were allowed to elect their own officials and to live according to their ancient customs. The famous letter of the emperor Claudius to the Alexandrians and the many municipal decrees cited by Josephus, granting similar rights to Jewish residents of Roman cities, demonstrate the same basic principle.[23]

Above the magistrates stood the council of decurions, or *bouleutai*, as the highest local authority. In addition to their normal political duties, the decurions were expected to make regular contributions to local causes (spectacles, schools, temples, baths, libraries, etc.). As a reward for these often onerous services, the councillor could anticipate a series of honorific titles from the city, at a higher level an appointment to the Roman *ordo equester,* and for the fortunate few promotion to the rank of senator. Thus, these local aristocrats were given a vested interest in supporting the rule of Rome in the conquered territories.

With certain notable exceptions, the system of local clients worked to the advantage of Rome. Only in the second century did relationships between Rome and the provincial cities show signs of serious erosion.[24] Jealousies developed between cities over honors from Rome. From the beginning there were tensions between the cities and colonies of Roman citizens (normally retired soldiers) who begrudged the privileges granted to non-citizens in the cities; and many cities simply resented subjection to Rome. However, this opposition rarely reached the level of outright revolt. Serious discontent, to the point of active resistance, arose primarily among the lower classes.[25] Such was certainly the case in Judea where armed rebellion centered among the proletarian Zealots, whereas the aristocratic Sadducees, who dominated the city councils *(Sanhedrin),* remained loyal to Rome. In Judea, as elsewhere, the local aristocracy was the municipal equivalent of the Roman Senate — conservative, wealthy, hereditary, and, above all, loyal to the purposes of the Empire.

No doubt this loyalty often included recognition of the Roman gods, but in the provinces its primary focus was the imperial cult.[26] Under republican rule the East had long been accustomed to honoring benefactors, whether local citizens or Roman governors, with official cults. Thus it was an easy transition when the imperial cult supplanted the earlier benefactor cults as the chief sign of loyalty to Rome. Naturally the main proponents of these cults were the local, pro-Roman aristocracies. The title of *flamen Augusti,* designating the chief priest of the local cult, soon became the most coveted honor which a city could bestow on a citizen and often led to the granting of Roman citizenship.[27] Much has been said concerning the essentially political character of these cults. G. Bowersock asserts that they reveal "little about the religious life of the Hellenic peoples but much about their ways of diplomacy." [28] M. Nilsson denies that they had any significant religious impact.[29] While it would be foolish to deny that the imperial cult was essentially political in function, there are indications that at least some participants experienced something akin to religious sentiments. In a recent article, H. W. Pleket has discussed an inscription from Pergamum which shows an imperial mystery cult, complete with a *sebastophant* who carried the emperor's image in a kind of sacred procession.[30] While the evidence is not overwhelming, it does suggest that the imperial cults and their aristocratic supporters could on occasion transcend their strictly political role.[31]

THE PLEBS

Having completed our survey of the *honestiores* or aristocracy of the Empire, we come now to the amorphous category of lower class free-born citizens, both urban and rural. Of the latter we know precious little socially or religiously, partly because they could not afford the expense of inscriptions and partly because Roman civilization was essentially urban. The situation with respect to the urban *plebs* is somewhat more favorable. In contrast with their rural counterparts they benefited from the fact that the emperor, as *defensor plebis,* assumed official responsibility for their physical needs. Inasmuch as this group numbered several hundred thousands in Rome alone, such imperial benevolence was no small consideration.

As citizens, the plebs enjoyed a social advantage over slaves, freed-men, and foreigners, but in the economic sphere citizenship often worked to their disadvantage. In business, commerce, and foreign trade they lacked the essential capital to compete with foreign entre-preneurs. In the labor market the availability of free slave labor hurt them considerably. So bad was their economic plight that Augustus had to restrict the number of citizens eligible for the grain dole to 200,000. Using Gagé's estimate of between 600,000 and 1,000,000 for the total city population this means that one third to one half of the city was on relief.[32] Little wonder that Juvenal could summarize the salient feature of the urban proletariat as a preoccupation with bread and circuses. For them there was little else, and the endless round of public games and festivals provided the only source of release or fantasy. "In Juvenal's day and after," says J. Carcopino, "it indeed seemed a happier fate to be a rich man's slave than a poor, freeborn citizen." [33]

At this point in our discussion the question of urban, lower class religion naturally arises. Did the proletariat turn to religion for re-lease and fantasy? If so, what kinds of religious communities were available to them? According to Max Weber's sociological theory of religion and social stratification, the level of religiosity increases as one descends to a certain point in any social system.[34] Established groups, including the nobility, the professional military, and the various bureaucracies, are past-oriented in religious belief and seldom become instigators of new religious movements. At the opposite end of the social scale, neither slaves nor peasants, for different reasons, become religious reformers. The remaining urban lower and lower-middle classes, says Weber, are privileged enough to recognize the potential benefits of higher social and economic status but are unable to attain this status. The result is a high degree of alienation from the social order and a consequent openness to religious movements which are future-oriented and congregational, especially if they offer some basis for future compensation. Thus far our analysis has borne out Weber's thesis in regard to those at the upper end of the scale. The question is whether the thesis applies to the urban *plebs* as well.

On at least one point the *plebs* retained some loyalty to traditional religion. Augustus had reorganized the city of Rome by quarters, with images of the *Lares Augustes* or genius of the emperor at a major intersection in each quarter. Each quarter then appointed officers from the local residents, most of whom were lower class, whose duty it was to oversee the local cult and to organize a calendar of festivals. But the religious significance of these cults, while not negligible, cannot have been very great.

In order to expand our sources of information concerning the religion of the urban populace we must take into account the religious practices of lower class non-citizens in Rome.[35] From republican times foreign groups had brought their cults to Rome. "I cannot abide," says Juvenal, "a Rome of Greeks; and yet what fraction of our dregs comes from Greece? The Syrian Orontes has long since poured into the Tiber, bringing with it its lingo and its manners. . . ." [36] Speaking of the Roman proletariat *(humiliores)*, A. D. Nock contends that

> the Capitoline gods meant nothing to them, not even the patriotic emotion which they inspired in sceptical senators. They worshipped Isis and the Syrian goddess and were so lacking in any feeling of Roman propriety as to erect shrines to their favourite deities on the Capitol, which was like holding a Salvation Army meeting in the square before St. Peter's.[37]

In short, there is solid evidence that foreign cults in Rome had a significant impact beyond their native devotees. Initially this impact was limited to the lower classes but eventually, as we have seen, it reached to the emperor himself.

THE FREEDMEN

We come now to the lowest social categories, freedmen and slaves. Freedmen *(libertini)* were slaves who had been granted freedom through the process of manumission. Although they almost always bear Greek or Latin names, Roman freedmen fall into the category of foreign groups in Rome because most Roman slaves came from outside Italy. Syria and Asia Minor gave the largest number, but Greece, Judea, Africa, and the western provinces contributed their share. In the late Republic manumission was a common practice.[38] Wealthy aristocrats often freed their slaves out of charity or gratitude (especially toward nurses and tutors), but just as often as a means of increasing their free clientele or even the size of their burial procession.[39] In fact, so common was manumission that the number of freedmen and their offspring, totaling perhaps as much as five sixths of all citizens, created something of a social crisis in the early Empire.[40] The aristocracy became alarmed at the melting-pot character of their cherished city.[41] Consequently Augustus established strict restraints on manumission by enforcing the tax on manumitted slaves, by sharply curtailing manumission by will, and by forbidding owners under twenty to manumit at all.

We should not imagine that manumission meant absolute freedom for the former slave. Apart from the permanent stigma of being an ex-slave, severe legislation governed relations of former slave to master (patronus). Above all, the freedman owed allegiance (obsequium et officium) to his former owner and had no legal rights over him. Thus it is not surprising that most freedmen continued in the same jobs which they had held as slaves: chief of the household, supervisor of the master's business and financial affairs, foreman in his factories, or obsequious client. But a minority of freedmen did eventually succeed in acquiring significant wealth. The most notable example is the famous Trimalchio, whose nouveau riche vulgarity was the target of Petronius' wit in his Satyricon or Cena Trimalchionis.[42] Trimalchio was worth at least 30,000,000 sesterces (approximately $1,000,000) and was much better off than Pliny who was considered to be a wealthy man.[43] To be sure, such wealth was by no means the rule, nor did it abolish the social stigma attached to freedmen, but as a class freedmen became a powerful force in Roman finance, commerce, and foreign trade. If one were to designate a middle class in the early Empire, it would consist largely of freedmen.

In religious matters freedmen show a remarkable, though under-standable diversity of interests. Augustus wisely sought to secure their loyalty by entrusting them with primary responsibility for certain religious functions. The office of magister vici in Rome seems to have been reserved exclusively for freedmen, while the similar group of seviri Augustales in the provinces was almost always of the same class.[44] Both were important elements in the civil religion of the Empire. Freedmen served as priests in the cults of Cybele and Mithras, while still others formed collegia under the patronage of Mercury, the god of merchants. In other words, those who had achieved some measure of success imitated the religion of their social superiors, while others remained loyal to what they knew of their native cults.

The category of imperial freedmen requires special consideration. As the largest slave holder, the emperor controlled a large number of freedmen. They served at every level of the official bureaucracy, and in the reigns of Gaius, Claudius, and Nero their power was enormous.[45] They managed three major administrative departments:

a rationibus (imperial treasury), *a libellis* (petitions and grievances), and *ab epistulis* (affairs of state). The private secretaries who supervised access to the emperor were freedmen, while quite different roles fell to imperial actors and concubines. Under Claudius, the power of Pallas and Narcissus became notorious, and in 53 Pallas succeeded in having his brother Felix appointed procurator of Judea (Acts 23:24ff.). It was not until the time of Trajan and Hadrian that the power of imperial freedmen was curtailed. In praising Trajan's administrative reforms Pliny indicates the power of the imperial freedmen under previous rulers:

> The majority of emperors, though masters of citizens, were slaves of their freedmen . . . They were governed by their advice and pleasure, they listened through them, spoke through them; through them also, or rather from them, pretorships, priesthoods and consulships were petitioned. You held the highest respect for your freedmen, but always in accordance with their station . . . for you know that the chief sign of a ruler's impotence is the power of his freedmen.[46]

Here, then, was a clear case where social status bore no relation to effective political power, and it was precisely this anomoly that rankled aristocrats like Pliny.[47]

A final word about the role of freedmen in the imperial cult. We have mentioned earlier the predominance of freedmen among the *magistri vicorum* in Rome. In the provinces, they also predominated among the *seviri* or *magistri Augustales*. These officials were generally responsible for the imperial cult in the towns and cities, but beyond sponsoring public games in honor of the emperor, their duties are uncertain. What is certain is that the title represented a significant local honor and must have provided a kind of revenge for those who knew nothing but disdain from proper Romans.

SLAVES

Slavery was a prominent feature of the ancient world and reached its highest proportion in the first centuries B.C. and A.D. [48] Although controversies abound as to the degree to which the Roman economy depended on slave labor,[49] there is general agreement that slaves constituted a significant segment of the Italian population in the early Empire.[50] We should not, however, regard slaves as a homogenous group. They came from many national backgrounds [51] and served many different functions in the Roman economy. Their condition varied greatly according to such factors as geographical location (Egypt was notable for care and protection of slaves), skills, attitudes of owners, and political conditions. The slave revolts in Italy and Sicily in the late republic attest to widespread discontent at the time, and Cato's account of slave labor in agriculture reveals a slave-driving mentality reminiscent of antebellum American slavery.[52] Under Augustus the fate of slaves suffered from the official policy of restoring the Roman citizen to a preferred position vis-à-vis foreigners, freedmen, and slaves. By contrast, the period following Augustus saw a gradual improvement in slave conditions.[53]

By the second century, possession of slaves had become a badge of social prestige, often at great cost to the owner. Juvenal remarks that the rise to social prominence was difficult in Rome "where you must pay a big rent for a wretched lodging, a big sum to fill the bellies of your slaves and buy a frugal dinner for yourself." [54] For the wealthy, slaves were no burden. Pliny the Younger owned at least 500; the freedman C. Caecilius Isidorus left 4,116 slaves at his death; and the emperor's retinue included at least 20,000.[55] If the emperor's household, with its extravagant system of specialized roles, is any indication, the life of the domestic slave cannot have been too rigorous.[56] This observation, taken with the fact that free citizens often competed with slaves for non-domestic jobs (in agriculture, mining, and pottery), would appear to support Carcopino's comment that "with few exceptions, slavery in Rome was neither eternal nor, while it lasted, intolerable." [57]

But we should not assume that the benevolence of owners like Pliny represents the norm. According to Roman law, a slave was a thing (res), and instances of brutality are not uncommon in the literature of the time. Paul's first letter to the Corinthians (7:21) and his letter to Philemon attest that escape from slavery was a common aspiration. Even the promulgation of humanitarian decrees, such as Claudius' edict granting freedom to sick slaves exposed by their masters, indicates that masters often exposed sick slaves. A similar judgment would have to apply to Seneca's lofty view that the soul might descend "into a Roman knight as well as into a freedman or a slave." [58] At the same time, the influence of men like Seneca and Pliny, especially among the aristocracy, should not be ignored as a factor in the gradual improvement of slavery in the Empire.[59] As for early Christianity, it never challenged the institution of slavery as such, nor did it exert any influence on Roman attitudes. Ephesians 6:5 and Titus 2:9f. enjoin slaves to be submissive to their masters; 1 Peter 2:19 even demands obedience to cruel masters on grounds that the patient sufferer is pleasing to God. By contrast, only one passage, Colossians 4:1, commands masters to treat their slaves fairly. Perhaps this discrepancy should be understood as reflecting the fact that there were more slaves than slave owners among early Christians. At their best, Christians accepted the Pauline idea that all believers were equal "in Christ" (1 Corinthians 12:13; cf. Philemon 15f.), but here again Paul's letters suggest that the best did not always prevail.

Before passing to the question of slaves and their religion, a brief word must be said about the special category of imperial slaves. Their number was large to begin with and grew constantly as wealthy citizens willed their slaves to the state. Most of these slaves performed menial household tasks, but some rose to subordinate positions in provincial administration or became unofficial advisers to the emperor himself.[60] Such a figure was Helicon who played an active role in the famous dispute between the Alexandrian Jews and their anti-Semitic opponents under Gaius and Claudius. Philo, the leader of the Jewish delegation, presents Helicon as a contemptible man who accepted bribes from the anti-Semites in return for pleading their case before Gaius.[61]

The picture of slave religion is at once puzzling and revealing. To begin with an apparent anomoly, we note that Paul's letter to the Philippians concludes with a greeting from "those of Caesar's household" (Philippians 4:22). While it is clear that the persons concerned were slaves and freedmen, not members of the imperial family, the presence of Christians among the emperor's slaves is something of a surprise. On the other hand, this bit of information suggests that slaves were free in their religious life as long as it did not interfere with their official duties. In his exhaustive study of slave religion in Greece and Rome, F. Boemer notes that although a *res* in many respects, the Roman slave was a *persona* in religious matters: his oath was binding, his grave was a religious site which could not be violated, and his curses were regarded as efficacious.[62]

In general, Roman slaves seem to have adopted traditional cults rather than forming a distinctively slave religion. Thus we find slave participation in practically all the cults and *collegia* of the Empire, with the natural exception of the official Roman cults.[63] In certain *collegia,* notably those of Bacchus-Dionysus, they appear to have associated with freedmen and freeborn citizens as complete equals *(fratres).* The general pattern, no doubt encouraged by Rome, seems to have been one of accepting slaves into Roman cults and of allowing them to form their own associations under the patronage of Roman deities. In this respect the example of Christians in the imperial household constitutes something of an exception to normal practice. They were not alone, however, for slaves were also active in propagating the *Dea Syria,*[64] and Tacitus records that a senatorial edict under Tiberius ordered the expulsion of four thousand slaves and freedmen "tainted" with the Egyptian and Jewish superstitions.[65]

If we may return briefly to Max Weber, it would appear that his theory concerning slave religion is supported by the results of Boemer's study. In religious matters, slaves in Rome formed a microcosm which reflected the macrocosm of their masters. Weber had theorized that slaves as a group were almost never bearers of a distinctive type of religion.[66] Even the willingness of slaves to accept the religious forms of their owners, which one might regard as somewhat surprising, is accounted for by his theory. One factor was surely the ever-present possibility of release from slavery which must have encouraged a superficial acceptance of traditional cults. Another is that the ambivalent attitude of depressed groups toward their social superiors always includes, along with hate and resentment, an element of admiration and an impulse toward emulation. Still another factor is the gradual improvement in the conditions of slavery in the early Empire which reduced the social distinction between slaves and lower class non-slaves and thereby impeded the emergence of a well-defined class consciousness among slaves. Finally, the fact that Rome allowed its slaves to find a degree of identity and solidarity in established *collegia,* whether the gods were Roman (Fortuna, Bona Dea, and Silvanus seem to have been particularly attractive to slaves) or foreign (Mithras, Dea Syria, Bacchus, or Jesus) may also have contributed to the non-formation of a distinctive slave religion.

EARLY CHRISTIANITY AND THE ROMAN SOCIAL ORDER

Very briefly I should like to examine early Christianity as a social phenomenon in the light of the preceding discussion. Unfortunately such an approach has not been popular among students of the early church, with the result that the initiative has often come from "outsiders" whose interests are sometimes less than purely historical. In a fascinating essay published in 1895, Frederick Engels likened primitive Christianity to the modern proletariat. He said:

> The history of early Christianity has notable points of resemblance with the modern working-class movement. Like the latter, Christianity was originally a movement of oppressed people: it first appeared as the religion of slaves and emancipated slaves, of poor people deprived of all rights, of peoples subjugated or dispersed by Rome.[67]

Subsequent reactions to this Marxist view have been varied and often violent. Max Weber rejected the economic factor as of little significance and attempted to view the early churches in their relation to the social structure of the empire. Ernst Troeltsch carried the reaction even further by claiming that the rise of Christianity was "a religious and not a social phenomenon" [68] and that the early communities "had very little to do with the most important socio-political events of the imperial period." [69]

Only in recent years and primarily among classicists, such as A. D. Nock, A. H. M. Jones, and E. R. Dodds, has early Christianity as a social phenomenon again come into focus.[70] Among this limited circle, something approaching a consensus has emerged on two aspects of the social question: first, that for more than two hundred years Christianity was essentially a movement among the lower and lower-middle classes of the empire,[71] and second, that its appeal among these groups was largely social in character. For example, E. R. Dodds notes that three social factors made Christianity attractive to these elements of the social structure: (1) its religious exclusivism, which offered a clear choice in an age of anxiety; (2) its openness in principle to all social classes and nationalities; and (3) its practical philanthropy.[72] To substantiate the latter claim, these critics point not only to Christian writings but to early pagan observers as well. Lucian of Samosata, for instance, comments that Christian believers lavished physical and moral support on Peregrinus (whom Lucian clearly regarded as an outright charlatan) while he was in prison.[73] Even more of a demonstration of this attitude is the emperor Julian's observation that the success of Christianity stems from its practical philanthropy. "Why do we not observe," he asks, "that it is their benevolence to strangers, their care for the graves of the dead, and the pretended holiness of their lives that have done most to increase atheism [Christianity]."[74] In the same letter he laments that "it is disgraceful that when no Jew ever has to beg, and the impious Galileans [Christians] support not only their own poor but ours as well, all men see that our people lack aid from us."[75]

At this point we must take account of two possible exceptions to the statement that early Christianity spread primarily among the lower and lower-middle classes. These exceptions are wealthy believers such as Marcion and highly educated figures like Valentinus and his followers.[76] In the first place we should recall that neither wealth nor education was a basic criterion in determining Roman social classes. From the lofty perch of the Roman senator, the dictum held that "once a freedman, always a freedman." On the issue of wealth, we should also recall that from its inception Christianity had demonstrated a distinct bias against the rich. Thus when men of wealth began to accept the new faith, the church was faced with a dilemma. Because the ideology of poverty had outlived the social conditions which had spawned it and because this ideology was too firmly imbedded in the sacred writings to be discarded altogether, it had to be adapted to meet a new set of social conditions. In the case of Hermas, the church reacted by insisting that God had provided wealth solely for the performance of his ministries,[77] while Clement of Alexandria, in his treatise *Who Is the Rich Man that Shall Be Saved?*, sought to modify the tradition by showing that only the misuse of money, not money itself, constituted a barrier to salvation. Thus in terms of its ideology of poverty, Christianity underwent a dual modification which brought it closer to the social center of the Empire. The influx of wealthy believers, very few of whom were aristocrats, provided a new base of financial support and at the same time forced a reevaluation of the traditional deprecation of wealth.

The issues raised by the presence of well-educated believers lead in a rather different direction. Again we note that education was not a decisive factor in determining class status and that there is little evidence of highly educated Christians until well into the second century. Even more significant, however, is the fact that when men of culture began to appear in Christian communities, they introduced a new and, for many, an unacceptable version of the faith. The cases of certain Gnostics (Valentinus, Ptolemy, and Heracleon), of Marcion, and to a lesser extent of Clement and Origen are highly instructive. The distinctiveness of their religious views is as apparent to us as it was to their contemporaries, particularly in the West. Less apparent has been the observation that these views, when approached sociologically, appear as the inevitable product of a new intellectual class, a class whose pursuit of salvation regularly shows distinctive features: a disposition toward illumination mysticism, a devaluation of the natural order together with a renewed emphasis on sexuality and a quest for the meaning of existence in theoretical and universal terms.[78] If we look at the bitter conflict between Gnosticism and Roman Christianity from this perspective, it would appear that social differences were at least as important as, and probably supported, the theological differences. In other words, the refusal of emergent orthodoxy to accept the Gnosticism of Valentinus and his school serves to corroborate other bits of evidence which point to the fundamentally nonintellectual, nonaristocratic character of Christianity in this period.

These considerations bring us back to the question raised in the opening paragraphs of our discussion: Is there a systematic correlation between the religious character of early Christianity and its social constituency? A. H. M. Jones has touched on the subject in his article on the social conflict between paganism and Christianity in the fourth century. He notes that the strength of Christianity even at that time lay predominantly in Greek-speaking urban areas among the lower classes.[79] In seeking to explain the aristocratic aversion to the movement, he points out that Christians, especially in the West, continued to regard pagan culture with grave suspicion, that the sacred writings of the church were written in a style utterly at odds with the strict Atticism then in vogue, and that the senatorial aristocracy regarded itself as the chief defender of ancient Roman religion, the very religion which most Christians so vehemently abhorred.[80] There can be no doubt that these factors stood between Christianity and the Roman aristocracy. But when Jones concludes his essay with the observation that the emergence of Christianity as the dominant religion of the Empire in the late fourth century "coincided with a social change which brought to the front men from the middle and lower classes," [81] he has opened up a rather different perspective.

Here we return to the theoretical framework of Max Weber. Weber had suggested that the religion of non-privileged classes bears three distinctive marks: a strong tendency toward congregational units, future-oriented systems of compensation (salvation), and a rational system of ethics. He further proposed that these marks were not accidental but derived directly from the particular position of lower classes in the social hierarchy.[82] Their sensitivity to new religious movements (Weber called them prophetic movements) was closely tied to the degree of their alienation from the immediate compensations and rewards of the socioeconomic order. In short, they looked elsewhere for their rewards. Early Christianity was such a religious movement — congregational in structure, future oriented with respect to promises of reward, and supported by a system of rational ethics. (In the New Testament, the ethical commands directed to husbands, wives, children, and slaves would clearly fall into Weber's category of a rational system of ethics.) Thus, according to Weber's thesis, it is no accident that early Christians came primarily from the urban lower classes. Before Christianity could and eventually did penetrate the official aristocracy, two significant and complementary changes had taken place. First, the religion itself underwent certain internal modifications (e.g., decline of eschatological emphasis and accommodation to classical culture) which rendered it more acceptable to the upper classes; and second, the aristocracy, as we have seen in our analysis of the Roman Senate, underwent a process of provincialization and democratization which revolutionized its social character. If we may indulge for a moment in a thought experiment, one wonders whether Christianity would have emerged as a world religion if these two changes had not taken place.

NOTES

[1] *Octavius* 36.

[2] Origen, *Contra Celsum* 3. 44.

[3] Other references to the predominance of the lower classes among early Christians include Justin, 2 *Apologia* 10. 8; Tatian, *Oratio ad Graecos* 32; Lucian, *De Morte Peregrini* 12; and Origen, *Contra Celsum* 1. 27; 3. 18.

[4] In geographical terms this paper will focus on the city of Rome, but with the assumption that conditions there prevailed more or less uniformly throughout

the Empire. In adopting this procedure, I have followed the example of Jean Gagé in his excellent book, *Les classes sociales dans l'empire romain* (Paris: Payot, 1964), hereafter cited as Gagé. Gagé, pp. 38f., notes that the reforms of Augustus resulted in a uniform social structure in the Empire and that local variations were few and relatively insignificant.

⁵ In his book *Social Psychology* (New York: The Macmillan Company, 1965), Roger Brown devotes a section to "The Reality of Social Class." Brown remarks that the definition of socioeconomic classes in modern industrial societies is a highly arbitrary affair and that consciousness of class shows no consistent pattern in the United States. He establishes four criteria which must be met before one can use class distinctions as meaningful categories: " (1) the population is conscious of classes, agreed on the number of classes and on the membership of them, (2) styles of life are strikingly uniform within a stratum and there are clear contrasts between strata, (3) interaction is sharply patterned by stratum, (4) the boundaries suggested by the three kinds of data are coincident" (p. 114). On these rather hard criteria, it makes good sense to speak of social classes and class consciousness in Roman society.

⁶ In a recent study on *Racial Prejudice in Imperial Rome* (New York: Cambridge University Press, 1967), A. N. Sherwin-White notes that while there was no racial prejudice in the sense of color barriers, "there certainly was some culture prejudice" (p. 1). Greek and Roman anti-Semitism comes close to racial prejudice but even here, as Sherwin-White correctly remarks, the issues were political and religious rather than ethnic. In early Christianity the only clear example of racial diversification is "Simon, who was called Niger (Black)" in Acts 13:1. Simon is numbered with Barnabas, Lucius of Cyrene, Manaen, and Saul (Paul) among the prophets and teachers in Antioch.

⁷ See the discussion in Gagé, *op. cit.*, pp. 71–77, 191–216.

⁸ On the significance of the client system in the late Republic and the early Empire see Glen Bowersock, *Augustus and the Greek World* (New York: Oxford University Press, 1965), pp. 1-61.

⁹ See the excellent discussion in Ramsey MacMullen, *Enemies of the Roman Order: Treason, Unrest and Alienation in the Empire* (Cambridge, Mass.: Harvard University Press, 1966); on opposition to the Principate in the Greek East see Bowersock, *op. cit.*, pp. 101–111.

¹⁰ Jerome Carcopino, *Daily Life in Ancient Rome* (New Haven: Yale University Press, 1940), p. 61.

¹¹ *Annales* 3. 55. Reprinted from The Loeb Classical Library by permission of Harvard University Press.

¹² The provincialization of the Senate, though clear in its broad outlines is vague on many points of detail. Gagé, *op. cit.*, p. 91, estimates that by A.D. 200 senators of provincial origin comprised one half of the total body. Bowersock, *op. cit.*, pp. 141f., cites the names of sixty-nine senators from Asia Minor down to the time of Commodus and notes that other senators came either from Greek colonies in Italy or from families of mixed Greek and Italian blood.

¹³ Mikhail Rostovtzeff, *Social and Economic History of the Roman Empire*. 2nd ed. revised by P. M. Frazer (New York: Oxford University Press, 1957), p. 185.

¹⁴ See the extensive discussion in J. Beaujeu, "La religion de la classe sénatoriale à l'époque des Antonins," *Hommages à Jean Bayet* (Brussels: Latomus, 1964), pp. 54-75.

¹⁵ *Ibid.*, pp. 56ff.

¹⁶ On Aristides' religion see *ibid.*, pp. 60-64, and Eric R. Dodds, *Pagan and Christian in an Age of Anxiety* (New York: Cambridge University Press, 1965), pp. 39-45.

[17] On the rise of foreign cults in the second century see Beaujeu, *op. cit.*, pp. 64-74, and Arthur D. Nock, *Conversion: The Old and the New in Religion from Alexander the Great to Augustine of Hippo* (New York: Oxford University Press, 1933), pp. 74-76, 125ff.

[18] See the discussion in Beaujeu, *op. cit.*, pp. 68f. On the general issue of brotherhood in pagan religious associations see F. Boemer, *Untersuchungen über die Religion der Sklaven in Griechenland und Rom., I: Die wichtigsten Kulte und Religionen in Rom und im lateinischen Westen*, (Wiesbaden: Steiner, 1957), pp. 172-179.

[19] Carcopino, *op. cit.*, p. 56, notes that several emperors were also of provincial origin: Trajan and Hadrian were born in Spain, Antoninus Pius in southern France, and Septimius Severus from Semitic stock in North Africa.

[20] On the equestrian order see the standard work of A. Stein, *Der römische Ritterstand* (Munich: C. H. Beck, 1927), and Gagé, *op. cit.*, pp. 107-122.

[21] The internal hierarchy of the equestrian order gave rise to a corresponding hierarchy of titles: *egregius, perfectissimus, eminentissimus*. Among equestrian procurators, it was customary to designate them according to the level of their salary: *sexagenarii* earned 60,000 sesterces, *centenarii* earned 100,000, and so on.

[22] On the subject as a whole see the extensive discussions in Bowersock, *op. cit.*, pp. 85-100, and Gagé, *op. cit.*, pp. 151-185.

[23] For a general discussion of the relevant issues see Victor A. Tcherikover, *Hellenistic Civilization and the Jews*, trans. S. Applebaum (Philadelphia: Jewish Publication Society, 1959), pp. 296-332.

[24] For discussions of the so-called municipal crisis in the second century see Gagé, *op. cit.*, pp. 182ff., and Bowersock, *op. cit.*, pp. 101-111.

[25] Bowersock, *op. cit.*, pp. 101ff.

[26] See *ibid*, pp. 112-121, and Gagé, *op. cit.*, pp. 169-173.

[27] Bowersock, *op. cit.*, p. 117, suggests that the "Asiarchs" of Acts 19:31 were high priests in the imperial cult of the Asian provincial assembly; cf. also A. N. Sherwin-White, *Roman Society and Roman Law in the New Testament* (New York: Oxford University Press, 1963), pp. 89f.

[28] Bowersock, *op. cit.*, p. 112.

[29] M. P. Nilsson, *A History of Greek Religion*, trans. F. J. Fielden, (New York: W. W. Norton & Company, Inc., 1964), pp. 301f.

[30] "An Aspect of the Emperor Cult: Imperial Mysteries," *Harvard Theological Review*, 58 (1965), 331-347.

[31] *Ibid.*, p. 334, n. 14, and the examples cited by Nilsson, *op. cit.* (above n. 29).

[32] Gagé, *op. cit.*, 125; cf. Carcopino, *op. cit.*, p. 65.

[33] Carcopino, *op. cit.*, p. 64.

[34] Max Weber, *The Sociology of Religion*, trans. E. Fischoff (Boston: Beacon Press, 1964), pp. 80-117.

[35] On the subject as a whole see G. LaPiana, *Foreign Groups in Rome during the First Centuries of the Empire* (Cambridge, Mass.: Harvard University Press, 1927); Franz Cumont, *Oriental Religions in Roman Paganism* (Magnolia, Mass.: Peter Smith, Publisher, 1911, reprint New York: Dover, 1956), and Nock, *op. cit.*

[36] *Satire* 3. 60-63. Reprinted from *The Loeb Classical Library* by permission of Harvard University Press.

[37] Nock, *op. cit.*, p. 123.

[38] On the background and procedures of manumission see the standard work on freedom by A. M. Duff, *Freedmen in the Early Roman Empire* (New York: Barnes & Noble, Inc., 1958), pp. 12-35. Josephus, *Jewish War* 6. 420, states that 97,000 Jews were taken captive by Titus in A.D. 70. Of these, the strongest were sent as slave laborers to Egypt, *Jewish War* 6. 418.

[39] Dionysius of Halicarnassus (4. 24) writes of cases where dying aristocrats would free their slaves in order to increase the number of free persons attending their funeral.

[40] Duff, *op. cit.,* pp. 199f., suggests that as much as 80 percent of Rome's citizens were either freedmen or their descendants.

[41] The epic historian Lucan remarks caustically (*Pharsalia* 7. 405) that Rome was "filled with the scum of the world" (*mundi faece repletam*).

[42] See Duff, *op. cit.,* pp. 125ff., for references to other satirical sketches of wealthy freedmen in contemporary Roman literature.

[43] See Carcopino, *op. cit.,* pp. 67f.

[44] On the *seviri Augustales,* see Duff, *op. cit.,* pp. 132-137.

[45] The poet Statius describes the power of Claudius Etruscus, a freedman who served as imperial treasurer under Nero and received equestrian status under Vespasian: "Now to you alone is given the control of our holy ruler's wealth. In your charge alone are the riches all nations send and the vast world's tribute . . ." (*Silvae* 3. 3. 85ff.) . Josephus, (*Jewish Antiquities* 18. 145) records that Herod Agrippa exhausted his fortune in vain attempts to win imperial favor by bribing the emperor's freedmen.

[46] *Panegyricus* 88. 16.

[47] Duff's comments (*Freedmen,* pp. 205-207) culminating in the remark that "freedmen and their descendants in a great measure ruined Rome" must be taken *cum grano salis.* He appears to have appropriated uncritically the aristocratic prejudices of his sources.

[48] On slavery in classical antiquity see W. Westermann, *The Slave Systems of Greek and Roman Antiquity* (Philadelphia: American Philosophical Society, 1955) .

[49] See, for instance, the collection of essays edited by M. I. Finley, *Slavery in Classical Antiquity. Views and Controversies* (Cambridge: W. Heffer & Son, 1960, reprinted 1968, with bibliographical supplement) . For a Marxist perspective see also K. Kautsky, *Foundations of Christianity,* trans. H. F. Mins (New York: Russell & Russell Publishers, 1953) , pp. 25-59 ("The Slave Economy").

[50] See Gagé, *op. cit.,* pp. 43f.

[51] See M. L. Gordon, "The Nationality of Slaves under the Early Roman Empire," *Journal of Roman Studies* 14 (1924) , 93-111; Duff, *op. cit.,* pp. 1-11; and Westermann, *op. cit.,* pp. 96-102.

[52] See Westermann, *op. cit.,* pp. 76f.

[53] *Ibid.,* pp. 102f.

[54] *Satire* 3. 166ff.

[55] On these figures see Carcopino, *op. cit.,* pp. 69f.

[56] Among the many official positions occupied by imperial slaves, Carcopino, *op. cit.* pp. 70f., lists the following: bathers, masseurs, barbers, bakers, pastry-cooks, wine-tasters, and custodians for every conceivable public and private occasion.

[57] Carcopino, *op. cit.,* p. 56. In a similar vein, Ramsey MacMullen, *Enemies of the Roman Order,* p. 198, notes the scarcity of slave uprisings in the Empire and cautions against regarding slaves as a clearly defined social class or interest group.

[58] *Epistulae Morales* 31. 11.

[59] For a discussion of the factors behind the change in attitude and legislation concerning slavery in the first two centuries of the Empire, see Westermann, *op. cit.,* pp. 113-117.

[60] This period of slave power came to an abrupt end with the administrative reforms of Hadrian and by the third century slaves had disappeared from even the lowest bureaucratic positions; see Westermann, *op. cit.,* p. 112.

[61] *Legatio Ad Gaium* 166-178, 203-206.

[62] Boemer, *op. cit.,* (above n. 18) pp. 184ff.

[63] On the cult of Bacchus-Dionysus at Tusculum see above p. 110; on a similar cult at Lanuvium see Carcopino, *op. cit.*, p. 57, and Westermann, *op. cit.*, p. 108.

[64] See F. Cumont, *Oriental Religions*, p. 106.

[65] *Annales* 2. 85. Cumont, *The Mysteries of Mithra*, trans. T. J. McCormack (New York: Dover Publications, Inc., 1956), pp. 63f. notes that slaves often participated in the cult of Mithras.

[66] Weber, *op. cit.*, pp. 99-101.

[67] Karl Marx and Friedrich Engels, *On Religion*, introduction by Reinhold Niebuhr (New York: Schocken Books, 1964), p. 316. For a similar view see Kautsky, *Foundations of Christianity*, pp. 280-284.

[68] E. Troeltsch, *The Social Teaching of the Christian Churches*, trans. O. Wyon (New York: Harper & Row, Publishers, 1960), I, p. 43.

[69] *Ibid.*, p. 41.

[70] See especially the chapter entitled "The Spread of Christianity as a Social Phenomenon" in Nock's *Conversion*, pp. 187-211; See A. H. M. Jones, "The Social Background of the Struggle Between Paganism and Christianity," in *The Conflict Between Paganism and Christianity in the Fourth Century*, ed. A. Momigliano (New York: Oxford University Press, 1963), pp. 17-37. See also the chapter entitled "The Dialogue of Paganism with Christianity," in Dodds, *op. cit.*, pp. 102-138. The only notable exception to this pattern is E. A. Judge, *The Social Pattern of the Christian Groups in the First Century* (London: Tyndale, 1960).

[71] Naturally there were some exceptions, but these never included the aristocracy and were often already converts to Judaism. Pliny's statement in his letter to Trajan, dated A.D. 98, that Christians came from every class *(omnis ordinis)* is too vague to be of any real value *(Ep.* 10. 96. 9). Harnack's attempt in his *Mission and Expansion of Christianity in the First Three Centuries*, ed. J. Moffatt, (New York: Harper & Row, Publishers, 1962), II, 35 and 46, to claim that T. Flavius Clemens and his wife Domitilla, who were relatives of the emperor Domitian, were Christians fails for want of adequate evidence; see the discussion of H. Leon, *The Jews of Ancient Rome* (Philadelphia and New York: Jewish Publication Society, 1960), pp. 33-35, who argues on the basis of evidence from Suetonius *(Domitian* 15. 1) and Dio Cassius (67. 14. 1f.) that Clemens and his wife were convicted of being converts to Judaism not Christianity. (See also Benko, p. 67 and Kraft, p. 94.)

[72] Dodds, *op. cit.*, pp. 133-138.

[73] *De Morte Peregrini* 12f.

[74] *Ep.* 84a. Bidez-Cumont-*Ep.* 22 Wright (Loeb edition) 429D.

[75] *Ibid.*, 430D.

[76] For a survey of the evidence on wealthy and educated Christians, see Harnack, *op. cit.*, II, pp. 33-40.

[77] *Similitudo* 1. 9.

[78] See the excellent discussion of intellectuals and their religion in Weber, *op. cit.*, pp. 123-125.

[79] "Social Background . . ." (above n. 71), pp. 17f.

[80] *Ibid.*, pp. 19-22.

[81] *Ibid.*, p. 37.

[82] See Weber's discussion, *Sociology of Religion*, pp. 95-113.

FOR ADVANCED READING

In addition to the works listed under "Standard Reference Works" (pp. 32-33), the following titles may be helpful:

Carcopino, Jerome, *Daily Life in Ancient Rome.* New Haven: Yale University Press, 1940 (paperback).

Dill, Samuel, *Roman Society from Nero to Marcus Aurelius* (paperback). Cleveland and New York: Meridian Books, 1956.

Duff, A. M., *Freedmen in the Early Roman Empire.* 2nd ed. New York: Barnes & Noble, Inc., 1959.

Finley, M. I., ed., *Slavery in Classical Antiquity: Views and Controversies.* New York: Barnes & Noble, Inc., 1968.

Frank, Tenney, *Aspects of Social Behavior in Ancient Rome.* New York: Cooper Square Publishers, Inc., 1969.

Gagé, Jean, *Les Classes Sociales dans l'Empire Romain.* Paris: Payot, 1964.

Jones, Arnold H. M., "The Social Background of the Struggle between Paganism and Christianity," in *The Conflict between Paganism and Christianity in the Fourth Century.* Edited by A. Momigliano. New York: Oxford University Press, 1963.

Judge, E. A., *The Social Pattern of Christian Groups in the First Century.* London: Tyndale, 1960.

Kahrstedt, U., *Kulturgeschichte der römischen Kaiserzeit.* Bern, 1958.

Lewis, Naphtali, and Reinhold, Meyer, eds., *Roman Civilization: Sourcebook II, The Empire.* 2nd ed. New York: Harper & Row, Publishers, 1966 (paperback).

MacMullen, Ramsay, *Enemies of the Roman Order: Treason, Unrest and Alienation in the Empire.* Cambridge, Mass.: Harvard University Press, 1966.

Mattingly, Harold, *The Man in the Roman Street.* New York: W. W. Norton & Company, Inc., 1966.

Maxey, M., *The Occupations of the Lower Classes in Roman Society.* Chicago: University of Chicago Press, 1938.

Meyer, Eduard, *Die Sklaverei im Altertum.* Kleine Schriften, 1910.

Parsons, Talcott, *Societies: Evolutionary and Comparative Perspectives,* (Foundations of Modern Sociology Series). Englewood Cliffs, N.J.: Prentice-Hall, Inc., 1966.

Rostovtzeff, Mikhail, *Social and Economic History of the Roman Empire.* 2nd rev. ed. 2 vols. New York: Oxford University Press, 1957.

Sherwin-White, Adrian N., *Racial Prejudice in Imperial Rome.* London: Cambridge University Press, 1967.

Sherwin-White, Adrian N., *The Roman Citizenship.* New York: Oxford University Press, 1939.

Stein, A., *Der römische Ritterstand.* Munich, 1927.

Tanzer, Helen H., *The Common People of Pompeii.* Baltimore: The Johns Hopkins Press, 1939.

Weber, Max, *The Sociology of Religion.* Translated by Ephraim Fishoff. Boston: Beacon Press, 1963 (paperback).

Westermann, W. L., *Slave Systems of Greek and Roman Antiquity.* Philadelphia: American Philosophical Society, 1955.

Clarence L. Lee

5
Social Unrest and Primitive Christianity

The precise relationship between early Christianity and what are believed to have been various forms of social unrest in the Roman Empire has long been the subject of intense debate among historians. Basically the debate has involved the question of whether the remarkable diffusion of the Christian religion throughout the Roman Empire was a cause or merely an effect of certain disruptive forces which led to the breakdown of the traditional structures and values of Roman society. For some historians, notably Edward Gibbon, Christianity was the primary cause of this breakdown. Gibbon's conclusion entailed at the same time, of course, an indictment of Christianity for destroying a society which was, in his opinion, superior in every way to the one which replaced it.[1] Other historians, while sharing Gibbon's conviction that early Christianity was primarily responsible for the ferment which radically altered Roman society, have gone on to reach a totally different verdict with respect to Christianity. Instead of judging Christianity guilty for the role it played in effecting social unrest and change in the Roman Empire, many historians have credited Christianity with having created a more vital and humane society than the one which preceded it.[2] In either case, Christianity was a factor in bringing about the changes.

Against this causal interpretation of the relationship between early Christianity and social unrest in the Roman Empire, another group of historians have argued that Christianity simply inherited, and then went on to exploit, a revolutionary undercurrent in Roman society. It was this undercurrent rather than anything distinctive in Christianity itself which provided the basis of Christianity's appeal to the Roman world and the impetus for its involvement in the ongoing process of social transformation. According to this view, early Christianity — at least insofar as it was a social force within the Empire — was merely a part or result of a deeply entrenched revolutionary tradition and consequently deserves to be neither overly praised nor overly blamed for the role it played in effecting social change.[3]

Although our investigation of the phenomenon of unrest in Roman society is to be limited to the period of the early Empire, it is hoped that the present study will be able to achieve some basis for evaluating both of the interpretations outlined above. This is possible, we believe, because an understanding of the period of the early Empire is determinative for both interpretations. One position assumes that there was no serious social unrest in the first two centuries of the Empire, an assumption which then permits Christianity to play a much more creative role than would have been the case if social unrest had existed earlier. The other position assumes that social unrest was a "fact of life" in the world in which Christianity first made its appearance. This assumption permits the phenomenon of unrest to become the explanation for virtually everything that happened within the early Empire including Christianity itself.

In large part, our investigation will be an attempt to assess the accuracy or inaccuracy of these assumptions. Having an accurate picture of the status and character of social unrest in the early Empire is valuable in and of itself, but it is of even greater value if it helps to clarify what has long been one of the most puzzling aspects of early Christianity's relationship to the Roman world.

THE EVIDENCE OF SOCIAL STABILITY

A look at the evidence available to us from the period of the early Empire discloses what appear to be two irreconcilable descriptions of Roman society. On the one hand, as is more or less expected of the period which has come to symbolize the achievement or near achievement of "peace on earth," there is a large body of evidence which points either implicitly or explicitly to stability and harmony as the most prominent characteristics of the social life of the period. Perhaps the most exuberant spokesman for this view of Roman society is the Greek rhetorician Aelius Aristides, whose panegyric *To Rome* was delivered toward the close of the period we are investigating (*ca.* A.D. 150), but was meant to apply generally to the entire history of the Empire to that point. Extracting liberally from the panegyric, the following analysis of conditions in the Empire emerges:

No envy sets foot in [the] Empire. You [the emperors] have set an example in being free from envy yourselves, by throwing open all doors and offering to qualified men the opportunity to play in turn a ruler's part no less than a subject's. No hatred creeps in either from those who fail to qualify. . . . So, of course, things as they are satisfy and benefit both poor and rich. . . . The whole world.

as on a holiday, has doffed its old costume—of iron—and turned to finery and all festivities without restraint. All other competition between cities has ceased, but a single rivalry obsesses every one of them—to appear as beautiful and attractive as possible. . . . Cities shine in radiance and beauty, and the entire countryside is decked out like a pleasure ground. . . . Before [your] rule, things were all mixed up topsy-turvy, drifting at random. But with you in charge, turmoil and strife ceased, universal order and the bright light of life and government came in.[4]

Even after we have made the necessary allowances for rhetorical embellishment, Aelius' description still leaves a strong impression of an orderly and settled society. Most interesting for our purposes is the attention drawn in the panegyric to the absence of class hostility in Roman society. The socially privileged are not alienated from the socially disadvantaged; the rich are not hated or envied by the poor; the inhabitants of the cities are at peace not only with themselves but also with the surrounding countryside. We will have to refer to Aelius' portrait of Roman society a bit later on, to examine it from a somewhat different perspective, but for the moment it is enough to say that Aelius himself, as an observer of the social scene, was totally unaware of the existence of anything that could properly be called social unrest.

A similar impression emerges from other parts of the record of the early Empire. Toward the beginning of the period, under Tiberius, the historian Velleius Paterculus outlined society in much the same terms as Aelius. The entire Roman world, he claimed, was marked by *stabilitas* and *securitas*. Feuding and class-conflict had been put aside in order to promote the general good.[5] Seventy years later, this sanguine vision remains essentially intact in the extensive portrait of social life drawn by Pliny the Younger.[6] Although Pliny seems to have been aware of potentially explosive conditions in the social life of the Empire,[7] he is satisfied, for the most part, that tranquillity and harmony actually reigned. Even Tacitus is forced to admit somewhat grudgingly that the Empire has managed to remove almost all traces of class warfare — in an overt form, at least — from the Roman social experience.[8]

This kind of evidence, of course, is used by those who are anxious to ascribe a creative role to Christianity in the process of social transformation in the Roman Empire. The evidence, in effect, permits the advocates of this position to postpone the appearance of significant social unrest until Christianity itself had become a significant social phenomenon in the Roman world — sometime toward the end of the second century, in other words — thereby increasing the likelihood that Christianity was responsible in some way for the unquestionably disruptive and unsettled age which followed.[9] As we have already indicated, however, there is another side to the record of social life in the early Empire. There is once again a large body of evidence which projects a totally different image of society than the one found in the writings of men like Paterculus and Aelius Aristides. Instead of celebrating the social blessings of *pax romana,* this evidence points unremittingly to the injustices and flaws within the society of the first two centuries. Instead of *stabilitas* and *securitas,* it confronts us with the twin enemies of the Roman order, *discors* and *turbatio.*

THE EVIDENCE FOR SOCIAL UNREST

We should recognize, as we begin our investigation of the sources which reflect the unsettled character of Roman society, that evidence for the more dramatic forms of social unrest is difficult to adduce. If we look, for instance, for public protests or riots or demonstrations which were socially inspired, we will, to a large extent, be disappointed. Social unrest in the period we are examining was a much more subtle phenomenon, which is not to say that it was any less intense or significant, but rather was expressed in most instances without recourse to violence or overt displays of discontent. There is, to be sure, some evidence in the sources of open clashes of a social nature, and undoubtedly there were many others which went unrecorded, but these were scattered occurrences which broke the normal pattern of unrest in the early Empire and reveal little about the actual character or scope of the phenomenon. What we are saying, in effect, is that social unrest was most often found beneath the surface of Roman life during this period, a fact which helps to explain how someone like Aelius Aristides could seriously offer his roseate description of Roman society as an accurate picture of existing conditions.

Perhaps the succinct analysis of the meaning of *pax romana* which is put into the mouth of a Celtic chieftain by Tacitus comes as close as anything in expressing the real state of affairs with respect to the social life of the early Empire. The Romans, he said, "create a desert, and call it peace." [10] As we shall see, the well-ordered and smoothly functioning society created by the Roman state was a veritable desert for many elements within that society. Discontent and disaffection were easily bred in a world in which surface appearance and living reality had so little to do with each other.

We would naturally expect that a particularly acute form of discontent and disaffection would have existed among the poor in the early Empire. Such, indeed, was the case, but only in a qualified sense. As in every society, there were degrees of poverty among the inhabitants of the Roman world and important differences in the circumstances under which poverty was experienced. Somewhat surprisingly, those who lived at the lowest levels of indigency and for whom poverty was essentially an hereditary fact show the least signs of having been restless or socially dissatisfied. The poet Martial suspected that the man who lived in complete poverty was, in reality, a stoic who cared little about his social condition or his chances for achieving a better life.[11] The one concern which occupied most of his attention was the very simple one of avoiding starvation. This, together with the psychological need of an indigent class to be entertained, provides the background, of course, for the state's carefully contrived program of "bread and games." By meeting both the material and psychological needs of this class through a system of doles, the Roman state was attempting to insure itself against possible revolts by the class.[12] For the most part, the attempt seems to have been successful. It is interesting to note, in fact, that in the few instances in which the impoverished "mob" — whether in Rome itself or in the provinces — did indeed revolt, its revolt was usually an expression of dissatisfaction with the supply of bread or the quality of the games, not the condition of poverty itself.[13]

At a different level of poverty and with different circumstances surrounding the condition, we encounter a much less stoical attitude toward life in the Roman world. Basically, the poor who comprised the "mob" described above were the urban poor. They were unemployed, uneducated, and most often had a history of nothing but poverty. Although the percentage of the unemployed was much lower in other cities throughout the Empire, particularly in the East, every city seems to have had its "hard-core" poor who exhibited much the same mentality as the Roman indigent.[14] The more disaffected among the poor, on the other hand, were a diverse group. They included the small farmer, the day laborer, the soldier, the teacher, and the recently dispossessed or the "new poor," as we might call them. Common to all these groups, which in turn distinguished them from the impoverished "mob," was a deep-seated frustration or anger over the inequities of a system which kept them chained to the social liabilities of poverty in spite of their ambition to enjoy a better and more meaningful life.

The Clientela

Perhaps the group which best illustrates the basic issue involved in the unrest of the "ambitious" poor in the early Empire is the one associated with the peculiar Roman institution known as the *clientela*. The original purpose of this institution which can be traced all the way back to early Republican times was to provide a useful social and economic relationship between the wealthy and the poor. In exchange for protection and material support from a wealthy man (or patron), a poor man (or client) provided companionship, advice, and service.[15]

By the middle of the first century A.D., however, the institution had degenerated into a cheap parody of the oriental courts.[16] The patrons surrounded their presence with paid lackeys who were expected to fawn over them and beg for favors. Occasionally, some of these clients were freedmen who, in spite of their own fortunes were required to maintain the bond of *pietas* to their former masters. But the vast majority were poverty-stricken and were forced to rely almost completely on the small handouts they received from their patrons.[17]

Most important for our purposes is the fact that many of these clients were men of former position and wealth who found themselves reduced for a variety of reasons to a way of life which was totally degrading even under the best of circumstances.[18] Two such men were the poets Martial and Juvenal who appear to have been members of the equestrian order.[19] Both have left vivid portraits of clientship during the early Empire, portraits which reveal the humiliation and disgust which permeated the lives of the clients. The basic complaint of both men was that under this cruel system individuals of real worth and ability — many of them teachers and men of letters — were forced to grovel before their patrons simply because they were poor.[20] Many of the clients felt themselves to be the social equals, if not the superiors of their patrons, and yet, because of their poverty they were denied the social privileges and opportunities given to the man of wealth. Juvenal sums up his frustration and anger when he writes: "Poverty's greatest curse, much worse than the fact of it, is that it makes men objects of mirth, ridiculed, humbled, embarrassed." [21]

Poverty itself, then, does not appear to have been the main issue for this disgruntled class. The main issue was the social disadvantage which automatically accrued to poverty.[22] Juvenal provides us with an extensive catalogue of social privileges which he as a poor man was denied. He had a distinctly inferior standing in the courts; he had little chance of securing any kind of political job; his chances of marrying "well" were virtually nil; he was forced to experience all the terrors and discomforts of city life while enjoying none of its blessings.[23] Juvenal vehemently protested the privileges enjoyed by the rich:

"Out of the front-row seats!" they cry when you're out of money. Yield your place to the sons of some pimp, the spawn of some cathouse, some slick auctioneer's brat, or the louts some trainer has fathered or the well-groomed boys whose sire is a gladiator. Such is the law of place, decreed by the nitwitted Otho: "All the best seats are reserved for the classes who have the most money." [24]

We are, in fact, in Juvenal's description of clientship very close to the formal and legal distinction which would be drawn in the third century between the *humiliores* and the *honestiores*. The condition of poverty — regardless of the ability or background of those who were trapped in it — was automatically equated with social inferiority. Conversely, affluence — no matter how obtained or by whom — was automatically equated with social prestige and privilege.

As spokesmen for their class, both Juvenal and Martial cry out against this system. Their cry, however, was not accompanied by anything that could properly be called a revolt or uprising against the system.[25] Instead, they were content to harbor a deep hatred of the patrons themselves, especially those whose origins were humbler than many of the clients. Of all the forms of class hostility within the early Empire, none was as bitter as that found in the system of clientship; for here, more than anywhere else, the potential of the Roman social structure to humiliate and degrade became an everyday actuality. Although the urban *clientela* as described by Juvenal and Martial seems to have been unique to Rome itself, the social relationship implicit in the system — that is, the humiliating deference owed to the rich by the poor — was a fact of life everywhere in the Empire. The Empire itself was a system of client-states or cities with Rome (actually the emperor) as the patron.[26]

The Peasantry

Another group among the poor which displayed a lively tradition of disaffection and discontent was that of the small farmers or peasants. The role of the peasantry in the social and economic upheavals of the third and fourth centuries is well known, but what is sometimes forgotten is that this rural unrest can and must be traced back to the more outwardly stable period of the early Empire. The countryside was probably just as restless in the first and second centuries as it was in the third — the big difference being that the countryside did not have the military and administrative support under the early Empire which it was to find in the third century.[27]

The basic complaint of the peasantry under the early Empire was what it has always been in every age — exploitation.[28] Significantly, however, the manner in which the peasantry was exploited during this period followed much the same pattern as that of the urban *clientela*. Essentially, this is what the average peasant had become — a rural client.[29] Instead of being a small independent landowner living a free life in his tribal or rural community, the peasant had become almost everywhere in the Empire the tenant of an absentee landlord, and as such, was forced to accept the same kind of humiliating servitude and social inferiority with which the urban client lived every day. Moreover, since most of the landlords were to be found among the wealthy bourgeoisie of the city, the rural and urban clients frequently shared the same enemy.

Although a kind of "urbaphobia" was manifested by the urban clients (this would certainly be true of Juvenal), a smoldering hatred of the city was added by the peasants to the lengthening list of social tensions within the Empire.[30] In part, their hatred of the city stemmed from the fact that the exploiters lived there; but more important was the fact that the city represented a specially privileged, even pampered society from which the peasants felt they had been systematically excluded. They felt totally alienated from the culture and society of the urban centers, and as more and more rights and exemptions were lavished upon these centers by the emperors — usually at the peasants' expense — their hatred of the city became more intense.

As in the case of the urban clients, the peasants' hatred of the city did not normally express itself in open revolt during the first two centuries of the Empire;[31] yet, even when it was nothing more than a mood or attitude, it must be accounted one of the more serious forms of unrest in the period of the early Empire. The peasantry, after all, was by far the largest social class in the Empire,[32] and although the full implication of its hatred for the city would not become obvious until the third century, it is quite clear that the mere fact of its alienation from what had become the social ideal of *Romanitas,* namely urbanization, constituted an important and insidious force in the subversion of that ideal.

The evidence from Egypt is particularly helpful in illustrating the character and scope of rural unrest. As the most rural of all the provinces, Egypt experienced the most extensive and determined program of social protest by the peasants or *fellahîn.* Of special interest is the way in which this protest was often coupled with the folk-religion of Egypt. Revisions of ancient sagas such as the *Instructions of Onchsheshongy* and the *Oracle of the Potter* became the vehicles for a vicious attack against urban society, which in the case of Egypt meant the city of Alexandria.[33] In addition to the usual peasant complaint about their economic exploitation by the city, these documents reveal a deep resentment of the way in which the city — with the support and encouragement of the Roman *imperium* — tampered with the social and religious institutions of the countryside. The local temple, for instance, which traditionally served a social as well as a religious purpose for the *fellahîn,* was turned under Roman rule into a support system (as the place where taxes were collected, in other words) for urban civilization. The priests were similarly corrupted by being transformed into tax-collectors, a transformation which had the effect of discrediting them in the eyes of the people and making them, for all practical purposes, members of the hated urban society.[34] Against the city-led attempts to alienate them from their cherished social and religious institutions, the peasants reacted

predictably and effectively. Occasionally they revolted; but contin-
ually they engaged in a subversion of the social ideal of Imperial
Rome by refusing to identify themselves ideologically with the dom-
ineering culture and society of the city.

The Sibylline Oracles provide another example from the early
Empire of an Egyptian-based attack against the policies of Rome and
the civic life which it promoted. Here, however, the Jews, who were
within the city, joined the peasants in their ideological alienation from
the dominant culture and society of the city. In the revolt of the
Jews in Egypt during the reign of Trajan and/or Hadrian, the peasants seem to have supported the cause of the Jews against the government and the Hellenized city bourgeoisie.[35]

The Urban Working Class

The disastrous effects of this alienation of the poor from the social
program favored and subsidized by Rome can be seen most clearly,
perhaps, in the case of the urban working class. Unlike the peasantry,
the petty merchants, the artisans, and the workmen of the cities found
themselves totally immersed in an urban civilization and yet were not
allowed to share in the benefits and privileges which urban society
had been designed to promote. They were, in fact, refused the very
thing which defined the idea of *civitas* itself: full participation in
determining and enjoying the common good. As second-class citizens,
or in some instances, as no citizens at all, the poor workmen of the
Empire were made to feel that they were outsiders who contributed
materially through their labor and goods to the attainment of the
civic ideal but remained unrelated to it on a personal or social level.[36]
The "common good" was from their point of view a most uncommon
privilege enjoyed only by the wealthy. Therefore, their support of the
status quo could not be taken for granted.

This kind of situation lay behind the richly documented outbreak
of class hostility in the eastern provinces during the Principates of
Trajan and Hadrian.[37] More than likely these instances of unrest
were typical of a general mood which existed in most cities throughout the Empire. They reveal — particularly as described by Dio
Chrysostom — that the basic issue between the working class and the
wealthy citizens of the cities was social in character.[38] The tumults
and disorders raised by the linen workers in Tarsus, for instance, do
not appear to have been raised for economic reasons.[39] What this
particular group of workers was protesting was their exclusion from
the dimensions of social life which were considered to be the essence
of urban civilization. Similar instances of *stasis* are to be found in
Sardis, Nicaea, and especially in Smyrna where a long-standing feud

seems to have existed between the men of the "upper city" (evidently the wealthy) and the "men of the seashore" (the working class).[40]

Dio Chrysostom was not at all surprised that the workers were dissatisfied, and were, on occasion, disrupting the peace and tranquillity of the cities. "Of necessity," he concludes, "they stand aloof in sentiment from the common interest, reviled as they are and viewed as outsiders." [41] Social unrest, Dio continues, is the inevitable product of this imposed aloofness, for "nothing [can be] more harmful to a city than such a condition, nothing more conducive to strife and disagreement." [42]

Dio's judgment, it would appear, constitutes a convenient summary of the fundamental complaint found among the group we have called the "ambitious" poor. All of them — including certain elements within the military establishment and the professions, particularly the teachers — felt a sense of betrayal by the social program which was promoted by Imperial Rome.[43] This program was plainly designed to favor the rich; only the rich could really feel that they were included within the benevolent purposes of *Romanitas*. Hence, as Dio says, the poor stand aloof *in sentiment* from the Roman dream of bringing order out of chaos through what was essentially a timocratic urbanization of society. Far more significant than an occasional riot or local disturbance created by the poor during the early Empire was the aloofness or alienation of a group which comprised the vast majority of the population of the Empire. The hatred of the rich by the poor was, in reality, a hatred of the Roman social system. If the system failed — as it clearly did in the third century — the legacy of this particular form of unrest must be given much of the credit or blame.

The Slaves

Before we leave the poor as a group, there is another distinct element within Roman society that must be looked at briefly. The institution of slavery, of course, was still very much an established part of the social structure of the early Empire.[44] As an institution, however, it was undergoing important modifications and changes, all of which combined to produce an attitude or sentiment which was quite different from the one generally found among the poor. First of all, the creation of new slaves was on the decline during this period. Secondly, a more humane treatment of slaves had emerged as a generally accepted social obligation. Most important of all, however, was a more liberal policy with respect to emancipation. As the large numbers of freedmen from this period testify, the average slave must have been able to look forward, through manumission, to a vastly improved and infinitely more respectable social status either for himself or for his children. Although many slaves never attained freedom, all of them could share in the hope for freedom.

The slave, in short, probably tended to see the Roman social system working on his behalf. He was, accordingly, more willing to cooperate and identify with a system which, in spite of its inequities, promised him a degree of reward which he could never know as a slave. This attitude very likely explains the almost complete absence of serious slave revolts during this period. Moreover, it helps to explain the prodigious social and economic achievements of so many slaves after they had been freed. Although these achievements and the relation of the freedman class to the problem of social unrest belong properly to another part of our study, it must be noted here that the prior condition of the freedman class, that is slavery, does not seem to have been marked by any deep resentment of the way in which social privilege and respectability were equated with the acquisition of wealth in the early Empire. Instead of feeling alienated from or humiliated by this system, the slaves, as a social class, appear to have been ready to take advantage of it in ways which had become legendary even during the period of the early Empire itself. The only class of slaves to whom this optimistic mentality would not apply was the agricultural slave. He undoubtedly shared much the same mentality or social outlook as the free tenant. Not surprisingly, the reports of slave uprisings during the early Empire come from this group.[45]

These last observations provide a convenient point at which to reopen the question of early Christianity's relationship to social conditions in the Empire. Although a final evaluation of this relationship must wait until we have seen the conditions and attitudes which were obtained at all levels of Roman society, it is worth noting here that the frequently assumed exploitation of a revolutionary undercurrent among the poor or lower classes by early Christianity is, on the basis of our findings, highly problematic.[46] In the case of the slaves, for instance, individual dissatisfactions of a social character undoubtedly lay behind the conversion of some members of this class to Christianity, but certainly there was nothing resembling a general "mood" of social discontent among this group which Christianity was able to exploit. The exact opposite would appear to have been more nearly the case. The social implications of Christianity were probably much less impressive or promising to the average slave than the prospects which were latent in the social system in which he lived. If Christianity was able to attract significant numbers of slaves — a fact which is not at all clear from the evidence — it must have been for reasons other than social ones.[47]

THE ROLE OF CHRISTIANITY

Where genuine unrest did exist among the poor, Christianity's exploitation of the phenomenon is no less problematic. Except for the appeal of Jesus in Galilee and Pliny's warning that the new religion was infecting the villages and farms of Asia Minor, there is little evidence that Christianity made appreciable headway during this period among the peasants who were probably the most thoroughly disaffected group within the Empire.[48] Their particular form of unrest — alienation from an oppressive urban culture — kept them, in fact, effectively isolated from a church which had almost exclusively identified itself with the great urban centers. Whatever responsive chord Christianity might have been able to strike among the peasantry was rendered largely meaningless by this isolation.

In the case of the urban working class, there is better evidence of a kind of instinctive attraction to Christianity, but again it must be questioned whether this attraction had anything to do with issues which can properly be called social. Purely in terms of social expectations, the workmen, as well as other disaffected groups within the urban population, were looking for ways of being *included* in the officially promoted social life of Imperial Rome, not a way of being further excluded as they were certain to be if they joined the Christian sect. These groups, as we have seen, were indeed alienated from the social ideal of Roman civilization, but this alienation did not include a disinterest in social status or privilege as such. Their insistence on full and equal participation in civic life was, in fact, the whole point of their unrest. To make Christianity, then, the vehicle for the social unrest of these groups would be to make it into the very thing which it was accused of *not* being. It was a movement which was indifferent, even contemptuous of the position and participation of its members in human society.

As we move into the next level of Roman society, the large and thriving urban middle class, it is even more difficult to find evidence of an alliance between Christianity and some form of social unrest. As a class, the urban bourgeoisie had little reason to resent or resist the social policies of the Roman *imperium,* for those policies were plainly designed to benefit and encourage the middle class.[49] This favoritism was, of course, the source of much of the hostility and unrest among the lower classes (and, as we shall see shortly, among certain elements in the upper classes, as well), but for the middle class itself, it provided a powerful incentive for investing in the social system promoted by the Empire.

Although the makeup of the middle class during the first two centuries of the Empire was extremely complex,[50] it is possible to single out one group as being rather typical of the social ethos which pervaded the class. The rise of freedmen to positions of great social prestige and responsibility is certainly one of the most remarkable aspects of the history of the early Empire.[51] Of particular importance for our purposes is the mentality or outlook which this group brought to the class which absorbed so many of them. As one writer has summarized it: "They [took] the world as it was . . . they were not encumbered with dignity or self-respect. They had one goal, and they worked towards it with infinite industry and unfailing courage and self-confidence." [52] Unlike other groups among both the lower and upper classes who deeply resented the social humiliations which were built into every level of Roman society, the middle class — particularly the freedmen — demonstrated an equanimity with respect to social relationships which permitted them to escape the frequently debilitating effects of social unrest.

Still, in spite of its favored position and the constructive, cooperative attitude typified by the freedmen, the middle class has been accused of a form of social sabotage which, in turn, raises the possibility of its alliance with the social ideals of early Christianity. The issue specifically is the great burden which was placed upon the class by assigning to it major responsibility for maintaining the system from which it received so many advantages. The claim has been made that by the end of the first century, the various social and economic "liturgies" heaped upon this class had become so annoying or exhausting that the class as a whole was beginning to look for ways of evading its social responsibilities.[53] This is the context in which Christianity, with its alleged endorsement of social irresponsibility, is believed to have provided a convenient means of escape for a disgruntled element within Roman society.[54]

The difficulty with this position is that it simply does not fit the conditions which existed in either the middle class or the church in the period we are examining. There were, to be sure, individual instances of socially uncooperative bourgeoisie during this period, but on the whole, the middle class maintained an almost unbelievable enthusiasm for its civic and social responsibilities right down to the end of the second century.[55] Moreover, there is no evidence of Christianity catering to this class by endorsing social irresponsibility. Instead, the members of this class who found their way into the church were expected to assume as much of a burden or responsibility for the well-being of the Christian community as they had for the "worldly" communities from which they had come.[56] At a later date — toward the middle of the third century, for instance — it is indeed possible to find an almost complete disenchantment among the middle class with respect to its civic duties, and with this disenchantment one can begin looking for signs of Christianity either exploiting or being exploited by this particular form of social unrest, but during the early Empire what has commonly been interpreted as a kind of collusion between a restless middle class and an opportunistic church is simply untenable.

As we turn finally to the upper class, we are confronted with perhaps the most persuasive reason for being hesitant in assuming that Christianity swept across the Roman world on the coattails of a social revolution. Here we encounter the closest thing to open revolution which the early Empire faced, but we also encounter, in this same group, a disdain for Christianity which was to persist right down to the period in which the "fall" of Rome was completed. Both of these facts are so well known that it may seem somewhat gratuitous to pursue the question further; yet, some purpose is served by examining the character of aristocratic unrest in the early Empire, if for no other reason than that it helps to explain why Christianity was unable to capitalize on the disaffection of this group.

In one of the few studies made of the phenomenon of social unrest in the early Empire, Ramsay MacMullen has singled out the subversive activities and attitudes of the aristocracy as the most significant disruptive force in the Empire.[57] All other forms of unrest among the other classes were, in effect, the outer edges of this central core of aristocratic discontent. The basic complaint of the aristocracy was its loss of social and political ascendancy, a loss which was effected on the one side by the concentration of political power in the person of the emperor, and on the other side by the dilution of social privileges among the rising middle class. Frustrated by the atrophy of its former prerogatives, bitter because of its inability to exercise leadership, and deeply humiliated because of the cheapening of its once-unequalled position, the upper class struck back by attempting to subvert the new order which had been created by Augustus and modified by his successors.[58]

As MacMullen has demonstrated, this subversion normally was carried out in very subtle ways, but unlike the subversion which existed at other levels of Roman society, it operated according to a deliberate and well-articulated plan. The aristocracy was particularly anxious to glorify the Republican past as over against the tyranny of the present Imperial order,[59] a purpose which was effectively accomplished through the literature and philosophy of the period which was heavily committed to the cause of the aristocracy.[60] Moreover, it was anxious to repudiate the "vulgarization" inherent in the cosmopolitan civilization fostered by the Empire which threatened to undermine the traditional supports of an aristocratic society. The unrest of the aristocracy, in short, was a romantic reaction, an attempt to restore a departed social ideal.[61] It is in this context that its negative attitude toward Christianity must be seen. Christianity represented the worst in the vulgarization of society; it was for the aristocracy the logical outcome of the promiscuous social policies promoted by the emperors, policies which could only lead to chaos if they were allowed to continue.

The pessimism which accompanied aristocratic unrest during much of the early Empire proved to be prophetic. Chaos did follow as men such as Seneca and Tacitus predicted it would.[62] Interestingly, the reasons for the collapse of the Imperial system were better understood by these prophets of gloom than by many later historians who have had the advantage of hindsight in interpreting the process. The system promoted by Rome during the early Empire failed because of tensions and defects built into the system itself. A thin, but impressive veneer of social stability and harmony was created by catering to an ambitious and expanding urban middle class. As long as this class was expanding and thriving, the jealousies and resentments which existed on both sides of it could be contained; but with the decline of the middle class in the third century — with the removal of the props and opportunities which had given it strength — the antagonisms and hostilities which permeated Roman society spilled over and convulsed the system.

From a purely historical point of view, Christianity's relationship to all of this is, at best, incidental. Even if Christianity had never appeared on the scene, it is highly probable that Rome would not only have "fallen" but would have fallen in precisely the same way that it did.

NOTES

[1] E. Gibbon, *The Decline and Fall of the Roman Empire* (Chicago: Encyclopedia Britannica, Inc., 1952). See esp. chaps. 15 and 16 (on Christianity), 38 and 71 (summaries).

[2] This, essentially, is the position argued by Christians who lived close to the "fall" of the Empire. See esp. Augustine's *City of God*, Bks. 1-4. The position was later argued more elaborately by Bossuet in his *Discourse on Universal History*. For a more recent study favorable to Christianity, see A. Momigliano, "Christianity and the Decline of the Roman Empire" in *Paganism and Christianity in the Fourth Century*, ed. A. Momigliano (Oxford: The Clarendon Press, 1963), pp. 1-16.

[3] Marxist historians have been particularly anxious to promote this theory. See esp. Pöhlmann's *Geschichte des antiken Sozialismus und Kommunismus*, 2, 1901, pp. 583-617; K. Kautsky, *Geschichte des Sozialismus in Einzeldarstellungen*, 1, 1895, pp. 16-40.

[4] Aelius Aristides, *To Rome*, 59-60, 63-71, 93-104.

[5] Velleius Paterculus, *Compendium of Roman History* 2. 126. 2-5.

[6] See the excellent analysis in S. Dill, *Roman Society from Nero to Marcus Aurelius* (New York: The Macmillan Company, 1904), pp. 141-195.

[7] A sense of foreboding is particularly evident in Pliny, *Letters* 3. 14.

[8] Tacitus, *Histories* 1. 1 ("the interests of peace demand the concentration of power in the hands of one man"); see also *Annals* 11. 24.

[9] A good example of the use of this technique—in addition to Gibbon, of course —is found in E. Renan, *Marc Aurele et la fin du monde antique* (Paris: Calmann Levy, 1885).

[10] Tacitus, *Agricola* 30.

[11] Martial, *Epigrams* 2. 53.

[12] See esp. Juvenal, *Satires* 10. 78-81. ("The people don't give a damn any more . . . they play it safe, and ask for only two things, bread and games"); see also Fronto, *Elements of History* 17; and Dio Chrysostom who describes the mob in Alexandria as "a folk to whom you need only throw plenty of bread and a ticket to the hippodrome, since they have no interest in anything else" (*Discourse* 32. 31). On doles as imperial policy, see Rostovtzeff, *The Social and Economic History of the Roman Empire*, 2nd ed. (New York: Oxford University Press, 1957), 1, pp. 81-82 (for Rome itself), p. 149 (for the provinces).

[13] For evidence of bread-riots, see Tacitus, *Annals* 12. 43; Suetonius, *Claudius* 18. 2, Dio Chrysostom, *Discourse* 46. 6ff. On popular uprisings in connection with the games, see L. Friedländer, *Roman Life and Manners under the Early Empire* (London: G. Routledge, 1913), 2, pp. 1-19.

[14] One estimate states that the urban poor comprised between one third and one half of the population of the city, numbering somewhere between 400,000 and 600,000. See J. Carcopino, *Daily Life in Ancient Rome* (New Haven: Yale University Press, 1941), p. 65. See, also, Dio Chrysostom's description of the Alexandrian mob in *Discourse* 32.

[15] See Dill, *op. cit.,* p. 94; Friedländer, *op. cit.,* 1, p. 195.

[16] Lucian of Samosata provides a good illustration of this side of the institution in his *Nigrinus* 21.

[17] Martial discloses that clients were paid only about six sesterces a day. *Epigrams* 3. 30. See also Juvenal, *Satires* 1. 119-121.

[18] See Friedländer, *op. cit.,* 1, pp. 201-202. On poverty and its causes among members of the upper classes, see Dill, *op. cit.,* pp. 71-72.

[19] See Rostovtzeff, *op. cit.,* 1, p. 195; Dill, *op. cit.,* pp. 94-95.

[20] See, for instance, Juvenal's seventh *Satire.* Lucian describes the humiliations of a young man of letters in his *De Mercede Conductis.*

[21] Juvenal, *Satires* 3. 151-153.

[22] See Dill, *op. cit.,* p. 98.

[23] Juvenal, *Satires* 3.

[24] Rolfe Humphries, trans., *The Satires of Juvenal* (Bloomington, Ind.: Indiana University Press, 1958). Copyright, © 1963 by Indiana University Press. Reprinted by permission of Indiana University Press.

[25] The most "revolutionary" action Juvenal advocates is leaving the city. *Satires* 3. 1-5, and 162-163. Martial himself did eventually retire from the city and so withdrew from regular encounters with the system.

[26] See H. Mattingly, *The Emperor and His Clients* (Sydney: University of Sydney, 1948).

[27] See Rostovtzeff, *op. cit.,* 1, pp. 496-498; 2, p. 747, n. 64.

[28] See E. Kornemann, "Bauernstand" in Pauly-Wissowa, *Suppl.* iv, cols. 83ff.

[29] For Italy, see Rostovtzeff, *op. cit.,* 1, pp. 205-206; for the provinces, *ibid.,* pp. 344-345. A collection of texts illustrating tenancy can be found in N. Lewis and M. Reinhold, eds., *Roman Civilization* (New York: Columbia University Press, 1955), 2, pp. 166-188.

[30] The evidence has been collected by Rostovtzeff in his *Studien zur Geschichte des römischen Kolonats,* 1910.

[31] Uprisings of peasants in Egypt under the Flavians and Antonines were quite common. See Rostovtzeff, *Social and Economic History, op. cit.,* 1, p. 348. The most common form of violence resorted to by the peasantry seems to have been brigandage. See R. MacMullen, *Enemies of the Roman Order* (Cambridge, Mass.: Harvard University Press, 1966), pp. 255-268.

[32] See Rostovtzeff, *Social and Economic History,* 1, p. 347.

[33] See J. Fennelly, "Roman Involvement in the Affairs of the Egyptian Shrine" in *Bulletin of John Rylands Library,* 50 (1968), 317-335; MacMullen, *op. cit.,* p. 150.

[34] Fennelly, *op. cit.,* pp. 319-323.

[35] On the Jewish sections of the *Sibyllines,* see A. Kurfess, "Christian Sibyllines" in *New Testament Apocrypha,* ed. E. Hennecke and W. Schneemelcher (Philadelphia: The Westminster Press, 1963), 2, pp. 706-707. See also von Premerstein, "Alexandrinische Gesandte vor Kaiser Hadrian" in *Hermes,* 57 (1922), 305ff.

[36] The widening of citizenship under the early Empire generally was limited to men of property and wealth or individuals who had provided meritorious service to the state (e.g., soldiers). Although citizenship was somewhat more common among members of the lower classes in the West, the actual political (and social) rights of the poor were small or nonexistent everywhere in the Empire. See A. N. Sherwin-White, *The Roman Citizenship* (Oxford: The Clarendon Press, 1939), esp. pp. 167ff.

[37] See D. Magie, *Roman Rule in Asia Minor* (Princeton: Princeton University Press, 1950), 2, p. 600.

[38] Dio Chrysostom, *Oration* 32; 33; 34; 39; 46.

[39] *Oration* 34. 21-23.

[40] See Philostratus, *Life of Apollonius* 4, 2, 8, 75ff.

[41] *Oration* 34. 22.

[42] *Ibid.* A definite link appears to have existed between urban unrest in Tarsus and certain social and religious clubs *(collegia).* See esp. *Oration* 34. 21. The working men, in other words, very likely used what were ostensibly "lodges" or "guilds" as centers for the political activity which was denied them in the formal (curial) political life of the community, thus justifying to a large extent Trajan's extremely cautious attitude toward such societies (Pliny, *Letters* 10. 34).

[43] As the army came to rely more and more on recruits from the provinces—drawn especially from the peasant class—the soldiers' resentment of their unequal sharing in the urban civilization which they were defending increased greatly. See Rostovtzeff, *Social and Economic History,* 1, pp. 127-129. On the teachers, see n. 20 above.

[44] See W. Westermann, *The Slave Systems of Greek and Roman Antiquity* (Philadelphia: American Philosophical Society, 1955).

[45] See Pliny, *Letters* 3. 14.

[46] For an example of this approach, see J. Morris, "Early Christian Orthodoxy" in *Past and Present* (London: Cobbett Press, 1953).

[47] See E. Judge, *The Social Pattern of Christian Groups in the First Century* (London: Tyndale Press, 1960), pp. 49-61. During the period we are examining, the presence of slaves in the church almost always presupposes the conversion of the entire "household," i.e., slaves became Christians along with their masters.

[48] Pliny, *Letters* 10. 96.

[49] See Rostovtzeff, *Social and Economic History,* 1, pp. 378-379.

[50] See J. Wight Duff, "Social Life in Rome and Italy" in *Cambridge Ancient History* (New York: Cambridge University Press, 1932), 11, pp. 748-749.

[51] See A. M. Duff, *Freedom in the Early Roman Empire* (New York: Barnes & Noble, Inc., 1928).

[52] Dill, *op. cit.*, pp. 119-120. The classic example of the successful freedman in the early Empire is Trimalchio in Petronius' *Satyricon*. He describes himself as a man who has reached his present position by his ability. "What makes a man is the heart, the rest is trash. I buy well, and I sell well. . . . Believe me, have a penny, you're worth a penny; have something, you'll be worth something." *Satyricon* 75. 10; 77. 4-5.

[53] See Rostovtzeff, *Social and Economic History*, 1, pp. 380-392, esp. p. 388.

[54] This view is implicit in the well-known analysis of Christianity's anti-civic, anti-social mentality as delineated by J. G. Frazer, *The Golden Bough*, abridged edition (New York: The Macmillan Company, 1958), pp. 414-415.

[55] The evidence—much of it inscriptural—has been collected in Lewis and Reinhold, eds., *Roman Civilization*, 2, pp. 344-358.

[56] See A. Harnack, *The Mission and Expansion of Christianity in the First Three Centuries* (New York: Harper & Row, Publishers, 1962), pp. 147-198.

[57] See esp. MacMullen, *op. cit.*, pp. 242-243.

[58] For an analysis of senatorial-aristocratic unrest during the early Empire, see J. Wight Duff, *op. cit.*, pp. 746-748; Dill, *op. cit.*, pp. 1-57.

[59] A good example of "republican" opposition is Helvidius Priscus, the son-in-law of Thrasea Paetus who had been put to death by Nero. During the reign of Vespasian, Helvidius "attacked monarchical systems and praised republican, and to the people he openly advocated revolution." (Dio Cassius, *History*, 65. 12, 2).

[60] A recurring theme throughout the literature of the early Empire is the implication of philosophers as the instigators of social unrest and discord. The subject is so vast and complicated that a separate study would be required to explicate it properly. In general, it would appear that the cynic philosophers had their greatest success and impact upon the lower classes. They are accused by men like Dio Chrysostom (*Oration* 32. 9) and Lucian (*De Morte Peregrini*) of being rabble-rousers, inciting the mob to violence or social malcontent. The stoics, on the other hand, appealed mainly to the upper, educated classes, giving expression to many of the frustrations and dissatisfactions which agitated the aristocracy. See MacMullen, *op. cit.*, pp. 46-94; Dill, *op. cit.*, pp. 289-383.

[61] Dill, *op. cit.*, pp. 23-24.

[62] See *ibid.*, p. 26.

FOR ADVANCED READING

See titles listed in the foregoing chapter (Religion and Social Class).

John T. Townsend

6
Ancient Education in the Time of the Early Roman Empire

In order to understand ancient education, one must recognize the importance of educational theory and practice in the Hellenistic world. Failure to recognize this importance has caused many surveys of ancient education to project a somewhat distorted picture. General works like those of E. B. Castle, W. Barclay, and W. A. Smith[1] more or less jump from the situation in classical Athens to Roman education with scarcely a mention of the Hellenistic era. Such a perspective is hardly in keeping with the fact that in the Hellenistic era ancient education became molded into a single, universal system that would dominate the ancient scene until the barbarian overthrow of the West and the Muslim conquests in the East.

From the perspective of Hellenistic education, Roman education of late republican and imperial times is neither a separate entity nor a corruption of Athenian educational ideals. Roman education should be viewed as one aspect of Hellenistic education with Latin added to the curriculum and with less stress on physical training. In fact, even Jewish education was not exempt from Hellenistic influence; and, as will be shown below, it is possible to view Jewish education at least partly in terms of Hellenistic educational methods and curricula.

GENERAL CHARACTERISTICS OF ANCIENT EDUCATION

Evidence for the essential unity of Hellenistic-Roman education is impressive. This unity is more than a general similarity in curriculum. In the teaching of reading, for example, Quintilian advocates for late first-century Rome the same methods illustrated in papyrus remains from the schools of Hellenistic and imperial Egypt.[2] Gymnasia from Hellenistic and imperial times show a remarkable similarity in design. Thus, a treatise on architecture from Augustan Rome

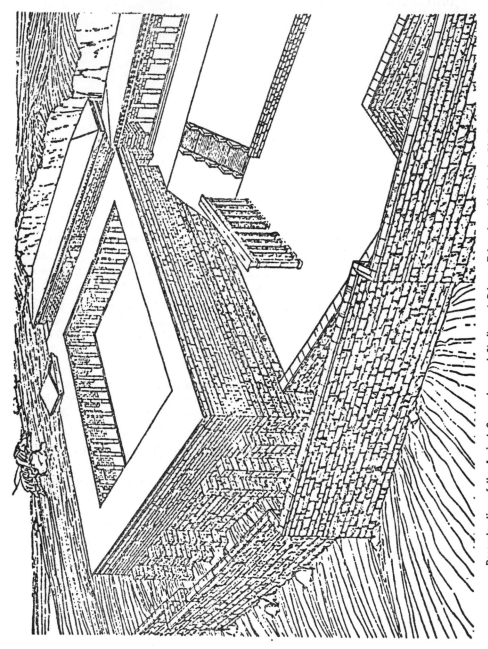

Reconstruction of the Ancient Gymnasium and Stadium at Priene. Taken from M. Schede, **Die Ruinen von Priene**, ed. G. Kleiner und W. Kleiss (Deutsches archaelogisches Institut, Abteilung Istanbul; Berlin: Walter de Gruyter, 1964), p. 88.

provides an excellent key for understanding the various excavated gymnasia like the one from before 130 B.C. at Priene in Asia Minor (see page 140).[3] Grammar as expounded by Dionysius Thrax in Rhodes during the second century B.C. is not essentially different from that taught by later grammarians, Greek or Latin.[4]

Of course, education was not entirely static during the long Hellenistic-Imperial era. There were exceptions and trends. On the island of Chios young aristocrats were serving three years in the 'ephēbeia, or finishing school for men,[5] while one or two years was more the norm. The study of law was increasing in importance although it did not approach its zenith until the later Empire. Physical education and music were constantly on the decline. Latin language and literature in the West were receiving greater emphasis along with Greek, although Greek continued to be of major importance in Roman education. This importance is reflected in the life of Roman Christians, who generally conducted their liturgical worship in the Greek tongue until the fourth century.[6] Thus, Paul would have had little language problem in communicating with the Roman church by letter or in person. In spite of such exceptions and trends, however, the general impression of education during the Hellenistic and imperial eras of the classical world is one of sameness rather than divergence.

Classical education usually involved attending a school, but such was not always the case. Many students were tutored, and in first-century Rome Quintilian felt it necessary to devote a whole chapter to arguing the advantages of school education over against home study.[7] It seems probable, however, that a Hellenistic or Roman boy studying at home with a tutor would have received an education substantially equivalent to that of his contemporaries attending school. Certainly there is no clear evidence to the contrary.

Ancient education progressed in three stages: primary, secondary, and advanced. The three stages are clearly outlined in the first century B.C. by the pseudo-Plato[8] and later by Quintilian.[9] Children began in primary school about the age of seven, and those who completed all three stages usually would have finished their schooling in their late teens or early twenties. Of course, then as now, relatively few received advanced schooling. However, we should not assume that ancient education was wholly reserved for the privileged few. Even the poor considered a certain degree of literacy to be essential, and near the end of the first century A.D. the Latin epigrammatist Martial writes of a cobbler whose parents, being poor and ignorant, taught him the ABC's themselves.[10] We tend to regard general literacy as a modern phenomenon. There were many places in the ancient world where literacy, if not general, was extremely common. Moreover, schooling was not limited to men only. In the Hellenistic age girls frequently went to primary and secondary schools just as their brothers.[11]

As mentioned earlier, physical education and music were declining in popularity during the period under discussion. One reason seems to have been that real proficiency in these areas was becoming the province of uncultured professionals. By the first century of the Christian era, music as a performing art had largely disappeared from the normal curriculum although musical theory continued as a branch of mathematics. In Rome excellence in performing music had always been looked upon with some suspicion. Typical of the Roman attitude is that of Sallust who in 43 B.C. casually referred to a lady as being able "to play the lyre and dance better than necessary for a virtuous woman," although in the same passage he spoke quite favorably of her having a good general education.[12] However, a little training in musical performance remained in some curricula because school children were sometimes expected to supply choral singing in the various religious festivals.[13]

PHYSICAL TRAINING

Although the importance of physical training was waning throughout the whole Hellenistic and Roman periods, it still played a significant role in all levels of education during the early Empire. Physical training and the gymnasia associated with it were particularly important in the East where the influence of traditional Greek education was strongest, and even as late as the fourth century, Basil the Great can still speak of the gymnasium as an institution with which he was familiar.[14]

At the head of each gymnasium was a gymnasiarch. Where a city had more than one gymnasium, there would be a gymnasiarch general over all the gymnasia. A gymnasiarch was held in high honor, but the honor was expensive. Not only did he serve without pay, but he was personally responsible for the running expenses of the gymnasium, not the least of which was supplying quantities of oil for the bodies of the athletes. In fact, in later times the office of gymnasiarch was not so much of an honor as a liturgy, i.e., a philanthropic obligation imposed upon the richer citizens as an added tax. Although in charge of the gymnasium, the gymnasiarch himself did not usually instruct. Actual teaching was left to assistants, gymnastic instructors, and lecturers.[15]

A gymnasium was often quite an extensive complex. A fairly typical example at Priene in West Asia Minor is depicted in the drawing on page 140. For most of the exercises there was at Priene a courtyard covered with sand and surrounded by porticos. This area was properly called the palaestra although in Hellenistic times the term "palaestra" had so broadened its meaning that it is difficult to define the word exactly.[16] In addition to the palaestra there were various rooms, such as the large lecture hall for students of college age, oil and dust storage rooms, a room for the punching bag, and a room for massages. To one side of the palaestra was the stadium. The Priene stadium was built on three levels into the side of the steep hill on which the city stood. On the lowest level there was an elaborate starting gate for the runners.

All gymnastic exercises were performed in the nude, a fact which partly explains the negative attitude on the part of certain Jews toward the gymnasium which the high priest Jason set up in Jerusalem about the year 175 B.C.[17] The athlete's naked body was prepared for action by first being rubbed with oil and then being sprinkled with various kinds of dust especially collected for the purpose.[18]

The major sports were *pankration,* boxing, and the pentathlon, which included running, jumping, discus throwing, javelin throwing, and wrestling. These ancient sports, however, did not always correspond to their modern counterparts. *Pankration* was a violent combination of wrestling, boxing, and kicking with no holds barred except gouging and biting. For boxing (cf. 1 Corinthians 9:26), the participants wore fingerless leather mittens which covered most of the forearm, and they fought without benefit of ring or rounds. Running was usually in a straight line and back (cf. Philippians 3:14). There were never any hurdles, but some races were run in full armor. Jumping was always for length, never for height; and the jumper carried a small dumbbell in each hand for balance. The javelin was thrown with a kind of catapult, or *ankúllē,* wrapped around it. Wrestling was performed standing until the loser fell on his back, shoulder, or hip, not merely his knees.[19]

We know much about how wrestling was taught. One interesting piece of evidence is part of a wrestling handbook for helping an instructor in putting two wrestlers, whom we can label A and B, through some kind of drill. The second column, which is the only one undamaged enough to understand, reads as follows:

[You] (A), turn your body sideways to your opponent and grip him by the head with the right hand.

You (B), clasp him around the body.

You (A), take hold under it [i.e., under the right hand].

You (B), stand firm and wrap your arms about him.

You (A), get your right hand down underneath.

You (B), grab where he is holding underneath. Put your left hand down on his side.

You (A), shove him away with the left hand.
You (B), turn him around and clasp him.
You (A), turn around.
You (B), bring your grip down around the thighs.
You (A), trip him.
You (B), grab him around the waist.
You (A), put your weight on him and force him backward.
You (B), lean forward, throw him back, turn around to him, and return to the attack.[20]

PRIMARY AND SECONDARY SCHOOLING

Most primary and secondary schools of the ancient world were private affairs. Without government support they were commonly small and inadequate, often in the hands of a single teacher. School buildings seem to have been any room where a class happened to be held, sometimes merely a curtained-off space on the market place and open to the air. Teachers themselves, especially those in the primary schools, fared little better than the buildings. Most were despised socially and had to eke out a meager living from the often unpaid fees of their students. In a few places, like Miletus and Teos in Asia Minor, teachers were elected by the municipality and paid from an endowed foundation; but, even in such situations, teachers received only slightly more income than skilled workmen.[21]

Boys and girls entered primary school more or less at the age of seven; and, especially where the culture was Greek,[22] they attended two institutions, the reading school (or *didaskaleion*) and the palaestra, which on this level was commonly a private institution separate from the municipal gymnasium.[23] Originally the children spent the morning at the gymnasium and the afternoon at the reading school.[24] During the period of the early Empire, however, physical education was receiving less stress. In this era the young students would leave for the reading school before dawn and proceed to the palaestra later in the morning. Then they would return to the reading school after lunch.[25]

Both Greek and Roman school children were accompanied to school by a slave known as a *paedagogus*. He acted as a kind of male nursemaid whose job was to accompany a student to school and see that he kept out of trouble. Of course, like all custodians, the *paedagogus* often received resentment from his charge, especially when the boy became an adolescent.[26] It is to this custodian, not to a school teacher, that the apostle Paul has compared the law in Galatians 3:24.

The teacher at the *didaskaleion* was properly known as a *grammatistēs*,[27] and his main job was teaching his pupils to read aloud (cf. Acts 8:30)[28] and to write. In all schools, Greek, Roman, and Jewish, children began with the alphabet and learned to recite the names of the letters both forward and backward.[29] Then in Greek and Latin schools the next step was to learn syllables, such as *ba, be, bi, bo, bu, ca, ce,* etc. Next came words of a single syllable. However, the words that the children learned were by no means limited to those in everyday use. Special emphasis was put upon rare and archaic words that tended to be tongue twisters. School vocabularies have been found consisting wholly of proper names, mainly Homeric. There are lists of gods, rivers, months of the year, etc.[30] After learning his word lists, the young student graduated to texts, not simplified primers like the ones in use today, but selections from the very best writers, especially Homer and Euripides, writers whose style would be worthy of later imitation. These selections the children would learn first to read aloud and then to recite from memory.[31]

Along with reading aloud came writing. We must remember that there were no blackboards until the late Empire. Texts had to be copied by hand on wooden boards, wax tablets, pottery fragments known as ostraca, or papyrus. The sooner a student could write, the sooner he could make his own copies. The teacher would have his copy of the necessary texts, and he would want the students to be making their own copies as soon as possible. The elements of writing were learned in the same order as those of reading. First came the letters. The teacher would draw a sample letter and guide the student's hand over it. Quintilian suggests having the student guide his stylus along letters carved into wood.[32] Having learned to write the letters, each student would proceed to syllables and words. At this stage no grammar or composition was taught. The one aim was to teach a student to write well enough to copy his own exercises.

In addition to reading and writing, a child in elementary school would learn some simple arithmetic. At this level arithmetic involved merely counting, a system of using the fingers for calculation, the simplest basic addition, multiplication, and other such matters.[33]

No discussion of the ancient primary school can pass over the question of discipline. While a progressive educator like Quintilian indicated that he disapproved of flogging and preferred that school be made stimulating,[34] he was almost alone in this view. Brutality was the rule. Herodes, writing in the third century B.C. vividly depicts a typical flogging in which the victim is raised to the shoulder by three classmates and beaten with a bull-tail lash.[35] Jewish schools from the beginning were no less severe. The Mishnaic opinion of the second-century authority, Abba Saul, which absolves the teacher who beats a pupil to death,[36] speaks for itself.

From the reading school those students who chose to continue entered grammar school where they studied the classics under a teacher known as a *grammatikós* or *kritikós*. Among the classical authors studied, Homer was preeminent. Next in importance came Euripides, Menander, and Demosthenes. The main Latin writers were Virgil first and then Terence, Cicero, and Horace.[37] This concentration on certain classical works tended to mold a man's thinking for the rest of his life. Sometimes the authors studied in grammar school are reflected in Christian writings. Clement of Alexandria, for example, in his *Exhortation to the Greeks* cited Homer far more than any other pagan author (thirty-three times), with Euripides placing second (nine times).

The study of the classics can be divided into four disciplines *(mérē)*: that pertaining to textual criticism *(diorthōtikón)*, that pertaining to reading aloud *(anagnōstikón)*, that which is exegetical *(exegētikón)*, and that which is evaluative *(kritikón)*.[38] The textual criticism was necessary because the texts were handwritten. Thus, after the students had copied the master's text, that text had to be checked for error.

After textual criticism came reading, which at the grammar school level involved more than merely uttering the correct words. The grammar school student was expected to read with expression.[39] Such a requirement was not an easy one. In the first place, "reading with expression" was understood to mean not only reading to convey the meaning of the text, but also taking into account things like meter and the general classification of a given work, namely, whether it was tragedy, comedy, heroic epic, or some other type. A second difficulty was that ancient manuscripts lacked punctuation and word separation. Reading such a text was almost as difficult for the ancients as it is for us; therefore, the students used to prepare their texts for reading by adding such things as accents and small marks between the words.[40] After the student had learned to read a text properly, as the final step he was expected to memorize it. Then examinations followed in the form of declamation contests which were held either in the classroom or publicly.[41]

The next discipline was exegesis, which involved, first of all, translating a text from classical, literary Greek into the common language of the day. Homeric Greek was so different from the common *(koinē)* Greek of the first century A.D. that it could almost be regarded as a different language. School children used to make vocabulary lists with the literary usages in one column and their *koinē* equivalents in the other.[42] Then came exposition of content and form which often took the form of a catechism. The following example of content exposition was found attached to a page of Dionysius Thrax's famous grammar:

Q. Who are for the Barbarians [i.e., the Trojans]?
A. Ares, Aphrodite, Apollo, Artemis, Leto, Scamander.

Q. Who is king of the Trojans?
A. Priam.
Q. Who is commander?
A. Hector.
Q. Who are advisers?
A. Polydamas and Agenor.
Q. Who are diviners?
A. Helenus and Cassandra.
Q. Who are Heralds?
A. Edaeus; Dolon's father, Eumedes; and likewise Dolon himself.[43]

An example of expounding form can be found in the work of the sixth-century grammarian Priscianus; for, although he writes long after the early Empire, he is following early writers and is giving the kind of exposition recommended by Quintilian.[44] Priscianus begins his exposition of the first line in Virgil's *Aeneid* with the following general statement on its meter:

> The line is uniform in genre, dactylic in species, simple in composition, dissimilar in feet, and in arrangement [dispositio] ends in a two-syllable foot. It is divided by colons into nine parts [caesurae]; by commas into two parts, a *semiquinaria* and a *semiseptenaria;* and by feet into five parts.

Then after digressing for a couple of pages into a discussion of meter in general and dactylic hexameter in particular, Priscianus continues his exposition of the line in the form of questions and answers:

Q. Scan the line.
A. *Arma vi/rumque ca/no Tro/iae qui/primus ab/oris.*
Q. How many parts [caesurae] does it have?
A. Two.
Q. What are they?
A. A *semiquinaria* and a *semiseptenaria.*
Q. How [are they distinguished]?
A. The *semiquinaria* is *arma virumque cano,* and the *semiseptenaria* is *arma virumque cano Troiae.*
Q. How many figures does it have?
A. Ten.
Q. Why?
A. Because it is composed of three dactyls and two spondees.
Q. How many parts of speech does this line have?
A. Nine.
Q. How many nouns?
A. Six: *arma, virum, Troiae, qui, primus,* and *oris.*
Q. How many verbs?
A. One: *cano.*
Q. How many prepositions?
A. One: *ab.*
Q. How many conjunctions?
A. One: *que.*
Q. Discuss each part separately. What part of speech is *arma?*
A. A noun.
Q. Of what kind?

A. Appellative.
Q. Of what gender?
A. Neuter.
Q. Why neuter?
A. Because all nouns which end with an *a* in the plural are unquestionably of the neuter gender. . . .[45]

The fourth and last discipline used in studying the classics was evaluation. Such evaluation was ultimately moral in character. Grammarians believed that from the poets in general and from Homer in particular they could extract a full system of moral values. However, a major problem in any moral evaluation of the classics was that the classics contained much that was immoral. Plutarch suggests that careful study will often indicate a poet's disapproval of an evil action that he is portraying.[46] Another method for treating embarrassing passages was to interpret them allegorically. Thus, some understood the well-known story of the adultery between Venus and Mars as representing movements of the heavenly bodies since Mars in conjunction with Venus portended adultery.[47]

Grammarians did more than teach their students to read and admire the classics; they taught them to write in the classical style. The teaching method described by Quintilian[48] was apparently widespread. First came the strict paraphrasing of a simple fable with careful analysis of each verse. Then would follow a freer paraphrase in which the student might abridge and embellish. Finally, the student would be allowed to compose simple pieces in various forms on given themes or texts. Quintilian suggests as a sample theme, "When Cratus had seen an ignorant boy, he beat his *paedagogus.*"

From the very beginning of a boy's education he was taught to admire the classics and to emulate their style.[49] This emphasis on classical style would, of course, hinder the acceptance of any work which happened to be written in an unclassical style. For this reason Josephus, who spoke Greek with an accent, felt compelled to have his works stylized by experts.[50] How vulgar the New Testament must have sounded to any educated Greek or Roman! Is it any wonder that Tatian must complain about those who reject the Bible because of its style?[51]

A further implication of ancient education for the early church is that, as the church came to acquire educated leaders, these leaders tended to use the classical style. For the unlettered in their congregations such a style must have sounded almost like a foreign language. How could uneducated Christians understand a church father's writings, when read aloud, or even his sermons? This problem, however, can easily be exaggerated. As shown above, literacy in the ancient world was far from uncommon; and a good percentage of Christians

must have received at least primary schooling. In fact, the gap between an educated Christian leader of ancient times and the illiterates
of his flock may not have been appreciatively greater than the gap
between certain modern philosophical theologians and a Christian
with substandard schooling.

The subjects studied in Hellenistic and Roman schools were col-
lectively known as the *encýclios paideía,* a Greek expression corresponding approximately to what we mean by the term "liberal arts."
Aside from reading and composition, which comprised the major
part of the primary and grammar school curriculum, the ancients
differed somewhat on what should be studied. Quintilian is typical.
On the grammar school level he would add mathematics and music
as part of the *encýclios paideía.*[52] In mentioning these subjects, especially music, he is somewhat defensive. They are subjects which he
feels he must justify. As mentioned above, music seems to have been
largely confined to musical theory. Mathematics was divided between
geometry and numbers. Geometry normally followed Euclid and led
into astronomy. Numbers included, not only arithmetic, but aesthetic
properties of numbers, such as perfect numbers and friendly numbers.[53]

Hellenistic schools as the educational institutions of a pagan society were inseparably associated with pagan religion. Not only did
the curriculum center around the pagan classics, which were taught
in classrooms decorated with representations of pagan gods; but also
the students were often expected, and even compelled, to take part
in pagan religious festivals.[54] In view of the religious affiliation of
the pagan schools, one should expect that the Christians would have
avoided them, but such was never the case. Christians attended pagan
schools as long as they lasted. Occasionally there were objections; but
even a rigorist like Tertullian, who was fully aware of the idolatry
implicit in attending school, would only ban Christians from becoming teachers. He specifically allowed that Christians study in the
schools because of what he regarded as the necessity of literary
erudition.[55]

HIGHER EDUCATION

Those who chose to advance beyond secondary school had a choice
among various types of higher education. Young Greeks of good
family commonly entered the *ephēbeia.*[56] Many others chose to study
rhetoric. Somewhat fewer would choose one of the philosophies. A
few would study medicine or law.

Legal specialists were known in the Hellenistic kingdoms,[57] but it
was at Rome that law became a major profession. By the second

century there were legal consulting offices and organized legal teaching at Rome.[58] In the later Empire, however, Beirut became the great center for studying law.

There were several great centers which were famous for their teachers of medicine. They included Alexandria, Cos, Pergamum, Smyrna, Corinth, and Ephesus. At these centers the medical professors were often somewhat organized into what might be regarded as the prototype of a medical faculty. At Ephesus there was a *synédrion* of medical teachers who sponsored public medical competitions each year, a kind of medical Olympics; and one of the competitions seems to have been in surgery.[59] Those physicians who went through grammar school and studied at one of the major medical centers would have had good training and education. A humble apprenticeship, however, was more the rule; and there were no government regulations to prevent apprenticeships as brief as six months.[60] Thus, even if we assume that tradition is correct in depicting Luke as a physician, this title tells us little about his education and training.

The *ephēbeia* was one of the more important institutions for higher education in the world of the early Empire. It had arisen in classical Greece as a means of training young men who were undergoing a kind of compulsory military service. In the Hellenistic age the *ephēbeia* had spread to most municipalities where Greeks comprised a sizable part of the population. In the process it had lost most of its original military character and had become an exclusive municipal finishing school, or junior college, housed in the gymnasium where budding aristocrats could pursue their studies with a major in physical education. Apart from physical education, learning in the *ephēbeia* must have been very superficial indeed. To be sure, lecture courses were given by various grammarians, philosophers, and rhetors on a variety of subjects in order to fill in the gaps of secondary education and round it off. Moreover, the curriculum was supplemented by visiting lecturers, and the *'ephēboi* usually had access to their own library. However, since students usually remained in the *ephēbeia* only a year or two and since they spent much of that time at the palaestra and stadium, it seems unlikely that much serious study was accomplished.[61]

More important was the social significance of the *ephēbeia*. The *ephēbeia* certified that a man was truly Greek in culture and outlook; therefore, it served to guarantee him a privileged position for life. Graduation from the *ephēbeia* was essential for full social and political acceptance. Thus, it is not surprising that at Alexandria in Egypt many Jews considered it worthwhile to enroll their children in the *ephēbeia* in spite of severe opposition by the Greek community, opposition which culminated in the edict of Claudius expelling all Jews from the gymnasia.[62]

Although the *ephēbeía* was a Greek institution, there arose in the West a fairly similar institution known as the *collegia juvenum*. These youth clubs had received their impetus from Augustus and by the end of the second century had spread throughout the whole western Empire. Like the *ephēbeía* these clubs stressed sports, and at Pompeii the *juvenes* owned a gymnasium as well as a *scholia*. Again like the Greek *ephēbeía*, most members came from the leading families in town; and, as the occasional presence of freedmen indicates, a few came from families seeking social advancement.[63]

More extensive education at the highest level usually centered in the study of rhetoric. Writers like Cicero and Quintilian considered normal academic advancement to proceed from reading master to grammarian to rhetor. Students in rhetoric were first introduced to classifications and definitions, a procedure which reflects the ancient tendency to reduce everything to rules and systems. The five steps for speech preparation were defined as invention of ideas, arrangement, style, memorization, and delivery.[64]

Invention of ideas included the gathering of necessary information according to prescribed rules. A good illustration of these rules is a treatise on preparing an encomium by Theon, an Alexandrian rhetor of the second century A.D.[65] Theon lists thirty-six categories under which one should seek material for lauding the subject of an encomium. Then he shows how to expand the material, for example, by making comparisons. He even indicates how to praise subjects who lack excellence in important categories such as citizenship.

The other four steps in speech preparation were all developed as fully as the invention of ideas. The arrangement of the oration proper was usually under five or six headings, each with its own rules.[66] Style included such matters as figures of speech, grammar, rhythm, etc. Even memorization was not without its techniques. As for delivery, this step involved not only voice production and the theory of musical intonation, but also a system of gestures so detailed that it could almost be regarded as a fully developed sign language. In order to express shyness or reserve, for example, Quintilian recommends the following: "With the first four fingers [including the thumb] brought gently to a point, the hand is brought to the vicinity of the mouth or breast and then relaxed in a drooping position and a little forward." [67]

In addition to studying rules of rhetoric, the student also studied and analyzed model passages from the great prose writers for admiration and imitation. Among the Latin writers, Quintilian preferred Cicero and Livy although some of his contemporaries apparently insisted on the older school of Cato and the Gracchi.[68] Of even more importance was the choice of Greek authors. Under Augustus the ten Attic orators from the fifth and fourth centuries B.C. became standard in schools of rhetoric.[69] Of course, with classical Attic as the standard, there was a constant attempt to turn back the clock by rejecting as vulgar the natural developments in the Greek language during the Hellenistic era. Thus each decade brought a wider separation between the language of literature and the language of everyday life.

The next step in the study of rhetoric was the writing of preparatory exercises. Then finally a student was ready for composing full speeches on given subjects. Many topics for classroom orations have been preserved by the elder Seneca. The following is typical:

> When a woman is ravished, she may choose either the ravisher's death or a quiet wedding. A certain man ravished two women in one night. One chose his death; the other, a wedding.[70]

The study of rhetoric involved far more than merely learning the art of public speaking. Since an orator should be able to declaim on any given subject, his education had to include most branches of knowledge. Therefore, in addition to speech composition and delivery, the student of rhetoric spent much of his time in studying philosophy, astronomy, and history, etc. In fact, the study of oratory was the ancient equivalent for earning a degree in liberal arts; it covered the whole *encýclios paideía*.[71]

As in the case of rhetoric, the study of philosophy usually presupposed a secondary education although some sects, such as the Epicureans, were not at all strict on this requirement. More important was the fact that becoming a philosopher demanded a break with ancient culture in general and rhetoric in particular. In this respect the Cynics were extremists. They had dropped out from society, but all sects to some extent expected a kind of conversion on the part of their adherents. This conversion was even expressed by a special philosopher's garb such as Justin Martyr once wore.[72]

Unlike rhetoric, philosophy was not a unified discipline. Each sect had its own tenets, and sectarian rivalry was intense and at times vicious.[73] The would-be philosopher had to choose among the philosophies or else, like Justin,[74] go from one to the other. In a general sense, however, one can describe philosophical teaching as progressing in three stages. First would come some instruction on the history of philosophy beginning with Thales. Then would follow a general course on the sect's own philosophy. Finally would come the study of the sect's classics, especially the writings of the founder. These classics were read and interpreted much as a teacher of rhetoric would read and expound the classics of literature.[75]

One could study philosophy in three ways. First of all, one could listen to various popular, wandering lecturers and preachers. These were usually Cynics or Stoics. The apostle Paul must have appeared to many who heard him as one of these philosophical preachers when he traveled about preaching the gospel (cf. Acts 17:18ff.). Such preachers, of course, were hardly learned professors, and their hearers could hardly claim to have studied philosophy. However, philosophical preaching was important in that it gave even the unlettered a chance to gain some philosophical understanding. Thus, Jews or Christians could have received a smattering of philosophy without ever having received a formal, Hellenistic education. We can never assume, therefore, from an occasional philosophical allusion in a Jewish or Christian writing that its author had ever studied philosophy or belonged to a particular philosophical school.[76]

More formal philosophical instruction, such as instruction in rhetoric, was given by private teachers who established themselves in a center and began to give regular lectures. Such a lecturer was the Stoic philosopher, Epictetus, when after A.D. 89 he was exiled to Nicopolis on the western coast of Greece by the emperor Domitian. Various Christian teachers, such as Justin Martyr, Marcion, and Valentinus, all of whom lectured at Rome, must have appeared to many like private teachers of a new philosophy.

Thirdly, one could study either philosophy or rhetoric in established institutions. The oldest center for such institutions was Athens. Here Plato had founded the Academy about 385 B.C.; Aristotle, the Peripatetic school at the Lyceum in 335 B.C.; Epicurus, his garden in 306 B.C.; and Zeno, the Stoa about 300 B.C. Athens was also the city where Isocrates had founded his famous school of rhetoric about 392 B.C. Almost as important as Athens for higher education was Alexandria. Scholarly study there centered around the great Museum. Ptolemy Soter had originally founded this institution about 280 B.C. as a research foundation. Because of the scholars that it attracted, Alexandria rivaled Athens as an educational center in the first century of the Christian era. In fact, Alexandria even surpassed Athens in branches of learning other than philosophy and rhetoric, and its excellence in astronomy ultimately led the church to turn there for calculating the date of Easter.[77]

A further development in ancient institutions of higher learning began with Emperor Vespasian, who began the practice of establishing imperial professorships. At Rome he inaugurated two chairs, one each for Greek and Latin rhetoric, to be paid for from the imperial treasury. The first appointment for Latin rhetoric was Quintilian. Vespasian's example was followed by Marcus Aurelius who added similar chairs at Athens for the philosophical schools and for rhetoric.[78]

JEWISH EDUCATION

Jewish schools became established at a relatively late date. Secondary schools are known to have existed at the beginning of the second century B.C.,[79] but Jewish primary schools were probably not widespread outside Jerusalem until after the first Jewish revolt (A.D. 66–73)[80] and possibly not until after the Jewish revolt under Hadrian (A.D. 132–135).[81] One reason for the relatively late development of Jewish primary schools was undoubtedly the number of biblical injunctions to children to learn basic matters like Scripture at home from their fathers.[82] Thus at the beginning of the Christian era Jewish boys[83] commonly were receiving at home rudimentary learning which would be necessary for taking part in the religious life of the community and which would be assumed if they entered secondary school.[84]

Since Jewish schools arose sometime after Hellenistic schools had been firmly established throughout the eastern Mediterranean area, one would almost expect to find Hellenistic borrowings in Jewish educational institutions. Various similarities between the two school systems indicate that such borrowing did in fact occur. Moreover, Hellenistic educational patterns affected not only the relatively liberal Jewish communities in the Greco-Roman Diaspora like the community in Rome where synagogue teachers were called *grammatei;*[85] Hellenistic influence also affected, consciously or unconsciously, education in orthodox, Rabbinic circles.[86] One example of such influence from Hellenistic education can be seen in the threefold division of Rabbinic education, which corresponds roughly to the threefold Hellenistic division. Hellenistic influence can also be seen in details such as Rabbinic methods for teaching the alphabet in primary schools and in principles of scriptural interpretation at the higher levels.[87]

The three levels of Rabbinic education are described in the Mishnaic tractate *Avôt* 5:21, where the third-century authority Judah b. Tema began an ideal outline of human life as follows:

> At five years of age [one is ready] for Scripture; at ten, for Mishna; at thirteen for [keeping] the commandments [i.e., at thirteen he is *bar mitsvah* and responsible for his own actions]; at fifteen, for *talmûd;* at eighteen for marriage; at twenty for pursuing [a trade]; . . .

In representing children as having learned Scripture by the age of ten, however, Judah probably was idealizing the actual situation somewhat. In the second century at Usha in Galilee it was decreed that a father ought to show patience with his son learning Torah until the age of twelve.[88] Such a decree would seem to presuppose that it was quite normal for boys to continue learning Scripture until that age.[89]

Jews who took their religion seriously provided for their children to receive at least a basic religious education whether the children attended a primary school or not. This fact is well attested not only in Jewish sources,[90] but also by pagans like the philosopher Seneca.[91] Above the elementary level, however, the number of students rapidly fell away. The situation probably was not much different from that reflected by a medieval source in the following saying: "One thousand study Bible, but only one hundred complete it. One hundred study Mishna, but only ten complete it. Ten study Talmud, but only one reaches rabbinical ordination." [92]

The primary school, known as the *bêt sepher* or *bêt sôpher,* was taught by a teacher who was usually called a *sôpher* or scribe. Originally such a title was reserved for leading scholars, but by New Testament times scribes had become mere manuscript copyists who had sufficient education to teach young boys to read and write.[93] The curriculum was not overly different from Hellenistic reading schools except for the use of the Bible in place of Homer and the pagan classics. Like their Greek and Roman counterparts Jewish scribes began by teaching their pupils the alphabet, which they learned to recite forwards and backwards.[94] After learning the alphabet, the students would proceed directly to Scripture and begin reading Genesis; although after the destruction of the temple, they began with Leviticus.[95] Of course, there could be no study of syllables in a Hebrew school because the language for the most part lacked written vowels. Thus reading became largely a matter of memory. In fact, school children were often asked by their elders to recite the passage which they had learned in school that day.[96]

Apart from the difficulties of teaching children to read a consonantal alphabet, there was the further difficulty of obtaining texts for study because of the many regulations surrounding the copying and handling of Scripture scrolls. For example, it was forbidden to copy Scripture from dictation or to extract isolated sections from biblical books although the latter regulation was avoided by an interpretation which permitted one to copy part of a book provided he intended to finish copying it later.[97]

While it is quite likely that Hebrew was widely spoken in Judea before A.D. 135,[98] most Jews of the ancient world grew up speaking other languages, such as Aramaic or Greek. Therefore, in addition to studying the Hebrew Scriptures, most Jewish school children would have had to memorize a standard translation known as a *Targum.*[99] Beside Scripture reading and *Targum,* elementary school children would also have learned to recite essential parts of the Jewish liturgy such as the *Shema* (originally Deuteronomy 6:4), the *Shemôneh Esreh* (or Eighteen Benedictions), the *Hallēl* (or Psalms 113–118), and the grace after meals. Writing also was probably taught in the elementary schools, at least in rudimentary form. Although there is little direct evidence for the inclusion of writing in the elementary curriculum, some evidence does exist.[100]

The secondary school, commonly known as the *bêt midrash*, was concerned with the study of oral Torah, which is referred to in the New Testament as the traditions of the fathers.[101] We can distinguish two kinds of oral Torah: *midrash*, in which the tradition was arranged in the form of commentaries on Scripture, and *mishnah*, where the tradition was arranged separately under topical headings. In New Testament times oral Torah was probably taught in both forms, but *mishnah* was becoming more and more popular so that Judah b. Tema, referred to earlier, could describe secondary education simply as *mishnah*.[102] Oral Torah, of course, was distinguished by the fact that it was not written down, at least not officially. In the classroom it passed directly from the lips of the teacher to the ears of the student, who committed it to memory.[103]

After a student learned oral Torah, he might be able to study at an academy, such as the one at Jamnia, or attach himself to some great scholar like Yôchanan b. Zakkai.[104] Early Christian tradition represents Jesus as such a scholar-teacher surrounded by disciples although Jesus was not a typical Rabbinic scholar and his disciples had certainly not received the necessary preparation for advanced Rabbinic schooling.[105] At this level students studied advanced scriptural interpretation and *talmûd*. In New Testament times advanced scriptural interpretation involved the application of certain exegetical rules to Scripture in order to search out from the written text various matters explicit in oral Torah.[106] *Talmûd* was a general term and involved advanced juridical learning and discussion.[107]

In two important areas Jewish children received their education outside the Hebrew classroom. These areas were vocational training and Greek studies. In regard to vocational training Jewish practice differed widely from the general culture of the ancient world which regarded manual labor and higher learning as incompatible. Of course, there were no trade schools, but it was considered a father's duty to pass on his vocational skills to his sons. Thus in his ideal outline of human life Judah b. Tema quite naturally included the pursuing of a trade alongside the learning of Scripture, *mishnah*, and *talmûd*.[108]

In regard to Greek learning, the picture is somewhat mixed. Rabbinic literature certainly contains many warnings against the study of Greek wisdom, but there seems to have been no absolute ban in effect. Greek studies were necessary for any communication with the world at large including the Roman government. There is no evidence that Greek ever became part of the regular curriculum in orthodox schools, but it was readily available from Greek teachers apart from Rabbinic schools. In fact some knowledge of Greek language and literature was probably quite common in orthodox, Rabbinic circles until A.D. 132 and certainly until A.D. 70.[109]

We may examine the educational background of the apostle Paul in terms of the Rabbinic school system since he claimed to have been a Pharisee who was brought up speaking Hebrew (Philippians 3:5). Of course, he had had some training in Greek, and he had learned a trade.[110] In fact, the apostle had little patience with anyone who thought labor beneath him.[111] In regard to Paul's training in Rabbinic schools, we have a clue in Galatians 1:14, according to which he said, "I advanced in Judaism beyond many of my own age among my people, so extremely zealous was I for the traditions of my fathers." Surely this statement means that he had at least studied *mishnah* in the *bêt midrash*. Had he progressed even further to the higher level of *talmûd* and the use of exegetical rules? Nowhere does the apostle cite any of these rules by name, but in Rabbinic works these rules were officially used and cited in discussing juridical problems quite unlike anything treated in the Pauline Epistles. However, the apostle's use of Scripture does seem to indicate that he often thinks in terms of Rabbinic exegetical rules although he does not seem overly adept at using them.[112] As a tentative guess, therefore, we might conclude that Paul had finished the step in his education known as *mishnah* and had begun *talmûd*. Such a conclusion would be some justification for assuming that he had studied at the feet of a well-known Rabbinic scholar such as Gamaliel.[113]

NOTES

[1] Edgar B. Castle, *Ancient Education and Today* ("Pelican Books," A 511; Baltimore: Penguin Books, Inc., 1961); William Barclay, *Train Up a Child* (Philadelphia: The Westminster Press, 1959); W. A. Smith, *Ancient Education* (New York: Philosophical Library, Inc., 1955).

[2] Quintilian, *Institutio Oratoria* 1. 1. 24-37. A good selection of school papyri can be found in E. Ziebarth, *Aus der antiken Schule* ("Kleine Texte," 65; Bonn: A. Marcus and E. Weber, 1913). See also O. Guéraud and P. Jouguet, *Un livre d'ècolier du III*° *siècle avant J. C.* ("Publications de la societé royale égyptienne de papyrologie: Textes et documents," II; Cairo: L'institut français d'archéologie orientale, 1938).

[3] Vitruvius Pollio, *De Archectura* 5. 11. For a good interpretation of the Priene gymnasium, see Henri I. Marrou, *A History of Education in Antiquity* (New York: Sheed and Ward, Inc., 1956), pp. 128–130 [pp. 180–183 in the Mentor paperback edition]. See also J. Delorme, *Gymnasion: Étude sur les monuments consacrés à l'éducation en Grèce (des origines à l'Empire romain)* (Paris: E. de Boccard, 1960).

[4] See H. Nettleship, *Lectures and Essays,* Second Series (Oxford: The Clarendon Press, 1895), pp. 163ff.; A. Gwynn, *Roman Education from Cicero to Quintilian*

("Classics in Education," no. 29; New York: Columbia University Teachers College, n. d.) , p. 157.

⁵ W. Dittenberger, *Sylloge Inscriptionum Graecarum*, 3rd ed. (Hildesheim: G. Olms, 1960) , no. 959.

⁶ See Archdale A. King, *Liturgy of the Roman Church* (Milwaukee: Bruce Publishing Company, 1957) , pp. 52ff. King also presents several other pieces of evidence on the importance of Greek in the early Roman church. On the rising importance of Latin in Roman education, see Gwynn, *op. cit.*, pp. 64, 154f.; Marrou, *op. cit.*, pp. 255–264 (pp. 342–357) .

⁷ Quintilian 1. 2.

⁸ *Axiochus* 366E-367A.

⁹ For an excellent summary of Quintilian's work, see Gwynn, *op. cit.*, pp. 180-241.

¹⁰ *Epigrammaton libri* 9. 73. 7.

¹¹ At Telos (Dittenberger, no. 578[9]) girls and boys received the same education. See also Sallust, *Bellum Catilinae* 25:2 and 5; Marrou, *op. cit.*, pp. 103 (148) , 144 (202); W. Jentsch, *Urchristliches Erziehungsdenken: Die Paideia Kyriu im Rahmen der hellenistische-jüdischen Umwelt* ("Beiträge zur Förderung Christlicher Theologie," 45:3; Gütersloh: C. Bertelsmann, 1951) , pp. 50ff., 79.

¹² Sallust 25:2 and 5.

¹³ See below, n. 54.

¹⁴ *Epistulae* 74. 448a.

¹⁵ On other gymnasium officials, see Marrou, *op. cit.*, pp. 110–112 (158–159) ; Martin P. Nilsson, *Die Hellenistische Schule* (München: C. H. Beck, 1955) , pp. 53–59.

¹⁶ See Marrou, *op. cit.*, pp. 127f. (180) ; Nilsson, *op. cit.*, p. 32.

¹⁷ 2 Maccabees 4:9-12.

¹⁸ See Philostratus, *De Gymnastica* 56.

¹⁹ On wrestling and *pankration*, see E. N. Gardiner, "Wrestling," *Journal of Hellenic Studies* 25 (1905) , 14–31, 263–293. On Greek sports generally, see Marrou, *op. cit.*, pp. 116–127 (165–177) .

²⁰ B. P. Grenfell and A. S. Hunt, *The Oxyrhynchus Papyri*, Part III (London: Egypt Exploration Fund [Graeco-Roman Branch], 1903) , pp. 137f., no. 466. The translation of this text is difficult due to the many technical terms used. On the translation of some of these terms, see Gardiner, *op. cit.*, pp. 29, 265, 280–288. Cf. Lucian, *Asinus* 9f.

²¹ See Marrou, *op. cit.*, pp. 102–115 (147–163) , 145–149 (202–206) , 266–268 (360–362) , 301–308 (403–412) : Gwynn, *op. cit.*, pp. 137f., 154, 184. For similar conditions in the later Empire, see A. Cameron, "Roman School Fees," *Classical Review* 79 (1965) , 257f.

²² For Latin children, however, physical training was not at all uncommon. See Quintilian 1. 11. 15.

²³ In some cities, however, there seems to have been more than one municipal gymnasium for the various age groups. See Nilsson, *op. cit.*, pp. 31f.

²⁴ See Menander, *Dis Éxpatón* as translated by Plautus, *Bacchides* 424–434.

²⁵ See Lucian, *Amores* 44f.; *De Parasito* 61; Marrou, *op. cit.*, pp. 397f. (517f.) , n. 15.

²⁶ Menander-Plautus, 422f.

²⁷ See, for example, the pseudo-Platonic *Axiochus* 366D. On other terms used, see Marrou, *op. cit.*, p. 144 (202) . In Latin primary schools the teacher was normally called the *ludi magister*. See Gwynn, *op. cit.*, pp. 84, 92, 189.

²⁸ Silent reading was exceptional. See G. L. Hendricksson, "Ancient Reading," *Classical Journal* 25 (1929/30) , 182–184, who also discusses Acts 8:30. Cf. W. P. Clark, "Ancient Reading," *Classical Journal* 26 (1930/31) , 698–700.

[29] See Ziebarth, *op. cit.*, p. 3. Cf. the Infancy Gospel of Thomas 6:3.

[30] For examples of such lists, see Guéraud and Jouguet, *op. cit.*, pp. 8f.; Ziebarth, *op. cit.*, p. 6.

[31] This method of teaching reading is outlined by Quintilian 1. 1. 24-37. For a modern study and defense of the method, see C. A. Forbes, "Why Roman Johnny Could Read," *Classical Journal* 55 (1959/60), 50-55.

[32] Quintilian 1. 1. 27.

[33] Marrou, *op. cit.*, pp. 157-158 (218-220).

[34] Quintilian 1. 1. 20; 1. 2. 15-29; 1. 3. 6-18, esp. 13f.

[35] Mime III *(Didáskalos)*. Such a beating is the subject of a painting found at Pompeii. See Nilsson, *Abbildung*, 10.

[36] *Makkot* 2:2. Cf. *Sukkah* 29a.

[37] Quintilian 1. 8. 5-11, recommends the following expanded list: Homer and Virgil first; then writers of tragedy, Horace and other lyric poets (with the licentious passages expurged), and Menander for comedy; then finally the early Latin poetic writers, i. e., Ennius, Accius, Pacuvius, Lucilius, Terence, Caecilius *et al.* Cf. Henry J. Cadbury, *The Book of Acts in History* (New York: Harper & Row, Publishers, 1955), p. 39.

[38] *Scholia in Dionysii Thracis Artem Grammaricam*, ed. A. Hilgard ("Grammatici Graeci," 1. 3; Leipzig: B. G. Teubner, 1901), *Prolegomena Vossiana*, p. 10, lines 7-9. Cf. Quintilian 1. 4. 3ff.

[39] Dionysius Thrax, *Ars Grammatica*, ed. B. Uhlig ("Grammatici Graeci," 1. 1; Leipzig: B. Teubner, 1883), 2.

[40] See W. Schubart, *Einführung in die Papyruskunde* (Berlin: Weidmann, 1918), pl. 3, 3.

[41] See Quintilian 1. 2. 23ff.; see also Marrou, *op. cit.*, p. 166 (231).

[42] For examples of school vocabularies on the opening of Homer's *Iliad*, see A. Erman and F. Krebs, *Aus den Papyrus der königlichen Museen* (Berlin: W. Spemann, 1899), pp. 232f.; S. Eitrem and L. Amundsen, *Papyri Osloenses*, Fasc. 2 (Oslo: J. Dybwad, 1931), no. 12, pp. 12-15.

[43] *Papiri Greci e Latini*, vol. 1 (Leipzig: O. Harrassowitz, 1912), no. 19, pp. 42ff.

[44] Quintilian 1. 8. 13ff. Priscian's use of the terms, "colon" and "comma," seems to follow Hephaestion (A.D. 130–169).

[45] *Grammatici Latini*, vol. 3, ed. M. Hertz and H. Keil (Hildesheim: G. Olms, 1961), *Prisciani Partitiones Duodecim Versuum Aeneidos Principalium*, pp. 459-461. For a commentary on this work, see M. Glück, *Priscians Partitiones und ihre Stellung in der spätantiken Schule* (Hildesheim: G. Olms, 1967), pp. 88ff.

[46] *Moralia, Quomodo Adolescens Poetas Audire Debeat* 4 (19A-E).

[47] See Plutarch 4 (19F). See also S. Lieberman, *Hellenism in Jewish Palestine* ("Texts and Studies of JTS," 18; New York: Jewish Theological Seminary of America, 1962), pp. 64ff.

[48] Quintilian 1. 9. 1-6.

[49] Most preferred Attic Greek, but there were exceptions. Cicero, for example, defended his own Rhodian dialect. See *Brutus*, §53, cf. §§284-291. Cf. also *Orator*, §25.

[50] Josephus, *Antiquities* 20. 263; *Apion* 1. 50. On the importance of style in writing history, see Josephus, *Jewish War* 1. 2; *Antiquities* 1. 2.

[51] *Oratio ad Graecos* 26-30. On deficiencies in biblical style, see J. Scherer, ed., *Le commentaire d'Origène sur Rom. III. 5-V. 7* (Cairo: L'institut français d'archéologie orientale, 1957), pp 218f., on Romans 4:23; Jerome, *Ep.* 22. 30. In the fourth century Apollinarius the Elder rewrote the Bible in suitable literary forms, e. g., OT history in Homeric hexameters. See also Socrates 3. 16; Sozomen 5. 18; A. M. H. Jones, "The Social Background of the Struggle between Paganism and Christianity,"

The Conflict between Paganism and Christianity in the Fourth Century, ed. A. Momigliano (Oxford: The Clarendon Press, 1963), pp. 20f.

[52] Quintilian 1. 10. 1-49. It is interesting that Quintilian uses the Greek term and not some Latin equivalent (§ 1). On the *encýclios paideia* generally, see Gwynn, *op. cit.,* pp. 82ff.; Marrou, *op. cit.,* pp. 176-177 (243-245); Jentsch, *op. cit.,* pp. 78f.

[53] On the teaching of mathematics and music, see Marrou, *op. cit.,* pp. 176-185 (243-255).

[54] See Nilsson, *op. cit.,* pp. 61-75; Marrou, *op. cit.,* pp. 116 (164), 136f. (191f.), 389 (507), n. 13. Cf. Jentsch, *op. cit.,* pp. 79f.

[55] *De Idololatria* 10. See also Marrou, *op. cit.,* 321ff. (427ff.)

[56] There is some dispute about the age that one entered the Hellenistic *ephēbeia.* Nilsson, pp. 34-42, argues against Marrou that the term *ephēboi* must refer to boys in their early teens. Marrou, in his review of Nilsson (*L'antiquité classique* 25[1956], 234-240), answers his arguments in detail and also gives some new evidence that *ephēboi* refers to an older age group.

[57] Mikhail Rostovtzeff, *The Social & Economic History of the Hellenistic World* (Oxford: The Clarendon Press, 1964), pp. 1094f.

[58] Aulus Gellius, *Noctes Atticae* (A.D. ca. 123-165) 13. 13. 1; Marrou, *History,* pp. 289ff. (387ff.)

[59] J. Keil, "Artzeinschriften aus Ephesos," *Jahreshefte des oesterreichen archaeologischen Instituts in Wein* 8 (1905), pp. 28f. Unfortunately the inscription pictured here is damaged at the word for surgery. On Hellenistic medicine in general, see Marrou, *op. cit.,* pp. 192-193 (263-266); Rostovtzeff, *op. cit.,* pp. 1088-1094.

[60] See Galen, *Opera quae exstant,* ed. C. G. Kühn (Leipzig: Officina Libaria Car. Cnoblochii, 1821-1833), vol. 1, *De Sectis ad Eos Qui Introducuntur,* pp. 82f., vol. 10, *De Methodo Medendi,* pp. 4f.

[61] On the *ephēbeia* in general, see Nilsson, *Passim;* Marrou, *History,* pp. 105-112 (151-159), 186-189 (256-260).

[62] V. A. Tcherikover and A. Fuks, eds., *Corpus Papyrorum Judaicarum* (Cambridge, Mass.: Harvard University Press, 1957-1964), vol. I, pp. 69-74; vol. II, no. 153, pp. 36-55, especially p. 41, lines 92f. On the general relation of Egyptian Jews to the *ephēbeia,* see *ibid.,* vol. I, pp. 38f., 59, 61, 64, 75f., and the papyri referred to in these sections.

[63] See Marrou, *History,* pp. 299ff. (400ff.) For an excellent study of the *collegia juvenum,* see S. L. Mohler, "The *Juvenes* and Roman Education," *Transactions and Proceedings of the American Philological Association* 68 (1937), 442-479. In comparing the *juvenes* to the *ephēboi,* however, Mohler errs in not allowing for the evolution of the Greek institution in the Hellenistic era.

[64] The general use of these five steps is attested to by Quintilian 3. 3. 1.

[65] L. Spengel, ed., *Rhetores Graeci,* vol. III (Leipzig: B. G. Teubner, 1854), pp. 109-112.

[66] Quintilian 3. 9. 1, says that most authorities prefer five headings although he recognizes that others add to this number. Cicero lists six headings in *De Inventione* 1. 19, and in *De Oratore* 1. 143; but only four in *De Partitione Oratoria* 27.

[67] Quintilian 11. 3. 96. The bulk of Quintilian's *Institutio Oratoria* (i. e., books 3-9) is simply an elaboration of the five steps of speech preparation from invention through delivery.

[68] *Ibid.,* 2. 5. 19-21.

[69] The Attic orators were even models for Latin orations. Cf. Quintilian 12. 10. 27, who feels that some were carrying Attic standards too far. On the ten Attic

orators generally, see R. C. Jebb, *The Attic Orators* (London: The Macmillan Company, 1876), especially the introduction.

[70] *Controversia* V. On classroom declamations generally, see Gwynn, *op. cit.*, pp. 158-173: W. Kroll, "Melete," Pauly-Wissowa, *Realencyclopaedie*, 15, 1 (1931), cols. 496-500; W. Morel, "Sausoria," Pauly-Wissowa, *Realencyclopaedie*, 4 A, 1 (1931), cols. 469-471.

[71] The first book of Cicero's *De Oratore* is largely a discussion of the importance of a general education for oratory.

[72] *Dialogus* 1; Eusebius, *Ecclesiastical History* 4. 11. 8.

[73] See Tatian, *Oratio ad Graecos* 25.

[74] *Dialogus* 2f.

[75] See Marrou, *History*, pp. 208ff. (284ff.).

[76] One example of such occasional philosophical allusions may be the various ethical lists of virtues and vices found in the New Testament, but such lists may not have any immediate philosophical origin. See A. Deissmann, *Light from the Ancient East*, trans. L. R. M. Stranchan (New York: Hodder and Stoughton, 1909), pp. 319-322; S. Wibbing, *Die Tugend- und Lasterkataloge im Neuen Testament* ("Beihefte zur ZNW," 25; Berlin: Töpelmann, 1959); A. Vögtle, *Die Tugend- und Lasterkataloge im Neuen Testament* ("NT Abhandlungen," XVI, 4/5; Münster Westfalen: Aschendorffsche Verlagsbuchhandlung, 1936).

[77] The right of the Alexandrian Church to determine the date of Easter each year was probably accepted at Nicaea on the basis of Alexandrian scientific superiority. See Cyril of Alexandria, *Ep. (Prologus)* 87, §2 (Migne, *PG*, vol. 77, col. 385).

[78] Dio Cassius 72. 31. 3.

[79] Ecclesiasticus 51:23. In the Hebrew version the school mentioned here is called a *bêt midrash*. See also S. Zeitlin, "The Temple and Worship," *Jewish Quarterly Review* 51 (1960/61), 238f.

[80] See E. Ebner, *Elementary Education in Ancient Israel* (New York: Bloch Publishing Co., Inc., 1956), pp. 38-50, especially pp. 48ff.

[81] N. Morris, *The Jewish School* (New York: Jewish Education Committee, 1937), pp. 14-23, especially pp. 21f.

[82] Deuteronomy 4:9; 6:7; 11:19.

[83] Jewish girls did not attend school in orthodox circles. See Morris, *op. cit.*, pp. 24-34; N. Drazin, *History of Jewish Education from 515 B. C. E. to 220 C. E.* ("Johns Hopkins Univ. Studies in Education," no. 29; Baltimore: The Johns Hopkins Press, 1940), pp. 117-133.

[84] See 4 Maccabees 18:10ff.

[85] See H. J. Leon, *The Jews of Ancient Rome* ("Morris Loeb Series," 5; Philadelphia: Jewish Publication Society, 1960), pp. 183-186. Unfortunately Leon misses the significance of this reference because he sees the scribe as the scholar that he once was rather than as the schoolmaster that he had become in New Testament times. See below, n. 94.

[86] See Morris, *op. cit.*, pp. 29f., 27f., 37-41, 72f. On the differences between Rabbinic and Hellenistic education, see Drazin, *op. cit.*, pp. 137-143. A basic difference in the matter of curriculum would be the absence of physical training and music in Rabbinic education.

[87] See Lieberman, *op. cit.* pp. 47-82.

[88] *Ketûrôt*, 50a, as interpreted by Rashi.

[89] See Ebner, *op. cit.*, pp. 70f.

[90] E.g., *yBerakhôt*, at the end of the tractate; Josephus, *Against Apion*, 1. 60; 2. 176f.; Philo, *De Legatione ad Gaium* 31. (§210).

[91] Quoted in Augustine, *De Civitate Dei* 6. 11.

[92] *Vayyiqra Rabbah* 2:1.

[93] B. Gerhardsson, *Memory and Manuscript* ("Acta Seminarii Neotestamentici Upsaliensis," 22; Lund: C. W. K. Gleerup, 1961), pp. 44f., 60; Ebner, *op. cit.,* pp. 51-60.

[94] *Shabbat,* 31a; Ebner, *op. cit.,* pp. 75f.

[95] See *Avôt deRabbi Natan* 6:2 (20b); *Sôpherîm* 5:9 (37a); Ebner, *op. cit.,* pp. 77-79.

[96] *Chagîgah* 15a; *Gittîn* 56a, 68a, *Chûllin* 95b; Ebner, *op. cit.,* pp. 79f.; Gerhardsson, *op. cit.,* p. 64.

[97] *Sôpherîm* 5:9 (37a); Ebner, *op. cit.,* pp. 67f.

[98] See M. H. Segal, *A Grammar of Mishnaic Hebrew,* (Oxford: The Clarendon Press, 1958), pp. 1-20.

[99] Ebner, *op. cit.,* p. 80; Gerhardsson, *op. cit.,* p. 61.

[100] *YTaanît* 4:8 (69a); *TShabbat* 11(12):17; *Shir ha-Shîrîm Rabbah* 1:15. Cf. *Berēshît Rabbah* 1:5.

[101] Galatians 1:14. Cf. Mark 7:3, 8f., 13, and the parallels in Matthew 15.

[102] See also the saying of R. Hôshaya (c. A.D. 225): "*Bêt Sepher* for Scripture and *bêt talmûd* (= *bêt midrash*) for *mishnah*" (*yMegillah,* 3:1 [73d],/*yKetûbôt,* 13:1 [35c]).

[103] See Gerhardsson, *op. cit.,* p. 115; H. L. Strack, *Introduction to the Talmud and Midrash* (Philadelphia: Jewish Publication Society, 1945), pp. 12-20, especially p. 17.

[104] On the disciples of Yôchanan b. Zakkai, see J. Neusner, *A Life of Rabban Yohanan ben Zakkai* ("Studia Post-Biblica," vol. 6; Leiden: E. J. Brill, 1962), pp. 64, 71-80. On academies, see L Ginzberg, *Students Scholars and Saints* (Philadelphia: Jewish Publication Society, 1928), pp. 36f., 48ff.; Drazin, *op. cit.,* pp. 49-53.

[105] See W. D. Davies, *The Setting of the Sermon on the Mount* (New York: Cambridge University Press, 1964), pp. 418f.

[106] On Rabbinic exegetical rules, see J. W. Doeve, *Jewish Hermeneutics in the Synoptic Gospels and Acts* (Assen: Van Gorcum, 1954).

[107] On advanced Rabbinic education generally, see Drazin, *op. cit.,* pp. 43-99.

[108] See Morris, *op. cit.,* pp. 179-200.

[109] See Lieberman, *Greek in Jewish Palestine* (New York: Philipp Feldheim, 1965), *passim; idem, Hellenism,* pp. 100-114; Ebner, *op. cit.,* pp. 84ff.; Morris, *op. cit.,* 72-77.

[110] See 1 Corinthians 4:12; 9:3ff.; 1 Thessalonians 2:9; 2 Thessalonians 3:8. Cf. Acts 18:3, according to which Paul was a tentmaker.

[111] See 2 Thessalonians 3:10.

[112] E.g., note how in the Old Testament texts cited in Galatians 3:6ff. various pairs of quotations tend to have the same key word or root in common.

[113] Cf. Acts 22:3.

FOR ADVANCED READING

Drazin, N. H., *History of Jewish Education from 515 B.C.E. to 220 C.E.* (Johns Hopkins University Studies in Education, no. 29) Baltimore: The Johns Hopkins Press, 1940.
    One of the better surveys on the subject in English.

Ebner, E., *Elementary Education in Ancient Israel during the Taanaitic Period (10-220 C.E.)* New York: Bloch Publishing Company, Inc., 1956.
    A detailed, scholarly study.

Gehardsson, B., *Memory and Manuscript.* ("Acta Seminarii Neotestamentici Upsaliensis, XXII) Lund: Gleerup, 1961.

Chapters four and seven contain a short but good study of Jewish schools in late Taanaitic and Amoraic times.

Marrou, Henri I., *A History of Education in Antiquity.* Translated by George Lamb. New York: Sheed and Ward, Inc., 1956. This translation is also available as a Mentor paperback (MQ552) with different pagination.

Marrou's work is the best English study of Greco-Roman education published in recent years. A more recent French edition, revised and enlarged (Paris: Éditions du Seuil, 1965), is probably the best and most complete work on the subject in any language.

Morris, Nathan, *The Jewish School.* New York: Bloch Publishing Co., Inc., 1937.

A good survey, but not as full as his later work in Hebrew, *A History of Jewish Education, Book I: From the Earliest Times to the End of the Talmudic Period* (Tel Aviv: Omanuth, 1960).

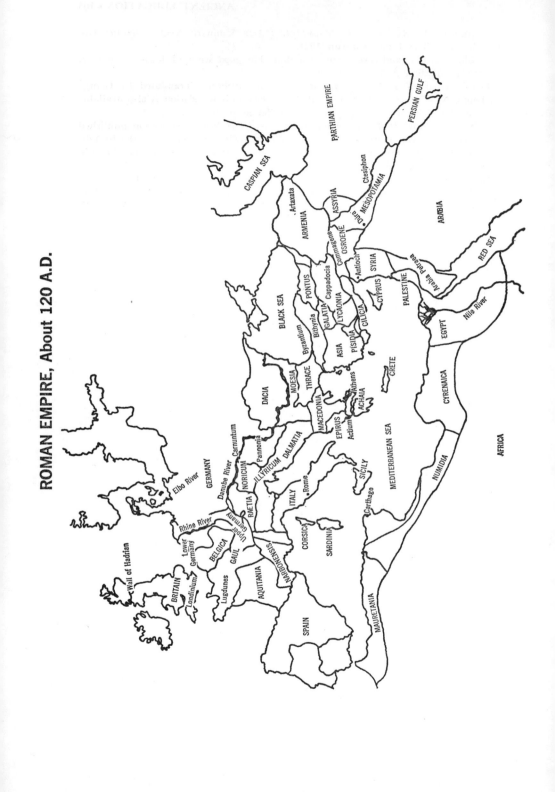

ROMAN EMPIRE, About 120 A.D.

John J. O'Rourke

7
Roman Law and the Early Church

The Roman Empire was the realm in which Jesus lived, died, and was proclaimed as risen Lord. Within that Empire most of the first Christian communities developed even though Christian preachers were certainly active beyond its political boundaries before the middle of the second century A.D.[1] Thus, Christianity began and developed amid peoples who were subject to what in a broad sense can be called Roman Law. This law had its effect, not only on the developing Christian church, but also on the one who was the center of its preaching. Jesus Christ was sentenced before a Roman tribunal that imposed upon him a typical Roman punishment, death by crucifixion.

INTRODUCTION TO ROMAN LAW

Roman Law is a general term describing what is actually a plurality of legal systems. Most of this legal complex can be roughly divided under two main headings: Italian law *(Ius Italicum)* and provincial law. Italian law, itself a conglomeration of various legal systems, was in force in Italy and in certain privileged colonies *(coloniae)* of Roman citizens outside Italy. Provincial law, as its name implies, concerned the peoples in subject territories although Roman citizens in these territories were largely subject to Roman Law as they would have been in Italy itself. Moreover, provincial law differed considerably from place to place, and in Egypt the legal situation was especially unlike that which existed elsewhere. In addition to provincial law and Italian law one might also distinguish Latin law *(Ius Latinum* or *Ius Latii)* although it is possible to consider Latin law as a subdivision of Italian law. Latin law applied to certain groups who enjoyed some, but not all, rights of Roman citizenship. These groups included the inhabitants of certain regions in the West as well as certain classes of freed slaves (or freedmen) in both Italy and the colonies. These latter originated with the *Lex Junia Norbana* of A.D. 19 and were known as Junian Latins *(Latini Juniani)*. They lacked the rights of suffrage and intermarriage with Roman citizens as well as the rights of receiving legacies or making wills. Nevertheless, they did possess the rights guaranteed under commercial law *(ius commercii)*.[2]

Roman history falls into three major eras according to the three successive modes of government that came to prevail. These eras are those of the Monarchy, the Republic, and the Empire. Roman legal history follows these divisions as the various legal institutions adapted themselves to the type of government in power. Thus the first period of legal history was the era of the monarchy from which later Roman Law inherited the concept of the *imperium,* i.e., the undefined royal power of the king that became the basis of authority for the leading magistrates of republican and imperial times. The legal history of the republican era is difficult to subdivide into smaller units. There is no obvious turning point. However, by the second century B.C. Roman Law had developed from its primitive beginnings into a system with the sophistication necessary for a people ruling the world.

The legal history of the Empire is commonly divided into three eras. The first is the classical period which extends from the ascension of Augustus to the death of the emperor Alexander Severus in A.D. 235. The second is the period known as post-classical which extends up to the ascension of the emperor Justinian, with his actual reign (527–565) comprising the third period during which Roman Law received its definitive codification. The first part of the classical period, therefore, is of the greatest interest to the student of Christian origins. Much of what we know about early classical Roman Law comes from the second-century jurist Gaius. His principal work, *Institutionum Commentarii Quattuor,* represents what in modern terminology would be called an introduction to Roman Law.[3] Unfortunately, however, during the first century of the Empire the legal situation was constantly changing. Therefore, the *Institutes* of Gaius may not always represent accurately the legal situation under a given emperor from Augustus through Hadrian.

With his military victory at Actium in 31 B.C. Augustus became the *de facto* dictator of the whole Roman Empire although he was careful to avoid the title of "dictator" which had last been conferred on Julius Caesar and which was never to be conferred again in Roman history. Four years later Augustus formally renounced his dictatorial powers and publicly proclaimed, "I have transferred the republic from my power to the authority of the Senate and People of Rome." [4] As his proclamation suggests, Augustus did indeed restore the old republican forms of government, but enough of these forms were concentrated in his hands and in the hands of his successors to give them total control of the government.

The forms of republican government which became the basis of imperial authority were proconsular authority *(imperium proconsulare)*, tribunician power *(tribunicia potestas)*, and a number of lesser powers, which in the aggregate were almost equally important. Proconsular authority, i.e., the authority of a provincial governor, gave the emperor ultimate power in the Roman provinces including the command of the various armies stationed there, and this authority was regularly renewed for him during his reign. Tribunician power gave him the necessary authority for convening the Senate and the popular assemblies as well as the right to veto the acts of any other magistrate. This power also protected his person, since those holding the office of tribune were protected by special right from attack or indignity. However, Augustus was not eligible for the office of tribune. Augustus was an aristocrat (or patrician), and tribunes were required to be from the common people (or plebeians) since their function had been to protect the plebeians from patrician abuses. Therefore the emperor satisfied himself with tribunician power apart from the office. Among the minor powers conferred upon Augustus were the rights to declare war and conclude peace, to present proposals to the Senate by letter rather than in person, and to "recommend" candidates for the more important magistracies. Thus the early Roman emperors did not immediately appear to have substituted the rule of one man for republican government. Actually no new office of emperor was really established, and as a result there developed no established legal basis for selecting an emperor.[5] The office of emperor was always in some sense an extraordinary one; and the emperor was simply the first citizen *(princeps)* who happened to hold various republican powers simultaneously, powers which enabled him to rule the Empire as he saw fit.

The Senate continued to function, and its prestige even increased. Its actual power, however, suffered a gradual erosion. For example, the Senate still exercised control over certain provinces; but these provinces were only those assigned to it by the emperor, who chose to exercise a more direct control over provinces of military importance. The Senate still administered the traditional republican treasury *(aerarium)*, but Augustus established a new imperial treasury *(fiscus)* which soon was receiving the bulk of the revenues, including tax revenues from senatorial provinces.

Most of the various republican magistrates continued to function, but their activities became mainly nonpolitical. The two consuls, who in republican times shared the executive power of the state, were still regarded as holding the highest titular office; and indeed they continued to exercise full power whenever there was no emperor. Praetors continued to be appointed in numbers varying from ten to eighteen. The urban praetor at Rome was the chief magistrate for civil suits between citizens. Other praetors presided over the various criminal courts known as *quaestiones perpetuae*.

THE IMPERIAL CIVIL SERVICE

The far-reaching powers of the emperor naturally involved far-reaching responsibilities. To manage his responsibilities, he needed various assistants responsible directly to him. This need led to the development of the imperial civil service. For the first time in Roman history a trained and paid group of professionals were active in government. Since wealthy Roman families commonly placed their freedmen and even their slaves in executive positions to administrate their vast holdings, the natural place for an emperor to seek needed assistants was from among his own household staff. Thus the early emperors came to use a growing number of freedmen to fill responsible government positions, and under Claudius the *de facto* governors of the Empire were these freed slaves. For example, Pellas, the chief aide to Claudius, and his brother, Antonius Felix, governor of Judea at the time of Paul's arrest (Acts 24:1ff.), were men of this class. Certain posts, however, were reserved for senators or for those belonging to the equestrian order, a class of wealthy citizens second only to men of senatorial rank. Moreover, after Claudius, various reforms by Hadrian and other emperors insured that the more influential posts formerly held by freedmen were to be reserved for equestrians.

Imperial appointments from the senatorial class included pro-praetorian legates *(legati Caesaris pro praetore)* and the urban prefect *(praefectus urbi)*. Propraetorian legates normally governed imperial provinces although the government of lesser provinces, such as Judea and Sardinia, was commonly entrusted to officials from the equestrian class. However, before Claudius made Felix governor of Judea, he scandalized Rome by making him an equestrian.[6] The urban prefect was originally merely an occasional delegate appointed to govern the capital during an emperor's absence, but during the reign of Tiberius he became a permanent officer who was responsible for maintaining order in the city. To discharge this responsibility, he had at his command the urban cohorts, a police force numbering four to six thousand men.

The only significant military force in Italy was the emperor's personal bodyguard known as the Praetorian Guard *(Cohors Praetoria)*, and the commander of this powerful force was the praetorian prefect (*praefectus praetorio*). So influential was this official that he was considered a potential rival to the emperor himself. Thus the office of praetorian prefect was regularly filled with equestrians instead of senators since only senators might become emperor, and at times it was jointly held by as many as three men. Among the duties of this prefect as commandant of the Praetorian Guard was probably the supervision of prisoners arriving at Rome from the provinces. However, although the Western Text of Acts 28:16 mentions that Paul was handed over to the military commander (*stratopedarchos*), the official in question was more likely some subordinate officer, possibly the *princeps castrorum*, rather than the praetorian prefect himself.[7] Two other important equestrian officers in the imperial civil service were the *praefectus annonae* and the *praefectus vigilum*. The first was responsible for providing grain in Rome at a reasonable price. The second was the Roman fire chief. He headed a department of over seven thousand men which Augustus had established in A.D. 6. This prefecture soon increased considerably in importance and came to include jurisdiction in minor criminal cases. There were also several prefects of lesser importance. Their number included officers in the imperial postal system (*praefecti vehiculorum*) and those in charge of aiding poor children out of public funds (*praefecti alimentarii*).

In Roman Law *procurator* was a technical term designating a legal agent entrusted with the management of property. Thus an imperial *procurator* was originally an official who managed a portion of the emperor's property; but, since the line between imperial property and state property was not clearly drawn, imperial *procuratores* were in reality public officials. In time there developed a whole hierarchy of *procuratores*, the more important of whom were equestrians. *Procuratores* commonly supervised financial matters. *Procuratores* employed at Rome were under a chief *procurator* (*procurator a rationibus*), who was in effect the Empire's minister of finance. Others collected taxes in the various provinces where they were empowered to act independently of the governor. Even senatorial provinces had *procuratores* to represent the interests of the new imperial treasury (*fiscus*). In addition to designating an officer entrusted with financial matters, the title *procurator* often denoted other officials. For example, from the time of Claudius it was applied to equestrian governors who administered any imperial provinces not governed by a propraetorial legate of senatorial rank. Under earlier emperors, however, these equestrian governors had been called prefects. Since Judea was governed by equestrians, Felix (Acts 23:24–24:27) and Festus (Acts 24:27–26:32) were known as *procuratores;* but the pre-Claudian Pontius Pilate was a prefect.[8]

Two other classes of imperial officials were members of the emperor's council *(concilium)* and the various imperial secretaries. Two of the more important secretaries were responsible respectively for dealing with the mass of imperial correspondence and for processing the endless petitions addressed to the emperor. Since the petitions often included requests for clarification on points of law, the petitions' secretary was at times a lawyer of some distinction. The imperial council grew out of a standing advisory council of magistrates and senators which assisted Augustus during the latter part of his Principate. His successor Tiberius also made use of a standing council, but later emperors preferred to appoint their advisers *ad hoc.* However, a standing imperial council was retained to supply technical assistance on legal matters.

TYPES OF LEGISLATIVE AUTHORITIES UNDER ITALIAN LAW

In the early Empire legislative actions came from several sources. As in the Republic, laws (in the technical sense of *leges)* could only be passed by the citizens of Rome gathered in official assembly. Other forms of legislative authority, developed in republican times, included magisterial edicts, legal interpretations by jurists, and practices sanctioned by custom. New imperial legislative actions were senatorial resolutions *(senatus consulta)* and the various categories of imperial decrees *(constitutiones principum).*

The Roman popular assemblies were of two kinds: those including all citizens, who voted either according to wealth *(comitia centuriata)* or according to tribe *(comitia tributa),* and the assembly which excluded the patrician upper class from its membership *(concilium plebis).* The legislative functions of these assemblies declined rapidly during the first century, and after the *lex agraria* of A.D. 97 they ceased passing laws. Outside of Rome other Italian municipalities had popular assemblies. Under Augustus they exercised a significant voice in local affairs, but like the Roman assemblies their powers had largely evaporated by the end of the first century.

Magisterial edicts developed from the fact that a Roman magistrate originally possessed considerable freedom in the exercise of his *imperium.* Each magistrate, therefore, when he took office, customarily issued an edict informing the people how he intended to administer the law. In time these edicts became set by custom so that a new magistrate would adopt the edict of his predecessors with few, if any, changes. Thus, from these edicts, especially the edicts of the urban praetor, there arose a body of magisterial law known as the *ius honorarium.* Under the Empire the right of magistrates to alter the edicts on their own authority gradually eroded and finally ended under Hadrian.

Juridic interpretations of law were known as *responsa prudentium*. They generally took the form of expert opinions rendered by noted jurists for given cases. Such opinions, while not legally binding, were in practice generally regarded as decisive. The authority of a *responsum* was not unlike the authority given to precedents in English and American courts, and the various *responsa* gradually became a legal code *(ius respondendi)*. The emperors did not curtail the authority of the jurists in giving *responsa* but rather increased it. Augustus did, however, initiate a certain indirect imperial control over the jurists by giving to certain of them the right to issue *responsa* with imperial authority.

In republican times the Senate exercised great influence on legislation although it could not enact legislation itself. One source of senatorial influence was the Senate's right to guide a magistrate in the use of his edict. Under the Empire the Senate assumed more and more magisterial guidance. Thus by controlling the magistrates who applied and modified the *ius honorarium,* the Senate exercised indirect legislative power. However, while the Senate was exercising more power, it was also becoming more subordinate to the power of the emperor; and in time the Senate merely passed what the emperor had proposed.

Imperial *constitutiones* were various legal actions by an emperor which included edicts, decrees, and *rescripta*. Imperial edicts were similar to the edicts of lesser magistrates. Unlike other magistrates, however, the emperor possessed almost unlimited jurisdiction and remained in office for life. Thus imperial edicts were often quite broad in scope; and they remained in force, not only during an emperor's lifetime, but even after his death until they were changed or abrogated. Imperial decrees were decisions in civil or criminal trials which were held before the emperor's tribunal either in the first instance or on appeal. *Rescripta* were written responses from the emperor on specific matters. They were also called either *epistulae,* when they consisted of letters in answer to requests from officials and public bodies, or *subscriptiones,* when they dealt with the petitions of private individuals.

There is some question concerning the constitutional basis for the emperor's legislative power. Later jurists assumed that the emperor could actually legislate because of his tribunician power, but the law which granted this power to Augustus did not provide for such an assumption. In fact, the growth of imperial legislative authority appears to have been gradual, and the first emperors generally achieved their legislative ends through action of the Senate.

JUDICIAL PROCEDURE UNDER ITALIAN LAW

Roman civil actions during the late Republic took place in two distinct stages involving two kinds of proceedings. The first took place before a magistrate, such as one of the praetors at Rome. In this procedure, which was referred to as being *in jure,* the plaintiff brought the defendant into court. Then the parties drew up a formula setting the ground rules for the second part of the trial which was *apud iudicem.* The formula generally included an exact statement of the matter in dispute, a clause limiting the scope of the action, and more or less precise directions about the consequences if the judge found for the plaintiff. In addition the defendant might add an exception directing the judge not to find for the plaintiff even if his charge proved to be true when certain circumstances were shown to have prevailed, and after such an exception the plaintiff might add a further condition of his own *(replicatio).* Another matter necessarily decided at the proceedings *in jure* was selecting the judge *(iudex)* before whom the trial *apud iudicem* would take place. This judge needed no special office or training, but his authority was limited, for he had to decide the case according to the formula agreed upon *in jure.* He listened to the pleadings, assessed the evidence, and rendered a judgment.

Occasionally the proceedings *in jure* followed a more ancient procedure known as *legis actio.* This type of action used prescribed oral forms instead of the usual agreed-upon written formulae and required the losing party to forfeit a sum of money *(sacramentum)* to the state. The trial *apud iudicem* usually proceeded normally, except for the fact the parties sometimes could choose to be tried before a group of judges selected from special panels instead of before a single judge.

Under the early Empire a new type of civil action found its place beside the older procedures. This new system was commonly known as *cognitio extra ordinem.* Under *cognitio extra ordinem* the emperor or one of his officials used this administrative authority to cut through the formalities inherent in normal civil actions. Now an authorized official could initiate legal action by issuing a summons instead of waiting for a plaintiff to bring the defendant before him. No longer was there any need to wait for the parties involved to agree upon a formula and a judge. The official could force them into a two-stage trial with the second stage before a judge of his own appointing. More commonly he chose to abandon the two-stage procedure and either appoint someone to conduct both parts of the trial or hear the whole case himself. Along with *cognitio extra ordinem* came the right of appeal *(appellatio).* In republican times there had been no appeal from the judgment of a *iudex.* Under the new system, however, one might appeal from the original decision of an official to have his case brought before a higher magistrate.

In the last century of the Republic and during the early Empire there existed special criminal courts known as *quaestiones perpetuae.* Each court *(quaestio)* was responsible for trying only one category of offense. Thus, for example, Augustus created a *quaestio de adulteriis* for dealing with sexual offenses. In such a court a criminal faced a judge with a council of advisers. The advisers reached their decision by majority vote, and that decision was binding upon the judge. These *quaestiones* were not allowed to deal with crime inquisitorially, i.e., they were not allowed to initiate investigations and to make use of any means at their disposal. Rather they had to await an accusation from an injured party before accepting a case.

The *quaestiones* had several deficiencies. For some crimes, such as theft and fraud, no *quaestiones* existed. Moreover, these courts sat only in Rome, and it was impracticable to bring all citizens accused of serious crime to Rome for trial. Therefore, under the early Empire there arose a new system in which the emperor and various other magistrates used their administrative powers to decide criminal cases either in the first instance or on appeal. Since this procedure was separate from what had been ordinary process of law, it was referred to as being *extra ordinem.* The emperor Augustus devoted much time to hearing cases *extra ordinem,* but many of his successors delegated their judicial role to others. In a trial *extra ordinem* there were no limitations placed upon a magistrate in arriving at his knowledge *(cognitio)* of the crime, but this lack of restriction was rarely misused. Apart from the regular torture of slave witnesses, inquisitorial methods were generally reserved for cases involving treason.

In deciding cases *extra ordinem,* the emperor's court was normally supreme, but the consuls, with the Senate as a body of advisers, comprised an alternate high court, which was the usual forum for hearing charges of treason involving members of the upper classes. However, because of the emperor's influence in the Senate, this tribunal also was subject to him. Technically the decisions of the senatorial court, like those of the emperor and his magistrates, were administrative ones[9] and therefore not a source of law; yet, in practice they were such a source since these decisions showed what the authorities were willing to tolerate.

The penalty for treason was commonly death either by execution or by forced suicide. The latter was preferable since the condemned man's property still passed on to his heirs, whereas the property of one executed went to the state. Punishments imposed by the various *quaestiones perpetuae* rarely resulted in actual execution. The usual punishment which a *quaestio* would inflict upon members of the upper classes was banishment *(relegatio)* which, from the time of Tiberius, might involve deportation *(deportatio)* to an island or oasis along with forfeiture of property and citizenship. A common punishment inflicted upon members of the lower classes from the time of Augustus was condemnation to forced labor which, if for life, brought loss of citizenship. Another punishment was condemnation to become a gladiator, which in practice was equivalent to a death sentence. Capital punishment usually took the form of decapitation, but for the lower classes capital punishment could take the more severe forms of crucifixion, burning, and being thrown to the beasts in the circus. Imprisonment and confining with chains were used as methods of assuring that a person would appear for trial, as in the case of Paul awaiting trial in the court of the emperor (Acts 28:19f.), but neither method of confinement was used as a legal penalty.

LAW IN THE PROVINCES

Laws and legal customs of provincial peoples generally remained in force save insofar as they might prove embarrassing to Roman rule. For example, Roman citizens were not subject to local laws except where specifically provided for by Roman authorities. Also local, non-Roman officials may well have lacked the power to impose the death penalty except in cases which were clearly exceptional. Thus Jewish authorities were allowed to execute on the spot any non-Jew entering the inner court of the Jerusalem Temple,[10] and a similar right was granted the guardian of the sanctuary of Eleusis with regard to those who had not been initiated into that cult.[11] However, any restrictions on imposing capital penalties may simply have depended upon the whim of the Roman governor rather than on any definite general policy in view of the fact that governors enjoyed practically absolute power except where limited by imperial mandate. A governor's power even included the *ius gladii,* i.e., the authority to execute Roman citizens who were members of the armed forces, although this particular right he could not delegate to others. In regard to Roman citizens who were civilians, whether a provincial governor had the authority to execute them for capital crimes is disputed, although there is evidence that by the time of Nero, at least, some governors did possess this power. In view of the general nature of the authority exercised by Roman governors, it may well be that the famous dispute about the rights of the Jewish Sanhedrin to execute criminals in the time of Jesus[12] cannot be resolved by adducing examples of presumed exercise of that power at other times and places during the first century. The rights of the Sanhedrin at the time of the crucifixion would have depended more upon the policy of Pontius Pilate, the governor, than upon any general policy practiced throughout the Roman Empire.

In ruling a province a governor generally followed the emperor's example in choosing a council of advisers to assist him. In conducting trials also he commonly followed the procedure of Roman trials that were conducted *extra ordinem*. A charge was made. The defendant presented his case against the accusers after they had adduced their evidence before the governor and his council. Then, the governor consulted with these advisers and rendered whatever verdict he thought proper. Brief examples of this process are the trials of Paul before Felix (Acts 24) and before Festus (Acts 25:14-21; cf. 26:30-32) .

Subject peoples enjoyed no right of appeal from a governor's decision unless this privilege had been specially granted. However, there was at least one general exception. From the time of the *Lex Calpurnia* (149 B.C.) , provincials had had the right to appear at Rome and accuse a governor of extortion, and the fifth edict of Cyrene (4 B.C.)[13] established two possible procedures for doing so. They might bring suit to recover the extorted moneys, or they could bring a capital charge against a governor. Another possible exception to the finality of a provincial governor's decision lay with the emperor who could receive any appeal, even an appeal from a person with no right to make one.

Scattered throughout the provinces were colonies *(coloniae)* which enjoyed the rights of an Italian municipality. In theory they were inhabited by veterans from the army, but others lived in them as well. Several colonies are mentioned in the New Testament as being of some importance in the activity of the apostles, in particular of Paul: Philippi, Corinth, Antioch, Iconium, Lystra, and Troas. In the first century A.D., the local magistrates in such colonies were called *duoviri iuri dicundo.* These officials had formerly been called *praetores,* the Greek equivalent of which was *stratēgoí;* and it is by this term that Acts 16:22 identifies the magistrates of Philippi, apparently because the author knew of no other Greek equivalent for *duoviri iuri dicundo.*[14] There is some doubt concerning the authority of these magistrates to inflict corporal punishment such as was meted out to Paul at Philippi (Acts 16:22f.) However, the fact that each magistrate was attended by two *lictores,* who carried rods symbolizing judicial beatings (cf. 2 Corinthians 11:25) , suggests that *duoviri* were permitted to impose minor punishments, although their authority to do so upon Roman citizens was probably limited (cf. Acts 16:38) . The usual method for assuring good order was the threat of imposing fines or of seizing property, and at times a peace bond was required from potential troublemakers (cf. Acts 17:9) . Whether or not in the first century A.D. these local authorities also possessed a power similar to a provincial governor's power to expel undesirable persons from his jurisdiction (cf. Acts 16:35-39) is uncertain.[15]

Not all territories conquered by Rome became provinces in the Empire. Some retained a semi-independence and remained under nominal internal control of native kings. Judea was such a satellite state until A.D. 6 and again from A.D. 38–44. However, Rome could assume control at will and did so in Judea in A.D. 6 and again in A.D. 44. The rights of associated or allied kings who ruled these semi-independent states were only those that Rome chose to allow, and such rulers were always subject to demands from Rome.

ROMAN CITIZENSHIP

Roman citizenship was obtained in various ways. It was, of course, granted at birth to children of true Roman marriages, i.e., those marriages contracted between two persons who had a legal right to marriage (iustae nuptiae or iustum matrimonium). It was also granted to the children of a Roman woman by a slave or an unknown father. Furthermore, slaves manumitted in proper legal form acquired citizenship as did army veterans who had fulfilled their enlistment. Finally, the emperor might confer citizenship upon whomever he pleased, although the grant of citizenship to a whole community required the advice and consent of the Senate.

Proof of citizenship was given to former soldiers in the form of a document placed on metal. Other citizens normally were given no documentary proof of citizenship, but their names were inscribed in local registers of Roman citizens. Anyone needing to prove his citizenship could obtain through a magistrate a copy of his original registration upon a small wooden diptych. If anyone had his document of citizenship challenged, he needed the testimony of seven witnesses to support his claim.

Whenever a foreigner became a Roman citizen, he acquired various privileges and responsibilities, but he did not lose any other citizenship that he happened to possess. Among the privileges acquired with full citizenship was the right of suffrage at Rome according to one's social class, a right of some importance for those of senatorial and equestrian rank although relatively meaningless for the lower orders. Thus a new citizen was enrolled in one of the Roman tribes. Roman citizens living in the provinces were also listed on the tax rolls. They were subject to the Roman land tax, i.e., the tax imposed on all land outside of Italy and the coloniae; however, they were not required to pay the poll tax imposed on those living in Italy. Moreover, unless a grant of immunity had been given, Romans living in the provinces were subject to municipal taxation.

Juridically an Italian Roman citizen was subject to Roman magistrates, and a citizen from the provinces was subject to the governor of his native province. However, a citizen could accept the jurisdiction of the authorities in a different region. Thus Paul, a native of Tarsus in Cilicia, accepted the local jurisdiction of the authorities in Judea (Acts 24:1-21).[16] Moreover, with certain exceptions, any Roman citizen had the right to be judged by the emperor although by the time of Nero, the period of Paul's appeal to Caesar (Acts 25:10), the emperor rarely heard a case himself but delegated the task to others.

SLAVERY

Several Roman legal writers held that according to natural law no man should be enslaved, but such theoretical disapproval did not prevent the number of slaves from being quite large. Under Roman civil law (ius civile) a slave was not a person, but a thing (res), and subject to the whim of his master. During much of the era of the Republic a slave had had no rights; however, by the imperial era this situation had begun to change. In the past a master had sometimes allowed a slave to accumulate a peculium, i.e., property which, while remaining the master's legal possession, the slave was allowed to administer; but during the republican period the peculium was becoming recognized as a slave's property. Although a slave was still unable to contract any legal relationship, including marriage, he might now enter into a relationship similar to marriage, a form of conturberium, which, while without immediate legal effect, did convey some of the results of marriage if both parties should be freed. A slave was also regarded as something more than a mere thing in the area of legal responsibility. If a slave caused property damage, his master was held legally accountable; but in the case of some crime against a free person, the slave himself could be held accountable for his own actions and tried in the ordinary criminal courts. Other changes in the legal status of slaves involved the absolute rights of masters in the area of discipline. By the time of Claudius there were some rules against the killing of slaves, and a law made before A.D. 79 prohibited a master from punishing a slave by putting him into combat with the beasts in the arena without the authorization of a magistrate.

One generally became a slave either by birth or from capture in war. These common methods of enslavement were regarded as being part of the law of nations (ius gentium), i.e., those legal practices which Rome shared with other peoples. In addition Roman Law provided for enslavement under other conditions. Thus a man was subject to enslavement if he fraudulently sold himself as a slave in order to claim damages from the buyer. Also a free woman was subject to enslavement by a magistrate's decree is she cohabited with a slave after his owner had served notice that he forbade it. In such a case, however, there were certain restrictions if the woman was legally still under her father's protection or if she was a freedwoman, whose previous master would still possess what might be termed residual rights in her.

Slaves obtained freedom by various legal processes known as manumission (*manumissio*), but during the early years of the Empire, certain laws were passed making manumission more difficult in order to restrict the increasingly large numbers of slaves being manumitted. Under these restrictions only a master over twenty could free a slave, and the freed slave had to be over thirty to acquire Roman citizenship. Moreover, a limit was imposed on the number of slaves that a man could free in his will. Manumission, however, was not always an unmixed blessing. Freedmen still owed a former master (or patron) deference (*obsequium*) and aid (*officium*). Thus, for example, a patron could require certain services from his freedmen provided that these services did not involve the former slaves in risk of death or loss of personal dignity. Also in case of a patron's impoverishment, his freedmen must come to his aid; and the freedman named as sole heir in his patron's will became responsible for the latter's debts after his death.[17]

LAWS CONCERNING RELIGIONS

Romans generally tolerated established national religions unless they promoted debauchery or public disorder. There was somewhat less religious toleration in the capital city than in the provinces, but the introduction of many foreign cults at Rome during the late Republic and early Empire demonstrates that even there one could practice non-Roman religions as long as public order and morals remained intact. However, with the exception of the Jews, who enjoyed various special privileges,[18] adherents of all religions were expected to be willing to participate in the public worship of the Roman state.[19]

Throughout much of the first century, Christians were commonly regarded as adherents of Judaism and therefore shared the toleration and privileges afforded Jews. Only rarely was action taken against Christians on religious charges. One such action may be reflected in the charge against Paul and Silas at Philippi (Acts 16:20f.) According to part of this charge, they were Jews who "advocate customs which it is not lawful for us Romans to accept or practice"; yet, even in this instance the charge was also made on the basis of disturbing the peace, that "they are disturbing our city." Apparently the accusers did not simply denounce Paul and Silas for their preaching but because of the disturbance which their preaching caused. Therefore, both the trial and the beatings which followed it represent an attempt to quell public disorder.[20]

Whenever the adherents of a certain religion were causing disorder, Roman authorities commonly expelled them from the area of the disturbance. A notable example of this tactic was the expulsion of the Jews from Rome by the emperor Claudius, probably in A.D. 49. If sterner measures were called for, the emperor or one of his officials could take whatever other action thought necessary, including the proscribing of a religion. In regard to Christianity, however, there is no evidence that it was ever proscribed throughout the Empire during the first century. In the Neronian persecution the charge of incendiarism was invoked, even though Christians were generally considered a despicable group guilty of "hatred of the human race," an epithet which they earned by not sharing the usual religious practices of their neighbors.[21]

After the first Jewish revolt (A.D. 66–73) a change began to take place in the legal status of Christians. Due to the harsh measures taken against the Jews, particularly under Domitian,[22] Christians and Jews disassociated themselves to a greater degree than before so that Christianity no longer appeared in Roman eyes as part of Judaism. Since it was illegal to form new religions, Christianity as a new religion separate from Judaism gradually ceased to be tolerated. Thus for Romans, Christians were now not only atheists, that is, deniers of the Roman gods; they were also non-tolerated atheists liable to punishment or execution by the imperial authorities in the interests of preserving the religious foundation of unity within the Empire.[23]

Exactly when Christians came to be generally regarded as adherents of a new, illegal religion is difficult to determine. In the persecutions and threats of persecution toward the end of the first century (cf. Revelation 1:9; 2:13), there apparently was no general prohibition of Christianity as such. While Domitian fostered the traditional Roman religion and stressed the imperial cult, most of his concern was with the Roman upper classes. However, it is unlikely that all, or even most, provincial governors would have ignored sectarians like the Christians, who were not participating in the imperial cult. In any case, whatever was the exact status of Christians under Domitian, they were regarded as illegal sectarians within a few years after his death. In A.D. 112 Pliny the Younger, as governor of Bithynia in Asia Minor, was willing to take harsh measures against the Christians merely because they had ignored an official mandate against unauthorized religious societies *(hetaeria)* and stubbornly rejected his order to recant although he was fully aware that on other counts they were innocent. Nevertheless, in proceeding against the Christians, the governor acted with some moderation. He did not seek them out but acted only upon denunciation, and in this respect he was further cautioned by the emperor Trajan not to foster denunciations and to reject out of hand any accusations made anonymously.[24]

MARRIAGE LEGISLATION

Under Augustus a series of laws to foster and safeguard marriage had a widespread effect upon the mores of his age.[25] In particular this Augustan legislation would have been important for the city of Corinth in the time of Paul (cf. 1 Corinthians 5–7) since Corinth was a Roman colony and therefore subject to Italian law.

Italian law in the early Empire treated marriage as a duty for every man and woman. It imposed special taxes on unmarried men between the ages of twenty-five and sixty, on unmarried women between twenty and fifty, and on childless couples. It also imposed limitations on the rights of such persons to inherit. Even divorced women and widows were affected. In order to escape the special taxes levied on unmarried women, a divorcee had to marry within eighteen months after the dissolution of her prior marriage; and a widow, within two years from the death of her husband. Moreover, limitations were placed upon the right of a father to prohibit the marriage of his children. While under Augustus marriages still required consent from fathers or guardians, such consent could be compelled before a magistrate if difficult conditions were being imposed as an obstacle to a marriage. Similarly, masters who manumitted slaves were forbidden to impose conditions which would seriously impede their rights to marry as freedmen. In the case of freedmen who were Junian Latins there was a further incentive to marry and rear children. Through marriage such a freedman could acquire full citizenship for his wife and himself when their first child reached the age of one year.

Augustan legislation laid down revised standards defining who might legally contract marriages. Marriages were now permitted between freeborn citizens and freed slaves with the exception that senators and their descendants to the third generation were forbidden to marry ex-slaves as they were also forbidden to marry anyone from a family in the acting profession. Whether such prohibited unions were also invalid is not clear in view of the fact that Augustus at one time denied a divorce to a freedwoman married to the senator who had formerly owned her as a slave.

Italian law also contained various other restrictions on who might contract a legal marriage. Men over sixty and women over fifty were discouraged from contracting new marriages although they were not actually forbidden to do so. Entirely forbidden were marriages between those who were closely related. This ban included marriages between persons related in the direct line, between uncle and niece, and between aunt and nephew. In addition certain classes of people were barred from any legal marriage at all. These included known eunuchs, slaves, and soldiers. Also governors were forbidden to marry women from the provinces they governed, but this prohibition of itself imposed no great hardship since a governor's term of office was usually quite short.

Marriage formalities were generally quite simple, and sometimes there were no formalities at all. The mere fact that a couple lived together for more than a year created a presumption of marriage provided that there was no legal impediment to the union. Occasionally, however, somewhat more elaborate nuptial forms were required. Whenever a newly married couple did not commence living together at once, the marriage had to be attested either by a written document or by an oral declaration before witnesses. Another case involving a more elaborate ceremony was marriage with the *manus,* in which the authority over the woman passed from her father to her husband. In the vast majority of marriages during the early Empire, the wife remained legally under the authority of her father, but in rare instances the ancient nuptial forms were still practiced in which the bride passed from her agnate family to live under the authority (*manus*) of her husband.

Divorce was easy for either party, even in the case of a marriage with the *manus.*[26] Many have asserted that Augustus had tried to discourage divorces by decreeing that a grant of divorce had to take place before seven witnesses, but many jurists deny that even this formality was required for a valid divorce.[27] In Roman eyes, consent was the basic element making a marriage. Without such enduring consent there could be but a simulation of marriage. When the desire to live in a marital union no longer existed, all that remained was to dissolve the externals.[28]

As part of his program to improve Roman morals, in particular the morals of the upper classes, Augustus revised the laws dealing with adultery in order to facilitate legal proceedings against the guilty. Adultery was defined as sexual intercourse between a married woman and a man other than her husband. If a married woman's father caught his daughter in the act of adultery, he was allowed to kill the paramour; but, in order to escape prosecution for murder, he had to kill his daughter as well. A husband catching his wife and her lover *in flagrante* might kill the lover on the spot although he was not required to kill his wife. A husband did, however, have to divorce an adulteress at once or be punished as a procurer *(leno)*. Following the divorce, the charge of adultery had to be made in court by the woman's husband or father within sixty days, but after that time the charge could be made by anyone during the next four months since adultery was regarded as a crime against public morals. In most cases the guilty pair were banished to separate islands and heavily fined. The paramour lost half his estate; and the woman, a third of her property as well as half of her dowry.

In addition to adultery, sexual relationships between a man and a woman of honorable condition apart from marriage could be severely punished, but other forms of sexual relations without marriage were tolerated. Men were allowed access to public prostitutes. Another tolerated relationship was concubinage, a union similar to marriage but without juridic standing. Concubinage was generally practiced in situations where actual marriage was unacceptable. For example, the mores of the Roman upper classes almost demanded that one of their number desiring a freedwoman or the daughter of a man with a dishonorable occupation take her as his concubine instead of as his wife. Such unions were also popular with soldiers because of the legal ban against their contracting marriages. In spite of the fact that concubinary unions had no legal standing, custom demanded that they be more than mere transitory affairs. In the case of soldiers, it was common to raise such a union to the status of a legal marriage upon retirement from the army.

GUARDIANSHIP

In view of the mention of guardians by early Christian writers (e.g., Galatians 4:1f.), it is important to have some understanding of guardianship in Roman Law. Under Roman Law the oldest living male ancestor in a family *(paterfamilias)* had almost complete legal authority *(patria potestas)* over the persons of his legitimate descendants except for any female descendants who had been married with the *manus*. Whenever a person for some reason, such as his father's death, was left without a *paterfamilias,* he was said to be *sui iuris;* however, certain persons *sui iuris* were still required legally to be under a proper guardian. Such persons included minors, lunatics *(furiosi),* spendthrifts *(prodigi),* and women. Guardians could be appointed in various ways. Fathers commonly named guardians for their children in their wills. In the absence of a testamentary guardian, guardianship fell upon the nearest male agnate; and in default of other guardians one was appointed by the proper magistrate. Women were always under some kind of guardianship even after they had attained their majority at age twenty-five;[29] however, for women past this age, guardianship was little more than a legal fiction. An adult woman administered her own property and required her guardian's approval for important transactions only. Furthermore, for such important transactions a woman could force her guardian's approval or even have him replaced by another guardian more to her liking. Guardians generally were under the supervision of the proper magistrate. The magistrate might require him to give security, and in case the guardian caused the estate of a minor to suffer loss, either intentionally or through negligence, it was possible to recover damages. Another type of guardian was created exclusively in the interest of young men who had not reached the age of their majority. If such a man suffered loss in any transaction due to his inexperience, the transaction might be invalidated. As a result it was difficult to find anyone willing to do business with a minor. Therefore, to remedy the situation such a minor would request the proper magistrate to appoint a guardian to act for him and insure that his transactions were legally binding.

TAXES

Many were the types of taxes. The poll tax had to be paid for every adult including women and slaves, save for those over sixty-five. In the provinces this tax went to the provincial treasury. The land tax on Roman citizens owning non-Italic land, no matter where they lived, was paid to the imperial treasury. The central government could demand funds from the provincial treasuries. Throughout the Empire there was a 1 percent sales tax (though for some time it was reduced by one-half in Italy), a 5 percent tax on inheritances, a 4 percent tax on the sale of slaves, a 5 percent tax for manumission, a 2.5 percent tax on transport of goods, and a tax on immolated animals. There were also customs duties on goods passing from one region to another.

While the use of publicans to collect direct taxes on persons and property was declining in the first century A.D., they were still found in many places. Often they obtained a post by bidding for it; at times they merely received a portion of what was collected. Undoubtedly some were honest (see Luke 3:13); others were guilty of rapaciousness and thus even in the Gospels they are equated with sinners (see Matthew 5:46; 21:31-32).

Periodic censuses provided information necessary for determining future tax receipts. By A.D. 6 the system of taking a census every fourteen years in the whole Empire was firmly established. Prior to that time there had been periodic surveys of parts of the population of the Empire or of Roman citizens.[30]

NOTES

[1] On Christian expansion outside of the Empire, see W. Bauer, *Rechtgläubigkeit und Ketzerei im ältesten Christentum,* 2nd ed. rev. (Tübingen: J. C. Mohr [Paul Siebeck], 1964) ; Leslie W. Barnard, "The Origins and Emergence of the Church in Edessa during the First Two Centuries A.D.," *Vigilae Christianae* 22 (1968), 161–175.

[2] Originally the term *Ius Latinum* designated the law of Latium of which Roman law was a part. After the Social War the Latins and all other Italians were granted Roman citizenship so that there were no longer any Latins by birth. Thus the original *Ius Latinum* no longer existed. See R. Sohm, *The Institutes of Roman Law* (Oxford: The Clarendon Press, 1892), pp. 111, 118f.; John A. Crook, *Law and Life of Rome* (Ithaca, N.Y.: Cornell University Press, 1967), pp. 43f., 296, n. 29; Adrian N. Sherwin-White, *The Roman Citizenship* (Oxford: The Clarendon Press, 1939), pp. 91–111.

[3] For a text and translation, see Francis De Zulueta, *The Institutes of Gaius,* vol. 1 (New York: Oxford University Press, 1946).

[4] *Monumentum Ancyranum* 6. 13-16.

[5] Herbert F. Jolowicz, *Historical Introduction to Roman Law,* 2nd ed. rev. (New York: Cambridge University Press, 1952), pp. 352ff.

[6] See Adrian N. Sherwin-White, *Roman Society and Roman Law in the New Testament* (New York: Oxford University Press, 1963), p. 154.

[7] *Ibid.,* pp. 108–111.

[8] *Ibid.,* pp. 7f., 12.

[9] There is some question about the precise nature of these decisions. They appear in the form of *senatus consulta,* which were formally advisory in nature but which in practice could not be ignored. Cf. F. Miller in *Journal of Roman Studies* 58 (1968), 222.

[10] Flavius Josephus, *Jewish War* 6. 2. 4 (§ 126).

[11] See U. Holzmeister and C. Zedda, *Storia dei Tempi del Nuovo Testamento* (Turin: Marietti, 1950), p. 78.

[12] Recent works on the subject include Joseph Blinzler, *The Trial of Jesus* (Westminster, Md.: The Newman Press, 1959) ; P. Winter, *On the Trial of Jesus* (Berlin: de Gruyter, 1961) ; *idem,* "Trial of Jesus and the Competence of the Sanhedrin," *Commentary* 38 (1964), 39ff.; "The Trial of Jesus and the Competence of the Sanhedrin," *New Testament Studies* 10 (1963/64), 494–499. Sherwin-White, *Roman Society,* pp. 1–47; *idem,* "The Trial of Christ" in *History and Chronology in the New Testament* (London: SPCK, 1965), pp. 97–116.

[13] For a translation, see Allan C. Johnson, P. R. Coleman-Norton, and F. C. Bourne, *Ancient Roman Statutes* (Austin: University of Texas Press, 1961), p. 125.

[14] Sherwin-White, *Roman Society,* pp. 94f.

[15] *Ibid.,* pp. 71–78.

[16] It is not known how Paul acquired Roman citizenship. Possibly he was the son of a freedman. See Photius, *Ad Amphilochum.* It is unlikely that his family received Roman citizenship as part of a general grant since no ancient city gave citizenship to a Jewish community as such. See M. Adinolfi, "Stato Civile dei Christiani 'Forestieri e Pellegrini,'" *Antonianum* 42 (1967), 420–434. On the whole question of Roman citizenship, see Sherwin-White, *Roman Citizenship.*

[17] A brief but excellent treatment of slavery is found in William W. Buckland, *A Textbook of Roman Law,* 3rd ed. rev. (New York: Cambridge University Press, 1964). On slavery and marriage, see A. DeMañaricua, *El Matrimonio de los Esclavos* (Rome: Università Gregoriana, 1940).

[18] These privileges date back to Julius Caesar. For a translation of his decree on the subject, see Johnson, Coleman-Norton, and Bourne, *op. cit.*, pp. 91f.

[19] See William H. C. Frend, *Martyrdom and Persecution in the Early Church* (Garden City, N.Y.: Doubleday & Company, Inc., 1967), pp. 77–93.

[20] This point is not noticed by Sherwin-White, *Roman Society*, pp. 77f.

[21] Frend, *op. cit.*, p. 123.

[22] *Ibid.*, pp. 158f.

[23] *Ibid.*, pp. 160–162.

[24] See Plinius Junior, *Epistulae* 10. 96, 97. At one time it was claimed that Pliny moved against the Christians of Bithynia because of a Neronian proscription of Christianity, i.e., the *Institutum Neronianum* mentioned by Tertullian, *Ad Nationes* 1. 7 and *Apologia* 5. It is now generally recognized that what was referred to was at best a custom, not a law or edict, requiring or suggesting the suppression of Christians. See Frend, *op. cit.*, p. 126; Crook, *op. cit.*, pp. 278–280; B. Reicke, *The New Testament Era: The World of the Bible from 500 B.C. to A.D. 100* (Philadelphia: Fortress Press, 1968), pp. 291–317. For the view that Trajan's reply to Pliny *(Epistula* 10. 97) represents the first legislation against Christians, see T. D. Barnes, "Legislation Against the Christians," *Journal of Roman Studies* 58 (1968), 32–50.

The notion of illegal religion *(religio illicita* or *prava)* was common among the Romans and continued into the period of the Christian emperors. Cf. e.g., Suetonius, *Vita Divi Claudii* 25. 5, and *Codex Theodosianus* 16. 5. 52. Also used to describe foreign cults were expressions like *externus ritus* and *externa religio.* See, e.g., Livy, *Historia* 25. 11. 12. A religion could become illicit simply by a decree or an edict from a magistrate. See A. Berger, "Ex Post Facto in Roman Sources and Ex Post Facto Laws in Modern Juristic Terminology," *Seminar, Annual Extraordinary Number of the Jurist* 7 (1949), 58–65.

[25] The series of laws included *lex Julia de maritandis ordinibus, lex Julia de adulteriis coercendis,* and *lex Papia Poppaea.* Textual remnants of these laws can be found in G. Burns and T. Mommsen, *Frontes Iuris Romani Antiqui* (Freiburg im Breisgau: Mohr, 1887), pp. 111–114.

[26] The freedom of Roman women to initiate divorces undoubtedly influenced the wording of Mark 10:11f.

[27] See H. Last, "The Social Policies of Augustus," in J. Cook *et al.*, eds., *Cambridge Ancient History*, vol. 10 (New York: Cambridge University Press, 1966), pp. 445ff.

[28] See P. Bonfante, *Istituzioni de Diritto Romano*, 10th ed. (Turin: Giappichelli, 1951), pp. 180–194.

[29] One may interpret 1 Corinthians 7:36–38 as referring to guardianship. On this interpretation see J. O'Rourke, "Hypotheses Regarding I Corinthians 7:36-38," *Catholic Biblical Quarterly*, who in that article prefers the view that Paul is speaking of a relationship involving a slave girl.

[30] The problem of a Roman census in Judea during Herod the Great's reign is treated differently by different scholars; compare, e.g., Sherwin-White, *Roman Society*, pp. 162–171, and J. Finegan, *Handbook of Biblical Chronology: Principles of Time Reckoning in the Ancient World and Problems of Chronology in the Bible* (Princeton: Princeton University Press, 1964), pp. 234–238. See also chapter 9 in this book dealing with finances in the early Roman Empire.

FOR ADVANCED READING

Barnes, T. D., "Legislation against the Christians," *Journal of Roman Studies* 58

(1968), pp. 32-50.

Buckland, William W., *A Textbook of Roman Law*. 3rd ed., rev. New York: Cambridge University Press, 1964.

Frend, W. H., *Martyrdom and Persecution in the Early Church*. Garden City, N.Y.: Doubleday & Company, Inc., 1965.

Garney, P., "The Criminal Jurisdiction of Governors," *Journal of Roman Studies* 58 (1968), pp. 51-59.

Homo, Leon, *Roman Political Institutions from City to State*. Translated by M. R. Dobie. 2nd ed. New York: Barnes and Noble, Inc., 1962.

Jolowicz, Herbert F., *Historical Introduction to the Study of Roman Law*. 2nd ed. rev. New York: Cambridge University Press, 1952.

Jones, A. H. M., *Studies in Roman Government and Law*. New York: Barnes and Noble, Inc., 1968.

Sherwin-White, Adrian N., *The Roman Citizenship*. Toronto: Oxford University Press, 1939.

————, *Roman Society and Roman Law in the New Testament*. (The Sarum Lectures, 1960-1961) New York: Oxford University Press, 1963.

James L. Jones

8
The Roman Army

The battle of Actium on September 2, 31 B.C., marked a decisive turning point in Roman history. When the combined fleets of Antony and Cleopatra broke and fled, Octavian was left as the leader of the sole effective military and political force in the Roman Empire.

Octavian (subsequently known as Augustus Caesar) was not at first fully aware of his overwhelming victory. Contrary to normal Roman naval custom, the fleet remained at sea throughout the night in the event that fighting might break out anew. In the morning, however, it became obvious that Octavian was master of the sea and master of the world. There have been few such decisive moments in the world's history. The death throes of the Roman Republic were virtually at an end. In Italy, and particularly in Rome, there were, however, many emotional ties to the ancient republican institutions. Among the philosophers and the few surviving patrician families were some who sought to halt the course of events even to the extent of making several attempts to assassinate Augustus.[1] Most of the people, even in Rome itself, recognized that the old system was hopelessly obsolete, and Augustus found very little opposition to his program of reform.

THE AFTERMATH OF ACTIUM

In the months following the battle of Actium, Octavian was confronted with many crucial problems. Basically the issue was whether to attempt to restore the moribund structures of the Republic or to institute some form of stable autocratic regime. Octavian's compromise, the Principate, was a happy compromise which preserved much of the facade of the Republic but created the effective centralized control the times demanded. There were many factors to consider. Dio Cassius describes the issues and opportunities, which must have entered into the mind of Octavian, in the guise of lengthy but stylized and imaginary speeches of Agrippa and Maecenas.[2]

The military establishment created by Augustus was determined by the political and strategic requirements of the time balanced against the available financial resources. One of the striking factors in Roman civilian and military history is the narrow margin between solvency and bankruptcy upon which the Principate operated throughout most of its history. The need to provide an adequate force for defense while using the resources available was solved in a brilliant fashion by Augustus, and his solution to the problems remained with only minor changes throughout the next two centuries of Roman history.

On the political and military level Augustus could recognize that there was no organized opposing power or military threat within the Empire. At this time he alone controlled all effective military forces. Furthermore, Augustus recognized that Rome had extended itself to the geographical limit beyond which it could not hope to govern effectively. He established his policy and reached his military solution upon the assumption that there would be no further expansion of the Empire. This policy was followed more or less by his successors. Future military activities were directed primarily to the establishment of defensible military frontiers in Britain and on the Rhine and the Danube. Only in the East did the military problem remain fluid, where the Parthian, Armenian, and Sarmatian threats were factors for consideration.

Parthia constantly posed as a specter in the minds of the Romans. After the defeat of Crassus at Carrhae in 53 B.C., Rome was almost pathologically afraid of Parthia, and yet the threat was largely imaginary. Ronald Syme in *The Cambridge Ancient History* reminds us: "Between Ventidius' victory at Gindarus (38 B.C.) and the second year of Marcus Aurelius (A.D. 162) two centuries elapsed. In that space of time no Parthian was ever seen west of the Euphrates save as a hostage or a captive."[3] The threat of Parthia was, however, kept alive by the writers and poets of the Empire.[4] At this time Parthia was a collapsing feudal state and in no position to enter into military adventures against Rome save in defense. Both Parthia and Rome were under greater threat from the Sarmatian occupants of what is now southern Russia.

Armenia posed another essentially military problem to both Parthia and Rome because of its geographical location, forming a natural corridor deep into the territory of both powers much as the position which Kurdistan today occupies in relation to a number of nations in the Middle East. Control of Armenia by either Rome or Parthia would be regarded as a serious threat by the other side, and much of Roman military activity in the next two centuries was concerned with this problem.

The eastern frontier was not the only threat to the Empire, although it was the most vivid in the Roman imagination at the time of Augustus. The entire land frontier, Britain, the Rhine, the Danube, Arabia, and the Sahara, as well as Armenia and the Euphrates, were vulnerable to attack and had to be considered in the strategic military plan.

The military solution of Augustus was essentially the establishment of a military force as a border guard along the frontiers of the Empire. The force was stationed primarily in the imperial provinces, which were under the rule of legates holding power directly from the emperor. The Augustan military settlement is startling to military historians because it provided no strategic reserve. Throughout the Roman imperial period, until the reorganization of the army at the time of Constantine, Rome depended upon the movement of troops, either legions or detachments taken from legions (*vexilla*) or the transfer of auxiliary troops, from one area to another to meet military threats. At times this strategy led to serious trouble as one province was stripped of troops to meet an emergency in another. Not until Constantine's reorganization of the army into a field army plus border guards, each under its own military commander, was this basic defect in the Augustan settlement corrected.

In view of the strategic situation and the economic resources available, Augustus made certain far-reaching decisions about the structure of the army. He had to choose between raising temporary levies of civilians for short tours of service or continuing the development, begun by Marius about 106 B.C., of a professional standing army made up of career soldiers. The choice was crucial because throughout history professional career armies have usually placed their own interest on a level equal to or superior to that of the state.

Augustus decided to place the security of the state in the hands of a professional standing army. His decision seemed inevitable because military requirements demanded periods of service along the distant frontiers, and a levy of civilian soldiers inducted for short terms of service would not provide the effective trained force which the situation demanded. During the imperial period the army, with its discipline and arms, soon assumed a major role in the affairs of the Empire. At the death of Augustus and the accession of Tiberius, there were major uprisings of the army in Germany. Subsequently the army undertook an increasingly large role in the choosing, and at times the replacing, of emperors on the basis of its own interests or expected donatives. This development is clearly seen in the chaos that followed the death of Nero in which the four major armies of the

Empire struggled to establish their candidates on the throne. Eventually Vespasian was able to establish a stable government largely because he was supported by the largest army and his long period of service in the military had caused the army to identify itself with him as a fellow soldier.

The next question confronting Augustus was how large an army he would need and could afford. This decision was immediately necessary. After Actium some sixty legions in arms acknowledged the imperium of Octavian, and to this figure should be added perhaps an equal number of auxiliary troops. Some 300,000 to 400,000 men were under arms, far more than the need warranted or the resources could support.

Augustus quickly demobilized some 100,000 veterans, paid them bounties, and established them in colonies. His account of his career, *Res Gestae,* records that in his lifetime he restored some 300,000 soldiers to civilian life with bounties and other suitable rewards.[5] He also noted that he established some twenty-eight colonies of veterans in Italy, and he boasted of paying for the land so used. This policy was in contrast to previous practices: Sulla had founded homes for 100,000 of his veterans by ruthless seizure of land and property.[6]

After the immediate pressure of reducing the army was satisfied, Augustus established a special treasury, the *aerarium militare,* in A.D. 6, beginning it with a personal grant of 170 million *sesterces* to be added to by special taxes in Rome of 5 percent of the death duties and a 10 percent tax on auctions. From this treasury veterans were given a bonus payment upon their discharge from the army.

THE ROMAN ARMY BEFORE AUGUSTUS

Augustus admirably exemplified the complex personality of his Roman Empire. His mixture of cruelty and tenderness, licentiousness and stern discipline, made him the classic example of the virtues and vices of his race. Among other things, we may say that he was by no means a creative or adventurous thinker; rather, his genius was in his ability to take existing institutions and forms and remold them into viable and enduring institutions admirably suited to the needs of his time. This characteristic was especially true of his military solution.

We will be able to appreciate his policy better if we pause briefly to review the development of the Roman army in the republican period. Originally the Roman army consisted of the levies of citizens summoned yearly in the spring for the military campaign of the year, a practice which was customary in the city-states of the Mediterranean world of that time. A man's financial ability to provide weapons determined his place in the army. If he could afford a horse, he would be in the cavalry. If he could afford virtually no armor, he would be placed in the light-armed javelin throwers, the *velites,* who at that time would be stationed on the flanks of the heavily armored infantry, the main force of the army. If he had no property at all, he was excluded from the privilege of military service. Polybius describes the annual muster of the Roman army.[7] The total force available was divided into four quarters and each of these was called a legion. Each of the two consuls was given command of two legions. Later this practice was often modified, as, for example, at Cannae where the consuls alternated in holding command of the entire army on alternate days with disastrous consequences.

The conservative nature of Roman institutions is seen in the fact that the ancient practice of dividing the army into four legions was followed until the beginning of the Principate with the legionary numbers I through IV reserved for the designation of the legions commanded by the consuls of the year. Even Caesar and Pompey seem to have carefully observed this practice. The memory of this ancient practice was also preserved in the rule that command of an army of two or more legions or the governorship of a province in which two or more legions were stationed was reserved for consuls or former consuls (proconsuls). Such was the force of this custom that in the imperial period a lack of qualified proconsuls resulted in shortening the one-year term of office for consuls to six months, or even at times three months, to increase the number of qualified men available for appointment to proconsular offices.

During the course of history a number of significant changes were made in the organization, equipment, and tactics of the Roman army. These are properly the concern of a history of the republican period and are not directly germane to a study of the early Principate. Roman military history is an example of a fascinating paradox. The rigid, almost blind, conservative adherence to traditions was coupled with an audacious willingness to adopt new weapons and tactics and to improve on such innovations.

In the history of Roman military institutions two factors continuously influenced the military picture. One was that the privilege of military service, as also the right to enter the higher offices and ranks of the state, was dependent basically upon the amount of property possessed. The second factor was that eligibility for service in the legions was a privilege reserved for Roman citizens. Freedmen might serve in the navy and urban cohorts, and service in the *auxilia* was open to non-Romans. Slaves were excluded from all military service except in cases of grave national emergency. These two principles generally were observed even when rather flimsy legal fiction was required to preserve the principles. An example of this was the raising of two legions, the *I* and *II Adiutrix,* in the civil wars of A.D. 68–69. As the name implies, these were raised from the marines of the fleet, normally freedmen, who apparently were granted citizenship at the times that the legions received their names, numbers, and *aquilae.*

A basic change was made in the eligibility for service about 106 B.C. Much of the responsibility for this change is correctly attributed to Marius. In a crucial year when five Roman armies had been destroyed and there was urgent need for replacements, but only a nearly exhausted reserve of qualified replacements remained, enlistment in the legions was opened to the proletariat. All citizens were made eligible to volunteer rather than limiting conscription to those whose personal wealth made them liable for service.

There were several significant weaknesses in the Roman military establishment as developed by Marius and his associates. Most of the problems centered in the fact that as service in the army was increasingly opened to volunteers from the proletariat, the state was forced to assume the responsibility for the pay and maintenance of the soldiers while on duty and for their support after they had served their term of enlistment. There was, however, no plan for a fiscal policy either to pay the army or to provide for pension and retirement benefits. The need to find funds to maintain their armies became an increasing burden upon the commanders of the forces and led to a great deal of plundering and confiscation which forms such a dreary part of the record of the late Republic. In another extremely significant development in the Marian and post-Marian periods, the soldiers were enlisted by and bound by their oath of loyalty to the commander under whom they served. This practice began the era of personal armies so typical of the last century of the Republic.

The Roman army always had a peculiar sense of personal loyalty to its emperor and his family. This allegiance formed one of the bases of the subsequent conflict between the army and the Senate. The army by its temperament was dynastic, being willing to accept even totally inept emperors such as Caligula, Claudius, or Domitian if they continued in a dynastic succession. The Senate, on the other hand, attempting to preserve the ancient forms, always preferred an election of a new emperor.

Throughout the period we are considering, and indeed through the rest of the history of the Roman imperial period, this conflict over succession was one of the dominant factors in the government. Whenever a dynasty failed, as at the death of Nero or Domitian, there was always a danger that the armies would seek to set up their own commanders with the consequent dangers of a civil war.

THE AUGUSTAN ARMY

The Legions

Immediately after the battle of Actium, Octavian reduced the standing army to eighteen legions, retaining twelve of his own and incorporating into the imperial army six of the legions of Antony and Lepidus and disbanding the remaining forty-two.

About A.D. 3 this number was raised by the forming of eight additional legions. In A.D. 9 three legions were lost under Varus, and at Augustus' death there were twenty-five legions in the Roman army. That Augustus had planned his military requirements well was indicated by the fact that over one hundred years later Hadrian, one of the great military emperors, had only thirty legions in his army. Later Septimius Severus raised the number to thirty-three. This number was virtually unchanged until the reorganization of the army under Constantine when the number of legions was increased to sixty or more, but the strength of the legions was reduced from six thousand to approximately one thousand men.

Modern writers frequently fall into the habit of trying to equate ancient military ranks and organizations with those with which they are familiar. Therefore, terms, such as troop, company, battalion, squadron, or regiment are commonly used in translating Roman terms. These attempts to equate the ancient and modern military terms are misleading and should be avoided.

An exception can be made, however, in tracing some similarities between the Roman legion and the modern division. Both form the basic units of tactics, strategy, and fundamental planning for a military force. Then, as now, the contemplation of a military campaign would begin by estimating the number of legions or divisions required for the conduct of the operation. Both the legion and the division are essentially self-contained units capable of independent operation that can also be reinforced by the attachment of additional troops.

The basic unit of the Roman army was the *contubernium* of eight men. The unit, as the name implies, shared a tent in the field. In temporary camps the tent occupied an area of about ten feet square. In permanent barracks the *contubernium* shared two rooms, each approximately fifteen feet square, one for the storage of the baggage, gear, and armor, and the other for living quarters. These dimensions were sufficiently standard to enable archaeologists to determine the size of a military force, and often its composition, by the determination of the size of a camp or fort.

On the march the *contubernium* shared a pack animal, horse or mule, which carried the leather tent, the hand grinding mill for grinding the grain the soldiers were issued for food, and other heavy equipment. The *contubernium* also functioned as a messing unit and normally formed the basis for military details, either as a full or a half unit. It was customary, for example, to detail a half *contubernium* for small work details such as four men being assigned to perform a crucifixion.

We find unusual the absence of a "noncommissioned officer" in charge of this group, such as a corporal or sergeant who commands a squad in a modern army. In the military system of the Romans the senior man of the group would probably be the individual in charge, but there is no evidence that there was any title or any recognition of his position either in freedom from work details or increase in his remuneration.

Ten *contubernia* comprised one century. In the period of recorded history the Roman century did not consist of a hundred men, although obviously, as the name applies, this must have been the case at one time. The century was commanded by a centurion. For billeting purposes and perhaps for order of march, two centuries were formed into a maniple, but this unit had no tactical function in the imperial period. The maniple had been a basic tactical unit in the early republican legion.

Six centuries comprised a cohort and ten cohorts made up a legion. The first cohort was double the size of the other cohorts, and it included a rather impressive number of headquarter personnel, clerks, technicians, medical personnel, supply personnel, and even the early equivalent of a chaplain, the *haruspex*. The chaplain's major function was not the conducting of services or the counseling of soldiers but the determination of oracles and the reading of omens.

The total strength of the legion would be approximately 5,300 infantry. Because of the increasing reliance upon auxiliary forces and the relative difficulty in securing citizen volunteers, the legions were frequently under strength as much as 50 percent. In addition to the infantry there were 120 legionary cavalry. These were carried on the rolls of the various centuries and served primarily as messengers and liaison personnel and not as a tactical fighting unit. As a convenient approximation one could say that the Roman legion consisted of about six thousand men when at full strength.

Much of the combat support supplied in a modern army by artillery, engineer, signal, medical, and other branches was performed by the legionaries themselves in the Roman army. Artillery and siege operations were highly developed. Each century and each cohort had, or would manufacture, *ballistae* and catapults when a siege was undertaken. Missiles made of ceramic, stone, or metal were usually manufactured locally by the artisans in the legion.

Surveyors and draftsmen who planned fortifications and siege operations were assigned to the first cohort of each legion. These surveyors would also lay out and direct the preparation of the temporary marching camps and permanent forts.

The legions were normally designated by number. In the republican period there was considerable confusion in the numbering. Each general, Caesar, Pompey, etc., would number the legions of his own army according to his pleasure reserving, of course, numbers I through IV for consular commanders. With Augustus the numbering of legions became permanent. But since he incorporated into the imperial army legions from several sources, the armies of Antony and Lepidus as well as his own, there was some duplication of numbering which was resolved by the addition of a cognomen to the number. There are references to at least eleven legions bearing the number III. The most famous of these were the *III Gallica, III Augusta, III Italica,* and *III Cyrenaica.*

From time to time legions were disbanded or lost in battle. The loss of the *aquila* (the golden image of an eagle), the symbol and numen of the legion, was usually followed by the decommissioning of the unit and the punishment of its survivors, who might either be executed, dishonorably discharged, or reassigned to other legionary or auxiliary units. The record of the legion would suffer *damnatio* by being erased from the records of the army. Between A.D. 119 and 122 the *IX Hispana* was so erased from memory in northern Britain, and many of the earlier monuments of the legion show signs of attempts to erase its number and name. Three legions were lost with Varus in Germany in A.D. 9, the XVII, XVIII, and XIX, and these numbers were never reused in Roman designation of legions. The *XXII Deiotariana* left Alexandria to reinforce the Roman army in Palestine in the Second Jewish War and disappeared from history. It was apparently destroyed by Jewish insurgents.

A further help in the identification of units and particularly for dating them was the habit of giving additional honorific titles. In A.D. 42 Claudius gave to the VII and XI legions the titles of *Claudia Pia Fidelis.* Monuments and inscriptions are usually very accurate in the designation of a unit as it was known at the time the individual memorialized was a member of it. This developing list of titles gives a key to the history of the unit and also provides a guide to establishing the dating of Roman military inscriptions.

The Auxilia

A second major segment of the Roman army was the *auxilia.* These troops were composed of non-citizen soldiers. From the earliest times Rome always made a distinction between the Roman citizen eligible for service in the legion and citizens of allied cities who were allowed to serve in cohorts that were only used for secondary missions such as skirmishers, flank guards, and supporting units.

In the republican period the auxiliary troops were loosely organized into cohorts on a temporary basis in a specific campaign or for a limited period. These troops were reorganized and given a permanent status in the military establishment by Augustus.

Many of the units were composed of soldiers armed with special weapons. Often these units were recruited in areas where men were highly skilled in the use of the weapons. The Balearic Islands furnished cohorts of slingers; many cohorts of archers were raised in Syria; and much of the cavalry came from Spain and Gaul. The army of the early Empire depended entirely upon the *auxilia* for its tactical cavalry.

The large majority of volunteers for the *auxilia* came from the imperial provinces on the frontiers. Service in the army was a major factor in extending Roman culture. Soldiers in the *auxilia* would learn sufficient Latin to perform their duties; often they would assume Latin names, and as Roman citizens after discharge they would become enthusiastic supporters of the Roman way of life as they understood it.

In the early Principate most of the auxiliary forces served in or near the provinces of their original homes. There is some evidence of revolts when auxiliary units were transferred to remote areas.[8] Later, and especially after the Pannonian revolt (A.D. 6–9), a policy developed not to retain units in the area where they might form natural alliances with the populace, and most auxiliary units would be transferred to other areas for service. By the second century local recruitment for all military units became the norm, and ethnic distinctions, while often retained in the unit designations, were obliterated.

Because auxiliary troops were derived from the less literate population of the frontiers and therefore left fewer inscriptions and documents and because these troops were of less interest to the Roman historians, we know less about the details of their lives than we do of the legionaries. Auxiliaries were paid something more than half the salary of the legionary. A legionary considered it a promotion to become a *duplicarius* of an *ala* and receive twice the base pay of an auxiliary cavalryman.[9] The auxiliaries apparently did not ordinarily receive the donatives that the emperors gave to the legionaries and the praetorians (both units limited to citizens).

At least after the time of Claudius, the auxiliaries received citizenship upon the completion of their term of service which was longer than in the legions. This grant of citizenship was made by the issuance of *diplomata* which were given to the auxiliary at the time of discharge. Copies of these were made in small bronze or lead plates of which several are extant and form one of our basic sources of knowledge for the location of auxiliary troops.[10] Additional sources of information about the *auxilia* are the funerary inscriptions summarizing the *cursus honorum* of the equestrians who served as commanders of auxiliary units as a normal part of their public careers. The normal sequence of offices held by an equestrian began as a praefect of a cohort, then a praefect of an *ala*, and finally as a legionary tribune. After these military assignments, appropriate civilian appointments were open to members of the equestrian order.

Identification of auxiliary units was by a rather complex combination of number and names which might refer either to the weapons carried, the area from which the unit was raised, the area in which it had served, the name of a founder, or by a combination of names. Approximately four hundred units have been definitely identified, and it has been estimated that there may have been between six hundred and seven hundred in existence at one time or another. The auxiliary units would have been subjected to at least the same attrition or destruction or decommissioning as the legions.

One class of units of *auxilia* which are particularly interesting to the New Testament student are the *Cohortes Civium Romanorum* that were formed from volunteers from Italy. Italians were progressively excluded from service in the legions, and individuals desiring to enlist for military service were limited to the Praetorian Guard, the urban cohorts, or the Italian cohorts of the *auxilia*. One such cohort, the *Cohors II Italica Civium Romanorum* has been identified by inscriptions as stationed in Syria before A.D. 69.

The military forces of smaller provinces were composed primarily of auxiliary forces. The praefect of Judea ordinarily had six cohorts available, five at Caesarea and one in Jerusalem.

The client kingdoms, which in the first century were maintained as a series of buffer states along the eastern frontier, were expected to maintain armies of a reasonable size. These were organized basically on the pattern of auxiliary troops, and as the kingdoms were gradually incorporated into the Empire, their armies became units of the *auxilia*.

The auxiliary units were divided into *cohortes* of infantry and *alae* of cavalry. There were larger units of each, *cohors* and *ala milliaria* of about 800 men, and smaller units, the *cohors* and *ala quingenaria*, whose strength was about 480 men. Smaller units were favored in the early Principate, but after the time of Trajan most auxiliary units were of the larger type.

During the early Principate a third type of auxiliary unit was developed known as the *cohortes equitatae* in which a proportion of the men were mounted. This type of unit was especially suited to provide the combination of defensive power and mobility needed for the garrison of the small fortlets along the imperial frontier.

There was an increasing use of auxiliary forces in the Roman army. While military service became less attractive to the citizens of the Empire, the non-citizens on the frontier were finding in a military career an entrance into Roman life. After completing his service, the volunteer gained citizenship. His sons, as citizens, entered the legion, and they and their children had open to them the centurionate and following that perhaps entrance into the equestrian order. Many of the grandsons of barbarians are listed as the praefects of cohorts or even in higher offices as members of the Senate, and upon occasion held the imperial office itself.

Tacitus estimates that the auxiliary forces were approximately equal in strength to the legionary forces.[11] This proportion was probably correct for the period we are studying, although the *auxilia* became proportionately more important in the second century. After the enfranchisement of the entire Empire, the chief distinction between the legion and the *auxilia* disappeared, and service was increasingly made similar in both types of units.

In military campaigns the auxiliary units operated in support of the legions. There is no evidence that *auxilia* were permanently attached to, or under the command of, legionary legates. The Roman army normally recognized the military necessity of a fixed chain of command, and we may reasonably assume that auxiliary units would occasionally be attached to the legions for limited tactical operations. Normally they were under the command of the legate in command of an army or the provincial governor in whose area they were operating.

The Praetorian Guard

This famous body of troops formed a corps elite of the imperial army. Throughout the period with which we are concerned, they were of Italian descent and were required to meet rigid physical standards. They were characterized by distinctly more elegant equipment and armor, and they were better paid than the rest of the army. Early in the Augustan period they received twice the base stipend of a legionary. Later this rate was increased to three times the legionary's base pay. Gifts and donatives from the emperor or aspirants for the throne were also larger and more frequent. They were eligible for discharge and substantial discharge bonuses after sixteen years of service rather than the normal twenty years of the legion.

This organization had its roots in the practice of the republican armies in which the consul or general would be accompanied by a bodyguard comprised of the members of his own family and of his clients. As with so many organizations and institutions of the Roman world, the rather informal structure of the republican period was given definite form by Augustus. Originally Octavian, the future emperor, organized his personal bodyguard into a Praetorian Guard of nine cohorts. This number was raised to twelve cohorts by Caligula, and the Praetorian Guard remained a major factor in Roman political affairs until it was disbanded by Constantine.

With characteristic wisdom Augustus recognized the threat to the stability of his regime by the concentration of a large body of troops in Italy, and he distributed the nine cohorts of the Praetorian Guard throughout Italy, only three cohorts being in Rome at any one time. The entire Praetorian Guard was assembled in Rome by Tiberius where it established its famous camp northeast of the city.

The Praetorian Guard had little influence upon the military affairs in the eastern part of the Empire. Substantial detachments would accompany an emperor on his travels, but they were mainly stationed in Rome where they continued to exercise at times a decisive role in the power struggle which frequently occurred at the death of an emperor. The choice of Claudius by the Praetorian Guard was the first of a series of instances in which these troops, or their praefect, engaged in choosing an emperor.

The term *praetorium* in Philippians 1:13 is a factor in the introductory problems of that letter. If the letter were written from Rome, it would undoubtedly refer to the troops of the Praetorian Guard in their camp in the city. If it were from some provincial capital, it could refer to the military detachment assigned to security duties at the headquarters even though it was not part of the Praetorian Guard.

The Urban Cohorts and Vigiles

The *cohortes urbanae* were established by Augustus who formed three cohorts of one thousand men each. The corps was commanded by a *praefectus urbi,* a senator of consular rank. The urban cohorts were primarily established to provide police protection for the city. Later when the numbers were increased, one of the urban cohorts formed a military garrison at the mint at Lyons and was the only military force in the entire province of Gaul.

Closely related to the urban cohorts were the cohorts of *vigiles.* These were originally organized to afford protection from disastrous fires such as had plagued Rome in 7 B.C. and A.D. 6. In A.D. 6 Augustus organized seven cohorts of freedmen under the *Praefectus Vigilum,* a person of equestrian rank. The primary tasks of the *vigiles* were those of fire and police protection.

The Navy

It is always surprising to note how little the Romans knew, understood, and cared about sea power, although time and time again it had proved the decisive arm in military operations. However, throughout the period of our study, sea power was not important. After the battle of Actium the fleet was substantially reduced in numbers and established into two major fleets, those of Misenum and Ravenna, with auxiliary squadrons in Syria, Egypt, North Africa, the English Channel, the Rhine, and the Danube. The fleets, and particularly their marine components, formed a valuable source of emergency reinforcements of troops as in the period of the four emperors in A.D. 69 when two legions, the *I* and *II Adiutrix,* were formed from the marines stationed with the fleets at Misenum and Ravenna.

One of the few references to naval operations in our period is that described by Josephus.[12] He writes that Jewish ships from Joppa were engaged in piracy, which probably means that the Jewish ships were threatening the vital grain supplies from Egypt to Rome. Jewish ships were operating until they were destroyed by storms and by the Roman conquest and destruction of the city of Joppa. Otherwise not much is known of the Roman navy in the period of our study.

Numeri

In addition to the branches of the military establishment listed above there were loosely organized units known as *numeri* raised locally in the provinces. Very little is known of these units since their members were not Romanized enough to provide us with the inscriptions or funerary monuments which are so vital for our reconstruction of the military history of the Empire. Nor were these groups important enough to get a more than passing reference by any of the military historians. These were native troops organized and equipped in their own provincial style, speaking their own languages, and many of them commanded by their own tribal leaders.[13] We first find references to them in the time of Trajan although some *turmae* or informal levies of native troops raised by Julius Caesar in Gaul would have been a similar kind of military organization. We know very little about the organizations or the men who composed them, but it was in this type of organization that we first find the rise of the military force that was to dominate the later Empire and the feudal system, the *catafractarii,* the heavy-armor cavalry patterned on the Sarmatian and Parthian armored cavalry units. First reference to the use of these units is by Arrian writing in the reign of Hadrian. They were growing in importance during the later imperial period until by the time of Galerius they formed the major element in the centralized field army that was characteristic of the later Roman Empire.

THE PERSONNEL OF THE ARMY

The Officers

There were two basic classes of officers in the Roman army. First were the members of the aristocracy or nobility who were eligible for appointment as tribunes and legates. The other class of officers were former soldiers who had undertaken military service as a lifetime career and had risen on the basis of merit, bribery, or other factors to the rank of centurion or *praefectus castrorum* (the commander of a fort).

Augustus needed to provide his professional army with men from the aristocracy skilled in the strategy and tactics of war but at the same time to avoid creating any clique of military leaders who could be a focus of opposition to his reign. His solution was essentially simple. All imperium was vested in his person. His command was effected through the *legati* whom he personally appointed. The *legatus legionis* who was appointed from the rank of senators was usually of patrician rank. Augustus devised a unique process by which members of the equestrian and senatorial ranks could enter into a series of alternating military and civilian offices. This *cursus honorum* had its precedence in the series of offices which noblemen would pass during the process of rising to the office of consul during the republican period.

A senator of patrician rank might enter military service as a tribune. After a few years in this office, he would return to Rome and serve in one of the minor civilian positions. After this he would be eligible for appointment as legate of a legion usually for a term of three years. After this period of military service, higher civilian offices would be open to the candidate leading perhaps to election as consul. He would then be eligible for appointment as proconsular legate of a province. The literature and inscriptions preserve numerous examples of such a *cursus honorum*. Perhaps the most complete and vivid description is in the biography of Agricola written by his son-in-law Tacitus.

Other aristocratic officers of the legion were six *tribuni*. They were primarily members of the personal staff of a legate, although they are found occupying many different roles in the military organization. For the most part this experience was looked upon as a time to learn the principles and practices of military command for their later assignments. The appointment as a tribune came early in a young man's public career. There were two classes of *tribuni*. One class was the *laticlavii,* one of whom was appointed to each legion. The term *laticlavii* refers to the broad stripe of purple the individual was allowed to wear on his toga which indicated that he was of senatorial rank. The *tribunus laticlavius* would later be eligible for appointment as the legate of a legion as a part of his senatorial career.

The other five *tribuni* in a legion were the *angusticlavii.* These were men of the equestrian order which was indicated by the narrow band of color on their togas. This was usually the third and last of their military assignments in the equestrian *cursus honorum.*

This development of a *cursus honorum* with its alternating periods of military and civilian assignments placed these men completely under the observation of and responsible to the emperor. The short tours of military duty helped to avoid the danger of the development of personal loyalties and identifications of the legionary commanders with their legions and placed the entire military hierarchy directly under the control of the emperor.

The second class of officers might be designated the career officers. The basic continuity and stability of the legion and of the auxiliary troops rested with the career officers, especially the centurions. There were sixty centurions in a legion, each in command of a century. A rather involved series of ranks within the centurionate included the junior centurion called *hastatus posterior* who commanded the last century of the last cohort. The senior centurion in the legion was known as the *pilus primus* who commanded the first century of the first cohort and also served as chief adviser to the legate. The sequence and qualifications for promotion are not entirely clear.[14]

The soldier who rose to the rank of *pilus primus* would normally serve in that rank for one year after which he would receive his discharge from the service. He would retire as a wealthy man, and his wealth would qualify him for membership in the equestrian order. Many of these retiring centurions took their place in the local gentry of the region in which they had served. Others chose to enter the equestrian *cursus honorum* and accepted appointments as a praefect of a cohort or a commander of a fortress garrison.

Membership in the equestrian order was based almost entirely upon the financial resources of the individual. Many of the centurions, who had not achieved the rank of *pilus primus,* were able to enter this order upon their retirement. The centurions were extremely well paid, their base pay being over fifteen times the pay of a legionary, and a *pilus primus* would be paid over sixty times the annual stipend of a legionary. In addition to their pay, their share of the spoils of war and donatives was correspondingly greater than that of the legionaries, as was their discharge bonus. Also the number of complaints against centurions, who were accused of selling junior officer ranks or collecting money from soldiers for exemption from duties, meant that many of them were quite wealthy by the time they had completed their tours of duty. Many of the children of these centurions entered the equestrian *cursus honorum* as *praefecti cohortes.*

Probably the majority of centurions were promoted from the ranks, often entering through the series of minor offices described below. Occasionally men of the equestrian order would waive their rank and receive a direct appointment as centurion. They did so either because of the impoverishment of many of the equestrian families or because the individual felt a vocation to the military service. These former equestrians were favored in their promotion through the ranks of centurion to the higher positions of responsibility. While the legates and tribunes were from the senatorial and equestrian orders, the soldiers and career officers of the legions would be citizens but not members of the nobility. Centurions were frequently transferred from one legion to another and the inscriptions on their grave markers help greatly in determining the location of those legions. One centurion, Petronius Fortunatus, probably a native of Africa, enlisted in a legion and in four years rose to the rank of centurion. In his subsequent forty-two years of active service, he served in twelve legions from Syria to Britain.[15]

To accomplish the ever-increasing amount of paper work, the keeping of records, and the performing of the myriad duties within the military organization, a complex hierarchy of junior officers was developed in the legion. The extent of the paper work and records involved is to be seen in the fact that at the fortress of Dura on the Euphrates River, garrisoned by a *cohors equitata,* ten separate large rooms were occupied by the clerks and the archives of the fortress, and many additional records were stored in the surrounding temples.[16]

Through recent discoveries of papyri records and letters, many formerly obscure details of army organization are becoming better understood. At the same time the papyri provide firsthand contemporary records bringing a vividness that is welcome. MacMullen cites a letter of a newly appointed legionary accountant in Arabia which is preserved in one of the papyri fragments from Karanis: "I give thanks to Serapis and good fortune that while all are laboring the whole day through at cutting stones I as an officer move about doing nothing." [17] This papyrus letter is of further interest in showing that the legionaries were at least at times employed in various forms of manual labor as well as conducting the maneuvers and training peculiar to the military needs.

There were two classes of junior officers in the army, the *principales* and *immunes.* The former were equivalent to our modern noncommissioned officers with command and from whose ranks centurions could be appointed. Among this group was the *optio* who was second in command of the century. The *immunes,* on the other hand, were specialists in various activities of the unit and as such were excused from the normal duties of the legionaries. This group included such officers as the *signifer, custos armorum, librarius,* and the *medicus.* The relationship between these officers is discussed in detail by Domaszewski and Parker.[18]

There were large numbers of *principales* and *immunes* in the military organization. Cheesman has shown that in one *ala quingenaria,* which would consist of about 480 men, there were sixteen *decuriones* who were the commanders of the *turmae* into which the cavalry units were divided. In addition there were thirty-four *principales* and over one hundred *immunes.*[19]

The Soldier, Miles Gregarius

The soldiers of the Roman army were divided into two distinct classes, the citizens who were eligible to enlist in the legions and the non-citizens whose military careers were limited to the auxiliary troops with the grant of citizenship at the expiration of their term of service. While assignment in the legions was technically limited to citizens, there were various ways of circumventing this requirement in emergencies.

When two legions were raised from the freedmen of the marines at the navy bases of Misenum and Ravenna in A.D. 69, it would appear that the soldiers were given citizenship at that time. One can also recall that in earlier times Caesar had raised the *Alaudae* Legion in Gaul. Later, when this legion was recognized officially as a part of the army, it was given the number V and its *aquila* and the soldiers thereof were made citizens. Although the requirement of citizenship was retained, there was an increasing dependence upon non-Italian provinces, particularly Spain and Gaul, as sources for volunteers for the legions. By the time of Vespasian, Italians were specifically excluded from legionary service and were forced to enlist in the Italian cohorts of the *auxilia,* in the urban cohorts, or in the Praetorian Guard if they wished to enter military careers.

While freedmen were allowed to serve in the navy and perhaps also in some *auxilia,* there was a strong prohibition against the admission of slaves into the military service. This was usually meticulously followed except in times of grave emergency when ways would be found to give freedom, if not citizenship, to slaves willing to undertake military obligation. The correspondence of Pliny preserves this question regarding two slaves who had been enlisted and who had taken the military oath but were not yet assigned to a legion. His letter to the emperor describes the situation and asks for a decision as to the fate of the offending slaves.[20] The fact that it would be necessary to enter into correspondence with the emperor to determine the disposition of this case is evidence that it was not a common occurrence but rather one for which there was no precedent generally available. It is elsewhere recorded that Domitian returned to his master an escaped slave who had actually risen to the rank of centurion.

On the other hand, members of the senatorial and equestrian families were not allowed to enlist in the army. If they were interested in a military career, they could begin either by entering the *cursus honorum* as a *praefectus cohortis* or by resigning their status in the ranks of the nobility for the period of their enlistment in the legion.

During the early Principate, voluntary enlistment was for the most part adequate for the needs of replacement in the army. Some difficulty was found in supplying an adequate number of volunteers during the Pannonian revolt of A.D. 6 and after the disaster of Varus in the *Saltus Teutoburgiensis* in A.D. 9. Dio Cassius describes the difficulty in raising soldiers to replace the losses sustained in Germany.[21] This problem may be the reason as much as any other why the three legions destroyed at that time were not replaced.

Enlistment in the legions at the time of Augustus was normally for sixteen years. This period was based upon the ancient republican provision that the citizens were liable for military service for sixteen *stipendia* or sixteen annual campaigns. Later, because of the drain upon the financial structure of the Empire, this term was raised to twenty years. Part of the unrest in Germany at the death of Augustus was based upon the army's demands that the term of service be reduced from twenty back to the sixteen years that had been customary previously. Tiberius refused this demand because the military treasury would not be able to meet the increased demands upon it.[22] Enlistment in the *auxilia* was for a term of twenty-five years and in the navy for twenty-six years.

Qualifications for enlistments in the legions in addition to citizenship included an age requirement. During this period the normal age for enlistment was between nineteen and thirty-five, although some inscriptions show that on rare occasions men as young as fourteen to sixteen had been enlisted.[23] Applicants were given a physical examination, and at times there were some minimum physical requirements for enlistment. Grant states that in earlier times the minimum height for enrollment was four feet eleven or five feet, but in A.D. 367 this

requirement was raised to five feet five inches.[24] Grant does not indicate the source of his information, and it goes rather contrary to
some of our other evidence. Vegetius stated that it was far more
important that a soldier should be strongly built than tall. Some of
the special troops did have minimum height requirements: the first
cohort of the Praetorian Guard required a minimum height of five
feet ten inches for admission.[25] At the time of enlistment and the
administration of the oath of loyalty or perhaps at the time of assignment to a legion, the recruit was branded and given a lead identification disk and a certificate of recruitment indicating his military
status.[26]

Training and discipline were rather harsh in the Roman army.
During his period of training as a recruit, the enlisted man was required to go through two periods of physical exercise and training
per day. When he was enrolled as a legionary, this requirement was
reduced to one session a day. Along with physical drills of jumping,
swimming, and practice at arms, there were frequent reviews and
maneuvers and route marches, which were undertaken three times per
month in which the unit in full pack was expected to march twenty
miles per day at the rate of four miles per hour. There were occasional
forced marches to accomplish five Roman miles per hour.

In addition to military training, the soldiers were involved in a
great deal of construction and maintenance work, mainly the improvement of fortifications and the construction of roads and bridges. A
more extensive use of the legions in construction work can be seen
most clearly in the large number of buildings erected by the army in
North Africa where the *III Augusta* Legion was stationed at Lam-
baesis. In the course of some three hundred years that it was stationed
there, it undertook vast building projects. The same kind of effort
was probably carried on in other areas of the Empire especially in the
later years of the imperial period. The army was also involved in the
building of canals, harbors, and the operation and guarding of mines
and quarries. In the vicinity of each legionary camp there were
facilities for making bricks, pottery, and glass, some of the wares of
which appear to have been sold to the civilians in the area. At least
bricks and tiles stamped with legion signs are to be found in civilian
construction in areas adjacent to legionary camps. Legions also undertook agricultural work in the vicinity of the camps where they
were stationed.[27]

Arms and Equipment

Pay records, preserved in papyri in Egypt, indicate that the legionaries had stoppages against their pay for food and for clothing, al-

though there is no indication of stoppages for arms and armor. A normal policy seems to have been for the soldier to outfit himself at the beginning of his tour of service. This practice appears to be implied in the comments of Tacitus describing the Praetorian Guard that was required to provide its own armor.[28]

During the period under consideration between Augustus and Hadrian, the major sources of armor and arms were private factories and firms often operated by retired soldiers who set up their factories and shops in the vicinity of the legionary camps. Later, arms and equipment were manufactured in government factories, and this procedure was the normal practice after the time of Diocletian. In the ruinous inflation of the second and third centuries there came to be more stress upon the issue of food, arms, armor, and clothing in an attempt to keep the pay of the army realistic by issues in kind. Provision needed to be made for repair and maintenance of arms and equipment. Someone has estimated that a legion would require 120 cobblers and smiths to maintain itself and manufacture some of the required equipment in the legionary *fabrica*. The *fabricae* were found in every permanent camp of the legions.

In garrison, arms were apparently kept in rooms in or near the *praetorium* under the control of a *custos armorum or armentarius*. The arms of the legionary included two *pila* about seven feet in length with the upper third of the weapons made of soft iron shanks with highly tempered points at the heads. These were so designed that, when the *pila* were thrown on command at the beginning of an attack, the first *pilum* would be caught in the shield of the enemy and embed itself so that the soft shank would bend. This would render the shield difficult to handle and the enemy vulnerable to the casting of the second *pilum,* which would be followed by the rush into the attack on the part of the legionaries. The characteristic weapon of the legionary was the *gladius,* the short thrusting sword twenty to twenty-four inches in length which was developed from the Spanish sword.

Rations were ordinarily issued to the legionaries as whole grain which they then ground in the hand mill that was a part of the equipment of each *contubernium*. Legionaries in the field normally carried seventeen days of rations as a part of their equipment. The grain was usually ground and made into a form of porridge that the soldiers preferred to meat, which was rarely issued. There are records of the army protesting against an excessive issue of meat rather than grain. In the early Principate it appears that there was a deduction from a soldier's pay for the rations issued. Later, however, in the period of inflation in the second and third centuries, the issue of rations was a part of the perquisite of the soldier, and the number of rations drawn by an individual was determined by his rank and became a major part of his remuneration. In addition to the seventeen days' rations, each legionary normally carried his arms and equipment. Kromayer and Veith estimate that the average legionary's pack weighed approximately fifty kilograms or about 110 pounds.[29] Other, and probably more realistic, estimates place the weight of a soldier's arms and equipment at about eighty pounds. The best description we have of the equipment carried by a soldier is found in Josephus who states that each soldier, in addition to his weapons, armor, clothes, and rations, carried a saw, a basket, a spade, an ax, a thong, a bill-hook, and a chain.[30]

We are able to determine fairly well the pay of the various ranks of service at intervals during the imperial period. The following table based on the work of P. A. Brunt gives an illustration of the relative annual *stipendia,* in *denarii,* of the various ranks:[31]

	Augustus	Domitian	Severus	Caracalla
Private	225	300	500	750
Highest class of *principales*	675	900	1,500	2,250
Centurions	3,750	5,000	8,333	12,500
Primi ordines	7,500	10,000	16,666	25,000
Primi pili	15,000	20,000	33,333	50,000

From the time of Domitian on, the pay table does not accurately reflect the pay of the individual because there was an increasing issue of rations and armor in the period of radical inflation and debasement of coinage. Actually at the time of Caracalla the pay of the army, including its perquisites, was probably less than it was at the time of Augustus.

To the pay was added the donatives by the emperor at the time of his accession and a share of the spoils of war that a victorious army would acquire and distribute to the officers and men. The donatives and perhaps also the share of the spoils were divided, half of it going to the soldier and half of it going into his account in his unit's savings bank which he would receive at his discharge. Some soldiers were obviously quite wealthy either through independent means or the acquirement of wealth during their service.

The papyri give a number of indications of the wealth of soldiers both in wills and bequests and in arrangements for their burials. In addition many of the soldiers were able to acquire and to maintain a slave or slaves to assist them, perhaps in carrying their equipment. At discharge the legionary received a monetary grant of approximately 3,000 *denarii,* and the praetorians a grant of 5,000 *denarii.* This bonus plus their permanent tax exemption, provided a substantial fortune. The *auxilia* do not appear to have been given such grants but they were given their citizenship on the expiration of their service. Prior to the time of Augustus, soldiers at discharge were given grants of land. Augustus faced the problem of continuing the land grant to retired veterans when approximately 20,000 soldiers a year would have been retiring from the service, and he changed to a strictly monetary grant.

In the later imperial period with the depopulation of the countryside the soldier was encouraged to accept a land grant, which was approximately one square kilometer in size, in the vicinity of the place where he had been serving at retirement. Most of the soldiers upon retirement would live in the vicinity of the fortress in which they had served, perhaps entering into agriculture or more likely into the business of the manufacture of arms or the management of small shops or taverns.

THE MILITARY SITUATION IN THE EASTERN EMPIRE

The period of time between the reign of Augustus and that of Hadrian was one in which the Empire sought to establish its frontiers. By the time of Hadrian the Empire had essentially reached its maximum limits, and the emperor attempted to provide the boundary with defensible frontiers such as the famous wall in the north of England. Other frontiers were less well fortified. Some further readjustments in the Rhine and the Danube areas and in Arabia were attempted later, but for all practical purposes one could conclude that in the centuries following Hadrian the Roman Empire was attempting to defend gradually shrinking boundaries.

In Europe the principle of defense was based on the defense of well-recognized boundaries, either a line of fortified walls or a river line, such as the Rhine and the Danube. In the East the situation was somewhat different. Whereas the Euphrates formed a general line of demarcation, its nature and extent were such that the Empire, with the limited resources available to it, could not garrison it in strength as it did the other two *limes*. There were some outposts along the Euphrates such as the fortress of Dura, but for the most part in the East the Empire relied upon a thin screen of a frontier guard plus the concentration of strategic forces in reserve. In the Julio-Claudian period, 31 B.C. to A.D. 68, two legions were stationed in Egypt and four in Syria. Vespasian increased the Syrian army to six legions and Hadrian added two more, making eight legions in the Syro-Palestinian area. At this time approximately one third of the Roman military force was deployed along the boundary between Rome and Parthia. Reinforcements for this rather formidable army were drawn from the military forces of the client kings upon which Rome continued to place considerable reliance during the first century of the Christian era. These independent kings were allowed and encouraged to maintain armies often of considerable size. Josephus states that Antiochus IV of Commagene, Agrippa II, Soaemus of Emesa and Malchus of Damascus contributed 15,000 men to the army which Vespasian led into Palestine in the spring of A.D. 67.[32]

Some details are available to us concerning the structure of Herod's army. The Herodian armies were composed of mercenaries. The majority of the soldiers were Idumaean plus some Celts, Thracians, Germans, and Greeks. The Herods, as the Hasmonaeans before them, did employ Jewish mercenaries from the Diaspora but were reluctant to incorporate Palestinian Jews into their armies. Augustus gave Cleopatra's Celtic bodyguard to Herod to be included in his military force.[33] Herod followed the Roman custom of establishing colonies of retired veterans at various places in Palestine. One such colony was at Heshbon in Peraea, another at Gaba in Galilee, and there are references to others which have not been located.

Rome's policy in the East was dominated by its fear of Parthia and by its feeling of the need for control of Armenia. How real the Parthian threat was in the period we　re considering is difficult to evaluate. There was no support by Parthia for the Jews in the rebellions of A.D. 66 and 132. Rather it appears that the Babylonian Jews offered Trajan some military support in the campaign of 115. Recent studies of Parthia seem to indicate that the country in its quasi-feudalistic loosely organized structure was incapable of offering effective military reaction. The campaigns of Trajan seem to indicate the essential weakness in the Parthian military force at that time.

Communication between Rome and Egypt was vital. Threats to this line of communication by sea power, as happened during the First Jewish War when Jewish ships seemed to have posed such a threat to ships going between Alexandria and Rome, required the destruction of the city of Joppa. Also the land route from Egypt through Palestine was the means of communication between Rome and its vital province of Egypt during the months of the year when the sea was not suitable for shipping.

THE ROLE OF THE ARMY IN THE DEVELOPMENT OF THE EMPIRE

The military establishment that Augustus created was, as we have seen, a product of a series of compromises. An army of approximately twenty-five legions and an equal number of auxiliary troops meant that the slender resources of the Principate were required to maintain a standing army of approximately 300,000 men. While this appears to be a huge force, its strength was never adequate to the task of guarding the frontier of the vast empire.

The present knowledge of the financial structure of the early Empire makes it impossible for us to determine the proportion of the resources required for the maintenance of the army. Some of the financial problems are discussed in the next chapter in this volume. All of the evidence, however, agrees that the size of the standing army was always rigidly limited by the funds available for its support and that a great deal of the energy of successive emperors was devoted to securing funds for its maintenance.

While the maintenance of the army was a drain upon the economy of the Empire, almost too much for it to bear, there were certain contributions which the army made to the economic well-being of the Empire. The colonies established by the ex-soldiers throughout the Empire greatly helped to expand the civilization of the Mediterranean throughout the area where the ex-soldiers were living. Not least in its contribution was the road net built by Rome for the deployment of the army, and largely built by the army in the areas where it was stationed. Some 250,000 miles of road were built by Rome, and some of these roads are extant and in use today. Travel became relatively peaceful and safe. A person could average thirty to fifty miles per day traveling at a normal rate of speed on horseback or in a carriage. Tiberius once traveled two hundred miles in one twenty-four hour period. Also the sea was cleared of pirates and opened for travel to merchants as well as people traveling for enjoyment. By sea in merchant ships dependent upon the winds, a journey from Puteoli to Alexandria would take from seven to fifty days to accomplish. Irenaeus expressed the appreciation generally felt for the *Pax Romana,* "The Romans have given the world peace and we travel without fear along the roads and across the sea wherever we will." [34]

The Roman army tends to dominate the modern imaginary picture of Rome. The army was of great importance in the thoughts and plans of the emperor and his counselors. To the average inhabitant of the city of Rome, however, the army was remote. It was stationed along the frontiers, hundreds of miles away. Detachments might be brought to Rome for the triumphs of the emperors, and some of the sailors from Misenum were quartered in Rome to manipulate the canvas awnings of the arena. Otherwise one would see detachments of the Praetorian Guard and the urban cohorts in Rome, but the rest of the army was far away. There would not even be the interest aroused because of family ties, for during this period greater restrictions were being placed on Romans, and to a growing degree on Italians, to prevent their entering military service. The legions were being recruited from the enfranchised areas of Spain and Gaul, and the membership of the *auxilia* was limited to the non-citizens from the frontier provinces.

Few people in Rome, except the imperial household and the senatorial and equestrian nobles who served as higher officers of the services, had any direct contact with the army. The military tradition, however, was held up as expressing the ideal Roman virtues. The army with its stress on discipline and self-sacrifice and its obedience to organized authority held great attraction for many of the philosophers and religious teachers of the period. The pagan philosophers pointed to the discipline of the army as an ideal for members of their schools of philosophy. We also find that in the time of the Apostolic Fathers, especially in the writings of Clement, Ignatius, and Tertullian, many metaphors based upon military discipline and loyalty were used.

THE RELIGION OF THE ROMAN ARMY

The nature of the relationship between the *princeps* and the army was, to the Roman mind, a religious one. The *princeps,* as *paterfamilias,* was also *Pontifex Maximus* and his legate who commanded the legion was also the *pontifex* who offered sacrifices and directed the observance of the complicated *fasti* or calendar of religious festivals. The religious calendar of an auxiliary cohort has been found at Dura, and it helps us to understand how the observance of the cycle of ancient Roman festivals and the observance of the feasts of the reigning emperor helped to spread Roman civilization to the furthermost limits of the Empire.

Military service was basically religious in the oath or *sacramentum* by which the recruit was bound to the emperor and to his legion or cohort. This religious emphasis was constantly reinforced by the official religious activities of the unit.

Soldiers are usually religious in their attitudes toward life and death. The inscriptions around the camps and forts of the Roman Empire show that the soldiers of Rome were no exception. In addition to the vast number of military funerary monuments with a religious theme, there are the large number of altars and votive tablets to the gods, Roman or local, or to the deified military virtues, such as discipline, valor, and loyalty. The Roman soldier was also able to express his religious feeling in the cult of Mithras, the Persian mystery deity, whose worship was so congenial to the military mind and whose shrines are to be found associated with military installations throughout the Empire.

Against this religious background the relationship of the Christian church and the army needs consideration. The New Testament has a surprisingly large number of references to military men, and the view of the soldier in the New Testament is by no means condemnatory. Soldiers came to John the Baptist and were told to be honest soldiers. A centurion came to Jesus requesting the healing of one dear to him, servant or son. Another centurion, standing at the foot of the cross, expressed at least admiration for Jesus. In Acts, Cornelius and Julius were centurions friendly to the Christian movement. Paul frequently had recourse to military metaphors to convey his ideas to the churches.

In the subapostolic period the attitude of the church toward the army and especially the question of the compatibility of church membership and military service underwent a change. The most comprehensive study of this problem has been made by Adolf von Harnack in *Militia Christi*. His study does not fully recognize the favorable picture of the soldier and the army in the New Testament period, but he shows clearly the issues which forced the later church into a growing hostility toward military service. Later there developed an accommodation of the church to the state and to the army which culminated in the union of church and state under Constantine and the later Christian emperors.

The Roman army and its officers and men were regarded by the writers of the New Testament as an essential part of the Empire. The army was both an occupying force in control of Palestine and at the same time the force that established and maintained the peace which made the spread of Christianity possible.

NOTES

[1] Ramsay MacMullen, *Enemies of the Roman Order* (Cambridge, Mass: Harvard University Press, 1966), describes the opposition to the policies of Augustus, the several attempts to assassinate him, and the consequences of such attempts on his life.

[2] Dio Cassius, *Roman History*, Book 52.

[3] Ronald Syme, "The Flavian Wars and Frontiers," *The Cambridge Ancient History*, (New York: Cambridge University Press), XI, 142.

[4] Note, for example, the introduction of Josephus' *The Jewish War* seems to be warning the eastern peoples, including the Parthians, of the might of Rome. Horace, at the end of Ode 2, *Ad Augustum Caesarem*, prays for Augustus to protect against the threats from the East, "Nor mayest thou suffer the Medes [i.e., *Parthians*] to make incursions unavenged, you, O Caesar, being our leader."

[5] Augustus, *Res Gestae* 3. 16.

[6] Recorded in Appian, *Bell. Civ.* 1. 104.

[7] Polybius, *Historiae* 1. 16. 2.

[8] Tacitus, *Annals* 4. 46.

[9] Graham Webster, *The Roman Imperial Army* (London: Adam & Charles Black, Ltd., 1969), p. 260.

[10] *Corpus Inscriptionum Latinarum, (C.I.L.),* vols. 3 and 16.

[11] Tacitus, *Annals* 4. 5.

[12] Josephus, *The Jewish War* 3. 414-431.

[13] Arrian, *Tactica* 44, cf. Graham Webster, *op. cit.,* p. 150.

[14] Henry M. D. Parker, *The Roman Legions,* rev. ed. (New York: Barnes & Noble, Inc., 1928), pp. 201ff.; H. M. D. Parker, "A Note on the Promotion of Centurions," *Journal of Roman Studies,* 16 (1926), 45-52.

[15] *C. I. L.* 8. 217, cf. Graham Webster, *op. cit.,* p. 119.

[16] Ramsay MacMullen, *Soldier and Civilian in the Later Roman Empire,* (Cambridge, Mass.: Harvard University Press, 1963), p. 65.

[17] *Ibid.,* p. 32.

[18] A. von Domaszewski, *Die Rangordnung des römischen Heeres,* pp. 48f.; Henry M. D. Parker, *The Roman Legions,* has summarized the conclusions of Domaszewski, pp. 205ff.

[19] G. L. Cheesman, *The Auxilia of the Roman Imperial Army* (Oxford: The Clarendon Press, 1914), p. 45.

[20] Pliny, *Epistulae* 10. 29 and 30.

[21] Dio Cassius, *Roman History* 56. 23.

[22] Tacitus, *Annals* 1. 78.

[23] Johannes Kromayer and Georg Veith, *Heerwesen und Kriegführung der Griechen und Römer,* p. 487.

[24] Michael Grant, *The Climax of Rome, the Final Achievements of the Ancient World A.D.* 161-337, (Boston: Little, Brown, and Company, 1968), p. 42.

[25] E. H. Alton, "The Roman Army," *A Companion to Latin Studies,* pp. 482f.

[26] Arnold H. Jones, *The Later Roman Empire,* (Norman, Okla.: University of Oklahoma Press, 1964), II, 616.

[27] Pliny, *Naturalis Historia* 11. 106.

[28] Tacitus, *Annals* 1. 17.

[29] Johannes Kromayer and George Veith, *op. cit.,* p. 423.

[30] Josephus, *The Jewish War* 3. 95.

[31] P. A. Brunt, *Papers British School at Rome,* 18. 71; cf. Graham Webster, *The Roman Army,* p. 31.

[32] Josephus, *The Jewish War* 3. 68.

[33] *The Cambridge Ancient History,* 10. 115.

[34] Irenaeus, *Adv. Haer.* 4. 30. 3.

FOR ADVANCED READING

SOURCE MATERIAL

Much of the knowledge of the Roman army is derived from incidental references made by historians such as Caesar, Livy, Polybius, and Sallust who are invaluable for their references to military subjects in republican times.

For the period we are studying, i.e., between Augustus and Hadrian, we have the contemporary works of Josephus, Plutarch, Suetonius, and Tacitus. The writings of these men are informative for their military history and are to be found in numerous critical editions and translations.

Few books devoted specifically to military organization and tactics have survived from this period. There are numerous books on tactics of the post-Constantinian period which were preserved because their emphasis on heavy cavalry made them applicable to the situation in the Middle Ages. Some of these, such as the works of Vegetius and Ammianus Marcellinus, preserve valuable earlier material.

From references in Herodian and Lucian we know that there was a technical military literature that has not survived. Outmoded books on military subjects, such as supplanted liturgical books, usually survive only by fortuitous accidents. We regret the loss of such books as Cicero's *Art of War* and Frontinus' *De re militari* which is referred to in his later *Strategemata* written *ca.* A.D. 84-96.

Of the writers on military subjects who are of value may be included the following in an approximate chronological order:

Velleius Paterculus, *Compendium of Roman History, ca.* A.D. 30. Particularly valuable for military affairs in the reign of Tiberius during which time he was a praefect of a cavalry *ala*, a tribune in the V Macedonia Legion, and a legate of a legion in Pannonia in A.D. 7-8. The most valuable single study of military subjects in our period. Available in the Loeb Library edition.

Onasander, *The General, ca.* A.D. 41-59. A treatise primarily on the various aspects of a commander's qualifications and duties.

Frontinus, lived *ca.* A.D. 35-103. One time military governor of Britain and later in charge of the water supply of Rome. Famous for his book on aqueducts. Also wrote *Strategemata, ca.* 84-96, a manual of strategic and tactical maneuvers which had been successful or unsuccessful, derived mainly from historical sources many of which are otherwise lost. Frontinus' earlier book, *De re militari,* is lost.

Flavius Arrianus, second century A.D. His military treatises are among the best records of the imperial army but are not available in convenient form.

Flavius Vegetius Renatus, *De re militari.* Written in the fourth century and called "the most influential military treatise in the western world from Roman times to the nineteenth century." Available in an abridged form in Maj. Thomas R. Phillips, *Roots of Strategy* (Harrisburg, Pa.: Mil. Service Publish. Co., 1940). Vegetius' desire at the time of Valentinian to recall the Romans to their former glory caused him to preserve and use sources which are valuable for our study of the early Principate.

Notitia Dignitatum, ca. fourth century and later, is of some secondary value. A detailed description of organization and location of units of the army at the time of writing.

Ammianus Marcellinus, b. *ca.* A.D. 330, the "last of the great Roman historians" according to *The Oxford Classical Dictionary.* While the part of his history dealing with the earlier period has been lost, his extensive knowledge of military affairs based on personal experience makes his works a valuable secondary source.

Zosimus wrote a history from Augustus to Theodosius II, *ca.* A.D. 410. He used many excellent sources otherwise lost.

In addition to the literary resources, much valuable information is to be found in the monuments and inscriptions. Many of the inscriptions and diplomas are published in the *Corpus Inscriptionum Latinarum (C.I.L.),* especially volumes 3 and 16.

Contemporary history increasingly stresses an interest in the life and thoughts of individuals, especially the common people. Ancient writers were totally disinterested in the ordinary citizen or soldier. These people are coming to life in the papyri which have accidentally preserved material that is of the greatest value to us today. In the papyri are found duty rosters, records of pay and allowances, discharge certificates, and the letters, wills, contracts, etc., which bring vitality and interest to the history of the ancient world. While most of these papyri are of the Egyptian province, they have a general application.

Among the published collections of papyri relating to soldiers and military subjects are:

Daris, Sergio, *Documenti per la Storia Dell'Esercito Romano in Egitto.* Milano: Società Editrice Vita Pensiero, 1964.

Martin, V., "L'État actuel des archieves de Flavius Abinnaeus et la biographie de cet officer," *Chronique d'Egypte* 2 (1931), 345ff.

Milligan, George., *Greek Papyri*. New York: Cambridge University Press, 1910.

Mondini, M., "Lettere di soldati," *Atene e Roma* 18 (1915), 241f. A survey of papyri letters published up to the time of writing.

Sijpesteijn, Pieter J., *The Wisconsin Papyri*. Leiden: E. J. Brill, 1967.

Smolka, F., "Lettres de soldats écrits sur papyrus," *Eos* 32 (1929), 153ff.

Youtie, Herbert C. *et al.*, *Papyri and Ostraca from Karanis*. Ann Arbor: University of Michigan Press, 1944 *et seq*.

MODERN STUDIES

There is a vast amount of literature on Roman military subjects both in books and periodicals. The items listed here are representative of the most up-to-date and readily available material.

Allen, G. H., "The Advancement of Officers in the Roman Army," *Supplementary Papers of Am. Sch. Class. Stud. in Rome* 2 (1908).

Alton, E. H., "The Roman Army," *A Companion to Latin Studies*. Edited by Sir John E. Sandys. 3rd. ed. pp. 458-501. New York: Hafner Publishing Co., Inc., 1935.

Batiffol, P., "Les Premiers chrétiens et la guerre," *Bulletin de la Société nationale des antiquaires de France*, 1911, pp. 226f.

Birley, E., "Senators in the Emperor's Service," *Proc. of Brit. Acad.* 39 (1954), 197-214.

Brand, C. E., *Roman Military Law*. Austin, Tex.: University of Texas Press, 1968.

Brunt, P. A., "Pay and Superannuation in the Roman Army," *Papers Brit. School at Rome* 18 (1950), 50-71.

Charlesworth, Martin P., *Trade Routes and Commerce of the Roman Empire*. 2nd ed. Hildesheim: Olms, 1961.

Cheesman, G. L., *The Auxilia of the Roman Imperial Army*. Oxford: The Clarendon Press, 1914.

Domaszewski, A. von., *Die Rangordnung des römischen Heeres*. Edited by Brian Dobson. 2nd ed. Köln: 1967.

Dorey, Thomas A., *Latin Historians*. New York: Basic Books, Inc., Publishers, 1966.

Durry, M., *Les Cohortes prétoriennes*. Paris: Ec. Fr. d'Atheñes et de Rome, 1938. Reprint, 1968.

Earl, Donald., *The Age of Augustus*. New York: Crown Publishers, Inc., 1968.

Enslin, Morton S., "Rome in the East," *Religions in Antiquity*. Edited by Jacob Neusner. pp. 125-136. Leiden: E. J. Brill, 1968.

Gilliam, J. F., "The Appointment of Auxiliary Centurions," *Transact. of Am. Philological Assn.* 88 (1958), 155-168.

Grant, Michael, *The Climax of Rome, the Final Achievements of the Ancient World A.D. 161-337*. Boston, Mass.: Little, Brown and Company, 1968.

Harnack, Adolf von, *Militia Christi*. Tübingen: J. C. B. Mohr, 1905. Reprinted Darmstadt: Wissensch. Buchgesellschaft, 1963.

Holmberg, E. J., *Zur Geschichte des Cursus Publicus*. Uppsala: 1933.

Jones, Arnold H. M., *The Later Roman Empire*. Oxford, England: Basil Blackwell & Mott, Ltd., 1964.

Kromayer, Johannes, and Veith, Georg, *Heerwesen und Kriegführung der Griechen und Römer*. München: C. H. Beck'sche Verlags Buchhandlung, 1928.

MacMullen, Ramsay, *Enemies of the Roman Order: Treason, Unrest and Alienation in the Empire*. Cambridge, Mass.: Harvard University Press, 1966.

MacMullen, Ramsay, "Inscriptions on Armor and the Supply of Arms in the

Roman Empire," *Am. J. of Arch.* 64 (1960), 23-40.

MacMullen, Ramsay, *Soldier and Civilian in the Later Roman Empire.* Cambridge, Mass.: Harvard University Press, 1963.

Mommsen, Theodor, "Die Gardentruppen der römischen Republik und der Kaiserzeit," *Gesammelte Schriften Historische Schriften.* Dritter vol. pp. 1-10. Berlin: Weidmannsche Buchhandlung, 1910.

Nesselfauf, Herbert, "Diplomata Militaria," *C. I. L.* vol. 16. Berlin: Apud W. De-Gruyter et Socios, 1936.

Nilsson, Martin P., *Imperial Rome.* New York: Schocken Books, 1962.

Parker, H. M. D., "A Note on the Promotion of Centurions," *Journal of Roman Studies,* 16 (1926), 45-52.

Parker, H. M. D., *The Roman Legions.* New York: Barnes and Noble, Inc., 1928. Reprinted with corrections and a new bibliography. Cambridge: W. Heffer and Sons, Ltd., 1958.

Pauly, A. D., Wissowa G., and Kroll, W., eds., *Real-encyclopäedie der Classischen Altertumswissenschaft.* Stuttgart: 1894ff. Contains detailed articles on organization, weapons, tactics, etc.

Reynolds, Paul K. Baillie, *The Vigiles of Imperial Rome.* New York: Oxford University Press, 1926.

Sandys, Sir John E., *A Companion to Latin Studies.* 3rd ed. Cambridge: University Press, 1935.

Skeel, Caroline, *Travel in the First Century after Christ with Special Reference to Asia Minor.* New York: Cambridge University Press, 1901.

Smith, R. E., *Service in the Post-Marian Roman Army.* New York: Barnes & Noble, Inc., 1958.

Southworth, John Van Duyn, *The Ancient Fleets.* New York: Twayne Publishers Inc., 1968.

Starr, Chester G., *The Roman Imperial Navy.* 2nd ed. New York: Barnes & Noble, Inc., 1960.

Syme, Ronald, "The Flavian Wars and Frontiers," *The Cambridge Ancient History.* Edited by S. A. Cook et al. Vol. 11, pp. 131-187. New York: Cambridge University Press, 1936.

Watson, George R., *The Roman Soldier,* Ithaca, N.Y.: Cornell University Press, 1969.

Watson, G. R., "The Pay of the Roman Army, The Auxiliary Forces," *Historia* 8 (1959), 372-378.

Webster, Graham, *The Roman Imperial Army of the First and Second Centuries A.D.* London: Adam & Charles Black, Ltd., 1969.

Webster, Graham, *The Roman Army.* Chester: The Grosvenor Museum, 1956.

Yadin, Yigael, *The Scroll of the War of the Sons of Light against the Sons of Darkness.* Translated by Batya and Chaim Rabin. London: Oxford University Press, 1962.

William White, Jr.

9
Finances

Finance, the science of monetary affairs is a modern concept for which there is no lexical equivalent in either Greek or Latin, the two dominant languages of the classical world. However, the ideas and practices assumed under the term were well known in Greece and Rome. For this reason the study of financial practices provides insight into antiquity, especially so, since both finance and financial policy were an integral part of the rise and expansion of the Roman Empire. Since the origins and character of the earliest period of the Christian church were formed during this era of Rome's economic expansion, a more extensive understanding of the Roman financial situation will shed light on some aspects of the nature of the early church.

HISTORICAL BACKGROUND OF ROMAN FINANCIAL PRACTICE

Like almost every other aspect of the Roman culture, the specific development of Roman financial practice came into being through the contact and conflict of the Roman people with the nations round-about them. The combination, dialectic, and recombination of Roman and non-Roman cultures as much determined and shaped the destiny of Rome as the peoples who were conquered. If the geopolitical expansion of Roman power may be schematized as a series of ever-widening concentric circles beginning with the conquest and unification of the seven hills sometime about the seventh century B.C. and reaching out finally to encompass the area from the borders of England and the shores of the Black Sea to the coastlands of the Persian Gulf, then the Roman world view must have been altered in the process. In fact, Rome's contact, first with Etruscans and Gauls, second with Greeks, third with Carthaginians and Western Semites and lastly with Balkans, Parthians, and Ural-Altais, structured both the Roman social system and the sensibilities of the Roman populace. The final result which became apparent in the imperial establishment was an elaborate construct collected and refined by trial and error but hallowed by tradition, a system at once archaic and yet pragmatic, fraught with bureaucratic encrustations yet capable of rapid and efficient action.

One central innovation separates the Roman achievement from all that had gone before it, the application of the mechanistic world view[1] to the everyday problems of the marketplace with the consequence of producing technological answers. By so doing, Rome reached a pinnacle of economic power and authority only equaled a millennium after the destruction of Rome and not surpassed until the Renaissance. It is impossible to isolate Rome's monetary and economic activities from her technological prowess. Roman success in exploitation of the natural and human resources of the Mediterranean basin was in direct proportion to her efficiency in obtaining, processing, transporting, and distributing those natural resources and the products made from them throughout her Empire. Aside from purely psychological factors, Roman coinage, like that of the other nations of antiquity, derived value from its content of precious, noble metals. Gold, silver, and electrum specie had appeared millennia previous, but Rome added the dimension of a controlled and fluid currency which could be utilized as an economic weapon to wage financial war.[2]

The meaning of Roman finance must then be sought in the historical roots from which it sprung and the systems which it ultimately supplanted. Attitudes die hard, harder than the men who forge them, and all evidence tends to lead to the conclusion that the man in the Roman street was hardly an innovator or a revolutionary apt to follow after any idealistic schemes of social philosophy or political engineering. Undoubtedly, the specter of change was intolerable, and the populace much preferred the continuance of the *status quo*.

The background of imperial finance was developed upon those notions of the economic process which Rome inherited from the earlier civilizations. It is necessary to consider just what specific elements Rome received from those civilizations, which elements she developed to fit her situation, and which she rejected.

Finance in the Archaic Religious-State

The archaeological evidence of ancient finance indicates that finance was a function of the township settlement which attended the neolithic food-producing revolution. The oldest known written documents from Mesopotamia and the newly discovered, and possibly earlier, texts from Tartaria[3] all contain what appear to be economic records. This finding accords well with the evidence from the same period of intensive building programs and the establishment of complex social structures. The resulting irrigation-cultures entered the historical scene through the annals and the epics of the Sumerians and their Eastern Semite successors. Items of intrinsic value, such as weights of the noble metals, semiprecious stones, and objets d'art, were all used as symbols and vehicles of trade and value. The dominance of the temple and its authoritative center, the cult of the city god, characterized all the early river-valley settlements, hence the term religious-states. In such social systems the ultimate source of wealth was the fecundity and fertility of the earth and its animal inhabitants. The generations of men and animals rendered a people wealthy while sterility and pestilence rendered them poor. Even the Latin language preserved this reminder of the age of sheep-shepherd cultures/cow-cowherd cultures in its terms *pecus*, "a herd," and *pecunia*, "wealth." The financial officers of the archaic religious states were essentially religious officers whose right to rule was derived from the theocracy itself. To the very end of her days Rome dispensed money through functionaries and associations whose origins could be placed in the murky past of astrological and sacrificial offices.

Ancient taxation was based upon percentages, usually weights or measures, of the produce of flocks and herds which were dedicated to king and temple at certain specified seasonal festivals. As early as the second millennium B.C., substitution of weight of precious metal for a specific animal or its vegetable equivalent had already taken place, and Babylonian school texts indicate that scribal students were drilled in solving problems involving the amount of work and percentage of pay due for a specific task. The economic decrees in the cuneiform law codes play an important part in our understanding of the pressures of price and expense in regard to taxation. Needless to say, the subtleties of tax assessment and collection were not lost upon the ancient potentates. An important part of this financial control were the royal monopolies on the mining, smelting, and minting of precious metals into coins. The sexagesimal arithmetic system developed by the Sumerians carried over into monetary systems and metrology for many centuries and was still in effect in the Roman Republic.

Ancient armies foraged as they conquered and languished in retreat; aside from metallic weapons and funds to pay mercenaries, there is little evidence that the archaic religious-states concerned themselves with enlarged levies for supplying armies in the field. War in deep antiquity was far from total, and booty or the promise of it was often sufficient motivation for volunteers. Police forces, as we know them, were a later innovation necessitated by the rise of urbanization and urbanized populations. On the other hand, civil administrators collected fees for their services, licenses, and commissions, all of which were thought to be the natural reimbursement for their positions. Many other petty officials were wards of the royal court and were paid by means of supplying their sustenance. The Middle and Late Egyptian ostraca indicate that often this payment was a ration of bread, beer (or the grain from which to brew it), and some protein substance, usually fish. This element of ancient kingly wealth was duly noted by economists of the Age of Reason.[4] During the period of Rome's flourishing, the alteration from qualitative to quantitative wealth took lasting hold on the states under her control. No longer, as in the archaic religious-states, was sheer maintenance at a subsistence level of a number of human beings outside of the extended family sufficient to indicate financial power; it became necessary to demonstrate the technical proficiency and extravagance which only vast sums of coinage, not volume of goods, could buy. Here again the technological aspect is involved.

Although the first expression of round coins with engraved images appears to have taken place among the mineral-rich states of Anatolia about 1000 B.C.,[5] this practice does not appear in Rome until after its introduction by the Etruscans about 480 B.C. Even then the value of the coins set by weight of their metallic content was based on the rates accepted by the wealthy cities of Asia Minor and Syria-Palestine which were long engaged in flourishing international trade. Among the colonies of the Western Semites, such as the Carthaginians of Spain and southern France, payment of import tariffs in coins by weight of metal as substitutes for equivalent values in goods was commonplace by the early third century B.C.[6] All of these practices passed on into the Roman sphere of influence.

Finance in the Greek City-States

The Ionian cities east of the twenty-fifth meridian were the first to throw off the *mort main* of the ancient theocratic aristocracy and establish the newer concept of an oligarchy based upon conquest by right of wealth. The debate over which group — whether Minoan, Eteocretan, Mycenaean or Doric — founded the island thalassocracies is not yet settled but somewhere in the coastal region of Turkey and upon the multitudinous islands of Greece the first merchant-tradership ships appeared. Systematized and philosophized, this culture was reflected in the mechanistics of Thales and his followers. By a quirk of destiny, the nascent science and technology thus formed bypassed

Attica and were transported to the Greek autocracies of southern Italy, Sicily, and Sardinia. In those locations the Romans first discovered the rational conception of the universe. Interestingly enough, the classical Roman writers were not highly impressed by Plato, Aristotle, or the Sophistical schools. They were much more interested in the last stages of the Greek accomplishment, namely neo-Platonism, Epicureanism, Stoicism, and the various mysteries. The temper of Rome was unsuited to either Greek democracy or Greek philosophical meandering. Nevertheless the Romans recognized the Greek genius for detailed analysis, and later Latin treatises on government and such matters as influence finance were largely quotations from Greek sources.[7] Finance in the Greek city-states was turned over to special officers elected for the purpose of overseeing the dispersion of public funds and accountable to the council or whatever body the citizens provided. With the growth of the amphictyonic leagues, such oversight was turned over to the more central temples at Delphi, Delos, and elsewhere. Here the monies, usually in the form of metal bars or coins of too large a denomination for practical private commerce such as the *talent,* were placed in a rite of incubation under the protection of the god and with mutual honor before the shrine binding all the participants.

The sources of revenue in the Greek states were levies on goods imported and taxes paid on value of possessions. Since most products requiring division of labor were produced under government monopolies, such as the famous Athenian pottery, the income from such trade passed directly into the treasury. Cases of serious misappropriation of the public treasury were frequent enough, for example, the charges brought against the architects of the Parthenon. The manipulation of the courts and safeguards of the rights of the citizenry by men of means was a continuous threat to the internal political harmony of the Greek states. This penchant of the Greek personality led the Persians to the cynical conclusion that every Greek had his price and could be bought off; all one had to do was find the right amount. There is no doubt that these flaws in the Greek character could not be solved by legal means; yet the obvious failures of the Greek financial system were regularly the subject of reform and reconsideration in an effort to check abuses. In this enthusiasm Sparta forbade private citizens to own gold. In the period following the Persian wars, Athens controlled the lucrative trade in the eastern Mediterranean, but her maritime expansion was blocked in the west by the oligarchic Grecian states of Magna Graecia, the Carthaginians of North Africa, and the Etruscan metal monopoly on the western edge of the Italian boot. In effect Greece looked east for expansion and the most cosmopolitan of her leaders saw the domination of the Orient, Syria-Palestine along with Egypt, Persia, and India, as the destiny of her people. Alexander sent his armies in this direction and subjugated Asia to the domination of Greece.

Finance in the Hellenistic Kingdoms

The conflict of late Greek idealism with the practical colonialism of the Persian satrapical system produced the new entity of Hellenism. Superficially eclectic but effectively quite novel, Hellenism spread a veneer of Greek speech, culture, and enlightenment over the ruins of the archaic religious-states. During Alexander's short career many features of the opulent Persian royal house were accepted by the oligarchy of Greece. Alexander's soldiers and their commanders were infatuated with the resplendence of oriental cultures two thousand years older than their own. The harems, gowns, slaves, manners, and morals of the vanquished potentates, all of them war booty by right of conquest, swept over the new military aristocracy of Macedonia and changed forever the democratic simplicity of the Greek world view. In such a world order all subjects became slaves and the collective wealth of the citizenry became the royal exchequer. In the states such as Egypt with a long history of kingly absolutism, the state controlled monopolies were continued under the new masters. The disposition of the national wealth was at the whim of the overlord and the only necessary authority a kingly decree. In the face of the disruption of the ancient solidarity and the loss of security, the upper classes found respite in a sordid fatalism based on a profoundly pessimistic judgment about the life of man. If pleasure alone rendered life meaningful, then the pursuit of money was the necessary *summum bonum*. This alteration in attitude basically changed the common psychology of value and therefore elevated the financial aspect of life to ultimate importance. Taxation enforced by tyranny and exacted by terror was a chief characteristic of life in many of the Hellenistic states. Continual repression of the natives of the countries bred revolution which was met with squads of mercenaries who had to be paid, and so a vicious cycle was set in motion.

In the more important theater of international relations, the rivalry between the Hellenistic states was rooted in their competition for the India trade. The Ptolemaic income from careful exploitation of the commerce of Syria-Palestine and the harbors of North Arabia was very large and a source of constant warfare with the Seleucids, who sought to control the Indian and Parthian routes, to import the goods of the Ural-Altai, and to sell them at profit to the North and West. The ultimate goal may have been the growing trade which passed over the Caspian Sea and across the Eurasian steppes to the

Middle Kingdom, a trade which was to soon expand to incredible proportions and expand the horizons of western man. The minting of coins of the Indic rather than the Attic standard improved the Seleucid trading position and soon made Seleucia on the Tigris one of the richest cities of the age. The excavation of one of the fortress towns, Dura-Europas on the middle Euphrates, astride the caravan route to India and beyond, has greatly increased our knowledge of this economic facet of Hellenistic life. Although it suffered decay and disorganization, this elaborate trade and the supporting financial system were destined to fall into Roman hands in a large measure intact. These were the manifold traditions and cross-cultural alignments which Rome was soon to weld into one dominant and universal system, an Empire based on law and order.

FINANCE IN THE ROMAN REPUBLIC

The actual date and circumstance of the founding, or rather transition, of Rome from an archaic religious-state, under a birthright priestly monarch, to a republican order are lost in antiquity. Suffice it to say that by 400 B.C., and perhaps a half century earlier, Rome had achieved an organized republican system, the first one among western man. All the later offices were there in embryo, the Tribal Council, Tribunes, Aediles, Consuls, Censors, and Quaestors and that most prodigious of all bodies, the Senate. The Senate was to wax and wane with the waves of historical events, but its primary responsibility for the collection and dispersion of public funds rendered it the chief policy-making body of the republican era. The paucity of written sources makes any firm portrayal of the functions and responsibilities of the various republican offices impossible. Already Rome's wealth as demonstrated by archaeological finds was considerable and her commerce widely extensive and lucrative. The legal code known as the Twelve Tables contains some economic restrictions on excesses and elaborate, though fragmentary, passages governing inheritance, but the control of the financial organism was in private, not public, hands, a clear departure from the national policies of the contemporary states. In the war between Rome and Veii which erupted in 406 B.C., the new republic assumed the responsibility of paying the troops, the government's first great financial obligation. The final conquest of Veii a decade afterward brought into the treasury considerable booty and the difficult question of the distribution of the arable lands. This problem was to vex Rome throughout her existence, and failure to find any equitable solution was one of the causes of her demise. The newly acquired territories, both forest and field, were a considerable distance from Rome. They could only be used profitably by those who had sufficient capital to invest and who could wait for their gain. Such lands, *latifundia,* for any efficiency, had to be staffed with slaves and thus put a severe strain on the smaller farmer and the privately owned and tended farm. This situation hastened the rise of an aristocratic plutocracy consisting of old patrician families and newly rich plebeian families. In time the financial plight of the rural poor and the urban impoverished became the source of a bitter class struggle which was only partially settled by the tyrannical rule of Hortensius and the equalization of patrician and plebeian powers in the early third century B.C. However, the die was cast and the independent small landowner was ultimately doomed to disappear as an economic entity.

Rome began to follow the example of the Etruscans and Carthaginians and to mint her own coins in the late fourth or early third century B.C. The use of stamped metal bars of bronze was carried forth in the minting of large bronze coins. The system of valuation was one hundred weights of bronze equal to ten sheep or one ox. The republican bronze coinage consisted of the initial weight called an *as* (pl. *assēs*), of about one Roman pound, a half weight the *sēmis,* a third weight the *triens,* a quarter weight the *quadrans,* a sixth weight the *sextans* and a single weight, or one twelfth, the *uncia,* English cognate "ounce." In the course of the numerous wars of expansion, the process of inflation took place and the *as* was often lightened and devalued. Thus there appeared a sextantal *as,* one sixth of the original, and so forth until only the uncial *as* or one twelfth of the original was left. On one side of the coin appeared the head of a god or goddess, on the reverse a ship's prow. With the conquest of Asia by Alexander silver plate and coin brought back to Greece as booty caused a loss in the value of bronze. The old standard of 120 weights of bronze equivalent to 1 of silver became impossible to maintain. The Romans began to mint silver coin similar to the Greek drachma between the middle of the third century and the early second century B.C. The Roman *dēnārius* weighed about 70 grams but was reduced over the years. The basis of the silver coinage was the bronze so that the republican *dēnārius* was equal to ten sextantal *assēs,* later sixteen of the uncial *assēs.* The silver coins were minted in special installations located in a few temples. While bronze, silver, and even copper coins were struck under orders of the Senate and by the oriental cities of the later Empire, gold coins gained currency after the Second Punic War (218–201 B.C.). During the period of the two triumviates and the Empire, gold coins, *aurei,* were minted at the behest of the executive only, and Julius Caesar is said to have been the first to have his own likeness expressed upon a coin. Throughout Rome's history the frequent exchange of Oriental, European, and

African coinage was so commonplace as to require the trade of *argentārii* or "money changers."

The actual worth of the various Roman coins is difficult to estimate because of fluctuations in prices of goods and the relative economic state of the communities in which those commodities were sold. However, if we allow the weight of the late third–early second century B.C. Roman pound to stand at 327.45 grams, then it is equivalent to about thirteen and a fraction ounces of gold. Thus the Roman pound of gold was equivalent to about $475 with about twice the purchasing power of that amount in the decade 1960–1970. This valuation accords with the fact that one ox or ten sheep were equal to sixty *dēnārii,* or about $25, on that market which in turn matches the wage and private wealth statistics of the time. However, the debasement and reevaluation of the Roman currency, on which most of the Mediterranean world came to depend, was so frequent that only the most approximate estimates can be realized. On the above basis, taxes set at 5 percent would be considerable, given the generally lower standard of living and the lack of hard currency in an agrarian society where most metals had to be used for tools and other more practical and immediate purposes. The cost of large public works, until the time of the expansion of the provincial system after the Gallic Wars (58–49 B.C.), was such that subscriptions of funds by Rome's wealthier citizens were often sought. War was particularly expensive for the relatively small number of troops and horsemen in the field. The total cost of the First Punic War (264–241 B.C.) would have amounted to approximately $55,000,000 by the economic standards of 1960–1970. However, this seemingly large amount is a mere pittance if compared with the wealth of Sicily, Corsica, and Sardinia which Carthage was forced to yield to Rome.

From the period of the earliest extant records down to the end of the First Punic War, the revenue of the Republic was gained in three ways: direct taxes on capital, *tribūtum ex censu;* indirect taxes, such as customs and tariffs, *portōria,* and the 5 percent tax on the manumission of slaves, *vicesima manumissionum;* income from the state monopolies and lands, such as the *vectigal,* a rental for farm land, and the *scriptura* for pasture lands. When provincial governments were introduced with the continued successes in conquest, the colonies paid a fixed yearly amount, the *stīpendium,* which was set according to the wealth and produce of the individual settlement or province. As an alternative to this fixed sum a 10 percent tax on agricultural produce could be paid — the *decumae.* Harbor fees and tariffs on traded goods were also required. Throughout most of the republican period the Senate was solely in charge of the public treasury, and its officers were the only Roman officials capable of encumbering the treasury or authorizing debts to be paid from it. The chief positions were the quaestors and censors. The quaestorship was an annually elective office which was probably inherited from the old Sabine officialdom and transferred to Rome after 509 B.C. Upon the presentation of approved bills by the magistrates, the quaestors paid them out of the senatorial treasury, the *aerarium,* for which they collected and tallied the revenues. The censors allocated no funds, but during their brief incumbencies of usually eighteen months they let the government contracts, leased the state lands, and auctioned off the tax-gathering concessions. This last was one of the most vicious pitfalls of the Roman financial system wherein the right and authority to gather taxes was farmed out to the highest bidder who could then surcharge above the usual 5–10 percent for a tidy profit.

As the state lands grew and Rome faced the responsibilities of foreign colonial administration, the idea of making the colonial systems self-supporting gained currency. The necessary functions of colonial supervision — army, navy, civil administration, and tax collection — could all be made to pay for themselves out of exploitation of the colonies. Because the revenues from all forms of taxation were never very much and the vast resources of the Asian and African kingdoms were available, Rome by 187 B.C. had altered her course to that of relying on a booty economy. The simple formula was: let each subjugated state pay the cost of its subjugation and let each colony bear the expense of its colonization. So well did this system work that in 167 B.C. when Aemilius Paullus (d. 160 B.C.) won the battle of Pydna and paid an enormous sum of Grecian booty into the treasury, it was possible to halt the collection of the capital tax. As one authority has stated:

> This year of 167 was a turning-point in the history of the Roman State, for it saw the consecration of a financial system, arising from the conquest, under which the City paid as little as possible and the balancing of the budget depended almost entirely on the methodical exploitation of the conquered peoples.[8]

For this purpose and to this end, Rome utilized the most advanced technological system of transport and the widest degree of decentralization of functions the world had yet experienced. In retrospect the alteration to a booty economy and the change of Roman society from a producer state to a consumer state may have been the cause of the political and social turmoil that led to the reaction of imperialism. In the same fashion as the Senate utilized its prerogative of authority over the state finance to finance conquests abroad, it also applied its power to the engulfing of the magisterial functions of the old state and thus established its one sole and unique authority. The constitutional government of Rome fashioned in the productive era of the fourth and third centuries B.C., had given way to an oligarchy by 149

B.C., and finance had been the primary weapon employed. The political crisis which ensued was the stage for the rise, first of the Gracchi (133–131 B.C.), and second of the autocracy of the triumvirates ending in the personal government of the Caesars.

The financial situation in the last year of the Republic was one of action and response, both initiated by money. The response was that of violent civil disorder and the dissolution of public morality. The varieties of immorality were only exceeded by the multiplicities of graft. From the political payoff of both voters and rivals Rome witnessed the final plunge into assassination and rioting. The ultimate death of republican government was sealed by the failure of every attempt to solve the imbalance of large slave-run farms in competition with the private tenant. In the chaos of conflicting parties and the welter of financial irresponsibility, one force arose capable of establishing order and emending the constitution. This force was the military machine. Under its heavy hand the Republic perished and the Empire was born.

FINANCE IN THE EARLY EMPIRE

The rise of the Empire and its success is inextricable from the careers of two men, Julius Caesar and his nephew Octavius Augustus. The idea of a "first citizen" gained popularity throughout the last pre-Christian century and took form in Cicero's treatise, *De Republica,* which he wrote in 54 B.C. well after Pompey had actually begun his Principate. Under this system the entire monetary power passed from the Senate into the hands of the *princeps,* the visual, historic embodiment of the Roman citizen. Swiftly the principial notion passed on into the birthright monarchy established by Caesar in which the financial reins, as in the Hellenistic states, were firmly grasped by the monarch. With the monarchical formula in effect, violence became an accepted political tool, and the veil of constitutional respectability sought by Pompey for his Principate was torn aside. As censor Caesar removed senators and added handpicked henchmen raising the membership to an unwieldly nine hundred in which foul play and coercive threats could bring about the required result on any money matter. Although Caesar did not live to reap the final fruits, the title of *Rex* and the privilege of selecting his own and Rome's successor to power, yet he had launched for good or ill the monarchical ideal. The imperial concept was quickly seized and employed by his heir apparent, Octavius. With Octavius' assumption of the full tribunician power, *tribunicia potestas,* in 23 B.C., the Roman Empire and Caesar's dream of a dominion were accomplished. This imperial system was based upon the military, and the state now had the responsibility of paying out of the *aerarium* the costs of pensions and benefits for veterans. Ultimately a separate fund, the *aerarium militare,* was set up, and into it Octavius himself deposited approximately $16,000,000. As early as 28 B.C. Octavius had begun to reorganize the chaotic state of the financial system. He took certain specific steps to do so. He restored the fortunes of many of the old senatorial families, from donations for that purpose, in an effort to find support and assistance for his schemes to exclude foreigners from the army and to reinstate the old republican discipline. He set fixed salary figures for the provincial officialdom and newly appointed magistrates. He established a corps of accountants and scribes to attend to the massive tangle of bookkeeping that had arisen through neglect.

In the handling of the money itself, Octavius did not actually destroy the ancient organs of the Senate including the keepers of the treasure, the *praefecti aerārii Saturni.* In order to increase the available coinage, he presented bills for the minting of new coins and the reevaluation of the currency. He also planned and later carried out military operations in the Spanish areas of Cantabria, Asturia, and Salassi to reopen the gold mining operations there and exploit them for Rome. His long-term plan took many years to execute. Rome's resources were surveyed and tallied as a prelude to raising the amounts of tribute annually paid to Rome and to increasing the systematic exploitation of the colonies and provinces. On his journey to the East in 21 B.C., Octavius, revered as Augustus, took personal charge of the elaborate remains of the Hellenistic states and reorganized his colonial administration along those Greek lines upon which it had been begun.

FINANCE IN ROMAN SYRIA-PALESTINE

No Roman province was the source of more difficulty and disorder than Syria-Palestine, which was annexed to Rome by Pompey in 64 B.C. The ancient system of provincial administration was followed and, aside from the appointment of a governor and his staff, the social and political customs were allowed to continue. In Palestine, however, the situation was quite different from the outset because of the fact that Judaism and the Second Commonwealth were the only remnants of the old familiar archaic religious-state to survive the impact of Hellenism and still function in Roman times. The peculiar theocentric character of the Jewish system had become even more deeply entrenched in opposition to the Seleucid attempts to dislodge it. By the time of Augustus this feature of Jewish life had been reinforced and defended by the rise of the Pharisaic party which opposed any external influence in Palestinian affairs. The combination of elaborate ceremonial temple taxes, Hellenistic taxes, and Roman provincial taxes was not only a burden to the populace but nearly impossible to reduce to order.

Pompey installed John Hyrcanus in the seat of power and continued the policy of founding cities and towns in Syria-Palestine. He also continued the practice of farming out the tax-gathering concessions to the *publicānus* (Greek *telōnēs*), who were usually employed by their Roman overlords from the native population, thus building an insulation of native pawns against whom the conquered peoples could vent their frustration and rage. The financial burden of Syria-Palestine was as great as any of the provinces due to the Parthian Wars. The inability of the provinces, even under duress, to meet their tax levies forced an alteration in the imperial financial system such that the emperor himself saw to it the army was paid, the roads extended, and all other costs were met. In the East this change amounted to a personal assumption of all financial affairs by Augustus. Thus, the Roman emperor found himself collecting and dispersing the senatorial treasury in the same manner as the Hellenistic kings before him. To this end a new business-man class appeared which was made up of wealthy bourgeoisie from the native populations and whose positions of influence in their provincial towns enabled them to take on the tax-gathering functions. Efficiency in collecting and remitting the taxes due was probably motivated by a reduction in the personal taxes of these entrepreneurs. If so, then the position of Levi Matthew as portrayed in the Lucan narrative (Luke 5:27) is not strictly that of a "publican" as understood by the New Testament versions but in fact the Greek is better translated "tax gatherer." One important difficulty in tracing the financial administration of the Augustan age in Palestine is the confusion of Greek terms which exists between the standard, albeit meager, sources and the evangelists who seem to have utilized the common *koinē* equivalents for both the official Jewish and the Latin terminologies.

There can be no doubt that the economic conditions of Syria-Palestine improved greatly under Augustus' firm control and even more rapidly under his imperial successors. Many new cities and towns were built, and the full weight of Roman technology was used not merely for purposes of taxation but for the long-range goal of economic exploitation. Mines, quarries, smelters, ports, and food-processing facilities were built and operated along Roman lines. An interesting situation thus arose, in that many areas in Palestine along the watershed and basin of the Lake of Galilee and the Jordan valley actually supported more human beings than at any time before or since. Villages such as Caesarea and Sebaste were built by Herod along Roman standards while old public festivals and the great temple at Jerusalem were endowed and rebuilt with new enthusiasm.

Although the older aristocratic families who had come to power under the Maccabees were slowly impoverished, the majority of rural and town-dwelling Jews were better off than they had been for over a century, and the recent converts in the area of Galilee were experiencing the golden age of northern Palestine. The eclecticism of Herod's policy favored Judaism, revered the ancient sites of Greek culture, and honored Augustus with large monetary gifts bestowed all around. This approach, in effect, was an abomination of the solitary nature of the ancient theocratic state. This opposition from the Jews is represented in the Gospel narratives in the form of the bitter dislike of Herod and Rome.

The income of the Herodian court has been estimated at considerably more than the actual total of the taxes collected by reason of the advanced business practices of both Herod the Great and his predecessors. Thus the Jewish state income was a lesser burden upon the people than the taxes levied for Rome. Three separate systems of coinage were in circulation: the Jewish, the Seleucid, and the Roman, creating the need for the money-changers' office, Greek, *kollybistēs*, (Matthew 21:12; Mark 11:15). This need was all the more acute in view of the prohibition of the use of pagan currency, which usually bore the image of an idol, in the service of the great temple. There is no reason to imagine that the percent of taxation was above either the 5 percent level common to Rome or the 10 percent common to the Israelite theocratic state and enjoined in the Mosaic legislation. While the official documents give the impression of tranquillity and financial security, the more immediate and less encumbered sources show a scene of seething revolt and patriotic resentment against Rome and its financial agents no matter how cleverly concealed among the populace. After the dissolution of Herod's house occurred and Augustus revived the autonomy of the tetrarchies, the largess of the united kingdom faltered, and the necessity of stationing a legion in Jerusalem so irritated the already inflamed citizens that the stage was set for the scenes so familiar in the gospel tradition.

ROMAN FINANCE IN THE GOSPEL NARRATIVES

Finance plays a minor but important role in the Gospel narratives dealing with the life and teachings of Jesus Christ. Jesus' teaching about money can be summarized in three simple points: (1) Money is a gift of God's providence obtained through human agency; (2) its use can be for either good or evil, but the power it renders makes it potentially very difficult to handle wisely; (3) the ultimate test of one's religious sincerity is his liberality with his money. These three concepts are of course interconnected in the whole system of Jesus'

own messianic self-consciousness and the presentation of himself as
the exemplar of the older Hebraic covenant. Any assumption that
Jesus' speech in this regard supports any specific social or economic
theory goes beyond the evidence. The gospel tradition holds that the
immediate circumstances of Jesus and his followers were poor, although some, such as Peter, Andrew, James, and John, probably belonged to the lower middle class of fishermen who owned their own
small boats and supplied both the local market demand and the
Roman fishworks with their catch. Levi Matthew probably sat on the
beaching area at Capernaum to receive his customs toll on the catch.
A number of terms used in specialized senses for financial transactions
appear in the New Testament gospels. These terms by frequency are:
Greek *telōnēs,* "tax gatherer;" [9] Greek *telōnion,* "tax office;" [10] Greek
architelōnēs, "chief tax collector, head tax gatherer;" [11] and the very
special usage of Greek *apographē,* "list, inventory, census." [12] These
terms appear in contexts concerning the Roman taxation but are not
applied to the Jewish temple-tax. Of even greater interest are the
passages in which the quantitative estimates of price and value appear.
In statements regarding salary, as paid for a day's work by a peasant or
villager in an unskilled trade, the going rate was one Roman *denārius*
(Greek *dēnarion*), worth about twenty-five U.S. cents.[13] In the para-
bolic sections of the Gospel narratives even multiples of ten denarii are
given as possible values of lots of commodities. Although these are
quite probably realistic figures, the very nature of the discourses in
which they were given does not require them to be definitive values
of the items or quantities concerned.[14] Considerable critical effort has
been expended in the last century in attempts to deduce the genre or
types of literature or styles of discourse included in the evangelists'
records of Jesus and his speech. So far these attempts have been marred
by subjective theological and philosophical presuppositions of such
a nature as to bar their effective usage as semantic tools, and little in
the way of conclusive insight has been realized. In a more Hebraic
statement undetermined amounts of coinage are mentioned by the
names of their metallic constituents, but this only in Matthew 10:9
(Greek *"chryson . . . argyron . . . chalkon,"*) "gold . . . silver . . .
copper." However, the parallel account in Mark 6:8 gives only the
last term as a collective for all three and the other parallel account
in Luke 9:3 gives the most common middle term for all three.[15]
There is the probability therefore that the term *denārius* represents
the Roman usage and the Roman coinage used primarily to pay
Roman taxes and tariffs and never permissable for temple debts.
The most important text in this last regard is that contained in
Matthew 22:19 wherein two words appear referring to money, *denārius,* and the much less common Greek *kēnsos,* a Latin loanword

in Greek, the coin with which the head or poll tax, the "census," was paid. This word appeared with the Roman annexation of Asia Minor in the first century B.C. The gospel account contains the answer of Jesus to the Pharisees and Herodians, "Render therefore to Caesar the things that are Caesar's, and to God the things that are God's."

This simple text has been often misquoted and more commonly misunderstood as a clever but somewhat facetious put-off. The more profound and incisive meaning involved the divine image of Augustus and the evil imagination of the rich Pharisees. In essence Jesus meant,

> You are delighted to get the coins Rome issues; you do business with them, and you thereby do business with Rome; you hold we may not worship Caesar, that it is blasphemous to permit the image of Caesar as a god to enter Jerusalem, yet you permit it in the case of money, and thus you show that you yourselves worship money, as indeed Caesar does; that is, you worship power, power based on force and fraud; you cannot then grow squeamish if Rome, the champion of that sort of power everywhere, charges a modest commission.[16]

Nowhere in the New Testament is there a forthright condemnation of money, only of man made mad by it. No doubt many Jews other than the apostles saw the moral tangle and insidious evil involved in Rome's financial stranglehold on her Empire. They saw also that this encumbrance could not be tolerated nor compromised by the worshipers of the true God. This problem of ultimate sovereignty arose again at the trial of Jesus before Pilate, procurator of Judea, where Jesus made no attempt to deny his acceptance of the messianic kingship over the Jews (John 18:36ff.) .

One additional aspect of the meaning of Roman finance is found in the gospels and that is the equation of material benefits with security and the goal of human life. In the Sermon on the Mount Jesus stated, "Therefore do not be anxious, saying, 'What shall we eat?' or 'What shall we drink?' or 'What shall we wear?' For the Gentiles seek all these things . . ." (Matthew 6:31-32) . In this statement Jesus makes clear the basic distinction between the Roman and Jewish concept of wealth. For the Roman citizen the possession of wealth and its pragmatic fulfillment defined virtue; the effective way was the Roman way. In biblical Judaism, as interpreted by Jesus, all aspects of man's life were ultimately subservient to God's moral law. As the success of the Empire waned, the vacuity of the Roman premise was to become all too obvious.

ROMAN FINANCE IN THE APOSTOLIC AGE

The chief financial alteration between the era of Jesus' public ministry and that of his apostolic followers was the severe debasement of the currency under Nero. This was the outcome of Nero's extravagance and the internal strife it engendered. Under Nero the golden *aureus* was reduced by 10 percent in weight of gold and the silver *denārius* by an equal amount. In addition the habit of the Hellenistic cities of the East was followed in the alloying of the *denārius* with cheaper metals. The one positive outcome of this devaluation was that it brought Rome's monetary system into line with the debased coinage of the East, and this facilitated trade. However, it also forced up prices and enlarged the grain dole and the city mob in Rome. The overthrow and death of Nero in A.D. 68 brought the new dynasty of the Flavians to the imperial throne. The chief problem they faced was the reduction of Rome's treasury and the general rise in prices throughout the Empire. Finally, after two ephemeral emperors, Vespasian mounted the throne and quickly stabilized the tax, coinage, and expenditure systems. To achieve this result, he was obliged to levy even heavier taxes than his predecessors, and thus he started the process of grinding down the old private wealth which was to become uniform and totally oppressive with Constantine in the fourth Christian century. There are some references to the prices and exchange rates of commodities in the Epistles of the New Testament. The promise of the Revelation that goods would finally be exorbitant in price during the final judgment may well have had special meaning on the basis of the inflation throughout the Roman world at the end of the first century. Prices, wages, and taxes were as much a part of Roman man's existence as of modern man's, and to both men the gospel message was addressed by Peter in his encompassing statement: "You know that you were ransomed from the futile ways inherited from your fathers, not with perishable things such as silver or gold, but with the precious blood of Christ, like that of a lamb without blemish or spot" (1 Peter 1:18-19).

NOTES

[1] Cf. E. J. Dijksterhuis, *The Mechanization of the World Picture* (Oxford: The Clarendon Press, 1961).

[2] Note, for example, Cicero, *"Nihil tam munitum quod non expugnari pecunia possit," In C. Verrem* 1. 2. 4.

[3] Cf. "Writing," in *The Pictorial Bible Encyclopedia* (Grand Rapids: Zondervan Publishing House, 1970).

[4] Adam Smith, *The Wealth of Nations* (New York: E. P. Dutton & Co., Inc.,), IV.

[5] Developed from the practice of utilizing stamped bullion and bars.

[6] H. Donner and W. Röllig, *Kanaanäische und Aramäische Inschriften.* Mit einem Beitrag von O. Rössler. 2., durchgesehene und erweiterte Auflage (Wiesbaden: Harrasowitz, 1966), Band I, Nr. 69.

[7] E.g., Cicero's quotations from Polybius in *De Republica* 1. 26, 29, 35, 45-46.

[8] Leon Homo, *Roman Political Institutions from City to State* (New York: Barnes & Noble, Inc., 1962), p. 144.

[9] Matthew 5:46; 9:10; parallels in Mark 2:15, 16; Luke 5:29-30. Matthew 10:3; parallel in Luke 5:27; Matthew 11:19; parallel in Luke 7:34 et al. Matthew 18:17; 21:31-32. Luke 3:12; 7:29; 18:10-11 (Latin *Publicānus*)

[10] Matthew 9:9; Mark 2:14; Luke 5:27 (Latin *publicāneum*).

[11] Matthew 19:2 (Latin *princeps publicānorum*).

[12] Luke 2:1-2 (Latin *describi/descriptio*).

[13] Matthew 20:2-13; parallel in different circumstances in Luke 10:35.

[14] Matthew 18:28; Mark 6:37; 14:5; Luke 7:41; John 6:7; 12:5.

[15] In modern usage the Israeli cent or mill is a small aluminum coin equal to 1/100 (.01) of the lira or pound but it is called an *argorot* meaning literally "fine metals."

[16] S. Barr, *The Mask of Jove* (Philadelphia: J. B. Lippincott Co., 1966), p. 241. Copyright, © 1966 by Stringfellow Barr. Reprinted by permission of J. B. Lippincott Company.

FOR ADVANCED READING

In addition to the standard reference works (see pages 32-33) the following comprise our primary authorities:

SOURCES

Cicero, *De Republica*. Edited by Clinton W. Keyes. Cambridge, Mass.: Harvard University Press, Loeb Classical Library, 1928.
_____, *The Verrine Orations*. Edited by L. H. G. Greenwood. Cambridge, Mass.: Harvard University Press, Loeb Classical Library. Vols. 1 and 2. 1928, 1935.
Roman Documents from the Greek East: Senatus Consulta and Epistulae to the Age of Augustus. Edited by R. K. Sherk. Baltimore: The Johns Hopkins Press, 1968.
An Economic Survey of Ancient Rome. Edited by Tenney Frank. Vol. 1. Baltimore: The Johns Hopkins Press, 1933.

MODERN STUDIES

Abbott, Frank F., and Johnson, Allan C., *Municipal Administration in the Roman Empire*. Princeton: Princeton University Press, 1926. Reprint New York: Russell & Russell Publishers, 1969.
Breglia, Laura, *Roman Imperial Coins*. New York: Frederick A. Praeger, Inc., 1968.
Barr, Stringfellow, *The Mask of Jove*. Philadelphia: J. B. Lippincott Co., 1966.
Coster, Charles H., *Late Roman Studies*. Cambridge, Mass.: Harvard University Press, 1968.
Davies, Oliver, *Roman Mines in Europe*. New York: Oxford University Press, 1935.
Davis, W. S., *The Influence of Wealth in Imperial Rome*. New York: The Macmillan Company, 1910 (1933).
Forbes, Robert J., *Studies in Ancient Technology*. 11 vols. New York: James H. Heineman, Inc., 1964.
Frank, Tenney, *An Economic History of Rome*. 2nd ed. Baltimore: The Johns Hopkins Press, 1927.
Grant, Michael, *Roman Imperial Money*. New York: Barnes & Noble, Inc., 1954.
_____, *From Imperium to Auctoritas*. New York: Cambridge University Press, 1946.

Heichelheim, F. M., *Wirtschaftsgeschischte des Altertums*. Leiden, 1938.

Homo, Leon, *Roman Political Institutions from City to State*. Translated by V. Gordon Childe. New York: Barnes & Noble, Inc., 1968.

Kunkel, Wolfgang, *An Introduction to Roman Legal and Constitutional History*. Translated by J. M. Kelly. New York: Oxford University Press, 1966.

Levy, Jean-Phillippe, *The Economic Life of the Ancient World*. Edited by John G. Birain. Chicago: The University of Chicago Press, 1967.

Louis, Paul, *Ancient Rome at Work*. Edited by E. B. Wareing. New York: Barnes & Noble, Inc., 1965.

Mattingly, Harold, *Roman Coins*. 2nd ed. New York: Barnes & Noble, Inc., 1967.

Rostovtzeff, Mikhail, *The Social and Economic History of the Hellenistic World*. 3 vols. Toronto, Canada: Oxford University Press, 1941.

Scullard, Howard H., *A History of the Roman World, 753-146 B.C.* 3rd ed. New York: Barnes & Noble, Inc., 1961.

Starr, Chester G., *Civilization and the Caesars*. New York: W. W. Norton & Company, Inc., 1965.

Sutherland, Carol H. V., *Coinage in Roman Imperial Policy, 31 B.C.-A.D. 68*. London: Methuen & Co., Ltd., 1951.

Sydenham, Edward A., *The Coinage of the Roman Republic*. Chicago: Argonaut, Inc., Publishers, 1964.

Toutain, Jules, *The Economic Life of the Ancient World*. Translated by M. R. Dobie. New York: Barnes & Noble, Inc., 1930.

White, K. D., *Historical Roman Coins, 44 B.C.-A.D. 55*. Grahamstown, S. Africa, 1958.

Winspear, Alban D., and Geweke, L. K., *Augustus and the Reconstruction of Roman Government and Society*. Madison: The University of Wisconsin Press, 1935.

Donald Winslow

10
Religion and the
Early Roman Empire

Less than a year before his execution by the Nazis in April, 1945, Dietrich Bonhoeffer wrote of the great pleasure he derived from reading W. F. Otto's classic study of Greek religion, *Die Götter Griechenlands*. What struck Bonhoeffer, as he sat in his prison cell, was that Otto described a world of faith — albeit non-Christian — which sprang from the totality of human experience and not, as with much of Christian theology, just from its "cares and longings." [1] In a later letter, however, Bonhoeffer complained that too often Christianity is interpreted, after the manner of the oriental myths, as a "religion of redemption," i.e., a religion which arises from out of those "human boundary-experiences," such as fear, ignorance, and death, and seeks to redeem man from out of his human situation.[2]

Our purpose here is not to evaluate or to criticize Bonhoeffer's understanding of the Christian tradition but to point out that he was aware, and rightly so, of at least two major religious trends in the ancient world, whether or not these can accurately be assigned — the one to Greek religion and the other to Oriental religion. The trend with which Bonhoeffer was in sympathy was that religious impetus, often so lacking in modern Christianity, which claimed the whole world as the fitting arena for the religious enterprise, an enterprise in which the whole of man was involved. This trend we could not inappropriately designate as the "liberal" approach to religion. The opposite trend, the one with which Bonhoeffer was not in sympathy, we would label as "conservative." This religious style was directed almost exclusively toward the "beyond," and sought fulfillment only through an escape or redemption from the world, an escape undertaken only by a part of man, e.g., his soul or spirit or mind, or any combination thereof, but never his flesh or body. This conservative type of religion validated human experience only as it served the ultimate goal of extricating man from his secular humanity.

GENERAL CHARACTERISTICS

I have cited Bonhoeffer here because, in his subtle and often tantalizing way, he has given voice to a thesis that underlies this present essay, namely, that in the early Empire (indeed, as in the whole history of religions) there can be found these two religious trends, pulling in opposite directions — the liberal trend seeking to make sense out of man and his world, the conservative trend seeing value only in part of man in the next world. The religious man of the first and second centuries A.D. was caught, as it were, in the middle between these two trends since neither, in and of itself, proved wholly satisfactory. Unable to resolve the tension between the two trends, he found himself in a position of "religious ambivalence," to which the exceptional variety of religious expression in this period gives ample testimony.

To illustrate this point, we can look briefly at the concept of Fate as it emerges in the ancient world, a concept which has direct bearing upon the impetus, liberal or conservative, of man's religious identity. Fate was an impersonal, although sometimes personalized, power that controlled all the processes and interrelations of the cosmos, including the individual lives and destinies of men and nations. The religious conservative would conceive of Fate as so ineluctably connected with this world that the individual's sole recourse was to transcend this world noetically now and, it was hoped, to transcend it psychically upon death. Religion became for him primarily a matter of flight. The religious liberal, on the other hand, dealt with the existence of Fate in a considerably more positive, and sometimes even aggressive, manner. Rather than flee to some refuge beyond the reach of Fate, he would attempt to understand it, to control it, or to conform his life to it. If Fate was blind, he would try to lead it by the hand; if it was vengeful, he would try to propitiate it; if it was capricious, he would attempt to outguess it. If indeed Fate, whether divine, spiritual, astral, or what have you, was the central operating principle of the cosmos, the wiser course to the liberal was to align oneself to its operations rather than to spend one's life in a futile attempt to avoid it.

The two religious trends which we have described were both attempts to discover and to identify the ultimate value and meaning of life. Seldom did the trends, however, exist apart from one another. Most religious styles or attitudes were a combination of the two, often with a visible emphasis on one or the other. Whether cultic, cosmological, ethical, or idealistic, the religions of the Empire exhibited to a greater or lesser degree the tension which existed by virtue of the attempt to create a resolution between the conservative and liberal trends. As we begin our discussion of what some of these religions were, this fact should become manifestly apparent. We shall embark, therefore, upon a closer examination of the religious world into which Christianity was born and passed its adolescence.

Octavian, more properly referred to as Caesar Augustus, the first emperor of the new Imperial Age, is cited by his contemporaries and hagiographers, as well as by most history books, as the restorer of Roman religion, a religion which had fallen into decay during the years of the Republic. In fact, after nearly two hundred years of bloodshed, when Augustus established the justly famous *Pax Romana,* he became the restorer of almost everything of value from the traditional past as well as the founder of much that was new. That he played such a decisive role in the restoration of "Roman" religion, among other things, should not, however, lead us to conclude that the religion of the Empire was therefore Roman. Augustus did, in fact, restore many old temples and build some new ones; he revived the priestly colleges; he secured divine titles for his murdered father, Julius Caesar; and he made of the Secular Games a religious festival celebrating the birth of the new Golden Age. But these were all more or less cultic acts, deftly committed with overriding political interests and indicative of the truth of the Polybian axiom that "Roman power is due to Roman piety." As one historian of religions has written, "It was a characteristic Roman conviction that the primary function of religion was to serve the interests of the state and that as a guaranty of political prosperity the rites of religion were potent in the extreme." [3] Augustus seized upon this popular feeling and throughout his reign increasingly brought religion in to serve the state, so much so that when he himself assumed the title of *Pontifex maximus,* we have the first instance of what later, in Christian dress, was to be called "Caesaropapism." Accordingly, we may perhaps more accurately describe Augustus as the restorer of "state" religion, not of "Roman" religion. By virtue of his political pragmatism he knew how to "use" religion; and, more than this, the Ruler-Cult which developed out of his reign became increasingly more oriental and less Roman in its religious dimensions (as we shall see below) but always with its political implications for the whole Empire in the foreground. So when Suetonius speaks of the omens attending Augustus' birth or of his having been sired by Apollo, or when he records how the Senate consecrated the ground on Ox-head's Street in Rome which "the divine Augustus first touched upon coming into the world," [4] such sentiments reflect as much a loyal patriotism as they do a fervid religious imagination.

Neither in Rome itself nor in the Empire as a whole, however, was the major thrust of religious life politically oriented. Imperial religion satisfied the craving for peace and security, and its cultic acts were one way of dealing, largely through votive rites, with the ever-present problem of Fate on a rather grandiose national scale. But the "gods" of this state religion were cold, abstract, and formal. "The worship of the Roman gods," as Cumont has pointed out, "was a civic duty, the worship of foreign gods the expression of personal belief." [5] The alliance of the imperial throne with the cultic altar was not the root of the vitality of the religious life of the Empire. If formal patriotism could be expressed through superficial adherence to the designated divine "powers behind the throne," religious devotion was directed, in a multitude of forms, to other gods. If the religio-political fabric of the Empire was able, to some extent, to keep Fate under control and thereby preserve the *Pax Romana,* there was certainly no harm in ritual conformity — especially since later the refusal to give such formal worship was to be understood as political subversion, as a crime, not against the gods, but against the state, a *crimen laesae maiestatis.* Yet a truer picture of the religions of the Empire is found in the non-political domain, in the vast syncretistic hegemony of Oriental religions. Long before the time of Alexander various religions of the East had been slowly spreading West toward Greece and thence into Italy. When the soldiers, ambassadors, and merchants of Alexander's empire established their widespread footholds throughout the East, this process of religious intermingling was well underway.

Also prior to the time of Augustus we find that the respective Greek and Roman Olympian deities were arranged in complementary order, e.g., Jupiter is Zeus, Juno is Hera, Mercury is Hermes, etc. But even more striking is the extent to which the Olympians, Greek and Roman, were to find their Oriental counterparts, so much so that by the second century A.D. the nomenclature of the multitude of deities appears confusing beyond our capacity to decipher them.[6] In Apuleius' *Metamorphoses* (popularly known as *The Golden Ass),* for instance, the great goddess Isis proclaims to her convert, Lucius, that she alone is the "natural mother of all things, mistress and governess of all the elements," and that she is "adored throughout all the world, in divers manners, in variable customs, and by many names," among which she mentions Minerva, Venus, Diana, Proserpine, Juno, Hecate, etc.[7] It is not strange, therefore, that we find reported in Acts 14:8-17 that some of the more enthusiastic citizens of Lystra, impressed with the healings performed by Paul and Barnabas, decided that the gods had come down in human form and identified Paul with Mercury and Barnabas with Jupiter — a compliment that each of them was hasty to decline!

The direction of this growing syncretism, of which the interchangeability of divine names is but one indication, was generally East to

West, with the result that this movement, in the time of the early Empire, has been described as the "peaceful infiltration of the Orient into the Occident." [8] Further, this interaction between the variety of religions led to a general atmosphere of religious tolerance. The Eleusian Mysteries, for instance, originally an agricultural cult honoring the mythic career of Demeter, the cereal god, were open originally only to Athenians, thence to Greeks, and finally to foreigners as well. Hence Cicero's statement that "the most distant nations were initiated into the sacred and august Eleusinia." [9] Also, the Oriental Mysteries, many of which had begun exclusivistically, gradually became, through the process of syncretization, open both to geographical as well as cross-cultic expansion. To belong to one Mystery Cult, in the time of the Empire, did not forbid one's belonging to another. [10] Plutarch's friend Clea, for instance, was an initiate both of the cult of the Delphic Dionysius and of the Egyptian Isis; [11] and Lucius' spiritual pilgrimage, as reported by Apuleius, ended not with his climactic initiation into the mysteries of Isis but included adherence to the "religion of the great Osiris." [12]

The range of this tolerant syncretism can be further emphasized when its effects are illustrated from within the imperial household. Not only did Rome officially sanction foreign religions within the capitol (except when thought to be politically subversive) [13] and allow temples dedicated to foreign deities to be erected there (though not within the confines of the *pomerium*), but individual emperors manifested specifically syncretistic tendencies. Augustus, for instance, though hailed as the restorer of Roman religion, retained the Sibylline Books, consulted the Delphic Oracle, and, on the testimony of Suetonius, was given to superstition on a grand scale; he was afraid of thunderstorms, evidenced belief in augury and apparitions, and was concerned about whether putting his right shoe on before the left would bode ill. Augustus' "personal" religion, therefore, was not entirely political; as an individual he was open to the fears and haunts of any Roman and thus equally to the religious potential of Orientalism. In the words of Altheim, Augustus "was a Roman who observed in and about him the work of *fatum,* and was carefully prepared to neglect no indication that might bring him the tidings of this *fatum*. [14] So, too, were Augustus' successors: Claudius magnified the cult of the Great Mother Cybele; Gaius was a promoter of the cult of Osiris and gave Isis her first public temple; Nero built a huge colossus dedicated to the Sun (with his own features prominently displayed in front!); Hadrian was initiated into the mysteries of Eleusis; Alexander Severus worshiped every morning in his *lararium* before images of Christ, Abraham, Orpheus, Apollonius of Tyre, as well as before likenesses of his "deified" predecessors; and in 274, Orientalism triumphed within the imperial household when Aurelian designated the cult of the Invincible Sun *(Sol Invictus)* as the state religion to which he assigned a clergy of higher rank than the traditional Roman clergy *(collegium pontificum)*.

Yet, for all this multiplicity of religions, both at Rome and throughout the Empire, to describe the situation as one of unbounded polytheism would not be wholly accurate. Gods there were many, and indeed there always had been. But the "many" were often seen as local or temporal delineations of the "one." For all the polytheism of the Empire, for all the many religious approaches to the individual and corporate problem of Fate, monotheism was not strictly excluded. Nevertheless, as H. Mattingly has observed, the religion of the Empire was "in its essence . . . polytheistic; it worshipped the one and the many, with the stress on the many." [15] However, the vision of unity out of diversity was always a religious ideal, and not, as in the case of the state cult, a politically motivated program. Monotheism was not new to the Greco-Roman world, having roots at least as far back as the Eleatic philosopher Xenophanes who, in the sixth century B.C. stated that "One God there is, greatest of gods and men." [16] But never was this an absolute monotheism as in the case of the Judeo-Christian tradition. If there was one "greatest God," there were always several lesser deities. Yet in the Empire many voices did emphasize the "one" over the "many." Dion Chrysostom, for instance, spoke of those who said that "Apollo, Helios, and Dionysius are one and the same." [17] Maximus of Tyre, too, proclaimed that amid all the strife and tumult of the world there was "one generally accepted opinion," namely, that "there is one God, King and Father of all." [18] So it was possible to speak of *one* God, or at least of the *one* God who was above all the other gods (a phrase not foreign to Jewish as well as Christian literature). A further example of this "tendency" toward monotheism is to be found in the writings of a second century author whose works were circulated with those of Aristotle and under his name as well. In a treatise entitled *De mundo*, it is stated that "God being one yet has many names, being called after all the various conditions which he himself inaugurates." [19] The anonymous author goes on to enumerate these "various conditions" by describing them as Necessity, Fate, Destiny, Nemesis, etc. (all of which are lesser or greater deities in many mythologies) and pointing out that they are the direct operations (with no mediatorial intermediaries) of the one God whose chief characteristic is that of providence over his Creation. Here, then, is an example of a monotheistic tendency which is elaborated in the interests of a "providential" God who is superior to the multiple operations of Fate, because he works directly through them. To subsume Fate under the benevolent panoply of one Creator and Preserver answers, on the rational level at least, many of mankind's religious questions.

Thus far we have looked, very briefly, at the religious situation of the early Empire in an attempt to gain an appreciation of two major phenomena: first, that the religious enterprise existed between two opposite trends — which we have called liberal and conservative — with the result that the many religious styles of the period reflect an obvious tension of ambivalence, especially in regard to the problem of Fate. Secondly, we have noted that, in spite of the Augustan restoration, the religious life of the Empire was highly syncretistic, largely through the gradual adoption of Oriental religions in the West, but that this syncretism, although basically tolerant and polytheistic, was not without its monotheistic tendencies. We are now in a position to examine more closely what appear to be the major religious styles of the early Empire. In so short a space it is impossible to avoid a high degree of selectivity; yet our attempt will be to draw from a variety of sources so that the picture which emerges will not be totally divorced from reality. The religious styles we have chosen to consider are three in number: (1) the Oriental mystery religions, (2) religious philosophy, and (3) the imperial Ruler-Cult.

THE ORIENTAL MYSTERY RELIGIONS

"Fate and magic," A. D. Nock has said in reference to the religions of the Empire, "were part of a world picture which was nearly universal." [20] To this we may add S. J. Case's assertion that "it would not be a mere rhetorical figure to designate the religious history of the Mediterranean world in the early imperial period as the age of the mysteries." [21] If, then, Fate can be identified, along with its related concepts, as the major religious problem of the age, the appeal of the vast variety of mystery religions must have derived from their promise, in part at least, to provide an answer to this problem. We have already seen that, by the time of Augustus, the mysteries were not exclusivistic; they had an appeal that was both socially and geographically broad. But more than this, their appeal was largely to the individual as opposed to the group. On the one hand, most cults had mythic roots in some individual "hero" figure, such as the magical, healing cult, for instance, of Asclepius.[22] On the other hand, the initiations of the mysteries were directed more to personal longings and were more concerned with individual than with social experience. Whether the rites of the Phrygian Cybele, the Alexandrian Isis, the Syrian Baal, the Persian Mithra, or the Greek Eleusis, not to mention the popular Dionysian and Orphic cults, they all presented the potential convert with a variety of means whereby he could resolve his own religious ambivalence.[23] For some, the appeal lay in the drama of the cultus, in its imagery and sensuality, in its graphic presentation of an alternative to the cold traditionalism of Olympian formalism. To some the appeal was intellectual, with the promise of some insight into the hidden secrets of the universe, of an arcane *gnosis* by which one could decipher the sure way to salvation. For others, the appeal was largely ethical with the achievement of "righteousness" being the gateway to blessedness. For still others, the mysteries pointed boldly to the future life with the promise of immortality to the true believer. In Cicero's words: "In the mysteries we learn not only to live happily but to die with fairer hope." [24] Thus initiation into a mystery cult could be described as a *katharsis* or purification, as a new birth or regeneration, or as a conversion to truth. Even Tertullian, the early Christian apologist, although not easily given to charitable words about "pagan" religion, could describe the Eleusian initiation as a "baptism" where the individual is regenerated and receives the "remission of penalties" due his sins.[25] And there is an inscription over a Rhodian temple which reads like a "collect for purity":

[Those can rightfully enter here] who are pure and healthy in head and heart and who have no evil conscience in themselves.[26]

Precisely in the interests of this kind of purification the famous *Taurobolium* or bull's blood bath (sometimes it was a ram: *criobolium*) was conducted, a cultic rite continuing well into the fourth century and centering in Rome itself.

There is space to mention only in passing that associated with the mysteries, the most visible and dramatic part of which were the initiations, were very strong elements of both magic and astrology, so much so that Cumont has said that the "triumph of Oriental religion was simultaneously the triumph of astral religion." [27] One has only to look at the poetic *Astronomici* of Manilius, Lucian's *The Lover of Lies,* or to the *Anthologia* of Vettius Valens to realize that, in the Empire, magic ever remained the "bastard sister of religion," and the stars "the controllers of man's destiny." [28] Here again we see that if religion is thought to be manipulative, as with those mysteries which made use of magic or looked to the stars, the appeal lies in its proclaimed ability to conquer Fate. Two brief examples will serve to illustrate this point. The life of Lucius, for instance, is described by Apuleius as a long series of drastic encounters with a Fortune that was "ever bent on [his] distress," the most drastic of which was when he was unhappily turned into an ass. But upon his adherence to the cult of Isis, Lucius "is delivered from his former so great miseries by the providence of the goddess" in whose service (*ministerium*) he finds perfect freedom *(libertas)*.[29] A second example comes from the striking *Praises of Isis* in which are found these familiar lines: "I am the Lord of rainstorms. I overcome Fate. Fate hearkens to me." [30]

RELIGIOUS PHILOSOPHY

In turning from the Oriental mystery religions to the religious philosophy of the early Empire, we find ourselves in a radically different world (in spite of the fact that many philosophers of this period were initiates of one cult or another) and witness a manifestly different approach to the problem of "religious ambivalence," a calmer and more serene approach. As there were many religious "sects," so, too, there were many philosophical "schools," no one of them as original as the classical philosophies or as synthetic as the still-developing emergence of neo-Platonism. Philosophy in the first two centuries attempted, by and large, to answer the same questions as religion and simultaneously provided a critique of contemporary religion. Mattingly has reflected on the multitude of religions in this period and concluded that "atheists in the modern sense were rare; *atheos* was used more as a term of abuse than a description." [31] In fact, precisely the seemingly infinite proliferation of "gods" often drew from the philosophers the charge of "atheism." Even as late as the fifth century we find Augustine poking fun at the "pagans" for their absurd polytheism: gods for newborn children, for sleeping children, for crying children, for children when they suck, for children when they stand, etc. [32] The philosopher tended to be less than enthusiastic about all the "gods," since they watered down true religion. Asclepius in the Hermetic *corpus*, for instance, states quite simply: "Religious men, even if it were possible to take count throughout the universe, are not many." [33] The chief criticism levied against popular religion in the Empire by the philosophers was that of superstition. Lucretius the Epicurean, for instance, identified contemporary religion with superstition and confidently proclaimed that if everyone were to follow the teachings of his master, Epicurus, superstition would come to an end.[34] Witness also Celsus' ironic remarks directed against religion:

> Confronting the man who approaches their shrines the Egyptians have magnificent precincts, wonderful temples, splendid tents all around, and very superstitious and mysterious rites. But when he enters and goes inside he sees a cat being worshipped, or a monkey, or a crocodile, or a goat or a dog.[35]

That superstition would arouse such feelings in the philosophers stems first of all from the claim that philosophy was rational and superstition patently irrational, and secondly from the view that philosophy was indeed the *true* religion. Philosophy was the true religion not only because it revealed the truth about man and his destiny, but also because it provided the only sure bulwark against that kind of superstition that perverted man's true nature and clouded his destiny. H. R. Willoughby has said that the "growth of superstition in the Roman Empire during the first century A.D. was immense," [36] and the writings of Suetonius, Dio Cassius, and Plutarch underline this phenomenon. "The atheist," wrote the latter, "thinks there are no gods; the superstitious man wishes that there were none." [37]

Criticism of religion in general and of superstition in particular did not, however, prevent most philosophers from being initiates in the mysteries. Plutarch, for one, shared in the Orphic hope that the soul would attain divinity upon death, and both he and his wife were *mystes* of Orphism and he himself a priest of Isis at Delphi,[38] which is to say, the philosophers were not anti-religious as such. Even the philosophic schools had their initiatory rites;[39] philosophy was a "religious" stance to which one was "converted." [40] Of the many rival philosophies, two main classical branches stand out. Those schools which were associated with the "porch" of the Stoa (e.g., Seneca, Epictetus, Marcus Aurelius, etc.,) believed that they could teach that kind of *apatheia* which made the convert impervious to the blows of Fate. Here was a worldly optimism, a secular liberalism which came to terms with the ambiguities of human existence and then sought to rise superior to them. Accordingly, the emphasis on ethics was very strong. The second branch of imperial philosophy stemmed from the "academy" of Plato. Here the emphasis tended to be on the metaphysical, with its aspiration toward wisdom, its detachment and separation of the soul from the body, and a turning toward the intelligible world and those things which are eternally true.[41] This conservative pilgrimage was accordingly away from the world and toward God; it involved a disparagement of the physical and material in favor of the spiritual and immaterial. To know God, to be a friend of God, to participate in God, to become God — these were the verbal symbols by which these philosophers sought to escape the ambivalence and ambiguities of earthly life. Philosophy is here quite specifically religious, and Plato is viewed as the first of the great "theologians." [42]

THE IMPERIAL RULER-CULT

When we turn to a brief examination of the third and final religious phenomenon by which we are attempting to portray, as it were, the religious profile of the early Empire, we find ourselves back once more in the realm of the political. The imperial Ruler-Cult, a unique development of this period, was indeed politically "Roman," but its roots were manifestly Oriental. Since the time of the Egyptian Pharaohs, kings had been assigned the attributes of deity, sometimes while they were alive but more often upon death.[43] This practice spread in several directions and subsequently had its influence on the mystery religions as well as on philosophy. With the orientalization of Rome, it is not surprising, therefore, that the political goals of the state found an ideal helpmate in the religious concept of *apotheosis*.

During the Augustan restoration the imperial Ruler-Cult may be said to have begun. Its development was gradual, but by the time of the reign of Diocletian in the third century, the god-king concept was firmly entrenched. The cult began, more specifically, in 42 B.C. when the Senate voted to have the murdered Julius, Augustus' father, included among the gods of the state; and in 29 B.C. the first temple to Julius was dedicated. (One wonders, of course, to what extent these official actions took into account that at least three times during his lifetime there had been attempts to deify Julius.)[44] Two points are important here. First, the Ruler-Cult of the early Empire rendered deificatory honors only to a *dead* princeps. Neither Augustus nor his successors sought deification during their own reigns; they sought it only for their predecessors. Tiberius, for instance, is recorded as having to make it quite clear to some of his more enthusiastic supporters that they "should reserve special honor befitting the gods in keeping with the greatness of [his] father's services to the whole world." But, he continued, "I myself am content with the more modest honors appropriate to men." [45] The practice was, therefore, not to offer sacrifices to a living emperor, but only to his "genius" or *numen*. This imperial reticence is, we must add, somewhat qualified by the fact that, while they refused the title *Divus*, emperors were content to be referred to as *Divi filius*.

The second point to bear in mind is that the divine status of a deceased emperor was determined by the Senate. The implication of this is that only "good" emperors would be deified while "bad" emperors would be denied the honor. Thus, in theory at least, the imperial status was not, in and of itself, an immediate guarantee of divine status in the after life. As it turned out, for instance, Julius, Augustus, and Claudius were deified; Tiberius, Gaius, and Nero were not. The judgment of history, we might add, has not always paralleled that of the Roman Senate.

For all its use of religious terminology, for all its temples and priests, the Ruler-Cult was never really a religion; or, as Mattingly has said, it was but a "substitute" for one.[46] Its purpose was patently to provide a specific focus for the unity of the Empire, for the loyalty of its citizens, and, it must be added, for the control of subversive groups. On the popular level, the old idea of *Tyche* (Fate) in the hands of the god-king had been transferred to the emperor as "protector" of the City, and, by extension, of the Empire. But on the pragmatic level, the Ruler-Cult was a strong weapon in the hands of the Empire, a weapon both for the waging of war and for the keeping of peace.

When, upon Augustus' death in 14 B.C., the Senate declared him to be "immortal" and "assigned to him a college of priests and sacred rites" and had shrines "erected to him in Rome and in many different places," [47] the Augustan restoration, albeit posthumously, was established and became an integral part of the imperial ethos.

The mantle of "deification" did not fall lightly on the shoulders of all of Augustus' successors. For some it went beyond the boundaries of a political symbol with cultic paraphernalia and became a matter of personal ambition. We have already referred to Nero's erection of a Sun Temple with his own features upon it. Gaius (Caligula) seems to have gone the farthest in this respect. This unbounded ambition for deification elicited from Dio Cassius the sarcastic remark that when Gaius was eventually murdered, he then "learned by actual experience that he was not a god." [48] And Seneca was even more biting in his parody of the "deification" of Claudius which he entitled *Apocolocyntosis,* or "Pumpkin-ification." [49]

If the Ruler-Cult meant many things to different rulers, it also meant different things throughout the Empire. Its most traditional ritualistic supporters, as can be imagined, were to be found among the military. The reverence given the cult in Rome itself was often perfunctory, while in the East the cult seems to have had frenzied adherents, the excesses of whom were often an embarrassment to the imperial household. R. Syme has summed up the Ruler-Cult more than adequately in these words:

> The different forms which the worship of Augustus took in Rome, Italy and the provinces illustrate the different aspects of his rule—he is Princeps to the Senate, Imperator to army and people, King and God to the subject peoples of the Empire.[50]

THE RISE OF CHRISTIANITY

With this all-too-brief survey of some of the major phenomena which can be associated with the religious world of the early Empire, we are in a position now, by way of conclusion, to address ourselves to one final phenomenon, namely, the rise of Christianity. An historical perspective which allows one to view Christianity as the "obvious" answer to the problem of religious ambivalence, or one which designates the Christians as the "good guys" and the pagans as the "bad guys," will hardly be helpful to our understanding.

"Religion," it has been said, "is man's protest against the meaninglessness of events." [51] As we have seen, the ancient world was one in which men saw themselves as inexorably subjected to a personal (or impersonal) Fate so powerful that church and state were called into an otherwise awkward union to do battle with this common enemy; stars and planets and a whole host of deities symbolic of the natural order were cajoled and coerced, bribed and petitioned to become man's allies in the storm of life; and intricately devised escape routes away from the phenomenal world were planned, all with the goal of knowing and identifying with the one true God whose providence alone could master the wiles of Fate. How did the small Semitic band of untutored primitive Christians fit into this picture? On the surface it looks as though their "hero-god" had himself succumbed to the "meaninglessness of events." Did these early Christians have the answers for which mankind was so impatiently (or, in some cases, so resignedly) waiting? A close look at the pertinent documents might lead us to just the opposite conclusion, namely, that this "new" religion raised more questions than it provided answers. What strength lay in primitive Christianity's unpromising sectarian absolutism that led to their crucified Messiah's displacement of the traditional gods of the state and caused this minority foreign religion to become both the political as well as religious ally of the imperial household?

Several answers to these and other questions have been put forward. A. D. Nock's suggestion has had many supporters:

> The success of Christianity is the success of an institution which united the sacramentalism and the philosophy of the time. It satisfied the inquiring turn of mind, the desire for escape from Fate, the desire for security in the hereafter; like Stoicism, it gave a way of life and made man at home in the universe, but unlike Stoicism it did this for the ignorant as well as for the lettered.[52]

Cumont's thesis is also appealing. He has suggested that there was inherent in the ancient world a longing for one universal religion and that the orientalization of the West had "prepared all nations to unite in the bosom of a universal church." [53] Many other reasons have been offered to explain the success of Christianity within the pluralistic religious world of the Empire, some of them "pious," some of them deterministically informed, and some of them sociologically oriented. The success of Christianity has also been described as being due not so much to its own strengths as to the weaknesses inherent in "paganism." [54] A more positive approach, however, might be to attribute the meteoric rise of early Christianity to precisely the strengths of "paganism," i.e., its implicit recognition of both of the two trends which informed its religious style — liberal and conservative — as valid expressions of the religious consciousness. Christianity, in fact, was both liberal and conservative, and within its message it could speak convincingly to the religious ambivalence with a broadness which neither the mystery religions of the time, nor the religious philosophies, nor the Ruler-Cult, in and of themselves could wholly encompass. That this interpretation is not entirely an unfounded or speculatively farfetched thesis can be indicated by the documentary evidence which reveals that, for all the antipathy directed toward primitive Christianity by the Empire, it was viewed by some to be (1) another of the Eastern mystery religions, by some to be (2) a new philosophy, and by others to be (3) a more inclusive kind of Ruler-Cult. That Christianity could be simultaneously interpreted under all three of these contemporary categories of religious thought indicates a universality of appeal that has not, to my knowledge, been suggested before.

Three brief citations from contemporary sources will suffice to provide the reader with the initial steps toward a possible substantiation of this suggested thesis.

That Christianity was originally considered to be a sect of Judaism is well known. Thus, it was Oriental. Further, its "deified" Messiah, its rites of initiation, its cultic meal, and its eschatological doctrines all pointed toward its being one of the mystery religions. Indeed, even Lucian, no friend of the Christians, identified it as such when he referred to Jesus as the "man who was crucified in Palestine because he introduced this new mystery initiation into the world." [55]

That Christianity was identified as a new philosophy is also well attested. Its emphasis on revelation, its identification of Jesus with Truth, its reverence for Scriptures, its ethical ideals, and its concern for knowledge of and presence with God — all this was familiar to the religio-philosophical provenance of the period. Among the many charges brought against Christianity was that of atheism. We have already seen that this could mean many things. One reply to this charge, addressed by the Christian apologist Athenagoras to the emperor Marcus Aurelius is quite revealing for its "philosophical" sympathies with the age:

> We are of course not atheists. . . . Rightly, indeed, did the Athenians accuse Diagoras of atheism, since he not only divulged the Orphic doctrine as well as the mysteries of Eleusis . . . but he proclaimed outrightly that God did not exist. In our case, however, is it not mad to charge us with atheism, when we distinguish God from matter, and show that matter is one thing and God another, and that there is a vast difference between them? For the divine is uncreated and eternal, grasped only by pure mind and intelligence, while matter is created and perishable.[56]

That Christianity was considered originally to be an enemy of the state but gradually was accepted as its ally is also well known. Their strict monotheism forbade them to worship anything less than God; their belief that Christ had conquered the demons made it impossible for them to offer sacrifices to the "genius" of the emperor. But if early Christians could be termed social revolutionaries, political subversives they were not. They were, in fact, persecuted by the state for the wrong reasons. Rather than being disloyal, Christians approved of the state, of the imperial government, and, ironically, of the *Pax Romana*. A letter written by an anonymous Christian to his non-Christian friend Diognetus is a case in point:

> Christians cannot be distinguished from the rest of the human race by country or language or customs. They do not live in cities of their own. . . . Yet, although they live in Greek and barbarian cities alike, as each man's lot has been cast, and follow the customs of the country in clothing and food and other matters of daily living, at the same time they give proof of the remarkable and admittedly extraordinary constitution of their own commonwealth. They live in their own countries, but only as aliens. They have a share in everything as citizens, and endure everything as foreigners. Every foreign land is their fatherland, and yet for them every fatherland is a foreign land. . . . They busy themselves on earth, but their citizenship is in heaven. They obey the established laws, but in their own lives they go far beyond what the laws require. They love all men, and by all men are persecuted. . . . They are reviled and yet they bless; when they are affronted, they still pay due respect. . . . To put it simply, what the soul is in the body, that Christians are in the world.[57]

NOTES

[1] Dietrich Bonhoeffer, *Letters and Papers from Prison* (New York: The Macmillan Company, 1967), p. 173.

[2] *Ibid.*, p. 176.

[3] H. R. Willoughby, *Pagan Regeneration: A Study of Mystery Initiations in the Graeco-Roman World* (Chicago: The University of Chicago Press, 1929), p. 15.

[4] Suetonius, *Life of Augustus* 5.

[5] Franz Cumont, *Oriental Religions in Roman Paganism* (New York: Dover Publications, Inc., 1956), p. 44.

[6] See, for instance, the "Titles of Isis" in F. C. Grant, ed., *Hellenistic Religions* (New York: The Bobbs-Merrill Company, Inc., 1953), pp. 128-130.

[7] Apuleius, *Metamorphoses* 20. 5. This is not a novel approach; see, for instance, the Stoic *Hymn to Zeus* of Cleanthes: "Most glorious of immortals, Zeus all powerful/Author of nature, named by many names, all hail!"

[8] Cumont, *op. cit.*, p. 3.

[9] Cicero, *On the Nature of the Gods* 1. 42.

[10] See A. D. Nock, *Early Gentile Christianity and its Hellenistic Background* (New York: Torchbooks, Harper & Row, Publishers, 1964), p. 104.

[11] Plutarch, *Isis and Osiris* 35.

[12] Apuleius, *Metamorphoses* 11. 26-27. See also Philostratus, *The Life of Apollonius of Tyana* 4. 18.

[13] As, for instance, Claudius' expulsion of the Druids and astrologers.

[14] F. Altheim, *A History of Roman Religion* (New York: E. P. Dutton & Co., Inc., 1938), p. 426.

[15] Harold Mattingly, *The Man in the Roman Street* (New York: W. W. Norton & Company, Inc., 1966), p. 62.

[16] Cited by M. P. Nilsson, *Greek Piety* (New York: W. W. Norton & Company, Inc., 1969), p. 116.

[17] Dion Chrysostom, *Oration* 31. 11.

[18] Maximus of Tyre, *Oration* 17. 5.

[19] Pseudo Aristotle, *De mundo* 7.

[20] A. D. Nock, "The Development of Paganism in the Roman Empire," chap. 12, *Cambridge Ancient History*, vol. 12 (Cambridge: Cambridge University Press, 1939), p. 421.

[21] S. J. Case, *The Social Origins of Christianity* (Chicago: Chicago University Press, 1923), p. 18.

[22] See E. J. and L. Edelstein, *Asclepius* (Baltimore: The Johns Hopkins University Press, 1945).

[23] See Cumont, *op. cit.*, p. 196: "A hundred different currents carried away hesitating and undecided minds, a hundred contrasting sermons made appeals to the conscience of the people."

[24] Cicero, *On the Laws* 2. 14.

[25] Tertullian, *De baptismo* 5. See also Origen, *Contra Celsum* 3. 59.

[26] Cited by Willoughby, *op. cit.*, p. 44.

[27] F. Cumont, *Astrology and Religion among the Greeks and Romans* (New York: Dover Publications, Inc., 1962), p. 52.

[28] See also Celsus' description of the Mithraic mysteries in Origen, *Contra Celsum* 6. 22.

[29] Apuleius, *Metamorphoses* 7. 25; 11. 15.

[30] Cited by F. C. Grant, *op. cit.*, p. 133.

[31] Mattingly, *op. cit.*, p. 54.

[32] Augustine, *The City of God* 4. 21.

[33] Hermes Trismegistos, *Asclepius* 22.

[34] Lucretius, *On the Nature of Things* 5. 1194ff.

[35] Origen, *Contra Celsum* 3. 17. See also Lucian's biting satire on "homemade" oracles in his *Alexander the False Prophet*.

[36] Willoughby, *op. cit.*, p. 6.

[37] Plutarch, *On Superstition* 170.

[38] Plutarch, *Consolation to His Wife*, 10, and *Epistle to Clea*.

[39] On philosophic initiation, see Seneca, *Epistle* 90. 28.

[40] On conversion to philosophy, see A. D. Nock, *Conversion* (Oxford: Oxford Paperbacks, 1961), esp. chap. 11.

[41] Albinus, *Epitome of the Doctrines of Plato* 1. 1.

[42] Other than Albinus' work just cited, see Hermes Trismegistos, *Asclepius* 14. On the contemplative spiritual and "escapist" philosophy of the period, see A. Festugière, *Personal Religion Among the Greeks* (Berkeley: University of California Press, 1960), esp. chaps. 4 and 8. Even later Christians could refer to Plato as a "theologian; see Gregory of Nazianzus, *Oration* 28. 4.

[43] See Franz Cumont, *After Life in Roman Paganism* (New York: Dover Publications, Inc., 1959), pp. 113ff.

[44] See W. W. Fowler, *Roman Ideas of Deity* (London: The Macmillan Company, 1914), p. 107.

[45] N. Lewis and M. Reinhold, eds., *Roman Civilization*, vol. 2 (New York: Torchbooks, Harper & Row, Publishers, 1966), p. 561.

[46] Mattingly, *op. cit.*, p. 69.

[47] Dio Cassius, *Roman History* 56. 46; he goes on to say, however, that not all communities responded happily to the ordinance. For an excellent description of a deificatory rite, v. Herodian, *History* 4. 2.

⁴⁸ Dio Cassius, *Roman History* 59. 30. See also Suetonius, *Life of Caligula* 22 and the description of Caligula's death in Josephus, *Jewish Antiquities* 19. 1. 2.

⁴⁹ An edition of this treatise, *Divi Claudii apotheosis per saturam quae apocolocyntosis vulgo dicitur,* has been published under the editorship of Otto Rossbach, in H. Lietzmann, ed., *Kleine Texte für Vorlesungen und Übungen* (Bonn: Marcus & Weber, 1926) , vol. 154.

⁵⁰ R. Syme, *The Roman Revolution* (New York: Oxford University Press, Inc., 1939) , p. 475; cited by Lewis and Reinhold, *op. cit.,* p. 61.

⁵¹ Nilsson, *op. cit.,* p. 114.

⁵² Nock, *Conversion,* pp. 210-211.

⁵³ Cumont, *Oriental Religions,* p. 211. Later Christian thought, especially that of Clement of Alexandria, would view Greek philosophy as a parallel to the Mosaic Law, each equally preparing the world for the gospel of Jesus Christ.

⁵⁴ See G. Murray, *Five Stages of Greek Religion* (New York: Columbia University Press, 1925) , esp. chap. 4.

⁵⁵ Lucian, *The Passing of Peregrinus* 11. For others, that Christianity was a mystery cult meant that it was but another "superstition." See Suetonius, *The Life of Nero* 16. 2.

⁵⁶ Athenagoras, *Supplication for the Christians* 4. From *Early Christian Fathers,* vol. 1, *The Library of Christian Classics,* newly translated and edited by Cyril C. Richardson (Philadelphia: The Westminster Press, 1953) . Used by permission. See also the famous *Apology* (2nd) of Justin Martyr.

⁵⁷ *Epistle to Diognetus* 5-6. From *Early Christian Fathers, op. cit.*

FOR ADVANCED READING

The literature in this field is vast, and even a lengthy bibliography would fail to do it justice. The titles listed below, therefore, have been chosen (with one or two exceptions) with three criteria in mind: (1) they are relatively accessible, (2) they are relatively inexpensive (the large majority of them are paperbacks) , and (3) they are all in English.

SOURCES

Other than the Loeb Classical Library (currently being published by the Harvard University Press) in which are to be found the important works of Plutarch, Lucian, Seneca, Cicero, Dio Cassius, etc., the following collections of sources are helpful to the student of this period:

Grant, Frederick C., ed., *Ancient Roman Religion.* New York: The Liberal Arts Press, 1952.

Grant, Frederick C., ed., *Hellenistic Religions: The Age of Syncretism.* Indianapolis, Ind.: The Bobbs-Merrill Company, Inc., 1953.

STUDIES

E. J. Brill, a Dutch publishing house, is now in the process of publishing a definitive series of monographs under the general title *Preliminary Studies in the Oriental Religions of the Roman Empire* (Études préliminaires aux religions orientales dans l'Empire Romain) . These works, in several languages, and on several topics, promise to be of great value to anyone interested in the background of early Christianity. Another series currently underway under the general editorship of H. H. Scullard, and being published by Thames & Hudson of London, goes under the series title of *Aspects of Greek and Roman Life*. Titles in this series cover such subjects as medicine, architecture, the family, law, religion, etc. All these works are in English and should be invaluable aids to a student of the world and culture into which Christianity was born. Other important studies in the field are as follows:

Cumont, Franz, *After Life in Roman Paganism*. New York: Dover Publications, Inc., 1960.

_____, *Astrology and Religion Among the Greeks and Romans*. New York: Dover Publications, Inc., 1960.

_____, *Oriental Religions in Roman Paganism*. New York: Dover Publications, Inc., 1957.

Festugière, André, *Personal Religion Among the Greeks*. Berkeley: University of California Press, 1960.

Guthrie, William K., *Orpheus and Greek Religion: A Study of the Orphic Movement*. 2nd ed. New York: W. W. Norton & Company, Inc., 1966.

Mattingly, Harold, *The Man in the Roman Street*. New York: W. W. Norton & Company, Inc., 1966.

Murray, Gilbert, *Five Stages of Greek Religion*. New York: Anchor Doubleday & Company, Inc., 1957.

Nilsson, Martin P., *Greek Piety*. Translated by H. J. Rose. New York: W. W. Norton & Company, Inc., 1969.

_____, *A History of Greek Religion*. Translated by F. J. Fielden. 2nd ed. New York: W. W. Norton & Company, Inc., 1964.

Nock, Arthur D., *Conversion*. London: Oxford University Press (Oxford Paperbacks), 1961.

_____, *Early Gentile Christianity and its Hellenistic Background*. New York: Harper & Row, Publishers, 1964.

Toynbee, A., ed., *The Crucible of Christianity; Judaism, Hellenism and the Historical Background to the Christian Faith*. Cleveland, Ohio: The World Publishing Company, 1969.

Willoughby, Harold R., *Pagan Regeneration: A Study of Mystery Initiations in the Graeco-Roman World*. Chicago: The University of Chicago Press, 1929.

Gerhard Krodel

11
Persecution and Toleration
of Christianity Until Hadrian

The Roman policy toward foreign religions during the late Republic and the early Empire was one of toleration unless suspicion of
sedition or immorality prompted governmental counteractions. At
times repressive measures against foreign cults in Rome were motivated by the hostility of the Roman aristocracy toward the influx
of foreigners. But in either case the adherence to a particular religion
was not regarded as constituting a crime in itself. Temporary suppression of cults carried out by magistrative actions on the basis of the
power of *coercitio* was, from the Roman point of view, meant to restore "law and order." The suppression of the Bacchanals in 186 B.C.
was motivated by immoralities which allegedly had taken place, and
these crimes were punished while the cult itself was spared, though
for some time it was placed under certain restrictions. Devotees of
other cults and groups, such as the astrologers, were occasionally, and
in some instances even periodically, expelled from Rome on various
grounds of wrongdoing, only to return again and become part of the
syncretistic orchestra of coexisting religions that were tolerated by
the early Empire.

Only the Druids apparently were an exception. With utter cruelty
Rome crushed their rites because of their alleged practices of human
sacrifice and cannibalism, and because they fomented the fires of Gallic
nationalism and opposition to Rome. But once their political threat
to Roman imperialism had ceased and their obnoxious rites had been
forgotten, the Druids emerged with new respectability during the
second century of the Christian era.[1]

The Jewish people, though frequently maltreated by their Greek
neighbors and despised by Greek and Roman intellectuals,[2] were
protected as allies by Rome, which had granted special privileges to
them. At times they, too, were expelled from Rome during the first
part of the first century A.D. on grounds of alleged fraud and unrest,

and they, like other people, had to bear injustices meted out by Roman officials in Greek cities, as well as in their homeland. But they were permitted to practice their religion even though they rose three times in armed rebellions against the power of Rome. This treatment of the Jews is a good example of religious toleration by the Roman government.

Irrespective of the feelings of Roman aristocrats concerning the intrinsic worth of "foreign superstitions," Roman pragmatism tolerated, or even encouraged, the practice of their respective religions by its subjugated peoples. When, through the influx of *peregrini*, foreign cults penetrated the capital, some restrictions were placed on them until their deities were incorporated into the Roman pantheon, or the rites had risen in the esteem of the public. The Roman pragmatism, which granted citizenship to foreigners, went even further and invalidated, not by official decree but by actual practice, the old republican principle according to which participation in foreign cults was inadmissible for Roman citizens.[3] Confirmation for this change is found in the absence of official religious tests, in the lack of evidence of legal proceedings against citizens for participation in foreign cults, and in the absence of sections in the Roman civil and penal laws dealing with membership of citizens in foreign cults. The concept of *"religio licita"* did not exist during this period. Rome did not possess a department of religious affairs which licensed foreign cults, but it tolerated them and in this sense they were "lawful." A case cited for the Christian period as evidence of legal proceedings against Roman citizens for practicing foreign religions consists in the accusation and execution of Flavius Clements on the charge of "atheism" and the banishment of his wife Domitilla for the same reason. However, these executions took place in the later part of Domitian's reign of terror in which the ever suspicious emperor crushed all sorts of imaginary and real opponents on all kinds of pretenses. Hence Pliny's dealings with the Christians in Bithynia indeed represent an innovation and not merely the continuation of earlier Roman policies toward "foreign superstitions." The continuation of Roman policies lies in its pragmatism which did not enforce the principle that Christianity as such constituted a crime punishable by death.

ROMAN ATTITUDES TOWARD PALESTINIAN CHRISTIANITY

The crucifixion of Jesus, ordered by the procurator, Pontius Pilate, signaled the first in a series of encounters in which the Empire dealt with the newly emerging faith. Although a reconstruction of the events leading to Jesus' execution is well-nigh impossible, the fact of his crucifixion by Pilate's authority is indisputable. In all probability the Roman authorities of Judea regarded Jesus as a messianic rebel who constituted a threat to "law and order." But it is also possible that Pilate ordered his execution in order to oblige some influential Sadducees and to lessen their hatred in the hope that his deference to their wishes would strengthen his own position with them. His protector, the anti-Semitic Sejanus, had been deposed in A.D. 31, and it appears that subsequently Tiberius ordered his representatives in the provinces to treat the Jews with decency.[4] Although Jesus was not a political rebel plotting sedition against Rome,[5] his execution was also not a deliberate attempt by the Romans to stamp out particular religious convictions. However, it constituted one of countless cases of miscarried justice.

The proclamation of the messianic exaltation of the crucified Jesus could hardly gain popularity for the emerging church in Palestine; yet the Roman presence insured some measure of stability and toleration. Jewish opposition to members of the new sect varied in intensity from simple non-acceptance of their message to ridicule, social ostracism, occasional floggings in the synagogue, and occasional acts of mob violence which were directed primarily against preachers who were "dynamic," from the Christian point of view, or obnoxious, from the Jewish point of view. Persecution was strictly limited in scope and actual martyrdoms were few. One persecutor, Paul of Tarsus, declared (Galatians 1:13) that he had "persecuted the church of God violently and tried to destroy it." But it is by no means clear how he actually proceeded. Does "persecute" here mean to "harass verbally," or did Paul also employ more drastic measures? In the light of his experiences as a missionary apostle of Christ, the latter seems more likely, but no certainty can be gained about the nature and intensity of Paul's harassment of the church. In any event, the church was able to exist in Jerusalem in relative peace until the outbreak of the war, and Paul himself was able to visit there on different occasions.

Within the first decade of the church's existence, the Hellenistic Jewish Christian community, led by "the seven," was forced to leave Jerusalem, and Stephen, who was perhaps the spokesman of "the seven," was stoned by an outraged mob. But the community under the twelve was left unharmed and remained in Jerusalem. The reason for the expulsion of the others lay in their attacks upon cultic piety which aroused the antagonism of a segment of the population to action.[6]

The circumstances which led to Peter's imprisonment and James' execution by Herod are unknown (Acts 12:1-4). Herod's sudden death in A.D. 44 and the placing of Palestine under procurators ended this brief episode, and another period of relative calm began for the Palestinian Christians. While on occasion they experienced antagonism of various kinds from their countrymen because they sought to win them for Christ, their practice of the Torah and the presence of Roman power made their continued existence in Palestine possible. In the sixties, the deterioration of the political situation in Palestine and the corresponding growth of the zealotic movement produced enough confusion to leave its marks on the church also. During the interregnum of A.D. 62, between Festus' death and Albinus' arrival, the Sadducean high priest Annanus II brought James, the brother of Jesus and leader of the church of Jerusalem, to trial before the Sanhedrin on charges of "breaking the law." According to Josephus, James was put to death by stoning.[7] Because of the arrival of the procurator this condemnation on religious grounds remained an isolated incident, but it illustrated the hatred of the Sadducean Sanhedrin against the leadership of the church in Jerusalem.

When the flames of zealotic fanaticism, fanned by messianic hopes, drew the various groups of Judaism into rebellion against Rome, the Christian church, because of its faith in the crucified Messiah, was the one group which did not participate in the war against Rome. Hence it is reasonable to assume that many Christians who were unable to flee suffered persecution by zealots and their sympathizers during the general turmoil. Christian groups made their reappearance after the war. They continued to exist until the religious-patriotic hysteria of the messianic revolt under Bar Kochba delivered a blow to Jewish Christianity which only remnants survived.[8]

Also in the Jewish communities of the Diaspora the Christian proclamation aroused counteractions through which synagogues expressed their irritation with, and rejection of, the new heresy. Yet it seems unlikely that many Christians lost their lives directly or indirectly because of the Diaspora Jews. The successive failures of three Jewish revolts and the corresponding loss of prestige among the Romans, not to mention the anti-Jewish feelings among the Greeks, make it highly improbable that they should have commanded sufficient influence to draw Roman persecution upon the church.[9]

BEGINNINGS OF PERSECUTION IN ROME

Moreover, the genius of Roman policy tried to channel the emotions of its subjugated peoples into patriotism for the Empire, to establish security, and to crush opposition that threatened the peace and cohesion from within and without. Its pragmatic policy of "the carrot and the stick," which found it advantageous to tolerate Judaism and continued to tolerate it even after three rebellions, found it unnecessary to take note of the Christian groups that were emerging. When, on a local level, unrest of the populace caused by Christian preaching and behavior forced authorities to take note of them, then Roman officials would, on occasion, prosecute Christians.[10] At other times, they decided in favor of the Christians or refused to be drawn into religious quarrels. Naturally they would become suspicious when they heard that the founder of Christianity had been executed by a Roman procurator. The claim to Christ's absolute authority, the hope for an imminent end of the world "by fire," the polemics against paganism, the "obnoxious standoffishness" and clanishness of Christians, together with the fact that Christianity was not the "superstition" of a nation, were all factors not apt to gain the new sect the sympathies of the population or of the government of the Empire, especially when the distinction beween Jews and Christians became apparent.

Probably in A.D. 49 or 50, Claudius expelled some Jews from Rome on account of tumults which, according to Suetonius, were instigated by "Chrestus." Since Jews and Christians alike were involved in the tumults and expelled, the government at this stage was unwilling or unable to differentiate between them. Nor did the government, from its viewpoint, carry out a religious persecution. It rather meted out punishment for riots and unrest in the interest of public good. But the underlying cause may well have been Roman apprehension at the expansion of the Jewish population in the capital.[11]

Punishment of incendiaries was also the government's alleged reason for prosecuting the Christians of Rome in connection with the disastrous fire of A.D. 64 which destroyed almost one fourth of the city. Tacitus gives as the real reason for their execution Nero's attempt to counteract a persistent rumor that he himself had ordered the fire in order to gain space for his vast building programs. The emperor, intending to shift the blame on someone else, ordered the arrest and subsequent condemnation of Christians. "Covered with skins of beasts they were torn by dogs and perished or were nailed to crosses or were doomed to the flames and burnt, to serve as nightly illumination" in Nero's gardens.[12] Nero made the Christians into scapegoats for this catastrophe only because he was aware that the populace, segments of the *vulgus*, held the Christians in utter contempt and connected all sorts of abominations with this "mischievous superstition." Since the crime which the Christians supposedly committed and for which they were condemned to death was arson, one cannot speak of a religious persecution, even though they would not have been put to death had they not been Christians. The scope of the persecution, or, from the government's point of view, prosecution, was limited to the city of Rome. The action itself presupposes that the governmental authorities as well as segments of the populace could already distinguish between Jews and Christians, and the executions of the latter made that distinction clear to all.

Uncertainty exists concerning the legal basis of their condemnation,[13] but the notion that Nero issued a special edict proscribing Christianity lacks sufficient evidence.[14] Probably Paul and Peter lost their lives in this persecution.[15] Within less than half a decade the leadership of the church in Jerusalem, of the Pauline mission, and of the mission to the Jews had been extinguished by martyrdom even though there was no official policy of persecution.

The church in Rome survived the Neronian persecution as shown in *1 Clement,* and as far as our evidence indicates it was largely ignored and thus tolerated by the imperial authorities during the next decades. The suffering to which the Christians addressed in First Peter were subjected consisted in defamation by their pagan neighbors.[16] At times this may have led to police actions against them, where they, innocent of crimes, had to "suffer as a Christian" (1 Peter 4:16). Still Peter hoped that good conduct would be recognized although he was aware that this was not always the case (1 Peter 3:13, 16; 4:14, 16). Neither does *1 Clement* indicate persecutions by the government in the present or the immediate past.[17] The churches of the Apocalypse had suffered one martyrdom (Revelation 2:13) and the banishment of their prophet (1:9). Their chief threat was "Satan," manifest in the imperial cult.[18]

Neither Nero nor Domitian had any intention of destroying the Christian religion, and we have no direct proof that Christians were singled out by Domitian for special persecution.[19] Insofar as Christianity was known at the turn of the century, the image it had produced in the minds of its contemporaries was anything but good. For many its name had become associated with sinister activities. As the authorities and common people learned to distinguish between Jews and Christians during the second part of the first century, what appeared to them to be "atheism," obnoxious standoffishness, and lack of patriotism, evidenced by the Christians' refusal to participate in the imperial cult, was to them all the more scandalous because Christians were not a nation, like the Jews, to which Rome was bound by treaty and decrees. The unique offense of Christianity was its offense against polytheism and therefore against the Empire whose structure was based on polytheism. The monotheistic religion of the Jews could be tolerated because it was an ancient national religion which might win individual converts, but, by its very nature, could not permeate the Empire. The non-national "superstition" of Christianity wanted to win the world for Christ and thus was instinctively felt as a threat by those who rejected it. Hence, it was persistently associated with criminal activity. The unique and basic offense must manifest itself also in *flagitia,* in abominable activities.

Magistrative actions to deal with persistent rumors of wrongdoing, or with participation in illegal *collegia,* depended on the intensity of the animosity with which hostile crowds reacted to Christians in their midst as well as on the choice of action which individual magistrates thought fit to take. Actual persecution was, therefore, sporadic rather than general, accidental rather than organized, even though Christianity constituted a capital offense at Trajan's time.

This situation was unique in Rome's dealings with foreign superstitions. In the case of other religions and philosophies we hear of occasional banishments and expulsions because of some real or imaginary *flagitia* that were connected with them. Undoubtedly *flagitia* (whether actual, imaginary, or trumped-up is irrelevant here) had been the primary cause of the government's proceedings against individuals or groups of Christians. But at Trajan's time the unique development had occurred that the mere fact of being Christian had become a capital crime, irrespective of *flagitia.* This unique stance of the Roman authorities toward one particular foreign "superstition" was intentionally being blurred by them in that they continued to associate *flagitia* with Christianity, even after it had become apparent to them that such an association did not in fact exist.

A second unique feature which should be taken into account is contained in Trajan's order to Pliny, namely, that this particular capital offense was not to be prosecuted actively by the governmental authorities. Judicial or administrative action was to be taken against Christians only when others brought official accusations against them. The initiative in the prosecution of this particular capital crime rested, not with the government, but with the people. This unique feature once again exhibited the pragmatism of Roman policies toward foreign religions and simultaneously made the continuation of associating *flagitia* with Christianity possible, even when the falsity of this association was recognized by the authorities. On one hand, the Roman government regarded Christianity as a capital crime which should not be tolerated, but on the other, it did tolerate it to a large extent and capital punishment was inflicted on Christians only on rare occasions. For example, the condemnations of Ignatius and Polycarp were not followed by condemnations of the members of their respective congregations; nor is there any evidence of persecution in the communities to which Ignatius wrote.

However, an atmosphere of insecurity and unpopularity in which harassment was frequent surrounded Christians. Accusations against them must often have been ignored by magistrates. They could do so because neither the statutes of the *leges Corneliae* nor of the *leges*

Juliae, nor a special *senatus consultum,* nor an imperial edict had proscribed Christianity. In cases of conviction for the "name," that is, for being a Christian, the presiding official from Trajan's time was empowered to grant imperial pardon, *venia,* provided the accused met the sacrifice test or its equivalent.

DEVELOPMENT OF A LEGAL POLICY TOWARD CHRISTIANS

Our most important evidence for the government's dealings with Christianity after the turn of the century is found in the official consultation of Pliny (who had been sent as *legatus pro praetore* to Pontus and Bithynia in A.D. 111) with Trajan and the latter's reply. Since Pliny had never participated in trials *(cognitiones)* of Christians, he asked the emperor for guidance. Specifically, he asked: (1) whether the age of the accused should be taken into consideration; (2) whether their repentance *(paenitentia),* if it showed itself in sacrificing to the gods or calling on the gods and the emperor and in cursing Christ, should be rewarded by granting them pardon *(venia);* and (3) whether Christianity as such *(nomen ipsum)* was to be punished even when it was free from abominations *(flagitia)* or whether only these *flagitia* connected with Christianity were the object of punishment.[20]

Pliny then proceeded to tell the emperor how he had dealt with various groups of Christians. He interrogated them as to whether they were Christians. He apparently found it unnecessary to investigate whether or not they had committed *flagitia,* though he may still have thought at that time that *flagitia* were inseparately connected with Christianity. Nor did he offer the first group the opportunity to recant by offering sacrifices and cursing Christ. When the accused confessed to being Christians and persisted in their confession under threat of capital punishment, he ordered their execution. For Pliny it was self-evident that being a Christian constituted a capital crime, even though he had never before personally participated in proceedings against them.

However, in the interval between these first proceedings and the writing of his letter to Trajan, he had found out that *flagitia* actually were not *cohaerentia* in Christianity. Therefore he covered up his harsh verdict by stating that whatever the nature of their crimes might be, certainly their "stubbornness" and "inflexible obstinance" must be punished — as if these were legal reasons for the infliction of capital punishment.[21] In the absence of *flagitia,* "stubbornness" must serve as their substitute in order to uphold the fiction that there was a connection between Christianity and *flagitia.*

Christians who were Roman citizens had been sent by the legate to Rome. When informers found out that charges against Christians

were taken seriously by Pliny, new accusations by anonymous informers against people who were thought to be Christians poured in.
Some of the accused denied that they had ever been Christians. Pliny
used a threefold test to establish the veracity of their denials. Calling
on the gods, sacrificing before the emperor's image, and cursing Christ
were meant to distinguish Christians from the population. However,
refusal to perform these acts as such did not constitute the crime.
What was the criminal offense was *nomen ipsum*. When the accused
proved that they were not Christians by performing these acts, Pliny
set them free.

Another group confessed that they had been Christians in the past,
some of them as long as twenty years ago. They, too, performed the
cultic acts, but significantly Pliny did not set them free. Rather he
consulted Trajan asking whether their repentance should be officially
recognized by pardon, and therefore he delayed his verdict in their
case.

Pliny hoped that for pragmatic reasons the emperor would agree
to recognize their *paenitentia* as evidenced in their performance of
cultic acts to Roman divinities and grant pardon to them, so that "a
great number" of people could be healed from this contagious superstition which had already spread "not only into towns, but also into
villages and hamlets." [22] But Pliny's main argument as to why apostates from Christianity should be pardoned is the absence of actual
flagitia in Christianity. He told Trajan about the harmless nature of
their religious services, that they had pledged themselves to commit
neither crime nor "theft, robbery, adultery" nor to lie. This information which he had received from the above mentioned apostates, Pliny
checked out by interrogating under torture two slave deaconesses.
What he found was a *superstitio parva, immedoca*, but no *flagitia*.[23]

The obvious conclusion that in the absence of actual *flagitia* Christians should not be persecuted apparently never entered his mind.
The reason for this anomaly lies in the supposition that Christianity
as such constituted a crime for Pliny and his main question was
whether apostates in the past and in the future could receive pardon.
Trajan's rescript, written in terse style, informed Pliny of the absence
of fixed general procedures. The emperor agreed with his legate that
those who were convicted of being Christians must be executed, as
Pliny had done. Trajan, however, insisted that they were not to
be sought out by the authorities. If the accused met the sacrifice test,
he should receive pardon, though his past remained under a cloud.
Finally, contrary to Pliny's procedure, anonymous accusations were
to be ignored, for such "does not befit our age." [24]

The primary goal in dealing with Christians was their conversion,
as Pliny had suggested. The government could forego the initiative

of tracking down these criminals, and it rejected anonymous accusations because it knew of the absence of actual *flagitia*. Simultaneously, Trajan was unwilling and unable to state that Christianity without *flagitia* was to be tolerated.

A decade later, around A.D. 124–125, Hadrian's rescript to Minucius Fundanus, proconsul of Asia, in reply to a letter written by Fundanus' predecessor, Granianus, proceeded along the line of policy which Trajan had expressed in his reply to Pliny.[25] Hadrian's rescript has frequently been interpreted as "in practice the nearest to toleration that Christians were to attain before the end of Valerian's persecution." [26] Freudenberger, in a most careful analysis of this rescript,[27] has shown convincingly that it represents a continuation of Trajan's policy and not a departure from it. He and others before him have also made it clear why apologists like Justin, Melito, and Athenagoras misinterpreted Hadrian's rescript to the advantage of the Christian cause. Actually Hadrian demanded that due process of the law was to be observed in proceedings against Christians, lest insecurity prevail. This implies that magistrative *coercitio* was not to be employed against accused Christians, but regular legal procedure initiated by an accuser who was to be held personally responsible for his accusation. The accuser must make his case against the Christians in open court. The decision should therefore not be influenced by outcries of a mob or insinuations. If the people accused of being Christians were convicted of being Christians, that is, of acting against previously issued imperial rescripts, then judgment should be pronounced in accordance with the gravity of the crime, namely, capital punishment. But those who falsely accused people of being Christians should be subjected to the *calumnia* procedure and be punished in proportion to their crime.

Here lay the risk for the accuser in that he must take full responsibility for his accusation and face dire consequences if he could not prove his case. For then he became subject to the penalty which would have been visited upon the accused. Hence in practice this rescript inhibited, rather than encouraged, legal proceedings against Christians. If an accused should, for instance, deny that he was a Christian and prove it by sacrificing to the gods, then the tables were turned and the accuser became the accused. This legal safeguard represented the further development beyond Trajan.

In conclusion, while other foreign "superstitions" suffered temporary setbacks on account of the *flagitia* connected with them, Christianity, after the turn of the century, had become illegal and being a Christian was a capital crime. The rescripts applied first of all to the governors and province to which they were sent. But through Pliny's publication of his correspondence the directives of Trajan became known all over the Empire and thus acquired the force of legal precedent, with which other magistrates could orient themselves in similar cases without abandoning their right of decision on the basis of their own discretion. In practice, capital punishment, or its equivalent, such as exile into the mines, was seldom inflicted during the first two centuries of the Empire, because religious toleration was also a force in a syncretistic society and pragmatic reasoning endeavored to find ways that would inflict capital punishment on as few Christians as possible, especially when the absence of actual *flagitia* became known, at least to magistrates, through Pliny's correspondence.

NOTES

[1] H. Last, "Rome and the Druids," *Journal of Roman Studies* 39 (1949), 1ff.

[2] *Der Vorwurf des Atheismus in den ersten drei Jahrhunderten. Texte und Untersuchungen* 28, N. F. XIII, 4 (Berlin: 1905); Bo Reicke, *Diakonie, Festfreude und Zelos* (Uppsala: Lundequistska, 1951), p. 312.

[3] Cicero, *Laws* 2. 8; 10; 12.

[4] Philo, *Embassy to Gaius* 160f.

[5] In an age filled with revolutionary fever, some interpreters once again portray Jesus as a political rebel in the tradition of the zealots plotting rebellion against Rome "for God and country." J. Carmichael, *The Death of Jesus* (New York: The Macmillan Company, 1963); S. G. F. Brandon, *Jesus and the Zealots* (New York: Charles Scribner's Sons, 1967); similar views had been expressed by R. Eisler, *Iesous basileus, ou basileusas* (Heidelberg; C. Winter, 1929-30), and by Reimarus, cf. A. Schweitzer, *The Quest of the Historical Jesus* (New York: The Macmillan Company, 1956), pp. 13-26.

[6] F. J. Foakes Jackson and K. Lake *(The Beginnings of Christianity*, Part I, vol 2, [New York: The Macmillan Company, 1922], 148f.) and others hold that in Acts 6:8 and 7:54-60 two sources were fused by Luke, one in which Stephen's death appears as the result of juridical procedure, the other which narrated an act of mob stoning. But it is more likely that Luke had only the latter tradition before him to which he himself added the coloring of a "trial" before the Sanhedrin, suggesting that even the highest court acted like a mob. Cf. M. Simon, *St. Stephen and the Hellenists* (London: Longmans Green, 1958); J. Bihler, *Die Stephanusgeschichte im Zusammenhang der Apostelgeschichte*. Münchner Theol. Studien (Munich: M. Hueber, 1963).

[7] Josephus *(Antiquities* 20. 9. 1) speaks of "certain others" who were likewise put to death. Who they were is not stated, nor does Josephus indicate that the proceedings of the Sanhedrin were conducted in an illegal manner.

[8] Eusebius *(Ecclesiastical History* 4. 5f.) enumerated fourteen "bishops" of Jerusalem for the time between James' and Hadrian's reign. On the grandsons of Judas, Jesus' brother, who were brought before Roman officials, hardly before Domitian himself, cf. Eusebius, *Eccl. History* 3. 19. 1-6. On the crucifixion of Simon, son of Clopas, cf. Eusebius, *Eccl. History* 3. 32. 5f.; A Schlatter, "Die Kirche Jerusalems vom Jahre 70 bis 130," reprinted in: *Synagoge und Kirche bis bum Barkochba Aufstand* (Calwer Verlag: Stuttgart, 1966), pp. 99-173; R. T. Herford, *Christianity in Talmud and Midrash* (London: Williams & Norgate, 1903), pp. 120-151. Justin Martyr (1 *Apology* 31) briefly referred to the *timōriai deinai*, the terrible punishments of Christians ordered by Bar Kochba, unless they "denied

and blasphemed Jesus Christ." E. Schürer, *A History of the Jewish People in the Time of Jesus Christ,* First Division, vol. 2 (Edinburgh, T. & T. Clark, 1892), pp. 257-321; observations of N. N. Glatzer to revised edition of Schürer, *op. cit.* (New York: Schocken Books, 1961), pp. 276-308, and esp. pp. 300; 400, note 80. R. T. Herford, *op. cit.,* pp. 99-173. That the persecutions were simultaneously political and religious in nature lies in the character of messianic wars.

⁹ According to Acts 17:1-9; Revelation 2:9; *Martyrdom of Polycarp* 12. 2; 13. 1 some Jews occasionally spread calumnies about Christians. However, Justin, *Dialogue* 16. 4; 17. 1; 95. 4; etc., must be interpreted in the light of the *Birkath ha Minim* and of the Bar Kochba revolt, as well as in the light of the pre-Christian and Christian doctrine that Israel always persecuted God's prophets. (cf. Matthew 23:29-36; 1 Thessalonians 2:15f.) H. L. Strack, and P. Billerbeck, *Kommentar zum Neuen Testament aus Talmud und Midrasch,* vol. 1 (Munich: Beck, 1926), pp. 875; 943; Josephus, *Antiquities* 9. 13. 2; H. J. Schoeps, *Die jüdischen Prophetenmorde, Supplement häften till Svensk Exegetisk Arsbok* 2 (Uppsala: Lundequistska, 1943). Tertullian's famous statement that the "synagogue is the source of persecutions," *Scorpiace* 10, does not mean that synagogues contemporary to Tertullian were the source of all present persecutions but, as the context clearly indicates, he means to say that historically the beginnings of the persecutions of Christians took place in the synagogue.

¹⁰ Thus Paul was beaten with the rods of lictors three times (2 Corinthians 11:24). Nevertheless, he wrote Romans 13:1, 3.

¹¹ See Stephen Benko, "The Edict of Claudius of A.D. 49 and the Instigator Chrestus," *Theologische Zeitschrift* 25 (1969), 406-418.

¹² Tacitus, *Annals* 15. 44; Suetonius, *Nero* 38. 1; Dio *History* 62. 1-8.

¹³ Cf. H. Last, "Christenverfolgung II, Juristisch," *Reallexikon für Antike und Christentum,* vol. 2 (Stuttgart, 1954), col. 1211.

¹⁴ The reference to an *"Institutum Neronianum"* in Tertullian (*To the Gentiles* 1. 7; 9) has frequently been interpreted to mean that Nero issued an edict proscribing Christianity. (Cf. Jacques Zeiller in Jules Lebreton and Jacques Zeiller, *The Emergence of the Church in the Roman World,* vol. 2 of A History of the Early Church (New York: Collier Books, 1962), pp. 67-70. But *"institutum"* is also synonymous with *"consuetudo,"* custom. Cf. Cicero, *To Atticus* 4. 17. 1; Frend, *op. cit.,* pp. 126; 453, n. 48; R. Freudenberger, *Das Verhalten der Römischen Behörden gegen die Christen im Zweiten Jahrhundert. Dargestellt am Brief des Plinius an Trajan und den Reskripten Trajans und Hadrians, Münchner Beitrage zur Papyrusforschung und Antiken Rechtsgeschichte* 52 (Munich, 1967), p. 6f. The sporadic occurrence of persecutions of Christians and the absence of a reference to such an edict in the writings of Christian apologists support this interpretation of *"institutum"* meaning *"consuetudo."*

¹⁵ 1 Clement 4-7; Dibelius, "Rom und die Christen im ersten Jahrhundert," *Sitzungsberichte der Heidelberger Akademie der Wisseuschaften* 2. 2, (1941-1942), 1ff.; reprinted in M. Dibelius, *Botschaft und Geschichte, Gesammelte Aufsätze,* vol. 2 (Tübingen, J. C. B. Mohr, 1956), pp. 177-228, esp. pp. 194ff., 201ff. For a different view set forth by W. M. Ramsay, cf. F. W. Beare, *The First Epistle of Peter,* 2nd ed. (Oxford: Black, 1961), p. 12.

¹⁶ Cf. E. G. Selwyn, "The Persecution in 1 Peter," *Bulletin of the Studiorum Novi Testamenti Societas* I (1950), 39ff.

¹⁷ *Clement's* petition: "Save us from those who hate us without cause" (60:3) is placed before the petition, that we may "become obedient . . . to our rulers and governors on earth" and after the petition for doing "what is good and pleasing. . . . before our rulers." The threat of the imperial cult is not yet felt.

[18] The difference between the population of the Empire and the Christians is manifest in their different attitudes toward the imperial cult: "All who dwell on earth will worship it (the beast), every one whose name has not been written . . . in the book of life . . ." Revelation 13:8. Cf. Revelation 13:12, 15.

[19] Dio, *History* 67. 14. 1f.; Suetonius, *Domitian* 15; Tacitus, *Agricola* 2; 45: Eusebius, *Eccl. History* 3. 18. 1-4; 19. 1-6; K. Scott, *The Imperial Cult under the Flavians* (Stuttgart: Kohlhammer, 1936). Eusebius can report only two banishments of Christians during Domitian's reign, the author of the Apocalypse and Flavia Domitilla. On the other hand, Domitian released the grandsons of Judas. Eusebius, *Eccl. Hist.* 3. 19. See also Gager, footnote 71, p. 119.

[20] Pliny, *Ep.* 10. 96 and 97. Note this cagey way of expressing himself, *"an flagitia cohaerentia nomini puniantur"* (10. 96. 2), even though he knows that *flagitia* are not *cohaerentia nomini;* see also 10. 96. 1f.

[21] *"neque enim dubitabam, qualecumque esset, quod faterentur, pertinaciam certe et inflexibilem obstinationem debere puniri."* 10. 96. 3. Whatever the relationship between *flagitia* and the *nomen ipsum* may be, the obstinacy of Christians deserves capital punishment.

[22] Pliny, *Ep.* 10. 96. 9.

[23] *Ibid.,* 10. 96. 7 and 8.

[24] Pliny, *Ep.* 10. 97. 1 *"nam et pessimi exempli nec nostri saeculi est,"* A. N. Sherwin-White, "Trajan's Replies to Pliny," *Journal of Roman Studies* 52 (1960), 114 ff.

[25] Eusebius, *Eccl. History* 4. 8. 6–4. 9. 3.

[26] Frend, *op. cit.,* p. 169.

[27] Freudenberger, *op. cit.,* pp. 216–234; further lit. there.

FOR ADVANCED READING

An excellent bibliography is found in: Frend, W. H. C., *Martyrdom and Persecution in the Early Church: A study of Conflict from the Maccabees to Donatus.* Oxford, England: Blackwell & Mott, Ltd., 1965. Also, Garden City, N. Y.: Anchor Books, 1967, pp. 527-557. Cf. reviews in: *Journal of Theological Studies,* n.s., 18 (1967), pp. 217-221; *Novum Testamentum* 9 (1967), 155-157.

The following items might be added:

Borleffs, J. W. P., "Institutum Neronianum." *Vigiliae Christianae* 6 (1952), 129-145.

Freudenberger, R., *Das Verhalten der römischen Behörden gegen die Christen im 2. Jahrhundert. Dargestellt am Brief des Plinius an Trajan und den Reskripten Trajans und Hadrians.* Münchener Beiträge zur Papyrusforschung und Antiken Rechtsgeschichte. 12. Munich, 1967.

Getty, Robert J., "Nero's Indictment of the Christians" in *The Classical Tradition: Literary and Historical Studies—In Honor of Harry Caplan.* Edited by Luitpold Wallach, Ithaca, N. Y.: Cornell University Press, 1966.

Mayer-Maly, T., "Der rechtsgeschichtliche Gehalt der Christenbriefe von Plinius und Trajan." *Stud. et doc. hist. iuris* 22 (1956), 311-328.

Moreau, J., *Die Christenverfolgung im römischen Reich.* Berlin, 1961 (which is the *enlarged* German translation of the French original quoted by Frend.)

Rahner, H., *Kirche und Staat im frühen Christentum. Dokumente aus acht Jahrhunderte und ihre Deutung.* München, 1961.

Robert L. Wilken

12
Collegia, Philosophical Schools, and Theology

How did Christianity appear to men and women of the Greco-Roman world when it first began to emerge in public view? What conceptions were present within Roman "social thought" to identify and define a new phenomenon such as Christianity? What did men "see" when they looked at the Christians? In antiquity no one subjected the Christian movement to a social analysis or took a Gallup poll; nevertheless, the observations of outsiders are more concerned with the social side of Christianity than they are with its ideas and beliefs.[1] We do not have a great deal of evidence for our inquiry, but what we do have provides us with some very provocative clues to the route Christianity took as it climbed up the social ladder from the *"odium humani generis"* of Tacitus in the early second century to become the established religion of the Roman Empire under Theodosius I in the late fourth century.

One of the stages in this long and involved process was the apologetic movement which began under the emperor Hadrian in approximately A.D. 130. Widely viewed as the first Christian theologians, the apologists have been interpreted in light of their ideas on God, man, cosmology, *et al.*[2] This preoccupation with theological and philosophical ideas is justified, of course, by the character of our sources. The apologists were engaged in an intellectual task. Yet the more one reads early Christian writers and studies the non-Christian authors, the more one is convinced that something has been missing in our account of early Christian apologetics. It still seems possible and necessary to raise other kinds of questions. What, for example, is the relation between the intellectual work of the apologists and the social reality that they, as members of the Christian community, were experiencing? How do the apologists appear when viewed not in light of classical Greek philosophy, nor the history of theology, nor the Bible, but in light of the attitudes of outsiders toward the Christians?

268

In this chapter I should like to initiate a discussion of these questions by examining two specific problems: Christianity as a burial society *(collegium funeraticium* or *collegium tenuiorum)* and as a philosophical school. I hope to show that these seemingly unrelated social conceptions complemented each other and gave to those outside the Christian community as well as those within a basis for understanding Christianity in terms intelligible to the Greco-Roman world.

EARLY CHRISTIANITY AS SEEN BY THE ROMANS

We have an inflated view of the history of early Christianity. The historian of the Roman Empire, who by training and perspective could view Christianity within the larger historical picture, has seldom bothered to look closely at the Christian sources. The historian of Christianity, who knows the sources and the unique problems of early Christian history, has so enlarged his section of the canvas beyond all reasonable proportion that the general history of the times is granted only a small corner. The disjunction between Roman history and Christian history is also reflected in our sources. For almost a century Christianity went unnoticed to most men and women in the Greco-Roman world. When Christianity first appeared there was almost no common ground of understanding between Christians and non-Christians. The Christian writings, highly theological and directed primarily at Christian readers, present the Christian communities and the life of Jesus as the fulcrum of history, whereas non-Christian literature presents the Christians as a small, peculiar, troublesome, anti-social, irreligious sect drawing its adherents from the edge of society.

We would expect the self-understanding of the Christians to differ from the impression of them which was held by outsiders. Yet on many points we have, quite uncritically, accepted the Christian view of things and dismissed the views of their contemporaries. The Christians were sometimes said to be immoral, but seldom has anyone explored this charge to see whether it may have been true. More frequently we have simply passed it by, assuming that the early Christians spurned profligacy, behaved as puritans, and if anything were much too rigoristic in their moral expectations. On examination, however, the charge turns out to be quite accurate. Even our Christian sources show that Christian leaders, e.g., Paul, had to devote a good deal of their time and energy coping with moral laxity. A century later Justin complained that there are "those who are found not living as he taught . . . even if his teachings are on their lips. . . ." Origen echoes the same complaint in the third century.[3] In many communities the bishops and teachers presided over an unruly and undisciplined lot of Christians. We know also of some Christian groups who celebrated the Eucharist nude and who practiced an exotic rite involving *coitus interruptus* in which human semen was offered to God.[4] Among Christians one could also find opportunists, charlatans, and con men as well as the greedy, slothful, and perverse.[5]

To the outsiders the Christians did not present themselves as men of high moral standing, partly because they came from the lower strata of society and partly because there were enough bizarre practices to lead to such a view. Only when the Christians were able to discipline their own ranks and establish an orthodoxy as well as an orthopraxis did the judgment of outsiders begin to change. We know that the early Christian communities embraced a wide spectrum of beliefs and teachings. Not every Christian group believed the same things about Jesus, the Jewish Scriptures, and God; and since there were few fixed norms to decide such matters, the casual observer could hardly have been expected to know which Christian line was the correct one. Even the Christians themselves had trouble handling this question. The outside observer was inclined to consider those men Christians who called themselves Christians — an eminently sensible procedure. But if all Christians, i.e., those who called themselves Christians, did not *believe* alike, it is also true that they all did not *behave* alike. Just as everyone did not share Paul's views on Judaism, not everyone shared his moral or liturgical practices. A strong current of libertinism, offensive to the sensibilities of the middle- and upper-class Romans, runs through early Christianity. The Romans, not the Christians, were the puritans.

We should not be surprised, then, to find that the earliest references to Christians by non-Christians assume that Christians are guilty of shameful and degraded practices. Tacitus, who includes a few lines on Christianity in his *Annales,* says that the Christians were "detested because of their shameful practices" *(quos per flagitia invisos vulgus 'Christianos' appelabat)* and that the "deadly superstition" which originated in Judea now resided in Rome "where all degraded and disgraceful practices *(cuncta atrocia aut pudenda)* collect and flourish." [6] Tacitus was only peripherally interested in the Christians. He had not made an examination of the new religious sect on his own but had probably picked up his ideas from the prevailing opinion around him. The Christian communities, a world unto themselves, did not participate in the civic and cultural life of the towns and cities; they gathered in secret conventicles and were quite cavalier about their responsibilities as members of society. Consequently, information was hard to come by and if some Christians celebrated the liturgy without clothes, it would not have taken long for the word to get out that the Christians as a group were depraved.

Tacitus, Pliny, and Suetonius also call Christianity a crude, degenerate, and fanatical superstition *(superstitio prava, immodica; exitiabilis superstitio; nova et malefica superstitio)*. On the lips of an educated Roman or Greek the term *superstitio* had many connotations. Most frequently it designated religious groups or practices foreign to the Romans, e.g., Jews, devotees of Isis, *et al.* Such religions were thought to be fanatical — Jews refusing to fight on the sabbath — and exotic, irrational, and incompatible with Roman ideals or simply at variance with established religious rites and ceremonies. Superstition was at odds with genuine religion. Not only philosophers, wrote Cicero, but the *"maiores superstitiones a religione separaverunt."* [7]

In an essay entitled *On Superstition,* Plutarch argued that superstition is as destructive of genuine piety as atheism. He wrote:

> It occurs to me to wonder at those who say that atheism is impiety *(asebeia)*, and do not say the same of superstition. . . . The man who does not believe in the existence of the gods is unholy. And is not he who believes in such gods as the superstitious believe in a partner to opinions far more unholy? [8]

Superstition is opposed to *eusebeia* or *pietas,* the religious and ethical ideal so cherished during this period. Coins, statues, sarcophagi of the period frequently bear the familiar figure of a woman with uplifted hands, the *orans* which was the personification of *pietas,* and inscriptions as well as literary works testify to the same devotion to *pietas.* Superstition, then, was a form of impiety *(asebeia)* which promoted false and dangerous beliefs about the gods. "The superstitious man puts responsibility for his lot upon no man nor upon Fortune nor upon occasion nor upon himself, but lays the responsibility for everything upon God, and says that from the source a heaven-sent stream of mischief has come upon him with full force." Observing the life and attitudes of superstitious men, said Plutarch, one concludes that "it were better that there should be no gods at all. . . ." [9] Superstition, like atheism, bypasses "true piety." To say that the Christians were superstitious is not precisely the same as saying that they were immoral, but crude and fanatical religious beliefs and practices, especially about gods who are capricious, fickle, vengeful, or rash, could never to Pliny or Tacitus or Plutarch be a source of genuine piety and morality. Such gods undercut human responsibility and render moral life meaningless. The charge, then, that the Christians were guilty of shameful practices is closely related to the charge that Christianity was a degraded superstition.

PHILOSOPHICAL SCHOOLS

Not more than fifteen or twenty years after the publication of Tacitus' *Annales,* Justin, a native of Flavia Neapolis in Palestine, was converted to Christianity. As a young man Justin was educated in Hellenistic schools, and as he grew to maturity he, like other philosophically inclined men, set out on a quest from one philosopher to another in search of an acceptable way of life. Some time after his conversion to Christianity he wrote a book on Christianity and Judaism in which he presented an account of his conversion. Justin's description of his conversion, a highly idealized account, can be paralleled in other non-Christian works. The account may not represent Justin's own life history since Justin is relying on literary convention.[10] However, this does not discount the significance of Justin's account, for whatever the literary sources behind the passage, it shows that Justin wished to present his conversion to Christianity as a conversion to philosophy. And that is worth noting. Against the backdrop of prevailing opinion about Christianity as well as the character of the Christian movement up to that time, Justin's claim that Christianity offered men a genuinely philosophical way of life was so presumptuous that it probably appeared preposterous. Why does Justin present Christianity as a philosophy?

The philosophical schools held a dominant place in the Greco-Roman world.[11] Long before the appearance of Christianity, philosophy had become not so much a way of thinking about the world as a way of teaching men to live in the world. From the lofty and metaphysical heights of Plato and Aristotle, the new breed had brought philosophy down to earth to wrestle with the bread and butter questions of everyday life. In his study of *Conversion*, A. D. Nock cites the striking passage from the Roman satirist Persius who casually links philosophical speculation about the origin of the world and the purpose of life with the mundane question of how to handle money.

> O poor wretches, learn, and come to know the causes of things, what we are, for what life we are born, what the assigned order is, where the turning-point of the course is to be rounded gently, what limit to set to money, for what it is right to pray, what is the use of hard cash, how much you ought to spend on your country and on those near and dear to you, what kind of man God ordered you to be and where as a man you are placed.[12]

The various schools competed as much in terms of "life style" as they did in the realm of ideas. When a man chose to become a member of a particular school, the decision was viewed as a "conversion" or "break from the world" in favor of a higher and better way. Some philosophers took to the lecture circuit to become popular speakers and preachers on ethical and religious questions. Their sermons, called *diatribe*, a kind of *Volkspredigt*, dealt almost wholly with questions, such as suffering, poverty, old age, death, desire, pleasure, freedom, and they sought, not simply to instruct and teach, but to persuade and move men to change their way of life.[13]

The writings of Epictetus, Musonius, Plutarch, Seneca, and others reflect this philosophical style.[14] Seneca, for example, composed a lovely letter on philosophy in which he observed that through ingenuity, and technical skills man has learned to make bread from grain, invented ships to cross rivers and seas, discovered how to till the ground and grow crops, to weave, make tools, build houses, and make instruments of war. Thus, philosophy or wisdom did not "discover the arts of which life makes use in its daily round." "Philosophy's seat is higher; she trains not the hands, but is mistress of our minds." The function of philosophy is to

> discover the truth about things divine and things human. From her side religion never departs, nor piety *(pietas)*, nor justice, nor any of the whole company of virtues which cling together in a close-united fellowship. Philosophy has taught us to worship that which is divine, to love that which is human; she has told us that with the gods lies dominion, and among men, fellowship.[15]

Note here that philosophy promotes *pietas.*

What the Greeks and Romans of this time called philosophy approximates much more closely what we today call religion than it does our notion of philosophy. In his remarkable study of Hellenistic philosophy Paul Rabbow has shown that the philosophical schools devoted themselves to the "care of souls," *psychagoge,* i.e., the disciplined initiation into a noble way of life. The philosopher taught his disciples to cope with anger, lust, desire, fear of death, ambition, fate, and worldly goods. The letters of Seneca to Lucilius are marvelous examples of the techniques employed by the philosophers. Rabbow believes that many of the same principles employed in Ignatius of Loyola's *Spiritual Exercises* can be traced back to the moral philosophers of this period. Through memory verses, readings from the poets, meditation on proverbs and sayings, the philosophers sought to instill in their students a new way of life. "Wisdom's course," writes Seneca, "is toward the state of happiness; thither she guides us, thither she opens the way for us." [16]

The philosophical schools achieved great popularity in the Greco-Roman world because they could offer a compelling and credible way of life as well as an intelligible explanation of man, the gods, and the world. In short they gave men the certainty they were seeking in a world they found increasingly difficult to comprehend. The schools offered, writes Nock, "intelligible explanations of phenomena. . . . Secondly — and this is the point of cardinal importance — the schools offered a life with a scheme. One of the terms for a school of philosophy, whatever its kind, is *agoge,* which means way of teaching and way of living." [17] In one of his dialogues, Lucian, the satirist, pictures the various philosophical schools as slaves auctioned in the public square. When the Stoic appears, the best men of society — statesmen, lawyers — join the bidding because the Stoics sell virtue itself, "the most perfect of philosophies." The term used here for philosophy is *bios,* life. Lucian himself believed that the philosophers were so confused that they were no more help than the common man; yet he regularly gives us a picture of what most men expected from philosophers. Elsewhere he writes:

> While I was a boy, when I read in Homer and Hesiod about wars and quarrels, not only of the demigods but of the gods themselves, and besides about their amours and assaults and abductions and lawsuits and banishing fathers and marrying sisters, I thought that all these things were right, and I felt an uncommon impulsion toward them. But when I came of age I found that the laws contradicted the poets and forbade adultery, quarreling, and theft. So I was plunged into great uncertainty, not knowing how to deal with my own case. . . . Since I was in a dilemma, I resolved to go to the men whom they call philosophers and put myself into their hands, begging them to deal with me as they would and to show me a *plain solid path in life.*[18]

Justin was seeking for the same certainty, a safe and sure path in life. Justin, however, did not become a Stoic or a Platonist; instead he became a Christian. He claims to have examined the most important philosophical schools only to find them inadequate either because their explanation of the world was not satisfying, as in the case of the Pythagoreans, or because their teachings did not lead to a "further knowledge of God," as in the case of the Stoics, or because they did not live "philosophically," as in the case of the Peripatetics. The goal of philosophy according to Justin is to lead men to a genuine knowledge of God and a "happy life." [19] Of all the philosophies which Justin studied, the only philosophy which came close to this goal was Platonism, but even this he found wanting. Therefore he turned to Christianity, for it was the only school offering a "philosophy which is secure and profitable." [20]

Justin's somewhat innocent identification of Christianity with a philosophical school was a radical departure from earlier Christian views.[21] Few of his contemporaries and none of his predecessors would have felt at all comfortable with such an understanding of Christianity. In the few places where the term occurs in earlier writers it is always used to refer to pagans and never to Christians, and its sense is always pejorative. What is true for the Christians themselves, however, is also true for non-Christians. In the popular view of Christianity there was little to lead men to think that the Christians were rivals or competitors to the Stoics or Epicureans. Consider how Justin's account of his conversion would strike many readers of the *Dialogue.* He first mentioned the Stoics, and in the space of one sentence he dismissed the whole Stoic tradition. "I gave myself over," wrote Justin, "to a certain Stoic; and after spending sufficient time with him, since I had not acquired any further knowledge of God — for he did not believe himself, nor did he think such instruction was necessary — I left him and went to another." [22] With a sweep of the hand Justin rejected a way of life and thought stretching back almost five centuries and which would soon sit in the imperial throne in the person of Marcus Aurelius. It is as though someone today would, with a snap of the finger, write off the whole history of, let us say, Calvinism as inferior to the Four Square Gospel church. Justin was making a rather large claim. The Stoics boasted a venerable succession of teachers — Zeno, Cleanthes, Chryssipus, Poseidonius, Musonius Rufus, Seneca — and by the third century B.C. Stoicism had achieved recognition as a leading school of philosophy. During the next two centuries it had spread in the West, and by the end of the Republic it had captured the best and most influential men in Rome. At the time that Christianity was just beginning, Stoicism had reached the pinnacle of its influence. And during this period it had produced one of the greatest moral teachers of antiquity, Epictetus, who had traveled across the Empire gathering disciples about him.

Christianity could claim no such inheritance. As time went by Christian thinkers developed an argument legitimatizing the Christian tradition, but at Justin's time the claim was primarily moral and religious with the added support of appeal to the Jewish tradition. Our teaching is derived, wrote Justin, from "certain men more ancient than all those who are esteemed philosophers," namely the Hebrew prophets, and in these writings one will find "knowledge of the beginning and the end of things and of those matters which the philosophers ought to know. . . ." [23] By claiming that Christianity was a philosophy, Justin claimed that Christianity promoted genuine piety, i.e., belief in God and a way of life appropriate with this belief. "We cultivate," he wrote, "piety, justice, philanthropy, faith, and hope." [24] The first three of these terms are almost parallel to the passage from Seneca: from the side of philosophy "religion, piety, justice never depart." [25] In the preface to the *Dialogue* Justin wrote that it is only "men who are truly holy" who devote themselves to philosophy. The term "holy" *(hosios)* is often used interchangeably with piety *(eusebeia)* during this period. On sarcophagi of this time one sometimes finds piety represented by the *orans* figure on one side balanced by the *Chriophoros* (shepherd carrying a kid) representing philanthropy on the other side. On other sarcophagi, between these two figures is a third figure, a philosopher. The sarcophagus signifies that the person buried here lived a philosophical life, i.e., a life of piety toward the gods and of philanthropy toward mankind. [26]

Justin offered a new understanding of Christianity, as new to his fellow Christians as it was to the citizens of the Roman Empire. In response to the prevailing opinion that Christianity was a depraved superstition, he argued that it was a school of philosophy with vener-able teachers whose way of life was more acceptable than that of other schools. Furthermore, the Christian philosophy promoted genuine piety and should not have been classed with the immoral and bizarre practices associated with superstitious religious groups. In effect Jus-tin took the rather bold step to ask that Christianity be evaluated in terms of Greco-Roman ideals, i.e., whether the Christians promoted genuine piety. The Christian self-understanding and the understand-ing of Christianity among outsiders were beginning to find common points of contact.

All that Justin said was quite unbelievable at the time of Tacitus and Pliny and perhaps at the time that Justin was converted. By the time Justin was writing his apologies and preparing the *Dialogue,* a change was in the wind. Almost imperceptibly a different view of Christianity was emerging in some circles. About the same time that Justin was writing his *Dialogue* and living among the growing Chris-tian community in Rome, Galen, the philosopher-doctor, moved to Rome.[27] Except for a period when he returned to his native city of Pergamum to avoid the plague, he remained in Rome till the end of his life. As a physician Galen had already earned distinction, but his interests ranged far beyond medicine. When he was a young man, he had been introduced to philosophy by his father, and he, like Justin, had also made the grand tour to try on the current phi-losophies. First he went to a Stoic, then to a Platonist, next to a Peripatetic, and finally to an Epicurean. Like Justin he found none acceptable, but unlike Justin he did not become a Christian.

While in Rome Galen came to know about the Christians, and in his medical works he mentioned them several times in passing. Galen was not much impressed by the Christians; yet his evaluation was remarkably different from Tacitus or Pliny. To Galen the Christians appeared much like a philosophical school. However, they were thought to be little better than some of the other schools he had examined because they refused to submit their teachings to critical examination. Instead they asked men to accept their teachings and way of life on faith. Lucian made a similar complaint about philo-sophical schools in his *Hermotinus.* In his work *On the Pulse,* Galen scorned those who held opinions without sufficient critical investiga-tion. We would expect, said Galen, at least a "reassuring and suffi-cient explanation if not a cogent demonstration so that one should not at the very beginning, as if one had come into the school *(dia-tribe)* of Moses and Christ, hear talk of undemonstrated laws." The term *diatribe* is commonly used for philosophical schools during this period. Elsewhere Galen criticized the schools of Christians and Jews for slavish adherence to their own tenets without considering what others taught. Asked once about nose bleeding by someone whom Galen thought was really not interested in medical science, he retorted that he would not bother to tell him of advances in science, "for one might more easily teach novelties to the followers of Moses and Christ than to the physicians and philosophers who cling fast to their schools (hairesesi)." [28]

In some respects Galen echoed the earlier view of Christians by his charge of irrationality or undemonstrability of Christian teaching. Superstition and irrationality had much in common. Galen was especially troubled by the Jewish and Christian belief that God could do whatever he wished even if his wish were contrary to nature. Hellenistic thinkers found this idea, sometimes associated with the Creation and with the resurrection of Jesus, deeply offensive.[29] Worship of this kind of God could not lead to genuine piety. In other respects Galen differed from his predecessors. He had given up the view that the Christians were a degraded superstition or that they were guilty of gross acts of immorality. To him the Christians were a second- or third-rate philosophical school whose teachings were hardly worthy of serious examination. Yet even this was quite a change. For the first time a non-Christian observer used a socially acceptable category to identify the Christians, though he found them quite deficient by the standards he believed appropriate to philosophical schools. Christians were beginning to win a place under the sun.

Galen, like most Greeks, believed there was an intimate relation between clear and reasonable thinking and virtuous behavior or piety. The philosophers gave men insight into the world, man, and god and made it possible for men to live in a truly philosophical way, i.e., a life of justice, and piety. If a philosophical school fell short in reasonable proof of its views, one could hardly expect it to produce men of piety. In another passage Galen discussed Christian behavior and puzzled over the disparity between Christian teaching and Christian life. The Christians were weak in logical discourse, yet they seemed capable of leading men to a virtuous life. "We now see the people called Christians drawing their faith from parables and yet sometimes acting in the same way as those who philosophize." And in another place:

> For their contempt of death and of its sequel is patent to us every day, and likewise their restraint in cohabitation. For they include not only men but also women who refrain from cohabiting all through their lives; and they also number individuals who in self discipline and self-control in matters of food and drink and in their keen pursuit of justice have attained a pitch not inferior to that of genuine philosophers.[30]

Galen's view is almost precisely the reverse of what one might hear today. Instead of "Christian teaching is very admirable but the

Christians just do not practice what they preach," Galen said, in effect, "Christian teaching is quite inferior to what our better teachers offer, but Christians do achieve a high degree of virtue in their lives." [31] What Galen observed of the behavior of Christians forced him to take seriously their doctrines.

Galen was a lone and exceptional spokesman in his time. What he thought about the Christians could hardly have been the popular view. Most men did not view Christianity as a philosophical school — not even a third-rate school. Celsus' broadside against the Christians was written only a few years later. Yet Galen is too important a figure to dismiss. What his testimony reveals is that in one city, and this the capital of the Empire, some Christians were discovering an intelligible way to present themselves to outsiders, and that to some, at least, the model of a philosophical school seemed credible. Most Christians would have been quite uncomfortable with such an identification. They were content to let men think that the only road to Christian certainty was through "faith." "Do not ask questions, just believe" and "your faith will save you" were watchwords. Even in the third century Origen had to defend Christians against the charge of credulity.[32]

Galen may have been reflecting his experience with an exceptional group of Christians in Rome at that time, led by a certain Theodotus, a cobbler and leather dealer. According to Eusebius, Theodotus was attacked by his fellow Christians and excommunicated because he and his circle interpreted the Scriptures philosophically. They "dwelt treacherously with the rule of the primitive faith," Eusebius wrote, and "laboriously set out to find a form of syllogism to support their godlessness." They pursued the study of geometry, admired Aristotle, Theophrastus, and Euclid, and "some of them almost worship Galen." In short they "corrupt the simple faith of the divine Scripture. . . ." [33] The preface to Justin's *First Apology* corresponds to the kind of questions Galen addressed to the school of Christians. We ask, wrote Justin, that the Christians be examined "with piety" and in a "philosophical fashion."

> Reason requires that those who are truly pious and philosophers should honor and cherish the truth alone. . . . For in these pages we do not come before you with flattery, or as if making a speech to win your favor, but asking you to give judgment according to strict and exact inquiry—not, moved by prejudice or respect for superstitious men, or by irrational impulse and long established evil rumor, giving a vote which would really be against yourselves.[34]

Justin's challenge would still strike his readers as strange; yet what he said is not as preposterous as it would have appeared a generation earlier. The door was now ajar. A new philosophical school was in the making.

COLLEGIA

Understood as a way of life informed by ideas about God, the philosophical school approximated what we would today call a worldwide religious movement. As such it provided one model for interpreting Christianity within Greco-Roman society. Christianity was also viewed by some, within and without the church, as an "association," burial society, or *collegium*.[35] In contrast to the model of philosophical school, the model of an association called attention to the form that Christianity took in a given locality. The *collegia* were local associations seldom exceeding several hundred members. There is some evidence that in a given city or town certain philosophical schools would take the form of an association. Unfortunately the evidence is so scanty that we cannot say for certain what social form a philosophical school would take in a local area. However, there are many similarities between schools and associations.

Within the space of this chapter I cannot develop an argument for the similarities, socially speaking, between philosophical schools and associations. However, I can briefly set down some of the chief considerations which lead to this view:

1. At some points the terminology for associations and philosophical schools intersect: *secta, synodos, thiasos*.[36]

2. In Greece, philosophical schools sometimes took the form of *thiasoi* or religious associations. They met for common meals and discussion and may have assessed dues. They also celebrated the memory of the founder of the school, and sometimes the grave of the founder became a spiritual center for the adherents.[37]

3. To learn the philosophical way of life, disciples frequently came to live with the master in company with other disciples. In this setting the new disciple would listen to lectures of the master, study the writings of earlier teachers, memorize appropriate verses, and undergo rigid ethical instruction and guidance. Not a little part of this system was the support and interest of his fellows but also the disciple was inspired by sharing in a way of life which could trace its history back to venerable sages from earlier times. This memory was kept alive by the school.[38]

4. The neo-Pythagoreans did take the form of a religious association during this period, and they may provide the closest parallel to the early Christian community. Unfortunately we are badly informed on this school and cannot really explore the parallels in detail. We do know, however, that a group of Neo-Pythagoreans did build a basilica and meeting hall in Rome, and excavations of the basilica at Porta Maggiore have shown that the members of this school met regularly for religious worship and a cultic meal.[39]

Before proceeding to a discussion of Christianity as an association, let me clarify the direction of the argument. The question whether philosophical schools took the form of religious associations is important because Christianity not only appeared to outsiders as a philosophical school, but it also appeared as an association or *collegium*. My point is not that philosophical schools and associations were the same, nor even that one could have been mistaken for the other. My contention is that there were some similarities and that these similarities help us to understand, on the one hand, the social dimension of philosophy at this time, and, on the other hand, the religious and ethical dimensions of associations. In the case of the Christian movement, I do not think that, strictly speaking, it was either a philosophical school or a burial association. Nevertheless, to Christians and non-Christians alike it had elements of both and appeared to observers as one or the other or as a combination of the two.

The early years of the Roman Empire were times of great growth, sustained peace, and relative prosperity. The burgeoning industry and the demand for artisans, craftsmen, merchants, and similar skills and occupations became a ready avenue of economic and social betterment for slaves, freedmen, and freeborn persons throughout the Mediterranean world. Most of these men and women — bridlemakers, stonecutters, purple dealers, woolcombers, fruit dealers, *et al.* — were cut off from the social and cultural life of the senatorial and equestrian class. Devoting themselves to their crafts and small businesses, these people discovered the benefits of gathering together on holidays. The chief purpose of these gatherings was not to organize as "labor unions," though these associations were often formed along occupational lines, but for recreation, social intercourse, and religious worship. Eventually such gatherings grew into clubs or associations or societies. Initially they may have organized to provide for burial expenses of the members, but very quickly the social and religious aspects of the associations took on an equal, if not greater, importance.

A good example of such an association — in this case a burial club — is the society dedicated to Diana, formed in Lanuvium in Italy during the early second century, A.D. The bylaws of this society were inscribed in A.D. 136.

It was voted unanimously that whoever desire to enter this society shall pay an initiation fee of 100 sesterces and an amphora of good wine and shall pay monthly dues of 5 *asses*. . . . It was voted further that if a member dies farther than twenty miles from town and the society is notified, three men chosen from our body will be required to go there to arrange for his funeral. . . .

It was voted further that if any member takes his own life for any reason whatever, his claim to burial shall not be considered. It was voted further that if any slave member of this society becomes free, he is required to donate an amphora of good wine. It was voted further that if any master, in the year when it is his turn in the membership list to provide dinner, fails to comply and provide a dinner, he shall pay 30 sesterces into the treasury. Calendar of dinners: March 8, birthday of Caesennius . . . November 27, birthday of Antinous; August 13, birthday of Diana and of the society; . . . December 14, birthday of Caesennius Rufus, patron of the municipality.

Masters of the dinners . . . shall be required to provide an amphora of good wine each, and for as many members as the society has a bread costing 2 *asses*, sardines to the number of four, a setting, and warm water with service.

It was voted further that any member who becomes *quinquennalis* in this society shall be exempt from such obligations for the term when he is *quinquennalis*.

It was voted further that if any member desires to make any complaint or bring up any business, he is to bring it up at a business meeting, so that we may banquet in peace and good cheer on festive days. . . . Any member who uses any abusive or insolent language to a *quinquennalis* at a banquet shall be fined 20 sesterces.

It was voted further that on the festive days of his term of office each *quinquennalis* is to conduct worship with incense and wine and is to perform his other functions clothed in white, and that on the birthdays of Diana and Antinous he is to provide oil for the society in the public bath before they banquet.[40]

This society was organized as a burial club, but it is clear that the social and religious functions of the association were just as important for life in this world as the dues were in preparation for life in the next. Roman society was deeply divided along class lines, and most of the occupations of freedmen were despised by the ruling class. The only life worthy of a gentleman, in the eyes of a Roman, was politics, soldiering, or agriculture. Jean Waltzing wrote:

> The artisan, the small merchant, the worker were generally from the class of freedmen. They were placed always at the bottom of the political and social ladder; they saw in the association the only means to escape their isolation and weakness, to acquire some little consideration and even a little influence, finally to create for themselves in the society, in the city, an honorable place. . . . Religion, the care for funerals, the desire to be stronger, to defend their interest, to elevate themselves above the common herd, the desire to fraternize and to make their difficult existence more pleasant—such were the diverse sources of that urgent need of association which worked in the popular class.[41]

The collegia gave men a sense of identity and comradeship, a social unit larger than the family and smaller than the state where they could meet together with friends, eat and drink, worship, play, and share common experiences. The society at Lanuvium met once a month for business and more frequently for social and religious purposes. They joined in a common meal accompanied by a religious rite. The regular gatherings were interspersed with special days — a liturgical year — to recall the founding of the society, to honor the emperor, to remember patrons or celebrate the birthday of the goddess.

In the letter to Trajan on the Christians, Pliny called the Christians an *hetaeria,* one of the more pejorative terms used to refer to associations. According to Pliny the Christians were accustomed to meet together on a fixed day for religious worship and a common meal. In light of Trajan's instructions concerning associations Pliny had ordered the Christians to cease such gatherings. "They had given up this practice (meeting for a meal) since my edict, issued on your instructions, which banned all *hetaeriae.*" [42] In an earlier letter of that same year Pliny had dealt with the matter of a firemen's association in Nicomedia and this experience was probably in his mind as he dealt with the Christians. A group of citizens had requested that they be allowed to form a "fire department" since half of their town had just burned down while the populace looked on. Pliny wrote Trajan for advice and received this reply:

> I have received your suggestion that it should be possible to form a company of firemen at Nicomedia on the model of those existing elsewhere, but we must remember that it is societies like these which have been responsible for the political disturbances in your province, particularly in its towns. If people assemble for a common purpose, whatever name we give them and for whatever reason, they soon turn into an *hetaeria,* i.e., a political club.[43]

Pliny's reference to the Christians as an *hetaeria* is obviously not complimentary. In fact by so doing Pliny sought to find a legal basis to prohibit potentially troublesome assemblies. Yet the significance of his comment is not that the Christian assemblies were illegal, but that he viewed the Christians in the same terms that he viewed the proposed firemen's association.

Several generations later Celsus charged that the Christians had no right to exist as an association because they were secretive. "Celsus' first main point in his desire to attack Christianity," wrote Origen, "is that the Christians secretly make associations with one another contrary to the laws, because 'societies which are public are allowed by the laws, but secret societies are illegal.' " [44] Another tiny bit of evidence that Christianity was viewed as an association comes from the life of Alexander Severus in the *Historia Augusta.* Apparently a dispute had arisen about the right of two groups to occupy a public building for religious purposes. The one group was composed of cooks *(popinarii)* and the other of Christians *(Christiani).* We do know that there were associations of cooks, and it may be that this association was unable to afford its own meeting place and had requested use of public facilities. According to the *Historia,* the issue was decided in favor of the Christians.[45] Apparently this group of Christians had achieved recognition as an association and was able to make a claim on the meeting place.

These scraps of information[46] would be much less significant if we did not have the long passage on the Christian *collegium* in Tertullian's *Apologeticum* (chapters 38–39).[47] Tertullian was attempting to meet the charge that Christians had no right to exist as an association. He did this by arguing that Christianity was not a political club *(factio)* and that, in most respects, it was similar to the harmless associations one could find in most cities and towns. Should not the Christians be "reckoned among legal associations" *(factiones)*, asked Tertullian. "For unless I mistake the matter, the prevention of such associations is based on a prudential regard for public order that the state may not be divided into parties which would naturally lead to disturbance in the electoral assemblies. . . ." Other "sects" *(secta)* are allowed to exist, as for example, the Epicureans.

With this preface Tertullian proceeded to describe the Christian association. He wrote:

> The time has come to tell of the activities of the Christian association *(negotia Christianae factionis)*. . . . We are a *corpus* bound together by our religious profession, by the unity of our way of life, and the bond of our common hope. . . . We pray for the emperors. . . . We assemble to read our sacred writings. . . . With the sacred words we nourish our faith, we animate our hope, we make our confidence more steadfast, and no less by inculcations of God's precepts we confirm good habits. . . . The tried men of our elders preside over us, obtaining that honor not by purchase, but by established character. . . . Though we have our treasure chest, it is not made up of purchase-money. . . . On the monthly meeting day, if he likes, each puts in a small donation. . . . These gifts are, as it were, an offering for piety *(deposita pietatis)*. . . ."

The remainder of the chapter describes the Christian agape as a feast whose product is "piety" not licentiousness. After the feast is over, we go into the world to live modestly and chastely as though we had come from a "school of virtue" *(disciplina)* rather than a "banquet" *(cena)*. No one has ever suffered harm from our assemblies. "When the upright, when the virtuous, when the pious *(pii)*, when the chaste assemble together you should not call that a *factio* but a *curia*."[48]

The chapter is filled with technical terms used in connection with associations:[49] *factio, secta, illicita factio, corpus, curia, coitio.* The Christian community is called *factio Christianae, corpus, secta Dei, coitio, curia Christianorum.* In connection with the offerings, he uses terms for the common chest and dues in the collegia: *arca, honoraria summa, stips;* and for the regular meeting day he uses *menstrua die.* Some of these terms, namely *secta* and *disciplina,* are also used in connection with philosophical schools. What is most provocative about the passage is that Tertullian described the church in language quite foreign to the Christian biblical, liturgical, and theological tradition — body of Christ, people of God, etc., — but quite familiar to the ordinary citizen of a Roman city. The language used here to present Christianity would be quite intelligible to anyone, whether he was acquainted with the Christian tradition or not. To the observer the Christian community had a common chest, regular meetings for worship, and festive dinners, some type of official leadership, and perhaps, though Tertullian does not mention this, a common cemetery. To the casual observer, then, writes Jean Gagé, a recent historian of social class in the Empire, the Christian community "offered at first glance an astonishing resemblance to a type of confraternal association which had flourished since the second century . . . namely the *collegia funeraticia*." [50]

Tertullian capitalized on the resemblances as well as the differences between the Christian community and these associations. He used the similarities between the two to call attention to what he considered to be the differences. "We have our treasure chest, but it is not made up of purchase money." He shunned the Christian word for church, i.e., *ecclesia* in favor of *corpus, factio, secta, et al.* His readiness to present Christianity in this fashion is as radical a departure from traditional Christian thinking as was Justin's presentation of Christianity as a philosophical school. Tertullian could use traditional Christian language as well: "Nor is even our mother the church passed by, if, that is, in the Father and the Son is recognized the mother, from whom arises the name both of Father and of Son." And elsewhere: "After the promise of salvation under 'three witnesses' (Deuteronomy 19:15; Matthew 18:16; 2 Corinthians 13:1) there is added . . . a mention of the church; inasmuch as, wherever there are three (that is, the Father, the Son, and the Holy Spirit) there is the church which is a *corpus* of three." [51] The biblical and liturgical language views the church, not as a burial society or *collegium* similar to other groups, but as a wholly unique, elect community in fellowship with Christ and in union with God.

Compared to the rich imagery of the New Testament, Tertullian's description of Christianity as an association was modest, reserved, and remarkably non-theological. We have our own religious allegiance, said Tertullian. We follow a certain style of life; for example, we love one another, care for orphans and widows, seek a life of piety. We exhort one another to live according to this ideal in our gatherings. We have our own scriptures, leaders, and a history extending back to Tiberius. To legitimate the Christian association, Tertullian not only argued that Christians did not form a political club, but he also showed that Christians had a history and tradition extending back to their founder. "We date the origin of our *disciplina* . . . from the reign of Tiberius." Tertullian had already appealed to the Jewish tradition, but here he went beyond Judaism as a legitimation for the Christian *secta* to the origins of Christianity with Jesus of Nazareth. Having defended the founder of Christianity and the early beginnings, he concludes: "We have set forth this origin of our sect and name with this account of the founder of Christianity." [52]

In the *Apologeticum* Tertullian self-consciously adapted himself to conceptions current with the Greco-Roman world about associations, their customs and practices, their organization and gatherings, their history and tradition. It is noteworthy, however, that he regularly interchanged the idea of associations with that of philosophical schools. Even in chapter 39 he called Christianity the *"secta Dei"* and contrasted the Christian *disciplina* with a riotous banquet. In the preface to this section of the apology he compared Christianity to the "sects" of the Epicureans. Earlier in the *Apologeticum* he was even more explicit. Most sects, said Tertullian, take the name of their founder. Why do men revile Christians because they are named after Christ?

Tertullian was not using only the model of a burial society. He complemented that concept with the notion of "sect" or "school," particularly as the term was applied to philosophical schools. Tertullian relied on the precedent set by earlier apologists, notably Justin and Tatian, concerning the philosophical character of Christianity, but in his hands the earlier view assumed greater clarity and precision as it was blended with the idea of an association. Whereas the notion of "school" called attention to the "international" character of Christianity, "association" called attention to its local character. In its gatherings the Christian association promoted the ideals appropriate to philosophy, namely piety and virtue. We go from our assemblies, said Tertullian, not as thieves or vagabonds, not to commit licentious acts, but "concerned with modesty and chastity as if we had come out of a *disciplina* rather than a banquet." We are not a political club *(factio)* which promotes dissension and unrest but a school of the "upright, virtuous, pious, and pure." [53]

The restraint and diffidence of chapter 39 of the *Apologeticum* give way in the final chapters to the more typical style of Tertullian — bravado. When he had made the case that Christian associations were like other associations, though with notable differences, and that they, like the philosophical schools, nurtured piety and virtue, he turned the argument from the similarities between Christians and others to assert the absolute uniqueness of the Christian way of life. Some think that we are a "kind of philosophy *(genus philosophiae)* rather than something divine *(negotium divinum),*" because we practice what philosophers practice, namely "innocence, justice, patience, sobriety, chastity." But we are not "philosophers but Christians." "Where is any likeness between the Christian and the philosopher? between the disciple of Greece and of heaven? between the man whose object is fame and whose object is life?" [54] If one looks at the number of parties among us, he might be led to conclude that we are "to be equated with philosophers"; but we are really in possession of the "rule of truth which comes down from Christ by tradition" and this teaching is older than all philosophical doctrines. We are in possession of the "truth not the shadow." [55] Tertullian's conclusion, in light of the earlier argument, is not as contradictory as it may appear. If he was to establish the uniqueness of Christianity, he first had to show its similarity with other religious and social forms. If he had not done so, his claim about Christianity would have fallen on deaf ears. Before Christianity could be shown to be unique and without parallel, the apologists had to show what it was like, and, by implication, what it was unlike. What could Tertullian's words possibly have meant to Tacitus or Pliny? The Christian movement had come a long way from the days when it was known as a *superstitio,* and now it was ready to offer an intelligible argument for its claim of uniqueness.

CONCLUSION

In his book, *Treasure in Earthen Vessels,* James Gustafson pointed out that the church, when viewed from a social perspective, has many similarities with other groups and organizations in society. Though most Christians describe their religious life in terms of traditional biblical and liturgical language and concepts — body of Christ, true Israel, people of God, sons of God — this language does not tell the whole story. Gustafson writes:

> Reflective participants seek to understand the nature of any community in which they live. If they seek exclusively the differentium of that community, they lack an adequate understanding of it. If they think exclusively in the community's own characteristic language, e.g., the Biblical concepts, they will not see many phases of their own existence. Concepts from sociology and philosophy enlighten aspects of the life of the Church that traditional doctrinal or Biblical concepts do not.[56]

The choice of "philosophical school" and "association" as categories to identify the Christian community is not accidental. It rests on the social reality that men were experiencing as Christians. When men looked at the Christian community, they tended to see Christianity in light of the schools and associations with which they were familiar in everyday life. But the apologists had more in mind, for they also wished to avoid the designation *superstition.* The identification of Christianity with philosophical schools and associations provided, in the Greco-Roman world, the greatest possibility for interpreting Christianity to outsiders. At the same time these conceptions were able to express what the apologists thought to be the chief characteristics of Christianity and to do so in a way which was credible in terms of the

Christian tradition. Like the Stoics or Epicureans, the Christians were a "worldwide" sect whose adherents lived throughout the Mediterranean world and shared a common religious profession and style of life. A Stoic, no matter where he lived, was different from an Epicurean, and a Christian was different from either. Yet the Christian movement, from the very outset, organized itself into social units in each community, and these local associations of Christians engaged in much the same activities as other associations: worship, festive meal, fellowship, common treasury, cemeteries, burial of the dead. The combination of "philosophical school" and "association" suited the Christian community remarkably well.

There was a risk involved and it was not theological. Philosophical schools and burial associations had their own kinds of problems. Especially during the first century A.D. philosophers met with rebuke, censure, and sometimes exile. Indeed, as Ramsay MacMullen has shown, philosophy and subversion were frequently identified with each other in the eyes of Roman authority.[57] To claim that Christianity was a philosophy did not insure its acceptance. Yet the philosophers had more to commend them than, for example, magicians, astrologers, or some of the more exotic religious cults, and they had been able to align the cause of philosophy with the accepted ideals of piety and philanthropy. Similarly the associations frequently met hostility and suspicion, especially if their activities were unusually secretive or susceptible to political maneuvering.[58] The exiling of philosophers and restrictions on associations might have encouraged Christian thinkers to play down the "philosophical" and "collegial" character of Christianity. Yet they emphasized just these characteristics.

In his *True Word* Celsus had compared the Christians to the "begging priests of Cybele and soothsayers and to worshippers of Mithras and Sabazius, and whatever else one might meet, apparitions of Hecate or of some other daemon or daemons." [59] Origen replied that Christians prize reason, that they subject their sacred writings to reasonable exegesis, i.e., allegory, and that they bring about moral conversion by appeal to the rational belief in rewards and punishments, demonstrating their belief in free will. Other critics charged the Christians with fatalism and belief in astrology and divination. Christian ideas about a God who chose, elected, and predestined men appeared as a form of fatalism, as did belief in prophecy; and, not insignificantly, astrology and divination were practiced in some Christian circles.[60] Some liturgical practices, possibly the Trinitarian formula at baptism, appeared as a type of magical incantation.[61] The readiness to interpret Christianity as a "philosophical school" rested on the sound instinct that, if Christianity was to make its way in the

Greco-Roman world and remain responsive to its own tradition, it did better to cast its lot with the philosophers than with astrologers or with the oriental cults. The apologists sought to show that Christians were not ignorant and superstitious, that the Christian school was a reasonable option for men, and that in Christianity men could find a sure way of life leading to genuine piety.[62]

NOTES

[1] The summary of charges against the Christians by Minucius Felix in his *Octavius,* written in the third century when Christian beliefs were much better understood than in the early second century, is more social than it is theological and philosophical. As the years go by the reaction of pagans to Christianity becomes more philosophical and theological.

[2] Most recently see L. W. Barnard, *Justin Martyr* (New York: Cambridge University Press, 1967) and Niels Hyldahl, *Philosophie und Christentum. Eine Interpretation der Einleitung zum Dialog Justins* (Copenhagen, 1966).

[3] Justin, 1 *Apologia* 16. 8, from *Early Christian Fathers,* vol. 1, *The Library of Christian Classics,* newly translated and edited by Cyril C. Richardson (Philadelphia: The Westminster Press, 1953). Used by permission. Origen, *Contra Celsum* 4. 27. ". . . if you examine strictly who is a true Christian or if such sins were to be found, yet at least it would not be among those who assemble for worship and come to the common prayers and are not excluded from them." (H. Chadwick, *Origen: Contra Celsum* [New York: Cambridge University Press, 1953], p. 202.)

[4] Epiphanius, *Panarion* 1. 2. 26; esp. 26. 4. See S. Benko, "The Libertine Gnostic Sect of the Phibionites According to Epiphanius," *Vigiliae Christianae* 21 (1967), 103-119.

[5] Lucian, *Peregrinus* 12-16.

[6] Tacitus, *Annales* 15. 44; Pliney, *"nomen ipsum, si flagitiis careat, an flagitia cohaerentia nomini puniantur."* (*Ep.* 10. 96.) On pagan attitudes toward the Christians, see Pierre de Labriolle, *La Reaction paienne* (Paris, 1934); E. R. Dodds, *Pagan and Christian in an Age of Anxiety* (New York: Cambridge University Press, 1964), pp. 102ff. On Pliny, Rudolf Freudenberger, *Das Verhalten der römischen Behörden gegen die Christen im 2 Jahrhundert,* "Münchener Beiträge zur Papyrusforschung und antiken Rechtsgeschichte," vol. 52 (München, 1967); also A. N. Sherwin-White, *The Letters of Pliny* (New York: Oxford University Press, 1966). On Tacitus, Harald Fuchs, "Tacitus ueber die Christen," *Vigiliae Christianae* 4 (1950), 5-93; Freudenberger, *op. cit.,* pp. 180-189. On the charge of infant murder in the liturgy, see J. P. Waltzing, "Le crime rituel reproché aux chrétiens du II° siecle," *Bulletin de la Classe des Lettres et des Sciences Morales et Politiques, Academie Royale de Belgique,* 5° Serie, Book 9 (1925), pp. 205-239; F. J. Doelger, "Sacramentum infanticidii," *Antike und Christentum* 4, pp. 188-228. Doelger notes that certain gnostic practices may have given rise to such rumors.

[7] Tacitus, Pliny, *op. cit.;* Suetonius, *Claudius* 25. 3; *Nero* 16. 3. On *superstitio* see Freudenberger, *op. cit.,* pp. 189-199; Joseph Vogt, *Zur Religiosität der Christenverfolger im römischen Reich,* Heidelberger Akid. d. Wissenschaften, Philosophischer-hist. Klasse, Sitzungsberichte; 1962, 1 Abhand. D. Kaufmann-Buehler, "Eusebeia," in *Rivista di Archeologia Christiana* 6, 1016-1020. *De Natura Deorum* 2. 72.

[8] Plutarch, *De Superstitione* 169f-170a (F. C. Babbit, in the Loeb Classical Library, pp. 483-485); 168a-b, 171b-f (Babbitt, *op. cit.,* pp. 473, 491-495). On the

artistic representation of *eusebeia,* see Theodor Klauser, "Studien zur Entstehungs-geschichte der christlichen Kunst," *Jahrbuch fuer Antike und Christentum,* vols. 1-10 (Munster, 1958ff.) .

[9] *Ibid.*

[10] *Dialogue with Trypho* 2. 1-6. For parallels see the preface to the letter of Thessalus to Emperor Claudius (or Nero); text in Peter Boudreaux, *Catalogus codicum astrologorum graecorum* VIII, 3 (Brussels, 1912), pp. 134-136; also Lucian, *Menippus* 4ff. Other parallels and discussion of the literary form in Hyldahl, *op. cit.,* pp. 148ff.

[11] On philosophy during this period, see especially A. D. Nock, *Conversion* (New York: Oxford University Press, 1933); Paul Rabbow, *Seelenfuehrung. Methodik der Exerzitien in der Antike* (München, 1954); Anne-Marie Malingrey, *Philosophia, Étude d'un groupe de mots dans la littérature grecque des Présocratiques au IV siecle après J. C.* (Paris, 1961).

[12] Persius 3. 66ff. (Nock, *op. cit.,* p. 183) .

[13] W. Capelle, "Diatribe," *Reallexicon für antike und Christentum* (RAC) 3. 990-997.

[14] See Nock, *op. cit.,* pp. 164ff.; Rabbow, *op. cit.,* pp. 25ff.

[15] Seneca, *Ep.* 90. 3 (R. M. Gummere in The Loeb Classical Library, vol. 2, pp. 395-397) . Reprinted by permission of Harvard University Press.

[16] Seneca, *Ep.* 6. 1; 90. 28.

[17] Nock, *op. cit.,* p. 167.

[18] Lucian, *Menippus* 3-4; *Philosophies for Sale,* 20. In the fourth century the monastic life was called *bios philosophikos* by Christians; see Werner Jaeger, *Two Rediscovered Works of Ancient Literature: Gregory of Nyssa & Macarius* (Leiden, 1954) , pp. 19-22.

[19] *Dialogue* 2. 3; 3. 4; 8. 2.

[20] *Dialogue* 8. 1, *philosophian asphalē te kai sumphoron.* Justin's phrase is strik-ingly close to Lucian's "plain solid path in life." See also Plutarch, *De Superstitione,* pp. 171f. (Babbit, *op. cit.,* p. 495) : "But there is no infirmity comprehending such a multitude of errors and emotions, and involving opinions so contradictory, or rather antagonistic, as that of superstition. We must try, therefore, to escape it in some way which is both safe and expedient *(asphalōs te kai sumpherontōs)."*

[21] See Gustave Bardy, "Philosophie et 'philosophe' dans le vocabulaire chrétien des premiers siècles," *Revue d'Ascetique et de Mystique* 25 (1949) , 97-108. The term *philosophein* sometimes means "live as a Christian." See, for example, Tatian, *Oratio* 32-33. Anne-Marie Malingrey, *Philosophia,* p. 120. Also Melito in Eusebius, *Historia Ecclesiastica* 4. 26. 7; Miltiades, in Eusebius, *Hist. Eccl.* 5. 17. 5. Aristides and Athenagoras (Hyldahl, *op. cit.,* pp. 235ff.) speak of Christianity as a philosophy or identify themselves as philosophers.

[22] *Dialogue* 2. 3.

[23] *Ibid.,* 7. 1-2.

[24] *Ibid.,* 110. 3.

[25] *Ep.* 90. 3.

[26] See T. Klauser, *op. cit.,* 3 (1960) 112-133; D. Kaufmann-Buehler, "Eusebeia," *Reallexicon für antike und Christentum* 3. 1014; Justin, 1 *Apologia* 2. 1; 12. 5; 2 *Apologia* 15. 5.

[27] On Galen see Richard Walzer, *Galen on Jews and Christians* (London, 1949) . Walzer provides the text of Galen's statements on Christians as well as a very thorough commentary on their social and philosophical setting.

[28] Walzer, *op. cit.,* pp. 38-48. See also *Reallexicon für antike und Christentum* 3. 990ff. On faith and the philosophical schools, Lucian, *Hermotinus* 7.

[29] See Walzer, *op. cit.*, pp. 30-32 and especially *Contra Celsum* 5. 14.

[30] Walzer, *op. cit.*, pp. 57, 65.

[31] *Ibid.*

[32] See also *Contra Celsum* 1. 9 and Porphry, *Against the Christians* in Eusebius' *Praeparatio Evangelica* 1. 1. 2 (cited in Walzer, *op. cit.*, p. 54).

[33] Eusebius, *Hist. Eccl.* 5. 28. 13-14; Walzer, pp. 75ff.

[34] 1 *Apologia* 2. 1-3; also Tatian, *Oratio* 42.

[35] The literature on associations is endless, very repetitive, and frequently preoccupied with questions of legal history. Still fundamental is Jean Waltzing, *Étude historique sur les corporations professionnelles chez les Romains* (Brussels, 1895-1900), 4 vols., including texts of the relevant inscriptions. For a more recent discussion with extensive bibliography see F. M. de Robertis, *Il Fenomeno Associativo nel Mondo Romano* (Naples, 1955). For associations in the eastern Empire, Franz Poland, *Geschichte des griechischen Vereinswesens* (Leipzig, 1909).

[36] See F. M. de Robertis, *Il Fenomeno, Associativo nel Mondo Romano.* (Naples, 1955), p. 8; Gerda Krueger, *Die Rechtsstellung der vorkonstantinischen Kirchen* ("Kirchenrechtliche Abhandlungen," vol. 115-116; Stuttgart, 1935), p. 85; W. Dittenberger, *Orientis graeci inscriptiones selectae* (Lipsiae, 1903-1905), II, 712; *Corpus Inscriptionum Graecarium* III, 4315; Poland, *op. cit.*, p. 55.

[37] U. V. Wilamowitz-Moellendorf, "Die Philosophenschulen," in *Antigonos von Karystos* in *Philologische Untersuchungen* 4 (1881), pp. 232-306; Poland, *op. cit.*, pp. 154, 509. A society of philosophers is mentioned in Strabo 17. 1. 8 in connection with the Museion in Alexandria.

[38] See Rabbow, *Seelenfuehrung*, pp. 260ff.

[39] Jérôme Carcopino, *La Basilique Pythagoricienne de la Porte Majeure* (Paris, 1927).

[40] Text in *Corpus Inscriptionum Latinarum*, vol. 14. 2. 112; trans. Naphtali Lewis and Meyer Reinhold, *Roman Civilization* (New York: Columbia University Press, 1966), 2, pp. 274-275. See also minutes from the Bacchic society at Athens in A.D. 178 in *Inscriptiones Graecae* (Berlin, 1873—), II ², 1638; discussed in Marcus N. Tod, *Sidelights on Greek History* (Oxford: Blackwell & Mott, Ltd., 1932), pp. 71ff.

[41] Waltzing, *op. cit.*, p. 332.

[42] Pliny, *Ep.* 10. 96. See Rudolf Freudenberger, *Das Verhalten der römischen Behörden gegen die Christen im 2. Jahrhundert*, for an exhaustive commentary on the letter. A. N. Sherwin-White's commentary, *The Letters of Pliny*, adds nothing new on the question of *hetaeria*, except to reiterate the point that the legal base for persecutions could not have been the prohibition of illicit *collegia*.

[43] Pliny, *Ep.* 10. 33-34.

[44] *Contra Celsum* 1. 1; 8. 17. 47. Celsus's phrase in 1. 1 corresponds precisely to *collegia illicita*, according to Justinian's *Digest* 47. 22. 2. See Gerda Krueger, *Rechtsstellung*, p. 73, n. 1. For a consideration of the evidence for Christianity as an association, see de Robertis, *Il Fenomeno*, pp. 99ff.

[45] *Vita Alex.* 49.

[46] See also the somewhat obscure passage in Tertullian, *De Ieiunione* 13, as well as the later evidence collected in de Robertis, *op. cit.*, pp. 116ff.

[47] On this chapter see especially Krueger, *Rechtsstellung*, pp. 91ff.; as well as de Robertis, *op. cit.*, pp. 111ff.; J. Waltzing, "Collegia" in *Dictionnaire d'Archéologie chrétienne et de Liturgie* 3. 2107-2140; and J. Waltzing, *Tertullian. L'apologétique* (Paris, 1931), *ad loc.*

[48] *Apologeticum* 39. 1-2. On *factio* and *corpus* as terms for associations see Krueger, *Rechtsstellung*, pp. 86, 92ff.

[49] For similarities between *Apologeticum* 39 and Justinian's *Digest* 47. 22. 1 see

G. M. Monti, *Le corporazioni nell'evo antico e nell'alto evo* (Bari, 1934), 1. 284-285; Hardy, *op. cit.,* p. 145.

[50] Jean Gagé, *Les Classes Sociales dans l'Empire Romain* (Paris, 1964), p. 308. Also de Robertis, *Il Fenomeno,* pp. 119ff.; and E. G. Hardy, *Christianity and the Roman Government* (London, 1894). The idea that Christianity took the form of a collegium goes back to the study of T. Mommsen, *De collegiis et sodaliciis Romanorum* (1843) and to the archaeological work of Giovanni Battista De Rossi, *La Roma sotteranea cristiana* (1864-1877). De Rossi's thesis is based on the Christian cemeteries. These he took to be an indication that the Christian communities were recognized as burial societies.

[51] *De Baptismo* 6. 2; *De oratione* 2. 6.

[52] *Apol.* 7. 3; 21. 27. Collegia generally took note of the date on which they were founded. See Waltzing, *Corporations* 1. 362-363.

[53] *Apol.* 39. 19, 21.

[54] *Apol.* 46. 2, 5, 18.

[55] *Apol.* 47. 9, 14.

[56] James Gustafson, *Treasure in Earthen Vessels* (New York: Harper & Row, Publishers, 1961), pp. 5-6.

[57] Ramsay MacMullen, *Enemies of the Roman Order* (New York: Cambridge University Press, 1966), pp. 46-94.

[58] See J. Waltzing, *Corporations,* 1. 114ff.

[59] *Contra Celsum* 1. 9.

[60] Minucius, *Octavius* 11. 6. "*Nam quicquid agimus, ut alii fato ita vos deo dicitis; sic sectae vestrae non spontaneos sed electos.*" For divination among Christians, see Origen, *Commentary on Genesis* 3 (Genesis 1:16) in *Philocalia* 23. 1; also *Hom. in Joshua* 5:6 (Joshua 4:10ff.; *Soures Chretiennes* 71, 174).

[61] *Contra Celsum* 1. 6.

[62] See *Contra Celsum* 3. 9. Some Christians "have done the work of going round not only cities but even villages and country cottages," writes Origen, "to make others also pious towards God."

Stephen Benko

Vocabulary of Latin Terms

Aediles (of the people) —officers of the city of Rome in charge of public buildings, including temples and games. At one time they were also responsible for the corn supply of Rome.

Aerarium—the state treasury distinguished from the imperial treasury which was called *fiscus*.

Alimenta—plural of *alimentum*. The original meaning of the word is "food," "maintenance," later used for the public assistance program of Nerva and his successors.

Annona—literally "produce" or "harvest" almost always used for the corn supply of Rome.

Augur (pl. *augures*) —priest who took and interpreted the auspices.

Auspices—means by which the augur sought to find out whether the gods were favorable.

Censor—a public official elected for the purpose of taking the census of the people. There were always two censors whose duties also included the revision of the roll of senators. Because of this, the emperors often assumed censorial powers to exercise control over the Senate.

Collegium (pl. *collegia*) —guild, corporation, association, club.

Congiarium—donation distributed by the emperor to the people, or cash donation to the soldiers.

Consilium principiis—the advisory council (crown council) of the emperor.

Consul—there were always two consuls; they held the highest military and judicial powers. They were elected for one year. Under the emperors the power of the consuls declined; often they were elected for only three or six months, and the emperors themselves often held the office.

Cursus Honorum—the course of offices, see *Cursus Publicus*.

Cursus Publicus—the order in which a Roman citizen could hold public offices, also called *cursus honorum*. This order was: following ten years military service (i.e., not earlier than one's twenty-eighth birthday) , quaestor, aedile, praetor, consul. Usually two years had to elapse between two offices, i.e., consuls, as a rule, were men in their forties.

Decurio—member of a local senate of a Roman city.

Delator (pl. *delatores*) —informer, spy. Under Tiberius many were convicted upon the information supplied by these secret agents who received money for their services.

Equestrian Order—originally the "knights" who served in the cavalry. During the imperial era they no longer served in this capacity, but were the wealthiest class of citizens, engaged in banking, money lending, and similar financial activities. Because of their sharp business acumen, they provided the state with many able civil servants.

Fiscus—in the imperial era, the treasury of the emperor, distinguished from the state treasury called *aerarium*.

Fiscus Judaicus—the Jewish poll tax, which after A.D. 70 each of the Jews in the Empire had to pay into a central treasury in Rome. This was the continuation of the temple tax. After the destruction of the temple in Jerusalem, however, the principal beneficiary of the income was the temple of Jupiter Capitolinus.

Flamen (pl. *flamines*)—priest of a particular deity.

Honestioris (pl. *honestiores*) —persons of distinction; "upper class."

Humilioris (pl. *humiliores*) —persons of humble origin; "lower class."

Imperium—"the power to command" thus *imperium proconsulare,* the power of a former consul to command an army in a province. As a rule, this power ceased at the city limits of Rome.

Lar (pl. *lares*) —domestic deities.

Libertinus (pl. *libertini*) —freedman; a former slave emancipated by manumission.

Limes (pl. *limites*) —the fortified boundary line of the Empire.

Maiestas—the charge of high treason, especially impairment of the majesty of the emperor.

Manumissio—the act of emancipating a slave.

Obsequium-i—obedience, deference, submission.

Officium-i—obligation, ceremony, service, office.

Ordo Equester—see Equestrian Order.

Penates—family deities.

Pomerium—the sacred boundary of the city of Rome.

Pontifex—priest of the state religion.

Pontifex Maximus—high priest.

Praetor—the magistrate elected annually by the people to administer justice.

Praetorian Guard or *Praetorians*—the bodyguard of the emperor. Augustus organized it originally for the protection of Italy, and the guard was stationed at various points in Italy. Sejanus, under Tiberius, concentrated these troops in Rome. The Praetorians were regarded as an elite troop of soldiers.

Prefect of the Praetorians—the officer who commanded the Praetorian Guards. His power was first below that of the emperor.

Proconsul—a former consul whose authority was extended after the expiration of his term of office to carry out a military project or to govern a province.

Proconsulare Imperium—see *Imperium*.

Procurator—the financial agent of the emperor, usually a member of the equestrian order, whose duty was to supervise the revenues in an imperial province.

Proskynesis—form of worship in which the worshiper prostrates himself before the object of his worship.

Quaestor—Internal revenue officer. Originally two, later four and more in number, elected annually by the people.

Quindecemviri—a board of fifteen magistrates who took care of and interpreted the Sibylline Books.

Senate—the ruling body of the state. Its members were nominated by the censors, in the imperial era by the emperor, who assumed censorial powers. The Senate prepared legislative proposals, conducted foreign affairs, and passed resolutions which were called *senatus consulta*. This latter was often used by the emperors to promulgate a law. The Senate usually met in the Curia on the Forum Romanum.

Sesterces, sestertius—a silver, and later bronze, coin, which was divided into four "as"-ses. Sixteen asses (i.e., four sesterces) made a denarius. A sestertius was worth about five cents in terms of modern American money. Thus, when we read that Tiberius, at his death, left about 3,000,000,000 sesterces in the Treasury, we think in terms of some 150 million dollars.

Tribune—a magistrate whose office was the protection of the people. His power was great: he could veto the action of any other magistrate; his person was inviolable and he could call meetings of the people and propose changes of laws.

Tribunicia Postestas—the power and authority of a tribune, given to the emperor. This, of course, reduced the importance of the real tribunes to almost nothing.

Vicus-i—village, estate.

Stephen Benko

Early Christian Timetable

EMPERORS OF THE FIRST TWO CENTURIES

AUGUSTUS	31 B.C.–A.D. 14	The Julian-Claudian Dynasty
TIBERIUS	14–37	
GAIUS	37–41	
CLAUDIUS	41–54	
NERO	54–68	
GALBA	68–69	
OTHO	69	
VITELLIUS	69	
VESPASIAN	69–79	The Flavian Dynasty
TITUS	79–81	
DOMITIAN	81–96	
NERVA	96–98	
TRAJAN	98–117	
HADRIAN	117–138	
ANTONINUS PIUS	138–161	The Antonines
MARCUS AURELIUS	161–180	
LUCIUS VERUS (joint ruler with Marcus Aurelius)	161–169	
COMMODUS (joint ruler with Marcus Aurelius)	177–180	
COMMODUS	180–192	
PERTINAX	193 (January-March)	
DIDIUS JULIANUS	193 (March-June)	
SEPTIMIUS SEVERUS	193–211	Dynasty of the Severi 193—235

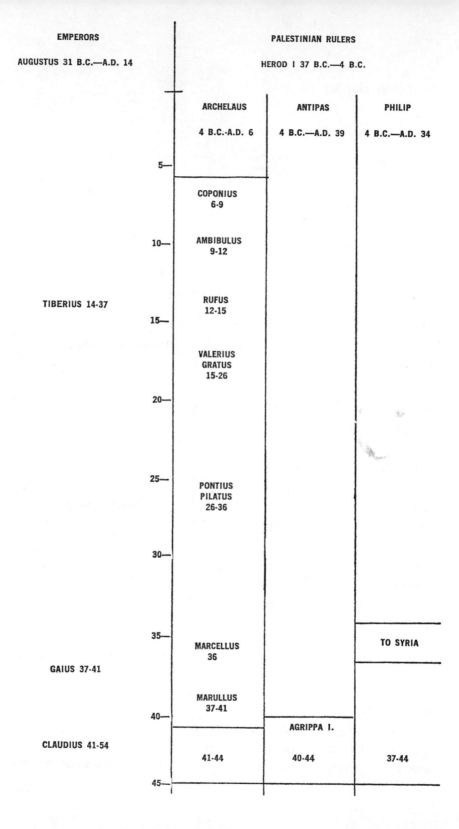

EMPERORS

PALESTINIAN RULERS

AUGUSTUS 31 B.C.—A.D. 14

HEROD I 37 B.C.—4 B.C.

ARCHELAUS	ANTIPAS	PHILIP
4 B.C.-A.D. 6	4 B.C.—A.D. 39	4 B.C.—A.D. 34

5—

COPONIUS
6-9

AMBIBULUS
9-12

10—

RUFUS
12-15

TIBERIUS 14-37

15—

VALERIUS
GRATUS
15-26

20—

25—

PONTIUS
PILATUS
26-36

30—

35—

MARCELLUS
36

TO SYRIA

GAIUS 37-41

MARULLUS
37-41

40—

AGRIPPA I.

CLAUDIUS 41-54

41-44

40-44

37-44

45—

THE CHRISTIAN CHURCH	ROMAN HISTORICAL EVENTS

JESUS CHRIST BORN

5—

THE CENSUS

ZEALOTISM—SICARII

10—

15—

20—

25—

JOHN THE BAPTIST

30—

CRUCIFIXION (33?)

35—

MARTYRDOM OF STEPHEN (36 ?)

40—

MARTYRDOM OF JAMES (42 ?)

45—

5—

REVOLT OF PANNONIA 6-9

DISASTER OF VARUS 9

10—

TIBERIUS GIVEN "PROCONSULAR IMPERIUM" 13
AUGUSTUS DIES 14

15—

TRIUMPH OF GERMANICUS 17
GERMANICUS GOES TO THE EAST 18
GERMANICUS DIES IN ANTIOCH 19; THE CASE OF PISO.
JEWS EXPELLED FROM ROME 19

20—

ACTORS EXPELLED FROM ROME 23; DEATH OF DRUSUS.

25—

TIBERIUS WITHDRAWS TO CAPRI 27
FRISIAN REVOLT 28-48

30—

SEJANUS' FALL 31

35—

PILATE'S FALL 36
TIBERIUS DIES 37
ALEXANDRIA RIOTS 38; PHILO GOES TO ROME.

40—

GAIUS ASSASSINATED 41

ANNEXATION OF SOUTHERN BRITAIN 43

45—

EMPERORS		PALESTINIAN RULERS
		CUSPIUS FADUS 44-46
		TIBERIUS ALEXANDER 46-48
	50—	VENTIDIUS CUMANUS 48-52
		ANTONIUS FELIX 52-60
NERO 54-68	55—	
	60—	PORCIUS FESTUS 60-62
		LUCCEIUS ALBINUS 62-64
	65—	GESSIUS FLORUS 64-66
		THE JEWISH WAR 66-73
GALBA; OTHO 68		
VITELLIUS 68-69	70—	
VESPASIAN 69-79		"FISCUS JUDAICUS"
	75—	JUDEA IMPERIAL PROVINCE
TITUS 79-81	80—	
DOMITIAN 81-96		
	85—	
	90—	
	95—	

THE CHRISTIAN CHURCH	ROMAN HISTORICAL EVENTS
APOSTOLIC COUNCIL (?)	EXPULSION OF THE JEWS FROM ROME 49
50— 50—	
ZEALOTISM INCREASES	
	CLAUDIUS POISONED BY AGRIPPINA 54
55— 55—	
PAUL TAKEN TO ROME	PARTHIAN WAR 58-63
60— 60—	
DEATH OF JAMES THE JUST (?)	
NERONIC PERSECUTIONS	
CHRISTIANS LEAVE JERUSALEM (64?)	
65— 65—	THE GREAT FIRE IN ROME 64
	NERO IN GREECE 66-67; REBELLION OF THE JEWS
MARTYRDOM OF PETER AND PAUL (?)	REVOLT OF VINDEX AND GALBA; NERO'S END 68
70— 70—	
75— 75—	
	ERUPTION OF VESUVIUS 79
80— 80—	DEDICATION OF COLOSSEUM 80
	TITUS DIES 81
85— 85—	DACIAN WAR 86-89
	REVOLT OF SATURNINUS 88-89
90— 90—	
PERSECUTIONS; CLEMENS AND DOMITILLA	
95— 95—	

EMPERORS		PALESTINIAN RULERS
NERVA 96-98		
	100—	
TRAJAN 98-117		
	105—	
	110—	
	115—	
HADRIAN 117-138		**JEWISH UPRISINGS IN CYRENE, EGYPT, CYPRUS**
	120—	
	125—	
	130—	
	135—	
ANTONINUS PIUS 138-161		**JEWISH REVOLT LED BY BAR/BEN-KOSEBA 132-135**
	140—	
	145—	
	150—	

THE CHRISTIAN CHURCH	ROMAN HISTORICAL EVENTS
1 CLEMENT WRITTEN (?)	DOMITIAN DIES 96
	NERVA DIES 98
100— DIDACHE (?)	100— FIRST DACIAN WAR 101-102
105—	105— SECOND DACIAN WAR 105-106 ARABIA PETRA ANNEXED 106
110— IGNATIUS OF ANTIOCH POLYCARP (to ca. 150) PLINY'S LETTER TO TRAJAN	110— ARMENIA AND LOWER MESOPOTAMIA OCCUPIED 114 PARTHIAN WAR 114-117
115—	115— ASSYRIA ANNEXED 116 REVOLT IN MESOPOTAMIA 116 TRAJAN DIES 117
PAPIAS OF HIERAPOLIS	
120—	120— HADRIAN ABANDONS ASSYRIA AND MESOPOTAMIA 117 HADRIAN'S FIRST TOUR OF PROVINCES 121-126
125— QUADRATUS ARISTIDES	125—
130— LETTER OF BARNABAS (?) SHEPHERD OF HERMAS (?)	130— SECOND TOUR OF PROVINCES 129-134
135— BASILIDES VALENTINUS	135— HADRIAN DIES 138
140— MARCION	140—
145—	145—
150— JUSTIN MARTYR HEGESIPPUS	150—

Index

BIBLICAL QUOTATIONS

CLASSICAL AUTHORS, NAMES AND QUOTATIONS

1.50	159	2.77	95
1.60	161	2.176f.	161
2.41	95	2.280ff.	82

Jewish Antiquities

1.2	159	14.228-	95
1.192	92	234	
1.214	92	14.233	94
4.198	93	14.235	95
9.13.2	266	14.237,	93
11.340,	93	240	
346		14.240	95
12.276	93	14.243	94
14.9	93	14.247	94
14.15	94	14.259	95
14.20	81	14.260	95
14.29f.	94	14.264	95
14.34	94	14.283	93
14.37	94	14.302	94
14.63	93	14.304	94
14.81	94	14.307	94
14.115	92	14.314	94
14.122	94	14.340ff.	94
14.137	94, 95	14.384	94
14.137ff.	94	14.403	93
14.143	94	14.489	93
14.146	94	14.491	93
14.190-	92	15.2	93
264		15.14	92
14.210	94	15.17	93
14.214f.	95	15.39	92
14.215	95	15.81	93
14.222	94	15.194f.	77n.
14.223-	94	15.220	93
226		15.267-	94
		276	

PEOPLES AND PLACES

SUBJECTS